To Worlds Unknown

To Worlds Unknown

The Letters of Clark Ashton Smith, Donald Wandrei, Howard Wandrei, and R. H. Barlow

Edited by David E. Schultz and S. T. Joshi

Hippocampus Press

New York

Contents

Clark Ashton Smith

Introduction

Clark Ashton Smith (1893–1961) began writing at an early age. His juvenilia, of which there is no small amount, consist of both verse and fiction with Arabian themes, inspired by the *Arabian Nights* and the *Rubáiyát*. These works date roughly to 1905 to 1911. In 1907, Smith read George Sterling's fantasy epic "A Wine of Wizardry" in *Cosmopolitan*. Inspired by Sterling, Smith's poetry, which he had been writing since 1904, turned from the Arabian themes to nature and to the fantastic. Smith began writing Sterling in 1911 and showing him his work. Sterling persuaded his publisher, A. M. Robertson of San Francisco, to issue a collection of Smith's verse titled *The Star-Treader* (1912). The book caused a sensation in San Francisco, but was slow in reaching a wider readership. But it did in time reach an audience more attuned to its themes.

An early appreciator of Smith's work was Donald Wandrei (1908–1987) of St. Paul, Minnesota. Wandrei learned of Smith's work from reading about it in a letter by H. P. Lovecraft published in the October 1923 issue of *Weird Tales,* in which Lovecraft mentioned "A friend of mine—Clark Ashton Smith, the California poet of horror, madness and morbid beauty." Wandrei's tastes undoubtedly set him on the trail of Smith, who by that time had appeared only once in *Weird Tales*, with two poems in the July–August issue. Smith had, of course, been published elsewhere, but only *Weird Tales* was a publication likely to capture Wandrei's notice. Wandrei's earliest extant letter to Smith dates to 1926, but Smith's reply to Wandrei's first letter dates to 11 December 1924, when Wandrei was only sixteen, and by that time Smith had appeared in *Weird Tales* twice more. In but the third sentence of his letter, Smith asked Wandrei if he had read Park Barnitz's *The Book of Jade* (1901). Smith himself had not, and young Wandrei was quick to offer to lend the rare book to Smith. It seems unlikely that so young a person as Wandrei would know of and be able to obtain such an item, but it is clear from his letters that he collected books with exotic themes and art, probably thanks to indulgent parents. Wandrei surely read Smith's early poetic contributions to *Weird Tales* in 1923–24, and learned soon thereafter how to obtain Smith's *Ebony and Crystal* (1922). In his initial letter to Wandrei, Smith remarked "It is good to know that one's work is not entirely unnoticed." Smith assumed that Wandrei must have had *The Star-Treader,* but that was not the case. And so Smith sold him a copy—twelve years after the book was published.

Smith and Wandrei soon were discussing favorite poets and exchanging manuscripts of their own work. By mid-year, Smith writes of hoping to publish a new book of poetry. Once again, having no success finding a receptive publisher, he decided to publish the book himself. Because *Ebony and Crystal* (a book issued by the printer of the local newspaper) was something of a physical disaster, Smith decided on a booklet in wraps rather than boards. When he said the book's appearance depended on whether he could come up with sufficient funds to pay the printer, Wandrei (remember: a boy of 16) offered to bear roughly half, or $50, of the cost—apparently without remuneration. Smith accepted the offer, and so in October 1925, *Sandalwood* appeared.

The two corresponded for the rest of Smith's life, although (as in the case of Wandrei and Lovecraft) the bulk of their letter writing occurred early on and tapered off over time. Nevertheless, Wandrei remained an ardent champion of Smith's work.

After Arkham House published the Lovecraft omnibus *The Outsider and Others* in 1939, August Derleth and Donald Wandrei contemplated an anthology of "all" Smith's stories and poems in a similar format. A ludicrous proposition, for Smith's verse and fiction could not be contained in one volume, even in the page size and typeface employed for *The Outsider,* and Smith remained an active poet and writer for years to come. Eventually, they decided on a book more modest in size and scope, similar in size to Derleth's own *Someone in the Dark*. Smith's *Out of Space and Time,* with a decidedly Poe-esque title not of his choosing, appeared in 1942 in an edition of 1054 copies—the third title from Arkham House, and the publisher's first title by a living author who was not associated with the enterprise.

In April 1942, with publication of *Out of Space and Time* imminent and just before he was inducted into the military in May, Wandrei stated that he wished to publish Smith's "collected, complete poems—everything." When Wandrei, who was stationed at Camp Adair, Oregon, was on leave in February 1943,[1] he visited Smith in Sacramento, at which time they doubtless discussed the planned book of Smith's poems. It does not seem that Smith started working on it, at least not in earnest, until more than a year later, when he wrote August Derleth "I'll get to work on the selection of titles for a third volume of prose [i.e., *Genius Loci*], also the selected volume of verse, before long. Your suggestion about arranging the poems is good."[2] And so in July 1944, Smith set himself on assembling an omnibus edition of his poetry. Smith toiled, probably on and off, for five years assembling the typescript (with two carbons) of what he called *Selected Poems,* not the complete poems that Wandrei had hoped for. (In November 1949, before seeing the final typescript, Wandrei still referred to it as *Collected Poems*.)

As with many other ambitious Arkham House projects, it took many years—in this case twenty-two—for manuscript to become book. Smith did not live to see its publication, having died ten years previous. However, Smith

---

1. In the extract by DW in D. H. Olson's "Of Donald Wandrei, August Derleth, and H. P. Lovecraft," he says he met up with CAS in Auburn (p. 378), but their letters speak of the meeting as occurring in Sacramento.

2. August Derleth to CAS, 13 July 1944, *Eccentric, Impractical Devils* 354: "I suggest also dividing or grouping the poems according to general subject—i. e., love lyrics separately; weird poems ditto" In the end, CAS did not follow this plan.

lived to see four of six fiction titles published by Arkham House and two slim editions of poems. Besides *Selected Poems* and two books of fiction, Arkham House posthumously published Smith's prose poems, his notebook (Derleth declined to publish the book, but his successor Jim Turner brought it out years later), and a book of selected letters.

It is sadly evident in Donald Wandrei's letters to Clark Ashton Smith that he played a key role in turning Smith against his young friend R. H. Barlow (1918–1951), with whom he had corresponded steadily for seven years and to whom he gave numerous manuscripts, paintings, and drawings. It remains unclear why Wandrei had a vitriolic hatred for young Barlow, but one can make some reasonable suppositions. Barlow's letters to Wandrei clearly indicate that the precocious youngster could be quite pestiferous. Barlow announced this loudly and clearly with his printed stationery, which declared him to be "R. H. Barlow Bibliomaniac." Tellingly, the stationery did not have a printed address, for as an Army brat, Barlow's family didn't stay in one place long. Their correspondence began cordially enough. Barlow ordered Wandrei's two books of verse, which he learned of from their mutual correspondent and friend, H. P. Lovecraft. In time, Barlow began to request from Wandrei any letters to him from Henry S. Whitehead for a planned book; for a copy of Wandrei's rare student publication *Broken Mirrors*; and then for manuscripts for his personal collection. Barlow had had great success in obtaining manuscripts from Lovecraft and Smith, and Wandrei was politely accommodating, although unlike Lovecraft and Smith, he was employed and also had residence in two locations—New York most of the time, and St. Paul in the spring—and so he did not always have the desired items at his immediate disposal.

Wandrei did send a manuscript ("The Atom-Smasher," a nonextant tale), which only induced Barlow to ask for more. At Barlow's insistence, Wandrei found a copy of *Broken Mirrors,* which he suggested might not be a book Barlow would actually want, since it had no fantastic material. Barlow purchased the book, but before long he was enlisting Wandrei to help dispose of it. One of Barlow's pet obsessions was to amass all the items that were to appear in a second issue of W. Paul Cook's *Recluse,* which never came to be. Barlow learned from Cook that Wandrei had submitted material, and so he asked Wandrei for copies of the items. He continued to beg for other manuscripts, even that for Wandrei's book, *Ecstasy.* Barlow's requests became more and more brazen. Surely Wandrei was somewhat taken aback when Barlow announced he wished to publish Wandrei's rejected series of fantasy poems, "Post-Historian Legends," as a booklet. Lovecraft expressed delight (out of politeness) when Barlow said he wanted to publish Lovecraft's *Fungi from Yuggoth,* but Wandrei was hardly flattered by Barlow's proposal, since he felt the first book from Barlow's press—Frank Belknap Long, Jr.'s *The Goblin Tower*—was quite amateurish, especially compared to his own two books of poetry. Barlow's plan to photograph and publish a portfolio of the artwork of Donald's brother Howard (1909–1956) must have been about the limit, for this encroached on Donald's own plan, initially unknown to Barlow. Barlow similarly stepped on toes by publishing material by the late Edith Miniter that others had plans to do. As is evident from the letters between Barlow and Howard Wandrei, there was some difficulty in getting Howard's art returned to him. The misadventure contributed to the brothers' dislike of and distrust for Barlow. The fact that Barlow half-jokingly and more than once suggested that he had kleptomaniacal tendencies when it came to borrowed manuscripts and art surely did not help. Wandrei seems to forget that he once wrote when he was only nineteen "I shall probably drive [Samuel] Loveman to distraction when I am in New York" (p. 61) and Loveman's "home may yet be burglarized of your paintings and drawings before I return to St. Paul" (p. 63). Despite all this, Donald Wandrei eventually allowed Barlow to publish some of his early stories in Barlow's mimeographed magazine, *Leaves*.

Howard Wandrei was a brilliant and distinctive pictorial artist, chiefly in pen-and-ink work. He illustrated Donald's book of poetry, *Dark Odyssey* (1931), and also did some illustrations for the weird and science fiction pulps. He also took to writing, publishing detective, horror, and science fiction tales in the pulp magazines, mostly under a variety of pseudonyms. He was selected to provide art for the cover of *The Outsider and Others,* and in fact obtained photographs of Lovecraft from Barlow so that he didn't have to draw Lovecraft from memory. But he was stricken with pneumonia, and so Virgil Finlay was enlisted to do the job.

In time, Barlow met the Wandreis—at a gathering of Lovecraft's friends in New York City in early 1935. Barlow was sixteen at the time—much younger than the others who attended—mostly members of the Kalem Club. Emboldened by having Lovecraft as his guest in Florida for seven weeks the previous summer, Barlow decided as early as the following May that he would go to New York, taking the bus from Washington, D.C. (where he lived in 1934 while seeking treatment for his eyes), so that he could meet all Lovecraft's cronies, about whom he had heard much from Lovecraft. Among those present were Lovecraft, the Wandreis, Frank Belknap Long, Samuel Loveman, James F. Morton, Rheinhart Kleiner, George Kirk, H. C. Koenig, Arthur Leeds, Wilfred B. Talman, Dean Phillips (and a friend of his), and one other individual. Many of those present were also friends and correspondents of Smith. One imagines that Barlow engaged in his usual pestering for collectables, since he now had a captive audience. Barlow's pesky requests for personal artifacts and his lack of social grace may have irritated people, notably the Wandreis and also Samuel Loveman. As Donald Wandrei described the occasion to Smith:

> . . . most of the evening we devoted to looking at Sam's immense collection of your drawings, water-colors, and grotesques. Barlow was positively ill with envy, and made a pest of himself by trying to beg, borrow, or buy one or all of them until Loveman patiently but flatly stated, "But Barlow, these are personal gifts from a very dear friend of mine." And even that did

not phase [*sic*] Barlow. I can admire the fervor of such hero-worship, but I wish to heaven it were accompanied by a little tact.

Reaction to Barlow's peskiness must have been obvious to him, for he wrote to Howard Wandrei shortly after the gathering, "I am afraid I annoyed you a great deal in NY with my incessant quizzing." Lovecraft may have been able to overlook such behavior readily—Barlow had been asking him for his manuscripts for more than four years, and he spent the summer of 1934 (and again 1935) with Barlow for weeks on end. And since Barlow was by far the youngest person at the gathering, those present may have been taken aback by the boy who invited himself into their annual gathering, intruding on their turf. Howard Wandrei later told August Derleth that no one in the New York circle liked Barlow, except James Morton, who may have been even more avuncular than Lovecraft and thus overlooked the boyish impetuousness. Wandrei himself wrote "Barlow undoubtedly has unfortunate traits, but he also has some excellent ones, not the least being his passionate devotion to weird literature and its exponents."[3]

Probably no one present truly understood the relationship between Lovecraft and Barlow; how Lovecraft had given Barlow many of his manuscripts, how he had confided in Barlow much about his own preferences for the disposition of his writings. And few of them knew, when Lovecraft died in March 1937, that in his "Instructions in Case of Decease," he had made Barlow his literary executor. Young Barlow probably was the person most qualified so serve in that capacity because of his intimate familiarity with Lovecraft's writings and his papers. But when it came to the ins and outs of publishing, Barlow was out of his element, although he was quickly becoming acclimated to it. Lovecraft also gave Barlow first choice to the many books in his library that he had not earmarked specifically for others.

It was Howard Wandrei who first informed August Derleth of Lovecraft's death. When the news got around that Barlow had, within days of Lovecraft's death, visited Lovecraft's grieving aunt and removed Lovecraft's remaining papers and books selected from his library, he was labeled a heartless and greedy predator.[4] Howard Wandrei wrote Derleth, "He is carrying around with him in his pocket two of HPL's note books, the ghoul. The kid's a ghoul. He hauls out these notebooks, tosses them at any interested party and says with a kind of supercilious morbidity, 'These are pitiful.' They are. One is a diary of HPL's last days, up to the time he went to the hospital, and is written mostly with the word pain. Not good reading."[5] It is evident that Barlow was no angel, and that much of his ensuing trouble following Lovecraft's death was partly of his own making.

3. DW to AWD, 25 March 1937, TLS, WHS.
4. Note that RHB ultimately deposited HPL's papers at JHL for preservation, although he did so over a five-year period (1937–42).
5. 1 April 1937 (ms., WHS). Note that the day after the encounter described by HW, RHB, at the William Sloane House (a Y.M.C.A. house) copied out much of the con-

And so the Wandreis and Samuel Loveman painted a portrait of Barlow as a vulture, out to capitalize on the death of their friend. In July 1938, as the campaign against Barlow raged (in correspondence with August Derleth, Donald referred to Barlow as "the rat" and the "menace"), Wandrei had the gall to write him, cordially, requesting that Barlow find him copies of *Weird Tales* missing from his collection for him to purchase, as Barlow had once offered to do. Once Barlow provided the final item Wandrei wanted, Wandrei himself severed ties with Barlow. Donald urged a lawyer in Providence to attempt to retrieve from Barlow the books and manuscripts he had taken from Lovecraft's library. The story Wandrei gave the lawyer was full of errors, as the lawyer found out when Barlow responded to a demand that he return all the material. Once the lawyer learned of Lovecraft's written instructions, he apologized and retracted his demand. Of course, this did not sit well with Wandrei, who was tremendously jealous of Barlow, feeling that the immature lad was assigned the role that he felt he and August Derleth deserved. He made every effort to have Derleth strong-arm Barlow for material needed for *The Outsider* and other projects, suggesting that Derleth not return material borrowed from Barlow but instead to send it to Annie Gamwell in Providence. In his memoir of Lovecraft, Barlow expressed regret that he had not published Lovecraft's "Instructions in Case of Decease," in which Lovecraft clearly spelled out his final wishes regarding his manuscripts and certain of his books.

Donald Wandrei had convinced Smith to retrieve the typescript for *Incantations*—a book Barlow hoped to publish, initially under his own imprint. When it became evident he could not do so himself, he approached the Futile Press, which had brought out Smith's *Nero and Other Poems* and also Barlow's edition of Lovecraft's commonplace book. Because the Futile Press was in California, and Barlow was going to meet with the proprietors, the Beck brothers of Lakeport, he wrote Smith that he would like to visit him. Barlow was mostly oblivious to the smear campaign under way, and so was astonished by Smith's last communiqué to him, telling him never to visit him or otherwise to write to Smith again.[6] In early December 1938, Smith destroyed Barlow's last postcard to him, in which Barlow proposed a visit regarding *Incantations,* but he did not destroy all Barlow's other previous letters to him. Barlow had been writing "Return by Sunset," "From a painting by Clark Ashton Smith," begun August 1938. It remained incomplete until June 1939, six months after Smith rebuffed him. Many factors contributed to Smith's virtual cessation of fiction-writing, but misunderstanding about Barlow was a major factor.

---

tent of the diary for AWD, and also a long list of names and addresses of individuals to contact for their letters from HPL and other items.

6. RHB deposited his letters and manuscripts from CAS at the JHL, along with numerous Lovecraft manuscripts, but this most painful and final communiqué (along with CAS's first letter to RHB) was found among RHB's papers following his death.

Donald Wandrei undertook a vendetta against Barlow and Claire Beck, going so far as to blacklist "Barlow there [i.e., with the Author's Guild], and . . . blacklist Beck on my next visit to the office, which will further help greatly to curtail any future machinations of them against other authors,"[7] vastly overreacting to a situation that by now he knew to be false. He saw that Barlow received no recognition for his assistance in preparing *The Outsider and Others* and *Beyond the Wall of Sleep*. Derleth was a little more gracious: he asked Barlow to write a brief memoir of Lovecraft to include in *Marginalia,* and in that book, since Wandrei was now in the military service and not able to assist in the book's production, Derleth could acknowledge Barlow's "unstinting" and "generous assistance." "The Wind That Is in the Grass" may be no more heartfelt than memoirs by Lovecraft's other friends, but Barlow's remains the most poignant. The memoir was written when Barlow was twenty-six and living in Mexico, seven years after Lovecraft had died, and farther removed in time from that event than most other recollections of the man.

Derleth's meager recognition of Barlow was too little and too late, for it seemed to pertain only to Barlow's memoir in *Marginalia* and a few rare bits of Lovecraftiana, and not at all to the provision of material for *The Outsider* and *Beyond the Wall of Sleep,* including many items Derleth and Wandrei could not have obtained on their own. Derleth also invited Barlow to write an introduction to Henry S. Whitehead's *Jumbee and Other Uncanny Tales.* This Barlow did, but it was the end of his involvement with the weird fiction group, for he was now living in Mexico, deeply immersed in his Meso-American studies. Derleth continued to publish various of Barlow's writings after his death. *The Shuttered Room* (1959) and *Fire and Sleet and Candlelight* (1961) contain selections of Barlow's poetry, and *Some Notes on H. P. Lovecraft* (1959) includes extracts from Barlow's journal of 1934 recording Lovecraft's visit to him in Florida.

Nevertheless, the damage wreaked by Donald Wandrei was done, and Smith and Barlow went their separate ways. A few years later, Barlow extended an olive branch to Smith. Rah Hoffman maintained that Barlow and Smith met once in person: "Barlow had made his only visit to Smith's cabin the day after our group had been there in 1941" (198). Not long after, Barlow sent Smith a copy of George Sterling's *After Sunset* (1939).[8] But there appears there was no further correspondence between the two.

And what of the friendship of Clark Ashton Smith and R. H. Barlow before that time? It began with Barlow writing Smith, at Lovecraft's suggestion, to ask if Smith knew of any weird fiction magazines published in England. Barlow was

---

7. DW to AWD, 3 January 1939, TLS, WHS.
8. In a letter to CAS (18 January 1943), RHB advised CAS that he was sending the book. RHB inscribed the book "For Clark Ashton Smith with the compliments of the Editor & Excavator" (Roy A. Squires, *Beyond the Bibliographies* [Catalog 7, 1973], p. 22).

soon asking Smith for manuscripts, and also drawings and paintings.[9] Over the years, Smith provided many manuscripts of both fiction and verse (now preserved among the Lovecraft papers at the John Hay Library). These Barlow secreted away in what he called "the vaults of Yoh-Vombis"—the closet in which he stored his precious manuscripts, magazines, and books, named for Smith's story of that title. As their correspondence grew, Barlow wrote of ambitious publishing plans. He proposed to bind the unbound sheets of Lovecraft's *The Shunned House*, but bound only a few. He started but did not finish *Caneviniana*, letters of Henry S. Whitehead, and also Lovecraft's *Fungi from Yuggoth*. His Smith projects were to include an edition of Smith's *The Hashish-Eater*, with illustrations by Smith (how he was to accomplish this is difficult to imagine) and Smith's long-planned *Incantations*. As noted, Smith requested the return of his typescript of *Incantations* before typesetting could begin. Nothing ever came of it, although he included it and "The Jasmine Girdle"—a subsection of the book—in his *Selected Poems*. Thus, Smith never saw the book he first conceived in 1925 in print.

It is unfortunate that the harshly critical comments of the Wandreis and others turned Clark Ashton Smith so violently against his young friend. The shock to Barlow is unimaginable. His friend and mentor Lovecraft had died unexpectedly in 1937, an event that he may never have gotten over. Little over a year later, his other great friend, whom he had never met but with whom he kept up a lively correspondence, inexplicably turned on him. Within a few months the smear campaign against Barlow became evident, and he surely was dismayed to find that August Derleth, with whom he had been cooperating and whom he was advising thanks to his personal knowledge of Lovecraft's wishes regarding his work, would not stand up to Wandrei in the matter.

Barlow gradually drifted away from the world of weird literature. In 1939, he became involved in the Activist poetry movement, led by Lawrence Hart in the San Francisco Bay area. The Activists sought to reject traditional poetic modes of expression, instead achieving emotional impact not through simple narration but through a succession of connected connotative phrases. Barlow remained associated with the Activists until he took up residence in Mexico in 1943. He attended San Francisco Junior College from 1939 to 1940, then went to Mexico in 1940–41 to study at the Escuela Nacional de Ciencias Biologicas and later at Universidad Nacional Autónoma de México. He returned to California to ob-

---

9. Around 1969, Roy A Squires offered for sale in his "Catalog II" "35. DRAWINGS BY CLARK ASHTON SMITH of Auburn, California. Acquired by R. H. Barlow from the Artist 1931–1938 and from the Lovecraft Bequest, 1937. (So reads the hand-lettered title-page of this volume.) A 'scrap-book' style volume of tipped-in drawings. Consists of 119 drawings in black-and-white and color." RHB presumably amassed most of the 119 items offered for sale. He acquired any drawings HPL may have had when he took control of HPL's papers. Thus it is difficult to know just how many of the items in the scrapbook may have belonged to either of them without direct consultation to see if CAS had inscribed any piece to one or the other.

tain B.A. and M.S. degrees in anthropology at the University of California in 1942. He returned to Mexico in 1943 as a permanent resident, joining the staff of the Universidad Nacional Autónoma de México, where he was an instructor in the ancient Aztec language of Nahuatl. He became head of the Department of Anthropology at Mexico City College, a position he held until he died in early 1951. He did write some pieces on Lovecraft for fan magazines in the early 1940s (including the *Acolyte*), but that was the extent of his involvement in the weird fiction community at the time.

For many years, R. H. Barlow was a shadowy figure in Lovecraft studies. Conversely, he became a major figure in Meso-American studies. These days, he can be recognized as a historically important figure in both, perhaps only because of a grave misunderstanding that arose as he sought to preserve the literary legacy of his friend and mentor.

—DAVID E. SCHULTZ

S. T. JOSHI

A Note on the Text

Donald Wandrei's letters to Clark Ashton Smith, R. H. Barlow (two only), and Barlow's letters to and from Smith, are mostly held by the John Hay Library. Some are held privately. Smith's final note to Barlow comes from a microfilm of various of Barlow's papers made by George Smisor, also held at the John Hay Library. That microfilm also contains letters by Donald and Howard Wandrei to Barlow. Smith's and Barlow's letters to Donald Wandrei are held by the Minnesota Historical Society. The editors have transcribed all the letters they could find. It is likely that a number of them have been lost. D. H. Olson mentions "tales of mail from Clark Ashton Smith laying unopened in the Wandrei living room for twenty years" (369), but this cannot be confirmed.

Acknowledgments

We are grateful to Douglas A. Anderson, Martin Andersson, Scott Connors, Stefan Dziemianowicz, Derrick Hussey, Ken Faig, Jr., Marcos Legaria, Charles D. O'Connor III, and Dwayne Olson for their assistance in the preparation of this volume. Mark Brown, Rosemary Cullen, Barbara Filipac, and Robin Wheelwright Ness of the John Hay Library, and the Minnesota Historical Society also provided valuable assistance. We are also grateful to CASiana Enterprises, Inc., for permission to publish the letters and other works by Clark Ashton Smith; and to the John Hay Library, Brown University, Providence, RI, and Donald Wandrei and Family Papers, Minnesota Historical Society, St. Paul, MN.

Abbreviations

AJ	*Auburn Journal*
AY	Smith, *The Abominations of Yondo* (1960)
BB	*The Black Book of Clark Ashton Smith* (1979)
C	*Colossus: The Collected Science Fiction of Donald Wandrei* (1989)

CF	Smith, *Collected Fantasies* (5 volumes; 2006–2010)
CP	Smith, *The Complete Poetry and Translations* (2007–2008)
DC	Smith, *The Dark Chateau* (1951)
DD	*Don't Dream: The Collected Horror and Fantasy Fiction of Donald Wandrei* (1997)
DS	Smith, *The Double Shadow and Other Fantasies* (1933)
E	D. Wandrei, *Ecstasy and Other Poems* (1928)
EC	Smith, *Ebony and Crystal* (1922)
EF	D. Wandrei, *The Eye and the Finger* (1944)
FF	*The Fantasy Fan*
GL	Smith, *Genius Loci and Other Tales* (1948)
LO	Smith, *The Last Oblivion* (2002)
LW	Smith, *Lost Worlds* (1944)
MW	Smith, *Miscellaneous Writings* (2011)
OD	Smith, *Other Dimensions* (1970)
OED	*Oxford English Dictionary*
OS	Smith, *Odes and Sonnets* (1918)
OST	Smith, *Out of Space and Time* (1942)
PM	D. Wandrei, *Poems for Midnight* (1964)
RW	Smith, *The Red World of Polaris* (2003)
S	Smith, *Sandalwood* (1925)
S&P	Smith, *Spells and Philtres* (1955)
SH	D. Wandrei, *Strange Harvest* (1965)
SP	Smith, *Selected Poems* (1971)
SS	Smith, *Strange Shadows* (1989)
ST	Smith, *The Star-Treader and Other Poems* (1912)
TSS	Smith, *Tales of Science and Sorcery* (1964)
WT	*Weird Tales*

ALS	autograph note, signed
ANS	autograph note, signed
AWD	August W. Derleth
CAS	Clark Ashton Smith
DW	Donald Wandrei
GS	George Sterling
HPL	H. P. Lovecraft
HW	Howard Wandrei
JHL	John Hay Library, Brown University (Providence, RI)
MHS	Minnesota Historical Society (St. Paul, MN)
RHB	R. H. Barlow
TLS	typed letter, signed
TNS	typed note, signed
WHS	Wisconsin Historical Society (Madison, WI)

Letters: Clark Ashton Smith and Donald Wandrei

[1]   [CAS to DW] [ALS]

[CLARK ASHTON SMITH
AUBURN, CALIFORNIA]

Dec. 11th, 1924

My dear Mr. Wandrei:

Thank you for your most appreciative letter. It is good to know that one's work is not entirely unnoticed.

Have you read the poems of Francis Saltus and Park Barnitz? Both of these poets had a **flair** for the exotic—and both are almost forgotten and extremely difficult to procure. I have never even seen Barnitz's one volume, "The Book of Jade."

I have a few "Star-Treaders," and will be glad to send you a copy, if you have not already procured one—(which is most unlikely.) The price is two dollars.

Lovecraft is great—his horror stories are totally unlike those of any one else. Victor Hugo would have found a "new thrill" in them, as well as in Baudelaire's "Flowers of Evil."[1]

Thanking you again for your appreciation,

I remain,
Cordially yours,
Clark Ashton Smith

Notes

1. Victor Hugo wrote in a letter to Baudelaire dated 6 October 1859, "Vous créez un frisson nouveau" [You are creating a new shudder].

[2]   [CAS to DW] [ALS]

[CLARK ASHTON SMITH
AUBURN, CALIFORNIA]

Jan. 30th, 1924 [i.e., 1925]

My dear Mr. Wandrei:

I hope you have received "The Star-Treader" before this—in spite of the Christmas rush.

The poems in this collection were all written before my twentieth year. Probably you will find them rougher and less melodious than the best of the later ones. Certainly they are less colourful.

You should read the poems of T. L. Beddoes (a contemporary of Keats) and the translation of Baudelaire in Boni and Liveright's Modern Library, if you are not familiar with them. Beddoes' "Death's Jest-Book," is a master-piece of weird and macabre imagination.

Thanking you again for your interest and appreciation, I am

Cordially yours,

Clark Ashton Smith

[3]   [CAS to DW] [ALS]

[Clark Ashton Smith
AUBURN, CALIF.
P. O. Box 388]

June 25th, 1925.

My dear Mr. Wandrei:

Indeed, your letter is anything but an imposition! I am always glad to hear from appreciative readers, who, as you must realize, are rather infrequent in my case.

"Odes and Sonnets" was privately printed in 1918 by the Book Club of California. The "Odes" were reprinted from the "Star-Treader;" and the "Sonnets" were afterwards included in "Ebony and Crystal." It would scarcely be worth your while to procure the book, which is rare and expensive . . . However, I may have a new volume out presently, under the title of "Sandalwood." Most of the poems are rather trifling; but I imagine you would like some of them, such as the enclosed clippings, taken from a local paper to which I contribute.[1]

No, I have never seen "The Book of Jade." Percival Pollard in his "Their Day in Court," mentioned it, saying that "it reeked bitterly of mortality."[2] And Floyd Dell, in "The Liberator" (I have given away the copy I had) wrote somewhat patronizingly and disparagingly on "The Book of Jade".[3] He gave the author's name, and some biographical details, of which I remember little, except that Barnitz was born in the middle west, was a scholar, travelled extensively, and died young from the abuse of opium and hashish. I believe "The Book of Jade" was his only production.

You are very kind to offer me the loan of this rare volume. Are you sure it isn't too much trouble?[4]

I have had several months of enforced leisure, from a crippled foot, and have spent much of my time in learning French, so that I could read and translate Baudelaire. The existing translations are somewhat Bowdlerized and scarcely convey the tonal qualities of the original. Translation is ticklish work; but I hope to achieve something if I keep at it.

Poetry of the more imaginative type is hard to find—and scarcely anyone writes (or reads) it in this iron age! But the strange, the magical, the marvellous, is the only **true** poetry. The present-day school is conceding more and more to utilitarianism, "social service", and other such fetiches—which to me are absolutely meaningless! Let us hope for a "romantic" revival, sometime!

Thank you for all the kind things you say about my work. It is usually more blamed than praised—and more ignored than blamed.

Very sincerely

Clark Ashton Smith

Notes

1. "Clark Ashton Smith's Column" had been appearing in the *Auburn Journal* since 5 April 1923 to offset the cost of having the *Journal* print and bind *Ebony and Crystal*.
2. *Their Day in Court* 378.
3. Two pieces by Dell are reprinted in *The Book of Jade: A Critical Edition*.
4. In September 1932, during his second visit to HPL, DW introduced HPL to *The Book of Jade*, held in the Harris Collection of American Poetry and Plays at JHL.

[4]   [CAS to DW] [ALS]

[Clark Ashton Smith

AUBURN, CALIF.

P. O. Box 388]

July 10th, 1925.

Dear Mr Wandrei:

I am greatly indebted to you for the loan of the Book of Jade, which I will return in a week or two. You are right about the mortuary poems being the best:[1] some of them, such as the "Sonnet of the Instruments of Death", "Sepulchral Life" etc. are truly impressive, and, it seems to me, very original. There is a tremendous idea in the "Grotesques", also, in the second of the "Fragments." In the first section, the sonnet "Ennui" impressed me as being perhaps the best, or at least, the most perfect. Ennui and sheer corruption are both extremely difficult subjects to handle. If I am ever in a position to edit an anthology, I will certainly include at least half-a-dozen of these poems.

There is no **certainty** that "Sandalwood" will be accepted by the publisher to whom I am sending it. Most of the poems are not in my best style; so maybe it will have a chance! "Reve Parisien," one of my Baudelaire is the best poem in the book. There are fourteen other attempts at Baudelaire; but I'm not sure yet whether most of them are good or bad. As far as I know, I am the only translator who has done them in the original metres. It is far harder to write good alexandrines in English than in French.

No, there is hardly any one who writes poetry of the imaginative type any more. There is a book called "Vanitas" by one Paul Eldridge, which is **said** to be in the Baudelaire style; but I've never seen it. It is easier to find imaginative prose[;] you should read the earlier book[s] of Lafcadio Hearn, particularly "Fantastics" and "Stray Leaves from Strange Literature," if you have not seen them. And you might find something in Lord Dunsany's "Book of Wonder" and "Dreamer's Tales."

I am planning a new book which will contain nothing but pure poetry—
no sentimentalities, no philosophical aridities—nothing but the strange, the
magical, and the gorgeous! "Incantations" might be a good title for this book
. . . which, in all likelihood, I will have to print at my own expense.[2]

Thanking you again for "The Book of Jade," and for the magnificent
compliments you pay me, I remain,

Very sincerely,

Clark Ashton Smith

Notes

1. DW's "The Corpse Speaks" repeats the word "dead," in imitation of Barnitz's
"The Grave," in which the word "dead" is repeated ten times in l. 6.

2. At this juncture, CAS had not written much of what he intended for the book. It
appears that he had some kind of manuscript by October 1928. More than a decade
after conception, he provided a typescript to RHB to publish, but DW served to dis-
suade CAS from working with the printer who took over the project when RHB
could not manage the job, and it was never published in CAS's lifetime. Ultimately it
appeared as a section of *SP* à la *The Star-Treader, Ebony and Crystal*, etc., as did another
unpublished book, *The Jasmine Girdle* (see CAS to DW 65).

[5]   [CAS to DW] [ALS]

[Clark Ashton Smith
AUBURN, CALIF.
P. O. Box 388]

Aug. 4th, 1925.

Dear Mr. Wandrei:

I am returning "The Book of Jade" to-day, with many,
many thanks. I liked it even better, on re-reading it. Most of the poems are
excellent, and some of the mortuary sonnets are *great*. I made copies of seven
of them, to keep.

The publisher to whom I submitted my last volume, writes me that he
can do nothing with it till next year.[1] I am inclined to fear that he is emulating
the courtesy of the Chinese!

Very sincerely,

Clark Ashton Smith

Notes

1. See CAS to Samuel Loveman, 27 September 1925: "G[eorge] S[terling] told me that
he had talked [George Steele] Seymour, of the Chicago Bookfellows, into promising to
bring out 'Sandalwood.' But when I submitted the typescript, it was returned to me with
an intimation that they could do nothing with it till next year" (*Born under Saturn* 328).

[6]   [CAS to DW] [ALS]

[Clark Ashton Smith
AUBURN, CALIF.
P. O. Box 388]

Aug. 7, 1925

Dear Mr. Wandrei:

Your letter came just after I had mailed "The Book of Jade", together with a brief note of thanks. I hope that both have reached you before this.

As I told you in the note, my prospective publisher will do nothing with "Sandalwood" till next year—if he does anything at all. I may print a couple hundred copies in pamphlet form myself, if I can steal, earn or borrow enough money.

Baudelaire is hard enough to read, let alone translate, for a beginner in French. I like the alexandrine, but dare say it's an acquired—or *un*acquired taste for most people . . . A perfectly literal translation of B. in verse would be impossible, I am afraid. Many individual lines and phrases, however, are as literal as I can make them. Here is my attempt at a little octasyllabic [*sic*] poem called *Horreur Sympathetique.*

> "From this bizarre and livid sky,
> Tormented like your doom and mine,
> On your void spirit passing by,
> What thoughts descend, O libertine?
>
> Insatiate of things unsung,
> Of shadow, and of lone surmise,
> I will not whine like Ovid, flung
> From out the Latin paradise.
>
> Skies torn like strands of ocean-stream
> In you is mirrored all my pride!
> Your slow, enormous clouds abide
>
> The dolent hearses of my dreams;
> Your glimmers mock with fluctuant lights
> The hell wherein my heart delights."[1]

"Flasks and Flagons" is included in a volume of collected sonnets by Saltus, which I have.[2] But I have never seen "Dreams after Sunset,"—a fine title, by the way . . . I can't understand the obscurity of Beddoes. He was a contemporary of Keats, and the world should have had time to find him out by now. Saltus and Barnitz, of course, are doubly debarred from fame by being Americans.

I like many kinds of poetry (not, however, all kinds of verse!) but I am sick of this eternal harping on the commonplace; and see no use in writing about the so-called "realities" of life, unless one can throw some new and strange light upon them, as Baudelaire often did. You are right: poetry should be an escape from life—or, at least, an extension or amplification of life. Anything else is unbearable. In an age of greater sophistication and increased leisure, imaginative poetry will be given its true value.

Probably you are right about prose . . . If anyone could "do" a novel of the kind that you specify, it would be H. P. Lovecraft.

I read "The Hill of Dreams" many years ago, and liked it. Machen's "The Great God Pan" is said to be very good, also. But I read very little prose, nowadays.

You pay me an overwhelming compliment! But most people have underpraised "Ebony and Crystal;" so perhaps your estimate will help to strike a balance!

I'd be grateful for the loan of "Dreams after Sunset."

Cordially,

Clark Ashton Smith

Notes

1. For lines 5–6, read the following as CAS's final version: "—Athirst for mortal things unsung / In shadowy realms of lone surmise,".

2. I.e., *The Bayadere and Other Sonnets.*

[7]   [CAS to DW] [ALS]

[Clark Ashton Smith
AUBURN, CALIF.
P. O. Box 388]

Aug. 25th, 1925.

Dear Mr. Wandrei:

Many thanks for the loan of "Dreams after Sunset." I agree with you that *some* of the poems are good, but most of them are more or less disappointing. Saltus seems to have written about ten times too much. I have never seen "Shadows and Ideals" (a good title) but will certainly keep an eye out for it. "The Bayadere and Other Sonnets" is the collection I have. Speaking of sonnets, you should see the "Collected S. of Lloyd Mifflin,['] which contains between three and four hundred! Some of them are fairly good, though not highly imaginative.

No, I have not seen "Les Paradises [*sic*] Artificiels," which is, in part, a translation of De Quincey's "Opium Eaters."[1] The original portion is a monograph on the effects of hashish. One of Baudelaire's translators—E. P. Sturm—speaks of it as showing a deterioration in his style.[2]

Robert Chenault Givler is a new name to me. I note that a book of poems called "The King of the Black Isles" by some one named Nicholson (I forget his initials)[3] has been published in Chicago. The title is attractive, and the specimen of the contents that I saw quoted, was uncommonly musical. Also, the book was severely "slated" by Harriet Monroe, editor of "Poetry" (?), which is a recommendation in itself.[4]

It will cost at least a hundred dollars to print a pamphlet of the sort that I am contemplating. Printers charge by the page; and I doubt if the material I have can be crammed into less than fifty pages, even by printing it continuously, with the shorter ones two to a page. But there should be no great difficulty in disposing of so small an edition as 200 copies. It will be a rare and precious item for collectors, some day!—if I can get the necessary hundred dollars.

As to the inadequate praise received by "Ebony and Crystal"—well, you ought to know that con[n]oisseurs are few and far between. However, the world usually accepts the judgement of the experts in the long run. There were few published reviews of the book, and most of these were more or less laudatory. Benjamin de Casseres was one who praised it highly[5] . . . Many copies, however, were sold locally, to people of the Babbit[t] type, who purchased it more from curiosity than any other motive. About all they would understand, was the erotic imagery in a few of the poems,—which gave the book a reputation for impropriety among the village Methodists!

My Baudelaires have been highly praised by people who know the original . . . It was hard to make anything of "La Fontaine de Sang", which I enclose. The last two lines, **literally** translated, ran thus: "But love for me is only a mattress of needles, / Made for to give a drink to the cruel girls!" Surely my last line is an improvement![6]

I'll return the Saltus in a few days.

Cordially,

C. A. S.

Notes

1. Thomas De Quincey, *Confessions of an English Opium-Eater* (1821), an autobiographical account of his addiction to laudanum.

2. Baudelaire's *Les Paradis artificiels: Opium et haschisch* was influenced by Thomas De Quincey's *Confessions of an English Opium-Eater* and *Suspiria de Profundis*. Sturm's comment can be found in *Baudelaire: His Prose and Poetry* 25.

3. J. U. Nicolson.

4. Harriet Monroe, "Familiar Glamours," *Poetry* 24, No. 2 (May 1924): 105–9.

5. Benjamin De Casseres, "And a Little Book Shall Lead Them," *Arts and Decoration* 19, No. 4 (August 1923): 47, 50. See Appendix.

6. "The Fountain of Blood," ll. 13–14. In final form, l. 14 reads: "Whereon, for thirsty girls, my blood pours many a rill."

[8]   [CAS to DW] [ALS]

[Clark Ashton Smith
AUBURN, CALIF.
P. O. Box 388]

Sept. 12th, 1925.

Dear Mr. Wandrei:

It is princely of you to offer to assume even half the expense of printing "Sandalwood!" I can't raise **all** of the remainder at present; but the printer, who is a good fellow, is to go ahead, anyway, and you will be glad to know that the linotyping of the book has already been begun. It will be bound in a heavy, bluish-green art-paper, tied with cord; and will, I think, present a fairly attractive appearance. I am including 43 new lyrics and sonnets, together with 19 of my Baudelaires.[1] Many of the poems are so brief that they can be printed two to a page.

When you send me your cheque, I suggest that you register the envelope containing it. Some of my mail (including the typescript of a short story) has gone astray during the past year.

I enclose two more Baudelaires. It is remarkable how few modern English poets have used the alexandrine at all. Dowson has the best ones; and Arthur Symons and Lionel Johnson have also used the line to good effect. There is an excellent specimen ("Ante Aram") in Rupert Brooke,[2] too. Most of Bergin Applegate's Verlaine alexandrines don't impress me as being any too good, but then, Verlaine is far harder to translate even than Baudelaire. Symons did the best ones, on the whole; but they are more Symons than Verlaine.[3]

Thanks for the book of Givler's poems![4] There seems to [be] a genuine poetic impulse in the "Dream-Flowers;" but most of the others are banal and didactic.

I will return "Shadows and Ideals" next week. A few of the poems are excellent; and the ones in French are quite pretty.

If the books you name were included in the Auburn library, they would all be relegated to the back closet—and would have a considerable circulation, since people could find them without hunting all over the shelves! However, you forget Balzac's "Droll Stories," the "Novellino" of Massucchio,[5] [*sic*] and Louys' "Aphrodite." I possess copies of these, and the ladies are always borrowing them. They think the "Heptameron"[6] dull by comparison!

I have tried to be faithful to the thought and mood of the original, in my translations. But you will notice, in several instances, that I have varied the image a little. However, I do not think that I have **essentially** altered, or falsified anything, as the other translators of B. have sometimes done. Even W. J. Robertson[7] offends in this respect. "Tu contiens dans ton oeil le couchant and [*sic*] l'aurore" is rendered "Thine eye is filled with dawn, with twilight dwindles"[8]—which is miles away from Baudelaire's meaning—and also sheer nonsense. My version of the fourth stanza in this poem ("Hymne á [*sic*] la Beauté") is perhaps more lurid than the original, since I have used "rosary" in place of "bijoux" and "jewelled crucifix" in lieu of "breloque" (trinket, or charm). However, the substitution seems "Baudelairian" enough.

Thanking you a thousand times in advance for the loan of the fifty, I am,
Cordially yours,
Clark Ashton Smith

Have you ever read "The Sphinx" of Oscar Wilde? You would like it, I think.

Notes

1. *S* contains only 42 lyrics.
2. *Collected Poems* 39.
3. Bergen Applegate's monograph *Paul Verlaine: His Absinthe-Tinted Song* (1916) contains translations of selected poems by Verlaine. Arthur Symons's translations of Verlaine appear in several of his poetry volumes, including *Silhouettes* (1892; rev. 1896) and *Knave of Hearts* (1913).
4. Probably his *Poems*.
5. Salernitano Masuccio (1410–1475), an Italian poet. His *Il Novellino* was a collection of fifty anticlerical stories, each dedicated to a famous person and containing an epilogue with a moral.
6. By Marguerite of Navarre (1492–1549). The work is a collection of 72 short stories written in the form of a frame narrative, inspired by the *Decameron* of Giovanni Boccaccio. Many deal with love, lust, infidelity, and other romantic and sexual matters. It was intended to contain 100 stories covering ten days, à la the *Decameron,* but at Marguerite's death it was completed only as far as the second story of the eighth day. It was published posthumously in 1558. The standard translation at this time was by Arthur Machen.
7. In his *A Century of French Verse* (1895).
8. *Baudelaire: His Prose and Poetry* 194. CAS himself rendered the line "The sunset and the dawn in thy deep eyes are holden . . ."

[9]   [CAS to DW] [ALS]
[Clark Ashton Smith
AUBURN, CALIF.
P. O. Box 388]

Sept. 27th, 1925.

Dear Mr. Wandrei:

I received your money order a couple days ago, and hasten to acknowledge it, with many, many thanks. The book will certainly owe its existence to you. I could not have raised anything like the necessary sum, myself; and I did not want to strain my credit too much, with the printer. I don't think he made anything on "Ebony and Crystal."

The volume ought to be ready by November. I'll send you an inscribed copy when it comes out. The price—to the public—will be one dollar; but I'd rather you didn't pay for the book . . . I don't expect to become rich from the sale of it, anyway. If I can sell enough to pay expenses, and refund your fifty within a reasonable length of time, I will be satisfied. As to the binding—well, you should know that books sell far more readily if they present an attractive appearance. The binding of "E. & C." was severely criticized by booksellers, and one of them even returned several copies to me, asserting that they were unsaleable because of the binding! I imagine that most people who buy verse at all, buy it for gift books . . . But anyone who really cares for poetry should be glad to get it in any form . . . . .

Yes, I have seen portions of the "Polybion."[1] [*sic*] I wouldn't advise you to read very much of it at a stretch: the verse flows easily enough, but becomes monotonous in the mass, since all the lines are end-stopped, and have the classical caesura. Anyway, the stuff is not highly imaginative . . . The alexandrine was also much used in alternation with the fourteen-syllable line, in early English verse. The combination was known as "Poulter's measure."[2]

I like James Thomson; but of course (like Leopardi and Beddoes) he will never be popular.[3] I am forced to conclude that even Baudelaire is valued most for the "realism" and "human interest" of some of his poems. A sot or a prostitute is more interesting to the average reader than the people on the dark side of the moon! Fantasy, imagination, and pessimism are not fashionable among fools.

Thanks for the list of curiosa. "Fantazius Mallare"[4] will go unpurchased, as far as I am concerned. I've no money for that sort of thing; and even if I had, I doubt if I would invest in Hecht, who impresses me as being rather flashy and blatant. Sexuality is getting to be too common and vulgar now-a-days, anyway. The newsstands are all cluttered up with it. I'm no prude; but too much of anything becomes a bore.

Here are some more translations. I haven't been able to put in much time on them lately—since I've had to earn a few dollars for grocery-bills.

Cordially yours,
Clark Ashton Smith

P.S. Hope you've received the Saltus book by this time.

Notes

1. Michael Drayton, *Poly-Olbion* (1613), a topographical poem describing England and Wales that runs to almost 15,000 lines of alexandrine couplets.
2. A meter with alternate lines of twelve and fourteen syllables. It was said that poulters gave twelve eggs for the first dozen and fourteen if a second dozen was purchased.
3. CAS refers not to James Thomson (1700–1748), author of *The Seasons,* but to James Thomson ("B. V.") (1834–1882), author of *The City of Dreadful Night* (1880), a celebrated poem of pessimism. Leopardi and Beddoes were also known for their pessimism.
4. By Ben Hecht.

[10]   [CAS to DW] [ALS]

[Clark Ashton Smith
AUBURN, CALIF.
P. O. Box 388]

Oct. 26th, 1925.

Dear Mr. Wandrei:

I am mailing you a copy of "Sandalwood", and hope it will arrive safely. I've had a tedious time getting the book printed in any sort of shape (somebody mixed two of the "galleys" on one occasion!) and feel about ready to take a rest.

Of course, you are right about bindings, etc . . . But how many people are there who love poetry for itself? A good way to find out would be to print a book in the way that you describe. Maybe I'll try it, some time.

Your offer about the fifty is most generous. But I hope I won't have to publish any more books in Auburn, or at my own expense. I have an intuition that my luck may improve before long. But, of course, intuitions are not always infallible.

"Weird Tales" took two of my Baudelaires.[1] The other magazines have been returning them with personal notes to the effect that they were "not quite suitable."

I should be delighted to see "Shadows and Ideals." I hope you will find a few things in "Sandalwood." I don't think I've included anything that was absolutely worthless. And I have left out some that the prurient might have seized upon.

Would you care to see a fantastic short story of mine, called "The Abominations of Yondo?" "Weird Tales" thought it was "more of a prose poem than a narrative"—and rejected it.[2] It contains some weird pictures, at any rate.

Your praise of my work is not "fulsome." Whether it is too excessive or not, only the future can decide. At any rate my fame seems to be spreading— I have received several enthusiastic letters of late.

Cordially yours,
Clark Ashton Smith.

P.S. Giacomo Leopardi was an Italian of noble birth—and a life-long invalid. He wrote poetry (all of which is said to be very pessimistic) and a number of philosophic essays, dialogues, etc. Some of his prose was translated by James Thomson. But I've never seen a version of the poems, with the exception of one called "The Leaf", which you will find in D. G. Rossetti.[3]

Notes

1. "Spleen" and "Horreur Sympathique."
2. See CAS to Sam Sackett, 30 June 1949, *Klarkash-Ton: The Journal of Smith Studies* No. 1 (June 1988): 19: "Then, incited by Lovecraft, with whom I was corresponding, I

wrote my first weird story, 'The Abominations of Yondo', which appeared in the revived *Overland* and drew many howls of wrath and derision from readers." GS wrote "Your 'Yondo' awoke many protests from the mentally infirm, I'm told" (18 April 1926), *The Shadow of the Unattained* 271.

3. In Rossetti's *Collected Works* 2.409.

[11]   [CAS to DW] [ALS]

> Auburn, Cal.
> Nov. 15th, 1925

My dear Wandrei:

Your welcome letter, and "Shadows and Ideals", are "both at hand"—to use the terminology of commerce. I am glad you were not disappointed in "Sandalwood"—I think, myself, that it contains much good work; though I hope to do something more purely imaginative presently. "Sandalwood" (as I meant the title to indicate) consists largely of incense at the shrine of Eros—at least, it is that, in one sense.

I find much good work in "Shadows and Ideals", but nothing, on the whole, that is very perfect or very great. My feeling about Saltus is that he could have done better if he had written less. But I may be wrong—poets differ in their methods of composition, anyway; and not all of them have the faculty of revision.

I enclose "The Abominations of Yondo", which you can read and return at leisure. It is possible that I may yet find lodgement for it in some magazine: my friend Sterling is on the staff of "The Overland Monthly", and I'll ask him if they can run it.

H. P. Lovecraft is still contributing to "Weird Tales;" but they have refused some of his best work as being too fantastic! The present editor (like nearly all other editors) seems to have more of an eye on the circulation, than on the literary quality of the stuff he publishes.

I wish I could get half as much out of any poet's work, as you seem to get out of mine! There are many others who seem to have a tremendous enthusiasm for my poems; but I don't think I have ever heard of any one who appreciates them *more* than you do.

I will make typed copies of some of my unpublished poems for you. But much of the unused work I have on hand is inferior, or in need of revision. I don't want to publish another volume till I have accumulated a considerable amount of first-class work. It is hard to say when this will be; but, at any rate, the title of the book will be "Incantations."

I enclose an experiment in French, which may amuse you. Here is a word-for-word translation, in case any of the French gives you trouble.

A Sunset[1]

Far-falling from a wounded heaven,
The sunset, on the pool of jet,
Is cast like a faded blood.

The darknesses, beyond the water,
Nest without sound in the cypress
With the tired and heavy crow.

Seized by a black enchantment,
The proud tombs, in the low shadow,
Are phantoms that sink

Like satiated ghouls,
The yew-trees, bowed above the ossuary,
Are drowsed and tranquil.

The day, a dying memory,
Is lost in the dismal wood,
And drowned beneath the black pool.

Far-falling from a wounded heart,
My love, on the water of Lethe,
Is cast like a faded blood.

This is very bald—but it gives the sense, at any rate.
Cordially,
CAS [ornamented]

Notes

1. The French version of the poem is "Un Couchant."

[12]   [CAS to DW] [ALS]

Auburn, Cal.
Dec. 4th, 1925.

Dear Wandrei:

Here are some of the poems I promised you—all of which you are to keep. Hope you received "The Abominations of Yondo."

I will return the book by Saltus before long.

"The Envoys" is a new poem; but most of the others are left-overs from my former volumes.

Yours, in desperate haste,
Clark Ashton Smith

[13]   [CAS to DW]   [TLS]

Auburn, Cal.
Jan. 1st, 1926.

Dear Mr. Wandrei:

I received "The King of the Black Isles" and find much good work in it, though your criticism is just, on the whole. The melody, and the romantic feeling for the past, are its best features. As to influences, I would say that Swinburne is the most obvious one, particularly when the meter is one that Swinburne has pre-empted. Compare the poem on Beauty with "Dolores," in the first series of "Poems and Ballads." Probably the journalistic "catchiness" of some [of] the verse is responsible for Nicholson's popularity—together with expert press-agenting. Publicity is nine-tenths of the battle, in selling anything. The main reason why my books don[']t sell better is, that they have never had much advertising.

I returned the book by Saltus yesterday, insuring it for ten dollars. "The Witch of Endor" [*sic*] is a good title. I've seen some of Eldridge's free verse, and didn't care greatly for it.

"The Fugitives" is still unwritten[1]—it was to have been a romantic drama concerning the elopement of a queen and a poet, with the scene laid in Poseidonis, the last island of Atlantis. Perhaps I will write it some day; but nothing interests me at present, except the unearthly and the superhuman. Unfortunately, I have been too busy to do any actual writing. One needs leisure, and plenty of it, for jewel-cutting. Later, I hope to go on with "Incantations". Some of the poems that I sent you will be included, though I have grown very tired of sonnets and quatrain poems. I want to devote more attention to novelties of stanza-form, and other melodic variations in the future.

Benjamin de Casseres, the well-known New York critic, has been showing a good deal of interest in my work of late. He puts me with Poe and Blake and Baudelaire.

I am interested in your project for a critical appreciation of my poems—though I fear you will have to publish it yourself. Let me know if I can help you in any way. I certainly appreciate, and am greatly touched by, your phenomenal interest in my work. I have long planned to dedicate "Incantations" to the memory of Poe;[2] but I should be delighted to inscribe some particular poem to you, if you would care for this.

Cordially, as ever,
Clark Ashton Smith

[P.S.] Pardon the typewriter: I have a sore finger, and typing is easier for me, at present.

Notes

1. The songs for *The Fugitives* appeared in *Sandalwood* ("The Song of Aviol," "The

Song of Cartha," "The Love-Potion," and "Song"). A fragment of *The Fugitives* appears in *SS* (225–26). The "blank verse" portion does not appear to survive.
2. "Incantations," as it finally appeared in *SP*, bore no dedication.

[14]   [CAS to DW] [ALS]

Auburn, Cal
Feb. 12th, 1926

Dear Mr. Wandrei:

Pardon my delay in acknowledging your letter, and the volume of Saltus. I've had a severe attack of influenza, and am scarcely over it even yet.

I like "Bel-shar-uzzur,"[1] though the songs are very poor. Some of the descriptive blank verse is barbarically impressive, and the rhythmic monotony seems to add to the effect, somehow.

I will return Nicholson volume very soon. It is certainly far above the average of modern verse. Some of the poems, though, could have been omitted to advantage.

I have not done any writing lately, but hope to before long. Did I ever tell you that I also paint and draw? The pictorial impulse seizes me like a fever, periodically; the last few days, I have done nothing but paint fantastic landscapes. The best of them was suggested by a phrase in Lord Dunsany, "the monstrous colours of the jungle decay."[2] Another depicted the valley of the Many-Coloured Grass in Poe's "Eleonora".

I wish you all success with your critical venture. Your appreciation, and that of some other enthusiasts, does much to encourage me. Did I tell you that De Casseres, the well-known New York critic, had praised my poems highly, likening them to Poe and Blake?

I want to re-read "The Witch of Endor" before returning it.

Cordially,
Clark Ashton Smith

The enclosed article on Barnitz may interest you.[3] The paucity and inadequacy of critical mention concerning "The Book of Jade" is remarkable.

Notes

1. *Bel-Shar-Uzzur: A Dramatic Poem.* In *The Witch of En-Dor* 183–279.
2. From "Idle Days on the Yann," in *A Dreamer's Tales* (1910).
3. In DW to CAS 21, DW comments that the item lent to him was in the *Overland Monthly*. A review of the book appeared around the time of publication: Grace Luce Irwin, "Current Books," *Overland Monthly* 48 [*sic;* should be 38], No. 2 (August 1901): 153–54. The article in question was Carey McWilliams, "The Poet of Montsalvat," *Double Dealer* No. 47 (January 1926): 298–301, and probably was obtained from GS, who read it and commented to the author about it.

[15] [CAS to DW] [ALS]

Auburn, Cal.,
April 18th, 1926.

Dear Mr. Wandrei:

I find, somewhat to my consternation, that I have left your letter unanswered for nearly a month. I could easily have written before, but had no conception of the lapse of time.

I hope your project for critical articles **will** materialize. Few have even *mentioned* "The Book of Jade"—let alone done justice to it.

My paintings, concerning which you inquire, are done mostly with coloured inks and water-colours. I have made hundreds of them during the past eight or ten years, but none are on a large scale. I have done pencil, crayon and India ink drawings, also, but prefer more and more to work in colour. I enclose a grotesque in pencil,[1] to give you an idea of one phase of my work. I did numbers of such grotesques at one time. Now, I confine myself almost entirely to landscapes of an exotic fantastic type. I will make you a present of one or two before long.

No, I haven't seen the Poe illustrations by Harry Clarke. I have made half a dozen or more designs for Poe, myself—pictures based on "Eleonora," "The City in the Sea," and "The Valley of Unrest" are among my latest set. But my pictorial inspiration seems to have exhausted itself for the present, and I hope to do some verse before so very long.

De Casseres has written fifteen volumes, only four of which have been published so far. He is one of the few Americans whose work will endure. You can count the others on the fingers of one hand. The pork-packer[2] school of literature will not be among them . . . So far, De C.'s only published mention of my work was a brief review of "Ebony and Crystal" in "Arts and Decoration," about two years back.[3] I'm sorry I haven't it on hand; however, he had not read my book very carefully at the time, and seems to have been far more impressed with it on a second reading.

Cordially, as ever,
Clark Ashton Smith

P.S. I enclose two grotesques, which you can keep if you like them.

Notes

1. See *Grotesques and Fantastiques* for examples.
2. Person with a morbid fondness for death and dead bodies.
3. See Appendix.

[16]   [CAS to DW] [ALS]

Auburn, Cal.
May 9th, 1926.

Dear Mr. Wandrei:

I am glad to know that you liked the grotesques, and will take pleasure in sending you something better before long. My exotic landscapes, done in coloured inks and water-colour, are my best work. They are **complementary** to my poems, in the expression of fantastic beauty, and the quest for the Otherwhere—"anywhere out of the world."[1]

Harriet Monroe is a typical product of the age. What do you expect? Few men—and fewer women—have initiative and courage enough to go against the current. But I predict that H. and her pets will be looked on as curiosities inside of fifty years. Literary taste will become better—providing it doesn't become **worse** and supersede the abominable with the unimaginable.

I wish you all success with your monographs, and await the one on myself with the greatest interest. I am told that De Casseres intends to "do" an article also. The literary pontiffs of America may hear of me yet! I hope you can arouse some interest in "The Book of Jade." Saltus *will* be harder to "revive", on account of his unevenness and diffuseness. It could best be done by publishing a selection of his finer poems.

Some of them, by the way, are included in Stedman's American Anthology. Stedman's taste, though, was damnably academic.

I doubt if I can claim credit for the phrase, "pork-packer school." I have the impression that it has been used before. Certainly it fits! Miss Monroe's magazine is the abattoir of poetry.

"We Shall Meet" was published in "The Wanderer," a San Francisco magazinelet which only ran for a year or two. Evidently there was not enough local interest in verse to support it.

Yours Cordially,
Clark Ashton Smith

Notes

1. The title of a poem in prose by Baudelaire.

[17]   [CAS to DW] [ALS]

Auburn, Cal.
July 4th, 1926

Dear Donald:

Many thanks for your fine essay on my work, which I have enjoyed immensely. Portions of it are prose-poetry. Of course, I want to keep this copy, if I may. I liked best the portion beginning with the phrase about "shadowed gold." Also, the paragraphs touching specifically on "Ebony and Crystal."

My comparative non-productiveness during the ten years given to "E. & C." was due largely to ill-health. Also, I destroyed much imperfect work. But this is inessential. The essay needn't be altered to include such details. I have no technical criticism to offer, except that the word "literature" is used with noticeable frequency in the first two pages. It might be better to vary it with "poetry". Flaubert, I believe, made it a rule never to repeat the same word on the same page. But one needn't go so far as that, even in prose. In poetry, repetitions may have a distinct value.

Glad you liked my paintings. Some day I will loan you a lot of the best ones. Four have been sold privately in New York, though at a poor price ($5.00 each). An exhibition, if it could be managed, might uncover a few patrons. But the market for pictures (outside of commercial art and illustrating) is pretty limited in America. Anyway, there are few connoisseurs of the exotic and bizarre.

Misanthropy is the inevitable end, if you have both sense and sensibility. But it's a waste of spiritual energy: people aren't worth despising. They seem to exist for the same reason that Coventry Patmore said the Cosmos existed: "To make dirt cheap."[1]

Write me when you feel like it. I always enjoy your letters.

As ever,

CAS [ornamented]

Notes

1. "The Two Deserts," ll. 14–17: "The Universe, outside our living Earth, / Was all conceiv'd in the Creator's mirth, / Forecasting at the time Man's spirit deep, / To make dirt cheap."

[18]   [CAS to DW] [ALS]

Auburn, Cal.
Aug. 3rd, 1926

My dear Donald:

I certainly appreciate your essay, which I have re-read a number of times. I am now loaning it to a friend, who will, I am sure, also enjoy it. My criticism was a trivial one. There is no **exact** synonym for "literature"; but you might use "letters", or "poetry".

As to the destruction of certain imperfect verses—well, I don't know of *any* poet whose published work could not be weeded out to advantage. There is considerable rubbish, or rubble, in Keats and Shelley; and even Poe has poems that might well have been eliminated. So little survives, in the long run, that it is just as well not to over burden one's literary baggage.

I have never read Tolstoi's "What is Art," but am familiar with his theories at second-hand. T. thought, if I am not mistaken, that all art should be brought down to the aesthetic and intellectual level of a Russian mujik;[1] otherwise it was not good art. A somewhat similar theory seems to prevail in America: "making art safe for democracy (or moronism)," you might call it.

Your theory concerning the future development of art and literature seems probable enough to me. I wish you *would* write a book, and work out the idea fully. The "humanists" would howl, of course; but, as the French say, "Q'importe?"[2]

I enclose a little grotesque, which you are to keep. Note the unusual pigment—a private mixture of my own containing bronze powder. Sometimes, I lay my colours on a ground of Japanese gold-paint, which gives them a similar metallic effect.

When I loan you the paintings (some time in the fall, perhaps) I will send them by express, insured, and will probably ask you to forward them to H. P. Lovecraft.

As ever,

CAS [ornamented]

Notes

1. A Russian peasant (esp. before 1917).
2. "What does it matter?"

[19]   [CAS to DW] [ALS]

Auburn, Cal.,
Aug. 23rd, 1926.

My dear Donald:

I had no difficulty in translating your French, which seems correct enough for me. However, I am no scholar; and French idioms are frightfully complex. I am told it is easier to write good French verse, than prose. It seems to me you have done marvellously well, for six months study.

Not having an unbound copy of "E. & C.", I tore the cover from one, and mailed it to you last week. I can see it would be a difficult task to re-bind the volume; but you are welcome to experiment with this copy.

I mentioned your essay "The Emperor of Dreams" to George Sterling; and he thinks that "The Overland Monthly" might print it, "providing it is not too long." I don't know just what would be considered "too long"; but your essay, it seems to me, is not of excessive length. If there is no prospect of having it printed elsewhere, you might send a copy to George Sterling, % The Bohemian Club, San Francisco.

A friend to whom I showed your essay, advises the revision of the phrase, "a million years hence". I think, myself, that "a thousand years hence" would be far enough in the future; hell knows what the human louse will evolve or devolve into, in a million!

A volume of the sort that you propose, written in gold on black or green vellum, would certainly be a novelty and perhaps a very beautiful one. I suggest that the lettering might be varied with copper, bronze and aluminium, or silver.

Some day, I will send you a landscape done in metallic colours. They are harder to handle than ordinary pigments.

As ever,

CAS [ornamented]

[20]   [CAS to DW] [ALS]

Auburn, Cal.,
Sept. 3rd, 1926.

Dear Donald:

I didn't expect you to *pay* for that copy of "Ebony and Crystal." It had a damaged cover, anyway, and would scarcely have been saleable. However, I'll even up the balance some other way.

I admit the force of your argument in favour of the million-year clause. Of course, it is nothing in a cosmic sense; and good literature is not produced at the same rate as periodicals, novels, etc. The point my friend wished to make was that a million years might bring about certain evolutional changes in the human ephemera,—changes not necessarily for the best. What he said was, "The Yahoos of to-day are bad enough: imagine what a million years may evolute them into!" Suppose the mechanistic tendency should ultimately prevail? (Baudelaire thought it would—see "Mon Coeur Mis à Nu")[1] A gloomy prospect, but after all, what matter? The people of other planets will take up the Promethean torch, perhaps more worthily. As to posthumous fame, I am not dazzled by that "sun of the dead", as Balzac called it ("La gloire est le soleil des morts")[.][2]

I am glad you like Oriental art—but, of course, you would. I'd rather have one painting by a Chinese master than a whole car-load of Rembrandts and Sargents. If I had the chance, I would devote years to studying Chinese, Japanese, Hindu and Persian art. All these are characterized by a freedom from the "bondage of real things", as Arthur Symons wrote, speaking of the Japanese influence in Beardsley's drawings.[3]

I think of doing some landscapes on black satin, or sateen, in which I will make use of metallic tints. You shall have one of these, if they turn out well. Gold, silver, copper, aluminium, etc. (at least, the first three) have long been used in art; but I've never seen or heard of a picture done in pigments mixed with metal powder. The effect would be difficult, perhaps impossible to reproduce by photography or lithography.

As ever,

CAS [ornamented]

Notes

1. *Mon coeur mis à nu* (My heart laid bare) was a series of aphorisms found among Baudelaire's effects and published posthumously in 1887. A translation can be found in

Baudelaire: His Prose and Poetry (1919).

2. From *La Recherche de l'absolu* [The Quest of the Absolute] (1834): "Glory is the sun of the dead."

3. Actually, Symons wrote of "release from the bondage of what we call real things" (*Aubrey Beardsley* 29), a sentiment evoked in CAS's "The Centaur," where he speaks of "the freedom of fantastic things."

[21]   [DW to CAS] [ALS, private]

St. Paul, Minn.
Sept. 18, 1926.

Dear Clark:

To the many other things I have had to thank you for I add my appreciation of the magazines and the two fragments. It is impossible to obtain publications like those hereabouts, and I have long wanted to see a copy of "The Wanderer". Can this "Overland Monthly" possibly be the magazine of the same title which published the review of "The Book of Jade" that you sent me? I note that you have your usual damnable luck in getting your poems published and published correctly; and also that you have made some changes from the typewritten version I have. The only one I question is that of the last line in the fifth stanza; I hate to see either omitted. You are more gifted than any poet has a right to be; though the original line comes easier to my mind since I had the poem nearly memorized. "The Envoys", "We Shall Meet", and "The Saturnienne", of your later poems, and "Solution" of the earlier have, I think, more than rewarded your experiment with new forms. They are treasures, even among the many others; and to make new, beautiful verse-forms in this day when man (small m) has forgotten how to write musical poems is a proud achievement.

I have been rather puzzled by the two fragments. How is it possible to prevent the colours from running along the cloth-threads? This must present a serious obstacle in such work.

It is fitting tribute to Oriental artisans that they have seen for thousands of years, perhaps always the futility and stupidity of depicting things as they are, without glamour, without illusion, without romance. The European pride in the "portraiture" of paintings, the American in "naturalness" and "humanity" are fatal to art. At the last Minn. State Fair, the board was fortunate enough to obtain a loan of paintings and potteries from the private galleries of T. B. Walker, said to be one of the richest men in the world (a dubious honor).[1] The paintings were English and Continental of the last few centuries, including originals of Hals and Turner.[2] They were hardly worth examining. But I wish you could have seen the Chinese, Japanese, and Persian potteries. I would have preferred the least of them in its poor condition to the whole group of paintings. There were "beakers", temple jars, hexagonal and octangular tall vases, Ming wares, "sang de boeuf" or "ox-blood" jars;[3] there were two old Persian vases described as of a group of five found in the ruins of the palace of Haroun Al Raschid; there was a Chinese vase beautifully decorated with symbolic figures; two Greek amphorae, decorated; and a fine Chinese temple jar with a teakwood cover surmounted with sculptured jade. The paintings were wretched beside such examples of Eastern art. In the Hill library here are two huge Japanese vases, over five feet tall, of mosaic and beaten brass, magnificent specimens, both; like you, I should treasure one of these more than a gallery of "masters". They called Lafcadio Hearn crazy when he adopted the customs of Japan and died there with a Japanese wife, himself transformed completely. I am inclined to believe that he was infinitely wise. It is incredible that the world can have so criminally ignored the priceless rugs of Turkey and Persia and China, the wares of China, the paintings of such as Hiroshigi[4] and the Persian or Indian or Chinese craftsmen, the rich and costly manuscripts of Arabia which have never been surpassed, all the artistic wealth of the Orient and the marvelous sense of colour-value, figuring, and decoration which the Western nations can not remotely approach—and pride themselves on the fact.

Well! our tastes would seem to be strangely alike, and at variance with the accepted. That reminds me, the sum of posthumous, contemporary or any other kind of fame has no right to appear larger than a pinpoint to you; fame is intellectual and artistic suicide; he with a vast audience must pasture innumerable asses. Your friend had more reason than I, but I think devolution will supplant evolution. Progress and civilization appear to be fatal to [the?] mind; a couple of years ago I read an item stating that there were nearly a million maniacs in the United States alone, to say nothing of harmless individuals not in institutions. What an appalling result shall some day come if the trend continues!

I sent another version of my essay to you earlier in the week. You will notice the additions and numerous changes. Some of them are experimental, as for example, the substitution of *lesser* words for superlatives. I believe that this actually strengthens the effect; the "blurb" writers and "ad" men have so prostituted English to commercialism that simple qualifying adjectives are becoming more effective than the superlative. The limit is just about reached; all that is needed is "the best and very finest and greatest masterpiece of masterpieces ever written in the entire history of the whole world" from some well-paid "ad" writer. I am still unsatisfied with the appreciation, however; perhaps when I am a centenarian—if I don't sooner become disgusted and nauseated by "idiot man" and take the way of Park Barnitz—the essay will assume the shape I wish and become an adequate estimate of your poems, an adequate expression of my passion for them. As before, any suggestion of yours will be gladly accepted; it seems to me that some essential part is missing, but for the life of me I can't discover wherein it lies. It may be that I have enjoyed your volumes too greatly; and having enjoyed them so much can not command that great prose which alone may express their profound aesthetic and intellectual and spiritual value; that prose must exist in some strange, unknown, ulterior language, whose symbols are all symbols of ecstasy and rapture, ineffable, golden, the secret song of Beauty.

As ever,
Daw.

P.S. I may have overlooked corrections in the essay; make any such needed, if you care to keep it. I think I neglected the extra "t" in "unforget[t]able".

Notes

1. Thomas Barlow Walker (1840–1928), an American businessman who acquired timber in Minnesota and California and was among the ten wealthiest men in the world in 1923. He founded the Minneapolis Public Library and became an art collector.
2. Frans Hals the Elder (1582?–August 1666), a portrait painter of the Dutch Golden Age. Joseph Mallord William Turner (1775–1851), British Romanticist landscape painter.
3. Referring to the color of the glaze, not the contents.
4. DW means Tarawa Hiroshige (1797–1858), renowned Japanese ukiyo-e artist.

[22]   [CAS to DW] [ALS]

Auburn, Cal.,
Sept 27th, 1926

My dear Donald:

I have your letter, and the revised copy of the essay. I think you were wise to "tone down" superlative adjectives, and I have no fault to find with the alterations. The whole paper seems excellent to me. As to bettering it, I fear I have no suggestions that would be worth offering. More criticism and less eulogy would make the paper more acceptable to editors and readers. However, you wanted to express your own "reaction" (which doesn't seem to include fault-finding!) as clearly and sincerely as possible. And it seems to me that you have done this.

I mailed you a picture last week—one of three experiments on a black fabric. It was necessary to lay the colours on quite thickly, and the result is more fragile than I had hoped. In future, I shall add white of egg to the mixture, to fix the paint and bronze powder more firmly.

I haven't had much difficulty in painting on fabrics, even with washes of ink and water-colour, since I use only fabrics that are close-woven. The colours *would* run, in an ordinary weave. Many of the old Chinese and Japanese masterpieces were painted on silk. But I can't afford a silk that would be suitable for the purpose. The cloth that I use is known to the trade as "Venetian sateen".

The difference between Oriental and Occidental art is most significant, it seems to me. The former is spiritual; the latter, with its insistence on literal form and realistic detail, springs from the infernal materialism of the Western peoples. Ideal design and colour are sacrificed to produce, at any cost, the illusion of "reality."

However, there are some European and American painters that you should like. If you have not seen them, I should advise you to look up any originals or reproductions that you can find, of Gustave Moreau, John Martin, Felicien Rops, and Sime, the London artist of the grotesque. Odilon Redon (I have been compared to him, but don't know his work) might be worth investigating; also, the American Romantic painter, Arthur [*sic*] P. Ryder.[1]

As ever,

CAS [ornamented]

P.S. The Overland has changed owners and editors several times, since the publication of the Barnitz review. In fact, I think it was defunct for a while.

I hope the painting will please you. I haven't thought of a good title for it. "The Chasm", or "The Gulf", would be the most obvious ones.

Notes

1. Gustave Moreau (1826–1898), French Symbolist painter of biblical and mythological figures; John Martin (1789–1854), British Romantic painter, engraver, and illustrator; Félicien Rops (1833–1898), Belgian printmaker; Sidney H. Sime (1867–1941), British artist in late Victorian and succeeding periods, known mostly for his fantastic and satirical artwork, especially for the work of Lord Dunsany; Odilon Redon (1840–1916), French Symbolist painter and printmaker; and Albert Pinkham Ryder (1847–1917), American painter, best known for seascapes.

[23]   [CAS to DW] [ALS]

Auburn, Cal.,
Oct. 26th, 1926.

Dear Donald:

Here is a letter for you from George Sterling. He had loaned your article, with address, to Miss Lee[1] of the Overland, so sent me the letter to mail.

I advise you to accept his offer, since I am convinced, myself, that no Eastern magazine would run your article. A far briefer and much less enthusiastic review of my work, written by one Alfred Galpin,[2] was turned down everywhere. But the Overland will be glad to run your paper—it will call attention to *them* as well as to me. Doubtless, as George says, there will be much derision and incredulity; but I take it that you care as little as I do. Anyway, few people around San Francisco can ever have read my work, if the S. F. sales are any indication. A hundred copies of "E. & C." and thirty of "Sandalwood" seem to have glutted the market.

Don't mind what G. says about your presumptive youth. As I'm pointing out to him, there are others, such as De Casseres and H. P. Lovecraft, men of middle-age, who would back you up, in substance. Everyone thinks your article well-written, especially Lovecraft, to whom I loaned my copy not long ago. He was curious about you, and wanted to know if you had written anything else. I'm asking his permission to loan you the typescripts of some new horror stories that he sent me.

Glad you liked the picture, which was at least imaginative enough. I thought of leaving out the back-ground rocks, but a similar trick has been done before. Goya has a picture of some people sitting on a rotten limb, over an abyss, with no suggestion of back-ground or bottom.[3] It will make you giddy, if you look at it long enough.

As ever,

Clark.

Notes

1. B. Virginia Lee (b. 1902), an editor at the *Overland Monthly* and later the *New American*.
2. "Echoes from Beyond Space," *United Amateur* 24, No. 1 (July 1925): 3–4. Galpin was an associate of HPL and for a time, fellow amateur journalist.
3. The etching "Disparate Ridiculo" (Ridiculous Folly), from the *Disparates* series, plate 3, by Francisco Goya y Lucientes (1746–1828).

[24]   [CAS to DW] [ALS]

Auburn, Cal.,

Nov. 11th, 1926.

Dear Donald:

Here are the two stories by H. P. Lovecraft that I mentioned in my last. I suggest that you return them to him directly (his address is on the typescript) and write him a letter. He will be very glad to hear from you. Your tastes and his are remarkably similar, it seems to me.

I understand that your article will be out next month. We shall see what we shall see. G. S. is pessimistic but I don't think the taste for Romantic poetry will die out entirely, unless the whole human race turns into a flock of sheep. Romanticism is revolt, the Promethean spirit ever seeking to overthrow the gods of the commonplace—and the marketplace. The latest ruse of the forces of Law and Order is to throw the Romantic-fantastic type of imagery out of court as being "non-vital." Even G. S. seems to be "falling" for this.

As ever,

Clark

[P.S.] Ben De Casseres is the man for your article. I'll see that he gets a copy.

[25] [CAS to DW] [ALS]

Auburn, Cal.,

Nov. 13th, 1926.

Dear Donald:

        I received your letter just after I had mailed you the two stories by H. P. Lovecraft. Hope you've gotten them by this time. "The Call of Cthulhu" is much the best, I think.

        G. S., as I said before, seems inclined to make concessions to the "vitalistic" school. There's no use arguing with him or anybody else about it. The viciousness and fallacy of the "vital" theory is patent to me,—it's only the old didacticism in a new disguise; but you can't talk to people in terms of pure logic,—unless they agree with you beforehand. I'll give it up, and go my own way, literarily speaking. "All concessions are made to the devil," in the brave words of Ben De Casseres.[1] From "vitalism" to the "ethical imagination" is only one step at best; and you can't get anywhere if you admit ethical considerations, which are purely relative, into the realm of the Absolute. The imagination becomes a mill-hand—or a Sunday-school teacher! Truth, if anyone ever discovers it, may prove to be the deadliest poison in the whole pharmacop[e]ia of the universe; certainly, there's no reason for inferring that it will be of any "social value."

        Not much of "Incantations" has been written, so far—my inspiration has taken a pictorial form for the past year. But don't worry—the poems will "out" sooner or later; when they do, I want them to go beyond anything else I have written in visionary scope and insight. At least, I don't want to repeat myself. I seem to be waiting for some sort of inner clarification at present. I want no finger-marks on my crystal, no cob-webs or vapours on my "necromancer's glass".

        Of course, I will be delighted to read your stories or anything else you have written, and will send them on to H. P. L. I think you are preternaturally modest not to have told me before,—or I was stupid not to have asked! Your English teacher's comment sounds like a tribute—if people call you "crazy", it is prima facie evidence that you have fathered something more or less uncommon. Well, I have an epigram on the subject: "Sanity is the madness of the greatest number."[2] If God exists, there is certainly no proof that he is sane, from the standpoint of a stockbroker or an alienist.

        Let's hope that you, I, Lovecraft, De Casseres, and perhaps one or two others can keep the Romantic revolt alive, in this age of Americanization—which is a process of making the world safe for mediocrity.

        Do you want to see my epigrams? I have written hundreds at one time or another, and will type a lot of them for you, if you wish.[3] You would like some of them, though others may seem too flippant and mundane.

As ever,

Clark.

Notes

1. "Emerson the Individualist," in *Forty Immortals* (New York: Seven Arts Publishing Company, 1926), 89.

2. From "The Epigrams of Alastor."

3. Published under various running titles: "The Devil's Notebook"; "Cocktails and Crème de Menthe"; "New Teeth for Old Saws"; "Points for the Pious"; "Unpopular Sayings"; "Paradox and Persiflage"; "The Epigrams of Alastor"; and "Epigrams and Apothegms." Now collected in *The Devil's Notebook*. The typescript CAS sent DW contained far more epigrams than the ten that appeared under that title in *Leaves* and included items taken from CAS's various appearances of epigrams.

[26]   [DW to CAS] [ALS]

1152 Portland Ave., St. Paul.
Nov. 27—[1926]

Dear Clark:

I have been profoundly moved by the news of George Sterling's death. The fragmentary accounts I have found in local and California newspapers are not very satisfactory; but their suggestion is infinite. He died a suicide, but I admire him for his art, for I have seen a quotation of one of his best lines: "Deeper into the darkness can I peer than most, yet find the darkness still beyond" and, "Until all friendship end[s] in death, the friend of friends".[1] He has gone the way of many another brave man, but he has left behind much more than they. I have not liked the tendencies displayed in his work of recent years, but his earlier volumes, especially "The Testimony of the Suns" and "A Wine of Wizardry," contain much that is beautiful, and much that deserves to endure. I have been slow in appreciating his poetry, for his volumes are quite difficult to obtain here, but having come to know him, I rank him very high. His death is a tragedy; but not more so, I think, than several other unhappy events in his life if I interpret the papers correctly. Memorials are not for us; his own poems are a more fitting and more lasting; we can only regret, as, from outside, we vainly peer into that deeper darkness wherein has gone George Sterling, a dreamer and a poet. We can only echo "Vale" to his silent "Ave atque Vale."

I have read the two tales of Mr. Lovecraft with the deepest interest. You are correct in your judgment, as usual, for "The Call of Cthulhu" is by far the better. I think it is one of the best tales he has written, at least of those which I have read. If this is one which "Weird Tales" returned, my steadily declining opinion of W.T. shall take another drop. I am returning them to the author this week, with a note of thanks and appreciation.

I shall also send this week a few of the things I have written. Some of the tales may interest you, if for no other reason than the subject. I have ceased showing them to people, after one or two trials; one does not seem to be admired for discarding the conventions. None of them is of recent composition; I have practically ceased writing, because the reward of the mental strain is so unsatisfactory. I am sometimes appalled at the effort and the time that must have gone into the making of your poems. Few people seem to realize that the mental strain of writing can be, and in the case of literary artists usually is, greater and more tiring than the hardest of physical labor.

I shall be delighted to see *all* your epigrams if it is not too much trouble to type them. I must confess that I have a weakness for them, because they say so much in so little. They are too often abused, unfortunately, but then, so are all types of literature.

I hope my essay finds favour with Benj. de Casseres. I have liked the few things of his which I have been able to find. You stated once that he also planned a criticism of your poetry. Do you know whether his plan has materialized, or will materialize? If it does, let me know where it appears.

The "vitalistic" school will eventually pass. It is unfortunate that it lingers on, but perhaps that very act will help bring about a return of Romanticism. I have no sympathy with contemporary schools and the bulk of their product; my hope is that the return will be stronger for having been delayed and suppressed so long.

As always,
Donald—

Notes

1. The first quotation actually appeared much earlier in *Lilith* 2.1.36–37 (but read "gaze" for "peer"). The second quotation appears in a syndicated story on Sterling's funeral; e.g., the *Santa Ana Daily Evening Register Chronicle,* 18 November 1926. There may have been other newspaper appearances. It is unknown if the lines are from an unfound or unpublished poem, or if GS composed them just before his death.

[27]   [CAS to DW] [ALS]

Auburn, Cal.,
Dec. 6th, 1926.

Dear Donald:

George's death was a great shock to me. We were intimate friends, and I have always had the highest admiration for his poetry. But I suppose he took the best way out. As Benjamin De Casseres wrote me: "We are all waiting to get out of this pig sty." I enclose a clipping from "The San Francisco Chronicle."[1]

I think his poetry (not the best of it, however,) will come in for considerable appreciation now ... "A Wine of Wizardry" had great influence on my own poetic development, and helped to confirm my flair for the fantastic. I think it is the longest poem that I know entirely by heart. I first read it when it appeared in the old "Cosmopolitan," about 1907, with an accompanying eulogy by Ambrose Bierce,[2] who ranked it among the greatest imaginative poems in literature. To this I subscribe whole-heartedly, in the teeth of all the proper and grand Moguls of poetic (?) realism. I have all of George's books, and would be glad to loan you anything you have not seen. The drama "Lilith" is one of his best works, and "Sails and Mirage" contains much fine work. My prime favourites, though, are the first three volumes, of which "The House of Orchids" was the third.

Your article on me is out, and reads even better in print, despite two or three typographical errors. I think you will receive five copies—the only payment that "The Overland" makes.

I have gone through "Ebony and Crystal" of late, and am struck by what Edgar Saltus would call "the resonant merit"[3] of the poems. There is something invidious, beyond a doubt, in the way my book has been passed over. Many presentation copies to literary "notables", such as William Rose Benet, Conrad Aiken, and Stuart P. Sherman, were not even acknowledged by the recipients. In fact, Markham and De Casseres were the only "notables" who really welcomed the book. You can draw your own conclusions, knowing the "trend of the times." "Vested Interests" are not confined to business and religion.

Note George's mention of "The Hermaphrodite" in his "Rhymes and Reactions" in the Dec. Overland—probably the last thing that he wrote.[4] The author is an old friend of mine, Samuel Loveman, **not** "Tweman", as the name is spelled by the Overland's linotyper,—who ought to be taken out and ganched from the parapet of the S. F. Ferry Bldg. The poem is a marvellous achievement, and has inspiration, beauty, and melody in excelsis. In it one may wander

"With halcyon feet by seas of rose
Against whose foam the ilex grows."[5]

It should be another "wild hair" in the eyes of the "vitalists", if any of them read it.

I am ordering ten "Overlands" for distribution among people who will appreciate your article. Lovecraft wanted two. The editor's note prefixed to your essay was not in any too good taste.[6] George was somewhat brow-beaten by the realists, toward the end, and even doubted the value of his own best work.

You shall have my epigrams before long.

As ever,

Clark.

Notes

1. Probably [Unsigned], "George Sterling Kills Himself in Bohemian Club," *San Francisco Chronicle* (18 November 1926): 1, 3.

2. Ambrose Bierce, "A Poet and His Poem," *Cosmopolitan* 43, No. 5 (September 1907): 575–77.

3. *The Philosophy of Disenchantment* 17.

4. George Sterling, "Rhymes and Reactions," *Overland Monthly*, 84, No. 12 (December 1926): 395.

5. *The Hermaphrodite*, in *Out of the Immortal Night* 49.

6. "'This may be a little too much of praise of Clark Ashton Smith, but at least it will bring comment and that is what we want,' said George Sterling when we brought this article into our office for the December issue" (380).

[28]   [CAS to DW] [ALS]

Auburn, Cal.,
Dec. 26th, 1926

Dear Donald:

A note to acknowledge your typescripts, which arrived before Christmas. I have run through most of them hastily, but wish to re-read them several times before I pass them on to Lovecraft. They are tremendously imaginative, and whatever stylistic flaws they possess (I haven't noticed any fatal ones) should be correctible by practice. "Art is long," but I advise you to go on, if you can stand the nerve-strain and mental tension of creative effort. I agree with you that these are deadly—"The Hashish-Eater", for instance, nearly killed **me.** I had the "hang-over" of a Babylonian debauch after writing it!

De Casseres liked your article,—and insists that you have not overpraised me. He is going to do one himself, but wants to feel in a creative mood. He has financial troubles, and is forced to do considerable pot-boiling. One Harold Hersey (editor of some cowboy magazine!) wrote Miss Lee that he was delighted with your article.[1]

I will send you the epigrams—also some verses—after New Year's. I have been asked to write an article on Sterling for "The Overland", and this means a lot of work.

I hope you will go on with your stories. You have an amazing fantasy. [*sic*]

In haste,

Clark Ashton Smith

Notes

1. Harold Hersey (1893–1956), science fiction editor and publisher. He edited the *Thrill Book* (1919), publishing CAS's poem "Dissonance," and *Ranch Romances* (1924–29), and took over the editorship of *Ghost Stories* during its final years (1930–31).

[29]   [DW to CAS]

1152 Portland Ave.,
St. Paul, Minn.
Dec. 28, 1926.

Dear Clark:

I owe you an apology for the inexcusably long time I have let your letter remain unanswered. I waited some time before I received my Overlands, and then it was the hectic holiday rush. With gratitude in my heart, I murmur, "Thank Heavens, it's over!"

My critique looks better than I thought it would in print, in spite of all the efforts of the "Overland's" thrice-cursed linotyper. I should agree with your suggestion of an appropriate fate, but it isn't quite adequate. I hope the essay will win you other supporters and enthusiasts, and call attention to some degree, at least, to your poetry. If it does, I shall be satisfied. Lovecraft has just sent me a copy of the magazine wherein Galpin's review appeared. I read it with much interest, and disappointment. His emphasis of inferior work intermixed with good, and rather flippant treatment are both unmerited and unjust. Perhaps my great admiration of your work has blinded me to flaws, but I confess that I can find very few. And I have been accused of being too harsh a critic rather than otherwise by most people who know me. I trust the copies of the "Overland" you are sending out will be appreciated. I have disposed of my ten copies except for a couple that I intend to send Arthur Machen and Vincent Starret[t].

I mailed you some—most—of my manuscripts last week. Perhaps one or another of them may interest you. Except for half-a-dozen, they are not really short stories; "fantasies" is perhaps a better name. "The Door to the Room" is the tale which brought upon my head the "crazy" remarks of a pious and puzzled professor. "The Twilight of Time" was written when I was sixteen, though I have made a few minor corrections since. It is a satire gone wrong, my intent having originally been to show standardization carried to its ultimate extreme. The "Fragment of a Dream" at one time made me think I had accomplished something, but I have destroyed half my manuscripts for various reasons, lately, and may add the "Fragment" to those which can now be perused only by wraiths. "The Messengers", you will observe, is in prose much what your "Envoys" was in poetry. I wrote it before I had read your poem, but it might be wiser for me to change or destroy it, since it has too many points in common with yours. Keep the manuscripts as long as you wish, but send them to Lovecraft when you are finished, if you believe he would care to read them.

I should be very glad to read others of George Sterling's books. All I could get in the various libraries here were "A Wine of Wizardry", "The Testimony of the Suns", "Beyond the Breakers", "The House of Orchids", and "Selected Poems". "Lilith" and "Sails and Mirages" I should especially be pleased to read, if you have them, or any others that I do not know. Send them express collect.

I have read the clipping carefully, and would like to keep it if you do not want it returned. I found it singularly difficult to get any material or data on Sterling during his life, and therefore filed all the clippings I could find in various papers for Nov. 18–20.

I am sending for Loveman's book "The Hermaphrodite" to-day, if copies are still available. I have always sought books recommended by you, Lovecraft, and Sterling, but when all three find merit in the same book, it is a tribute of the highest type.

Mr. Lovecraft has just loaned me some of his unpublished work, which, I take it, you already know. "The Doom that Came to Sarnath" and "The Strange High House in the Mist" were the best of the six he sent. "From Beyond" and "Beyond the Walls [*sic*] of Sleep" ought to be rewritten, but I don't believe "Psychopompos" will ever add to his reputation. These last three are a severe contrast to such tales as "The Outsider", "The Rats in the Walls", and "The Call of Cthulhu".

Later, if I have time, I shall type some poems I have written and send you them, if you care to read them. They might well be given the general title, "Laus Mortis"; unfortunately, they have none whatever of that great beauty present in your own poems. They are interesting, perhaps, rather than distinctive.

With thanks in advance for the loan of Sterling's volumes, and apology for my delay,

As ever,
D W.

[30]   [CAS to DW] [ALS]

Auburn, Cal.,
Jan. 13th, 1927.

Dear Donald:

I've sent your prose fantasies on to Lovecraft, and feel pretty sure he will like some of them. "A Fragment of a Dream" is the best-written of the lot, in my opinion. I liked also "The Door to the Room" and the companion prose-poems, "The Messengers" and "The Pursuers." I agree with you that "The Messengers" has a partial similarity to my "Envoys" but hope you will not destroy it on that account. It is very beautiful. Doubtless we both tapped the same sources of inspiration. . . . Anyway, there are no new ideas in the universe—so "why worry"?

"The Door to the Room" has a genuine shudder in it! It reminds me of the nightmares that I used to have! One isn't likely to forget some of the imagery.

I sent you some clippings, verses, etc., the other day. You can return the reviews of my work at leisure, and keep the other stuff; also, keep the notice of Sterling's suicide . . . There's a rumour current to the effect that he killed himself because he feared that he was losing his mind; but I don't know how much truth there is in it.

I discovered at least half a dozen flaws in the French poem that I sent you, when I came to look it over! Will give you a revised copy some time. One can't take anything for granted in regard to French idioms. The beastly little prepositions and conjunctions give me more trouble than anything else.

Hope you got the Sterling volumes. You can keep them as long as you like.

By the way, have you ever seen Baudelaire's last volume of verse, "Les Epaves"? I gather from Symon[s]'s mention of it in his book on B., that it contains about 160 pages of material, including the six poems that caused the suppression of "Les Fleurs du Mal."[1]

I'll be very glad to read your poems, when you can find time to type them for me. I'll copy a lot of my epigrams for you soon.

Hope you will enjoy Loveman's poem. It is not perfect, but has something—a breath of beauty or of ecstasy—that flawless poetry does not always achieve.

> As ever, your friend,
> C A S [ornamented]

Notes

1. *Les Épaves (Jetsam)* was a collection (published in Belgium to evade censorship) that included the poems excluded from the 1857 edition of the *Les Fleurs du mal*, consisting of some from *Nouvelles Fleurs du mal* and ten items Baudelaire judged unsuited for his other collections. The first edition of *Les Fleurs du mal* contained six poems condemned by the French court and ordered removed from the book. The poems were later restored under a section titled "Les Épaves." CAS translated these as I. Les Bijoux; II. Lethe; III. To Her Who Is Too Gay; IV. Lesbos; V. Femmes damnées: Delphine et Hippolyte; VI. The Metamorphoses of the Vampire.

[31] [DW to CAS] [ALS, private]

St. Paul, Jan. 20, 1927

Dear Clark:

I acknowledge with pleasure and the deepest gratitude all the things you sent. I was especially interested in the poems of yours and in the clippings concerning your works. My own French is not of sufficient extent to have any initial value concerning grammatical structure of the poem, but I don't see that it needs much change. The two English poems are peculiar, at least in their metrical form. I don't remember having seen any others like them, but then, you are the one who would invent new forms . . ! I disagree with the clippings in part. For example, the influence of Sterling on your work is greatly overestimated in one of them.

I have been busy of late, and have not had time to read the four volumes of Sterling, but have read two carefully and the others hastily. I did not realize what treasured possessions I was asking [for] when I desired the loan of the books, or I should have hesitated. I appreciate your courtesy more than I can express and the associations of the volumes has [*sic*] made me read them with more even than the care I would have given them in any event. There is exquisite poetry in these four works, and lines of unusual beauty are present to a degree almost unbelievable in this day, even for Sterling. I must thank you also for "A Day in the Hills."[1] The poems in it are erratic and very unequal in worth, ranging from the good to "stuff", but the pictures of Sterling make it of more than usual value.

Loveman's poems in the "Saturnian" (Is this still being published)[2] are likewise uneven; some I like, but some are scarcely mediocre. I have just received "The Hermaphrodite", and have taken a great liking to it. Whatever flaws it may have I am more than willing to excuse for the beauty of many of the lines, and for the high level of the poem as a whole. I have seen some lyrics of his in the United Amateur, which I also liked very much.

I shall return Sterling's volumes and the criticisms before very long.

I am glad that you found some of my fantasies worth reading. I have received an incredible amount of *discouragement* in this part of the country, and words of praise for the things I do are both rare and appreciated. However, a number of the things I sent are of no particular value, and one or two need revision. I think some of the typescripts were faulty; the last pages of "The Green Flame", it seems to me, were in process of revision, and some of the others need revision also. What you say of "The Door to the Room" struck me almost with the force of a blow, because parts of it were remembered from nightmares I had several years ago. The clawing arm picture was one of the most terrible nightmares I ever had, and affected me for weeks; then, I must have been only eleven or twelve when it came, for it occurred years ago. It is quite a while since I last was visited by nocturnal terrors.

A young artist I know and to whom I loaned my copy of "Sandalwood" returned it with a jacket and design. It's an interesting piece of work in black and white; it has a somewhat conventional border of vines and wreathes, [*sic*] but a great serpent rises upward from the lower left, coiling first around a beautiful and poisonous and lovely head of a woman; and where the woman's hair should be, a candle gutters, and the tallow forms queer apples as of exotic hair. The suggestion of the drawing is more powerful and effective than the work itself.

When is your article on Sterling to appear? I am quite anxious to see it, for it ought to be a valuable essay considering your knowledge both of the poet and his work. The note in "The Saturnian" prompts the question: Have any of your pictures or paintings been reproduced in magazines or elsewhere? I don't suppose this is very likely to be the case, however, in view of the usual magazine's preferences.

I have never seen "Le[s] Epaves". I am trying to locate a copy here again, but haven't yet succeeded; nor, if the libraries are in usual form, will I succeed.

Thanking you again for the loan of the books and the clippings

As ever,

Donald Wandrei

P.S. I have dropped the "D. A." henceforth and for ever for no particular reason except irritation at answering the questions of innumerable (at least they seem so) people who wanted to know the significance of the initials.

Donald

Notes

1. Edited by Henry Meade Bland; see Bibliography. Bland later included CAS' "Nyctalops" in an anthology.
2. The *Saturnian* was an amateur journal edited by Loveman. Three issues appeared: June–July [1920], August–September [1920], and March 1922. Loveman had announced in issue No. 1 that he was going "to present our readers with an appreciation and appraisal of the poetry and drawings of Clark Ashton Smith" (p. 8) and in issue No. 2 that the next issue of the *Saturnian* "will contain reproductions of two or three of the imaginative drawings, notably the magnificent 'Fear'." Neither of these appeared.

[32]   [CAS to DW] [ALS]

Auburn, Cal.,

Feb. 9th, 1927

Dear Donald:

I felt sure you would appreciate Sterling's work. His best is second to that of no one, in my opinion . . . As to my article (which will appear in the March Overland)—well, I fear its only merit is that it *does* convey my appreciation, in a measure. But critical essays or encomiums are not my forte; and I found it impossible to say much on the personal side, without indiscretion . . . There are too many others, however, who will not share my scruples.

Loveman printed only three issues of "The Saturnian", as I remember. Two of them were made up of translations from Heine, Baudelaire and Verlaine.[1] I imagine the Heines were the best. Some of the Baudelaires seemed to me to indicate a misreading of the original text. Loveman is uneven, but he is a true poet; and "The Hermaphrodite", at least, contains qualities that are seldom found in perfect art.

None of my pictures have been reproduced, except some hasty line-drawings that I made for a third-rate story of Lovecraft's, "The Lurking Fear", which appeared in a vile magazinelet entitled "Home Brew." I don't think they amounted to anything . . . Lovecraft, by the way, has a fine imaginative piece, "The White Ship," in the current "Weird Tales."

Here are some more French verses. I think they are better, idiomatically, than the last specimen that I sent you. The local French teacher went over them, and straightened me out on one or two points.

I am really very enthusiastic about your prose-poems; and I think you will find that Lovecraft is, too. Don't be discouraged by the bourgeoisie: I've had enough criticism of the sort you mention; in fact, I have been almost outlawed for the weirdness and alleged "wickedness" of some of my poems. Only yesterday, I was buttonholed by some would-be reformers (women, of course) and subjected to a lecture on the score of my various iniquities. Apparently they wanted to make a public bonfire of my best work, and confine myself, in the future, to poetic sermons, "uplift", etc., a la Edwin Markham and Edgar Guest.[2] I think they also wanted to reform my personal morality, which is locally supposed to be somewhat Byronic.

The cover design for "Sandalwood" that you describe is certainly a strange conception. Beardsley or Rops might have made something of it.

What about the verses you were to send me?

I will have the epigrams ready to send with my next. I haven't forgotten, but have been much pressed and harried.

As ever,

Clark.

Notes

1. Loveman's translations are gathered in *Out of the Immortal Night*.
2. Edgar A. Guest (1881–1959) was a prolific English-born American poet whose work became a byword for triteness and conventionality.

[33]   [CAS to DW] [ALS]

Auburn, Cal.,
March 13th, 1927

Dear Donald:

I have read your poems over several times, and like some of them. They are not as good as your prose; but I wouldn't be surprised if you were to write something very fine, in a few years. I hope you will keep on: masterpieces are one-fourth inspiration and three-fourths hard work, as a rule. I like the imaginative touches in some of your verses. "In Mandrikor" is suggestive of something that I once planned to write. I will return the poems presently, with more detailed comments.

I have typed a lot of miscellaneous epigrams—serious, flippant and sardonic—and enclose them herewith. Probably you will like some of them. There is more truth than poetry in most of them.

I am glad that "Weird Tales" showed a little good taste in accepting one of your prose fantasies.[1] As a rule, the editor seems to care only for "popular appeal."

I won a poetry prize the other day, much to my amazement. I was awarded fifty dollars for the best poem published in volume 5 of "The Lyric West", a Los Angeles poetry magazine. The poem was "To Omar Khayyam", which they had held for years before printing. I had forgotten all about it, in fact.

Lovecraft is very much taken with your work. I trust that his opinion—and mine—will help a little to offset any local discouragement. Remember always that you can't expect anything but opposition, misunderstanding and enmity from the mob.

I sent you an "Overland" with my article on "G. S." I meant to send one to Lovecraft, also, but have been unable to secure extra copies so far. There seems to have been a "run" on the magazine.

Yes, that encounter with the "reformeresses" was quite amusing. Obviously, they didn't realize what a contract they were undertaking! My two cardinal rules of conduct (or misconduct?) are these: Never to apologize for anything—and never to confess anything. Let the mob howl: it's the nature of beasts to howl.

I enclose a snapshot of myself, taken a year or two back. I am five feet ten inches in height, weigh 138 lbs, and very hard, muscular and agile. People often take me to be a "foreigner" of some sort. There are French and Celtic strains in the family.

> As ever,
> Clark Ashton Smith

Notes

1. "The Twilight of Time," published as "The Red Brain."

[34]   [DW to CAS] [ALS]

> 1152 Portland Ave.,
> St. Paul, Minn.
> March 25, 1927

Dear Clark:

I have read your epigrams with the utmost glee and an inward delight such as I have not experienced in a long time. They are choice; as a friend of mine remarked when I read some of the best, including the two on dancing, "They open out on you when you consider them." There are a few which seem to be statements of fact rather than epigrams, but the percentage of "luscious" cynicisms is extraordinarily high. I have read them several times now, and take particular delight in quoting certain ones at the moments that they will do the most good, and to individuals who will *feel*, if not appreciate, them. As you may gather, I am entranced by them, as a whole. If you do not want them returned,

I shall be overwhelmingly grateful and everlastingly proud to keep them for my private delectation. If you desire them, let me know and I shall copy most of them before returning the group. My only criticism pertains to the title; "The Devil's Note-Book" is an excellent title, but it resembles Bierce's "The Devil's Dictionary" and an anonymous author's "The Devil's Definitions".[1] This, however, is a minor point; merit places your epigrams on the shelf with Bierce and Wilde. The reading of these leads me to remark: you are a most versatile writer, one of the most gifted men of this, the twentieth century; poem, prose poem, short story, epigram, drawing, painting—Heavens! I do not know to what other goals you can possibly aspire, unless it be the novel and music!

I have read your critique, all too brief, in the Sterling number of the "Overland"; and I wish to express my gratitude for seeing that I received a copy. Add "critical essay" to the list in the paragraph above. Your taste is discriminating, but the essay is so well done that I wish there were more. Your work, and especially your poetry, has the singular and dual quality of satisfying me more than the writings of any other man, and yet leaving me eternally unsatisfied in its insufficiency of amount.

I am ever more profoundly grateful for the "snapshot" picture. For a long time I have had the most maddening desire to know *who* you were; but you have been a riddle, an enigma, ever since that memorable day of my life, two years ago, when I first read "Ebony and Crystal". I have often wondered and wondered what you were like, without having the audacity to ask; and now that I have the photo, I am surprised at the remarkably close resemblance of your visible picture and the imaginary portrait, the ideal image I had formed. You look Poesque and romantic. I am extremely pleased by your sending the photo, and am sorry that I can't return the favour; but the next time I have my picture taken, I'll send you a copy.

I had a piece of extraordinary good fortune a couple of days ago. While rummaging around in a second-hand bookstore in Minneapolis, I discovered hidden away in dusty shelves of books in the mysterious upper regions a copy of "The Star-Treader". How it got to this forlorn section of America is more than I can fathom. It is different from my other copy—it is larger in size, has the pages untrimmed and uncut, and is bound in gold-stamped brown boards instead of grey boards and pasted label and back strip. The date and publisher coincide with the other copy, however. How did it happen that the edition of the book was—apparently—made up in two different bindings?

Congratulations on your winning the poetry prize! It is only one of many that you ought to have received. The poem, I take it, is the same one which appeared in "Ebony and Crystal". Verily, the ways of the editor are strange and inexplicable; he is utterly unfettered by any consideration of Time, and hath eaten of the lotus in that the years are to him but as days. You might send out all your poems now so that you will have a comfortable annuity by the time you are seventy or eighty, if the prizes keep up and the dear editors run true to form.

I am glad that you liked some of the verse I sent, though I am skeptical about its value. I have written verse as an apology for doing nothing better. Not more than a half-dozen of the group are of any value; the rest, I think, could be dispensed with and not be a serious loss to the world's poetry. After a rather long absence, I am returning to prose, and probably shall write no more poetry, for some time, perhaps a year or more. With this letter I am enclosing a pagan rhapsody, "ΠΑΦΟΣ" (Paphos) which you may keep if you care at all for it. I suggest that you read it the next time the local Watch and Ward Society becomes interested in your morals. It must have some effect or another. This is the most indeterminate thing I have written as yet, and almost defies classification. At any rate, it's a new note in my writing. I wrote another fantasy last week which I meant to send with "ΠΑΦΟΣ", but Lovecraft has it. I'll send it along as soon as he returns it. I think you might like "The Woman at the Window", as I have titled it; it belongs to the class of "The Messengers" and "The Pursuers"; and is a study in blood reds and shades of red. I am almost through with another one of these brief poems in prose, and may be able to type it and send it with "The Woman at the Window." It will show the influence of "Ebony and Crystal" at least in its title, "Ebony and Silver" or "Ebony and Ivory."

As ever,
Donald Wandrei

P.S. If you have time, I'd appreciate mention of the worst or most obvious flaws in my verse.

D W.

[Enclosure: T.Ms. of "ΠΑΦΟΣ," inscribed] For Clark Ashton Smith, Grecian, and, as singers of Greece, singer of the ages.

Notes

1. No book of this title has been found.

[35] [CAS to DW] [ALS]

Auburn, Cal.,
April 5th, 1927

Dear Donald:

I am returning your poems in the same mail with this. "Song of Oblivion," "Sanctity and Sin," "In Memoriam: G. S.," "The Challenger," "In Mandrikor," and "Out of the Grave,"[1] seem to stand out most on re-reading. "In Mandrikor" has a truly imaginative atmosphere—in fact, it is so strong that I'd like to see you make it even stronger. I don't like the third line, somehow, but can't suggest an effective substitute at present. "And the faint stars are wisps that wave" is all I can think of; but there ought to be something better. I have a dislike for the word "glee," too; and would prefer "They hold in mirth their mad domain."[2] But these are only suggestions. "Song of Oblivion" is melodious, and has poignancy of phrase and feeling. The Poesque "Out of the Grave" is effective, too. I hope you will go on writing verse, as well as prose—the main thing is to persevere, and not become discouraged.

Thanks for the prose-rhapsody, "Paphos"; also, for the copy of "The Minnesota Quarterly." "Paphos" has much beauty, though I think you are more successful, so far, with the "weirds." I re-read "A Fragment of a Dream" with much pleasure. Who is Barbara Fawcett Craigie? "La Dame qui Avait L'Air Etrange"[3] has fine and unusual imaginative qualities.

I mailed you some more epigrams the other day. Hardly thought you would care so much for the cynical, flippant ones, of which I have a sufficiency.

I have written two or three poems. They'll have to get cold before I can tell whether they are good or bad. I am planning some prose, but feel indolent and unproductive. I need a change of environment, to mitigate the ultra-Baudelairian boredom from which I suffer. Probably I shall go to Berkeley next week, for a visit with some friends. It will be an improvement on Auburn. But I'd be glad to see the last of California—if some unknown rich relative would conveniently die and leave me a substantial legacy!

Later on, I will loan you some paintings and drawings (including "Fear," about which you inquired) and you can send them on to Lovecraft.

Send me on any new work that you have: it will be forwarded if I am not in Auburn.

As ever,
Clark

Notes

1. Unidentified. Possibly an early title for "The Corpse Speaks" (alternately "In the Grave").

2. The poem in question is that which appeared in *E*, not the one in *PM*. L. 3 reads "And faint stars fret the dead skies pain,"; DW used CAS's text for l. 22.

3. By Barbara Fawcett Craigie (1905–1998), in *Minnesota Quarterly* 4 No. 2, (Winter 1926): 16–17. Craigie was a friend of DW whom he met at the University of Minnesota; there is reason to believe that DW was in love with her and wished to marry her. She may have been the inspiration for the character Helione Forrest in his novel *Invisible Sun*.

[36] [DW to CAS] [ALS, private]

1152 Portland Ave.,
St. Paul, Minn.
April 14, 1927

Dear Clark:

I received the "Epigrams of Alastor" and read them with much pleasure. I liked the first group better, but there are many here that tickled my fancy quite as much as the best ones in the previous. I don't know why they make so strong an appeal to me, unless it is that they touched on topics concerning which I have been more or less cynical myself. I seldom carry epigram into writing, because I am rather caustic in conversation as a general rule, and don't like to repeat myself. At any rate, your epigrams give me great satisfaction, and I shall be more than glad to read whatever new ones you have chance to write. It was four o'clock in the morning before I got home the day "The Epigrams of Alastor" arrived; but I staid [*sic*] up to read them in the splendid silence of that hour of dawn!

I also received my poems, and am pleased that you found some to your liking. I made the changes which you suggested for the last stanza, but I'd like to get an even better third line for "In Mandrikor". Perhaps I'll think of a line before long, though I have had little success thus far. When you write your own poem, I'll be very glad to read it, as well as those you have just finished. It is with the greatest interest also, that I am awaiting the opportunity to see your drawings and paintings. They will have the best of care while they are in my possession. I have that somberly beautiful tapestry of yours on the wall of my room; I often admire it, or fix my eyes on it at night and lie down, dreaming.

"Paphos" is a peculiar, and I'm not altogether certain successful attempt. I tried to write another rhapsody, but it was not so good as the first and was scarcely intelligible to anyone except myself. I am enclosing with this letter two more poems in prose or "weirds", "The Woman at the Window" and "The Death of the Flowers". However, I have written a dozen of these the past year and am tiring of the form. I have begun a short-story again after a vacation of about eight months, and am also returning to work on a novel I began a year ago. I wish there were some new form of writing which had never before been known. I have experimented with the various types at one time or another, but never seem able to keep to one form for more than a few months.

Glad you found enough in "A Fragment of a Dream" to reread it. I meant to make some minor changes before it was "set-up" but forgot to do so. "La Dame sui [*sic*] Avait l'Air Etrange" seems to me to be a very beautiful piece of poetic prose. It was written a couple of years ago. The author is now twenty-one and a sophomore at the University of Minnesota. She doesn't write nearly so well now having spoiled her ability by taking imitative writing courses and by deliberately writing for an audience. She also possesses artistic talent, and is the one who made the jacket for my copy of "Sandalwood".

Your change of environment interests me. I have been suffering the same kind of boredom, and find St. Paul intolerable now. It was my birthplace, and in it my life so far has been spent, a few trips to small towns near by being the extent of my "travels". But I can hardly bear the thought of passing another summer here without a change of some sort. Consequently, I intend to go East for the next summer, and probably will leave in the middle of June. I can make the same wish concerning affluent relatives, but not having any, I must do without. For the first time in my life I can thank God that I'm young and don't have to worry about the manner in which I travel. I shall probably "hit the road" when I leave, and travel à la hobo; at least this will be my fashion unless my "finances" suddenly merit the _____. It won't be necessary, but I really believe that I would [travel?] without a cent if I had to, so weary am I of the city and especially of the tedium of summer. I plan to stop in Chicago for a few days, take a long "jump" to Providence to meet Mr. Lovecraft, and then go to New York for an indeterminate period, perhaps a week, perhaps all summer. I shall at least have a vagabond holiday if nothing else comes of the journey; and perhaps St. Paul will be endurable for another year until I am ready to leave it for good. What sort of place is Berkeley? And California? Off and on I am seized with a desire to go to San Francisco or Carmel, but probably shan't be able to do so for several years, if at all. A depression seems to be coming over me again; I feel that if I do not get a change soon, I shall return to the morbid brooding and hypochondriac spells that I had two years and one year ago. I wish I could absorb your precept that people are not worth hating; but the people, at least those I have met and seen in the Twin Cities, irritate me exceedingly. I suppose the inhabitants of all cities and surroundings will arouse my dislike, but I shall have a change, at any rate.

The best two comments on "A Fragment of a Dream" are in keeping with the ones I usually receive; one rather conventional middle-aged woman began to read the tale on a streetcar but was unable to complete it because it became too much for her; and another industrious soul spent much breath informing me how well I had imitated Machen's "The Great God Pan".! (??) I was so amazed that I could say nothing for a minute, but finally told him that I wrote the tale a couple of years ago, before I had read a line of Machen, and then asked him if by any chance he had ever read "The Great God Pan".

When I have a book published, I have a strong mind to make out a list of all the influences that have been ascribed to me and print it as a preface for the benefit and assistance of writers.

As always,
Donald.

[37]   [CAS to DW] [ALS]

Auburn, Cal.,
May 7th, 1927.

Dear Donald:

Your letter was forwarded to me in Berkeley, but I was caught in a "mad whirl"—a round of musicales, luncheons, walks, rides, picnics, etc, etc., and found it impossible to answer letters. I returned to Auburn day before yesterday, and am now trying to clean up my accumulated correspondence.

I thought you would like some of the epigrams: of course, they are not all of equal merit. But surely it is something to write even a few good ones.

Your prose-poems are excellent, as usual; but I think the phrasing might be strengthened and made more concise in places. Perfection is not readily obtained in these "bagatelles labori[e]use[s]" as Baudelaire called them.[1] One cannot work too hard over them. You have a fine gift, and the one thing necessary to its development is application. This comes well from me, since I myself work only by fits and starts!

I have arranged for an exhibition of my paintings at the Claremont Hotel, in Berkeley.[2] It will give me some local publicity, at any rate. The exhibition (two weeks) will begin June 19th.

I hope your eastern trip will do something to relieve your boredom. You might like San Francisco, which has more individuality than most cities. My happiest hours there were spent in Golden Gate Park—a place that one could not exhaust in weeks. Much of it has been permitted to run wild, and there are spots where one can forget that one is in a public park. Portions of Berkeley are charming, too, and I had some wonderful walks in the neighboring hills, which are crested with groves of eucalyptus. But (apart from my hostess) I met no one who interested me. The mob is the same everywhere.

However, I **did** meet Mrs. De Casseres, who was travelling in California with a friend, and we had a wonderful evening together. She is one of the most remarkable women I have ever met. I met Edwin Markham, also, and thought him a bit of a poseur. He was the roaring lion of a luncheon at the St. Francis Hotel (S.F.) which I attended.

I'll try to enclose some verses with this.

As ever,

Clark

Notes

1. Referring to his "Petits Poèmes en Prose."
2. The exhibit was put on by Henry Noyes Pratt (see CAS to DW 132n2).

[38]   [DW to CAS] [ALS]

1152 Portland Ave.,
St. Paul, Minn.
May 26, 1927

Dear Clark:

As usual, I am late in answering your letter. The nearer the time approaches when I intended to leave, the more colossal grows the number of things I have to do. I am rapidly getting to the point where I won't care two cents what happens and may from sheer rebellion procrastinate my going. This will not be likely; I can not imagine myself passing another summer here without some sort of relief.

And as usual, I like your poem, especially the form. I have tried to make something of verses of the same length—but of a different rhyme pattern—but did not have any too much success. Your metrical skill is uncanny; the only poem I have ever been able to write in a definite form is my one sonnet: "The Challenger"; practically everything else is experimental. I tried another poem last week after a vacation, but the thing puzzles me when I look at it. If I can manage to make myself like it, I'll send you it later. I am sending with this, however, a short story of a month ago. I hesitated a long time between destroying and keeping it, but at last decided to pass it on, to you at least. I think it's hyper-emotional.

Your trip to Berkeley must have been pleasant. If my plan for this summer has any success, I'll continue the experience next summer but follow my vagabondage in the Western world instead of Eastern. I may yet wander into Auburn and San Francisco and Carmel-by-the-Sea. The idea of a warmer clime than this appeals to me. A trite South Sea Island would be a perfect spot for me, as far as climate is concerned. Perhaps I am developing a wanderlust. I hope so. The only thing more dreadful than living here the rest of my life would be living somewhere else the rest of my life.

My younger brother is budding out into an artist of the fantastic to my great satisfaction.[1] He has done me six pen-and-ink drawings so far on handmade paper. One is of a misshapen dwarf hanging; a second, of an enormous spider holding the same dwarf after death. These two are black and white. The third, in sepia, is a girl caressing a satyr on a hilltop. The fourth, in green, a water-witch flying after a phosphorescent eel. The next, a negroid, repulsive creature done in gold on a solid black background. And the last, on an intensely blue background, a monstrous and poisonous gold flower rising on a single stem out of the breast of a dead girl, with one or two drops of reddish gold blood dripping from the center of the crimsoning bloom. The craftsmanship for one of his age—he is seventeen—is remarkable. The most notable feature of the drawings is the hateful and almost ferocious expression that he puts on most of his faces. He is going to make me sixty or a hundred of these drawings in various colours and ideas this summer; when done, they are to be bound in a book—they measure about $8 \times 5\frac{1}{2}$—and, while not a sequence, will be of one general type. I'll send you the volume when it is completed.[2] You may find the drawings very interesting. His promise is great; and I am encouraging him with all my heart.

The last work of mine that you saw was probably more imperfect than it should have been because I typed it and sent it on as soon as I had finished it, without waiting for it to cool. I have found this to be best, so far as I am concerned. When it cools, my writing so seldom pleases me that I never type it. This is what happened to the poem I mentioned above.

I am taking the liberty of keeping your poem, if you don't mind. Did you ever do anything more with your poem-drama?

As ever,
Donald Wandrei

P.S. Lovecraft tells me that Loveman has a large collection of your paintings and pictures. This was an unfortunate admission—I shall probably drive Loveman to distraction when I am in New York.

D W.

Notes

1. DW used seven of HW's illustration in *Ecstasy and Other Poems* (1928).
2. No such volume appeared.

[39]   [CAS to DW] [ALS]

Auburn, Cal.,
June 8th, 1927.

Dear Donald:

I have been dreadfully busy, or I should have answered your letter before. I have had scarcely an hour to myself for weeks.

Thanks for what you say about the last poem. Here is another experiment in French, which you may like. I made a failure of the last English poem that I attempted—strange that I should do better in French!

The summer trip you plan is a fascinating one; and I certainly hope that the following summer will bring you to California. If you care for scenery, you should find much beauty in the local milieu.

What you say about your brother is very interesting. I am sending on to you some fantastic drawings by one Bernard Dwyer, which were loaned to me through Lovecraft and the New York gang, and which you can return to Lovecraft at your leisure. You will find Lovecraft's monograph on weird literature enclosed with them.[1] It is a fine piece of work.

I am returning your story herewith. Can't say that I care as much for it as for some of the others, though it is brilliantly done, as usual.

My trip to Berkeley was most enjoyable, and I only wish it could have lasted longer.

No, I never finished the poem drama. God knows when I'll do anything with it now. I've thought sometimes of a re-handling of the old theme of Tristan and Iseult, but this, too, has come to nothing, so far.

Hope you'll forgive my silence, and write me soon.

As ever,
Clark

Notes

1. I.e., "Supernatural Horror in Literature."

Albert Christian Wandrei with his sons Howard and Donald
(Photo courtesy John Hay Library)

[40]   [DW to CAS] [ALS]

118 West 73rd St.,
New York, N. Y.
July 7, 1927

Dear Clark:

I have feasted on the offerings of the city, but am now acquiring indigestion. Under the first superficial glamour lies the same rabble, but worse, which you find almost everywhere. Next Monday I shall move on to Providence, and glad I shall be to leave. I have met most of the members of the old group which held forth when Lovecraft was here; now I shall trace the necromancer to his lair in Providence, and will undoubtedly acquire a vast amount of Colonial knowledge during my one or two week's stay. Long is travelling through with his parents about the 20th, and another member of the old group, Morton, will be there about the same time. There will thus be four of us.

I have been in the Chelsea bookshop several times; it is run by George Kirk, who knew you in California, and has been plagued [*sic*] of all his knowledge by now. I was very glad to obtain a copy of Nora May French's poems in his shop.

I hope you can come East for a time some day. I enjoyed my visit immensely the first week, and do still except for the people and the noise. I spent so much on books though that I have this added inducement to leave for Providence next Monday.[1]

I still hope and plan to go West next summer as I came East—à la hobo. It is pleasant to tramp the road if the rains don't interfere as much as they did with me.

I was disappointed to find that Loveman left almost everything of his in Cleveland. His home may yet be burglarized of your paintings and drawings before I return to St. Paul. But he read me the end of his marvellous "Sphinx," and showed me some lyrics and short poems that are the best find I have made in years. I hope I can get copies of them before my departure; Loveman is so darned indifferent about publishing them that if I don't get copies now, I probably never will. To this same Mr. Loveman I have yielded the privilege of completing this letter, and hope he does it with as much grace as he does lyrical poems. He too, I believe, is tiring of New York. He has a job with the Dauber and Pine bookstore that would almost kill me—two days a week he works from eight or nine in the morning till ten at night. I do not see how he can stand it, especially in New York. But he can speak for himself.

As ever
Donald

Dear Clark:

I can only add that I think of you often—very often—and that I am physically and mentally worked to death. I'll write at length soon. Wandrei is very fine and charming.

                                                            Your friend
                                                                  Sam
78 Columbia Hts.,
Brooklyn N.Y.

Notes

1. The visit is chronicled in DW's "Lovecraft in Providence."

[41]   [CAS to DW] [ALS]

                                                          Auburn, Cal.,
                                                          July 9th, 1927.
Dear Donald:

        I envy you that tramping-tour! Sooner or later, I intend to do
something of the sort, myself.

        I didn't imagine you would care much for New York. All big modern cit-
ies (or little ones, either) are monstrosities, anyhow. I never feel at home in
them, myself. Like the "stranger" in Baudelaire's prose-poem, "I love only the
clouds—the clouds that pass—over there—the marvellous clouds."[1]

        I want to thank you for the snapshots that you sent me before leaving St.
Paul. They show intellect, and sensibility; and I seem to read boredom in
them, too—if not actual unhappiness.

        I hope this will reach you before you leave Providence. I fear I'm a poor
correspondent: [*sic*] but I've had too many distractions (or too much of one
particular distraction) to write sooner.

        Here is a new poem ("Canticle"). I have some others, but they are still in
need of revision.

        I hope you will enjoy all of your eastern trip. Also, that you will be able
to visit California next year. I can assure you of a welcome!

        I worked hard for awhile—and now I'm playing hard. Next week, I shall
go on a camping-trip in the Sierras, with a harem of three women.[2]
                                As ever,
                                        Clark.

Notes

1. "The Stranger," in *The Poems of Charles Baudelaire* 91. For "over there" read "yonder."
2. I.e., Genevieve K. Sully and her daughters Helen and Marion.

[42]   [DW to CAS] [included with HPL to CAS, ALS, JHL]

                                                          [15 July 1927]
Dear Clark:

        If I weren't so indolent, I'd take a half-page and refute all the ridiculous statements H. P. L. made concerning me;* but I am lazily basking on top an enormous boulder shaded by a tall grove of trees, and overlooking an idyllic grotto. H.P.L. is alarmed at my proximity to the boulder's sheer edge; but I'm so darned extensive that if I did fall I really could act as my own shock-absorber. Poe's successor has been showing me marvellous scenery and woodland arcana of his old New England; but I think the California setting would also give me great pleasure, for I am not nature born to any section strong enough to hold my undivided appreciation as New England holds Lovecraft['s]. I look forward to my prospective Western tour; if you ever "hit the road" yourself, I'll be glad to give you all the tips that I can. It is a fascinating method of travel, and more adventurous than anything else I know on land. I had fine luck all the way East, and ended up with a long lift of 250 or 300 miles from Bridgeport, Connecticut, through Worcester to Boston and back to Providence with a truck driver. It was a twenty-three hour ride. I'm going back to St. Paul by the same method, with stops at Athol, West Shokan, and Chicago.

I sincerely hope you obtain recognition or sales with the Berkeley exhibition, though I am not sanguine from what I know of contemporary mentality & art appreciation. The criticism of the exhibition which you mentioned to Lovecraft amused me, but I can scarcely give it serious attention. I have my own aesthetic and artistic standards, which I feel certain are more intelligent than such as that.

I was fortunate to purchase some books I have long desired in New York, particularly Nora May French's poems. I looked for the "Odes and Sonnets", but had no luck. I'll write to a couple of California dealers whose address George gave me when I return to St. Paul. I was unable to find a single volume of Sterling's, but I shall order whatever ones are in print through regular channels on my return. At present, however, I am enjoying tours and trips through quaint old towns, and rural woods, and seashores too well to concentrate much attention on books. I'll be very glad to see your other new poems if you have time to type them. Your letters and poems and paintings have been a great and lasting pleasure to me.

    As ever

      Donald

*[HPL:] that would take industry, believe me!

[43]   [CAS to DW] [ALS]

                        Auburn, Cal.,

                        July 27th, 1927

Dear Donald:

      I returned from my camping-trip Monday night (or, rather, early Tuesday morning) to find your letters awaiting me. I am glad you are having so good a time: if one has lived long in one place, a complete change of environment and society is an almost infallible specific for the relief of boredom. I envy you your chance to meet Loveman, Kirk, Long, and Lovecraft—four of the rarest spirits in this land of holiness, hog-raising, and aesthetic hebetude and lippitude.[1]

The camping-trip was certainly a success: we prolonged it for six days beyond the proposed week and we were all heart-broken and lachrimose [*sic*] when the time came for our return to the *convenances* [2] and other curses of civilization. Our camping-place (we used no tents) was in a grove of fir and tamarack pine, lying between a snow-fed brook and a dark sapphire tarn, almost within sight of Donner Lake. The elevation is over 7000 feet; and, leaving Auburn, we passed from a sere and sultry midsummer to an Alpine spring, where dwarf willows were budding, and columbines, ultramarine larkspurs, pink heather, lavender daisies, tall greenish-white hellebore, phlox, Alpine lilies of purple-spotted nacarat, and pale aromatic rhododendrons, mingled with the towering centurial forests, or fringed the black, blue, bronze and opal tarns, or green in the interstices of river cliffs and great slopes of piled and folded granite. It was a land of "chasms and caves and titan woods."[3]

As to the "harem"—well, you mustn't take me too literally. My friends were a mother and two daughters; and I'm not Paul Fort's "Sailor Jack," "who loved the mother and the daughter too."[4]

I hope that next summer will find you in California. I am eager to meet you; and you may find other friends, also.

I'll try to send some verses in my next. I am pretty well "disorganized" just at the present moment.

As ever,

Clark

[P.S.] You were lucky to obtain a copy of N. M. F.—the book is not procurable in San Francisco.

Notes

1. *Hebetude:* the state of being dull or lethargic. *Lippitude:* soreness or bleardness of the eyes.

2. I.e., conventional proprieties.

3. Poe, "Dream-Land," l. 10.

4. The poem by French Symbolist poet Paul Fort (1872–1960) is titled "The Sailor's Song": "I loved the mother, and I loved the daughter. He sails for many a month, does sailor Jack. I loved the mother when I left her; I loved the daughter, too, when I came back" (tr. Jethro Bithell). In Albert Boni, ed., *The Modern Book of French Verse in English Translations* 257.

[44]   [DW to CAS] [ALS]

1152 Portland Ave.,
St. Paul, Minn.
Aug. 11, 1927

Dear Clark:

I returned home early yesterday morning and was highly pleased to find your letter awaiting me; it followed me across the country via Lovecraft and Dwyer. Now that my trip is over, I can only regret that it passed so rapidly; already it is like a dream out of some dim and fabulous epoch of my life.

I averaged about two hundred miles a day on the return trip. My nemesis of rain pursued me but eased after the first day. I slept in a field outside of Buffalo one night and almost froze. At Dover, Ohio, I became so exhausted late one night that I could go no further; I asked the sergeant at the jail there if I could get a bunk for the night, and they gave me a bunk and cell. They kept the door open so I could "escape" if I wished. Now I can say I've spent a night in jail! I got a lift of about three hundred miles into Chicago with three kids of sixteen or so who were heading west on motorcycles. The machine I was on broke down a couple of times, but when it was running, we went! We sailed down the streets of Chicago at 30 to 60 miles per hour during the rush hour. From a distance, and with the cut-outs open, we looked like cops and some of the traffic policemen held up traffic while we roared by!

I hope you can make a trip East some day just to meet Lovecraft, Long, Kirk, and Loveman, as well as Cook and Dwyer who are a little North and West of the Providence–New York gang. They are magnificent; I have never known a group whose general intellectual and aesthetic level was so high. Kirk you have met, and the others you will eventually, I trust. There is Loveman, genial, with an eternally young spirit, though often moody; and Long, the amazing child who is now rather cherubic in appearance, talks at so furious a pace when excited that he stutters, has an awful memory for places, and is an artist through and through in his violent enthusiasms, tastes, and eccentricities; there is Lovecraft, the intellectual, who is the epitome of New England conservatism but who goes far beyond New England in his scope; who has an extraordinary fondness for cats, cheese, chocolate, and ice-cream; who talks as he writes in amazing sentences and language; who writes all night, sleeps all day, does revision work and editing as a sideline, handles a huge correspondence, and writes stories in off moments, when he isn't exploring his beloved New England. There is Cook, the publisher, to whom books are almost everything; and Dwyer, who lives on a little farm near the Ashokan dam reservoir. Dwyer is 6 ft. 3 and weighs over two hundred; he is about 30 but looks 26, a stalwart son of Erin who is astonishingly careless of his drawings, which are stuck around chimneys and behind stones and under beds. Dwyer has a slight peculiarity of a speech which is neither brogue nor stutter, but consists, for example, in giving "th" a kind of Gaelic "dh" pronunciation. He is gifted with the desire to do good work coupled with a procrastinating indolence and an unbelievable appetite, and he is as congenial as all the rest of the group. All in all, it was a marvellous and most enjoyable trip which lacked only your presence to make it a complete unit. This is a detail, however, that I expect to attend to before I am superannuated.

I am eager to read your new poems, and hope you can enclose them with your next letter. I am also anxious to see as many of your paintings and drawings as possible when your exhibit ends. How did it turn out? I doubt whether it could have been successful on the financial end; knowing the artistic quality of your work, as I do, and the usual moron who makes up the population, I am firmly convinced that your paintings are too good for them.

What you say of your trip makes me believe that I would enjoy the California scenery. I am glad that you found it so pleasant, and look forward to a time when I can have the opportunity of making a similar one.

I spent most of yesterday unpacking books I got in New York and arranging them in my room. N. M. F. is the real treasure I acquired; I looked in vain for "Odes and Sonnets". My mother is away at present, and I have to get meals and generally watch the family. They'll be poisoned when she returns!

As always,

Donald

[45]   [CAS to DW] [ALS]

Auburn, Cal.,
Aug. 19th, 1927.

Dear Donald:

I think there is real inspiration in "Valerian," which has a touch of true cosmic fantasy.[1] You may want to make a few alterations, later. I've none to suggest, myself. I'm sending the poem on to a friend.

I'm glad you had such an enjoyable time in the East. Some time, I hope to duplicate your experience; but, as things are at present, I think you will have a chance to visit me beforehand. I agree with all that you say about our friends; and I know that I would enjoy meeting them as much as you did. Such men are rare—too rare, in this paradise of root-beer, dry-rot, and Rotarianism.

My exhibition at the Claremont, I am told, elicited much praise, but no purchasers. The paintings have just been returned; and—as soon as I can summon the energy—I'll re-box them, together with some others, and send them on to you.

My recent verses are amatory trifles; but I'll type some of them for you, such as they are. It is high time for me to do some real work. I played around all summer, and stored up a lot of impressions and sensations of the sort that an artist needs or at least can utilize for stimulus. Anyway, I was happy, and made some one else happy, and when you are as old as I am, you will realize that this is the only thing worth while.

Yours for Rum, Riot and Rape, as Ben de Casseres would say.

Clark.

Notes

1. DW dedicated the poem to CAS.

[46] [DW to CAS] [ANS, private]

Aug. 24——[1927]

Dear Clark:

Just a word to acknowledge your letter and poems. They were pleasant reading both! but I shall say more of the "amatory trifle" later, and try to send some of my own recent attempts.

Forgive the brevity of this note—I am in an angry and murderous mood. A friend of my father's left by auto last Saturday for Los Angeles, with room for a "space". And I had just $5.67 between me and Eternity!

The least I could do was spend the money in California. So I sent $15 to a San Francisco bookseller for "Odes and Sonnets". I haven't decided whether to buy a limousine or go to Europe on the remainder.

In Supreme Disgust,
Donald W

[47] [DW to CAS] [ALS]

1152 Portland Ave.,
St. Paul, Minn.
Sept. 1, 1927

Dear Clark:

"When you are as old as I am"—Ye Gods! When I am as "old" as you are, I shall consider that I still have two-thirds of existence to pass among our mutual friend, the human being, genus homonotonous! Maybe by that time I shall be able to write poems that will give me as much pleasure as yours; or become as tired of writing as I usually do of everything; or attain an epitome of cynicism and do just what everyone else does! I have read your "amatory trifles" again, and like "One Evening" best. They can't be classed with your really ambitious work; but they are much more distant from the atrocity which is a poem to the peepul than from your own heights. I shall be watching for the results of your stored-up energy.

I typed a good many of my own recent verses yesterday and enclose them. I have been riding on a prolonged crest of energy and impulse, resulting largely from my trip, I believe, and wrote about sixty of these poems in the last six weeks. Just at present I have come to the end. The past three days I have been engaged in the delightful pastime of scraping varnish off nine steps and a hall floor; and now I am absolutely barren of ideas, devoid of energy, and exhausted of enthusiasm. I couldn't even write an invective against varnish! Pass the poems on to Long when you finish them; if I possessed any real intelligence, I would have made a carbon copy, but with my usual brilliancy, the idea never entered my head till I was through. If I can summon the energy later, I'll type the rest of the six weeks' holocaust.

I expect to have Cook publish a book for me in three or four months; most of the copies will be absorbed locally. For once before I leave its pedagogic doors, the U. will be of some service to me. Many of the academicians hate my verse and stories like poison; but at least they have to read them in order to obtain the proper degree of maleficence and sarcaustic remarks!

Wright managed to make a kind of general mess of his October issue and at the last moment dropped out four pages of material by some fantastic method which I am unable to fathom. His first assault carried him clear through "The Red Brain" and left twenty-six lines in all smashed by the wayside. I'm glad he didn't commit the massacre *before* deciding how much ("much" is good!) to pay me! Wright takes all the blame frankly; and, after having met him, I can sympathize with his troubles.

"Odes and Sonnets" is beautifully printed. I received my copy yesterday and have not been so pleased by a specimen of fine printing in a long time. Now I can rest in peace in the possession of your four published volumes!

Three cheers for B. de C.*!

Donald

*I prefer wine, however.

[48]   [DW to CAS] [ALS, water damaged]

1152 Portland Ave.,
St. Paul, Minn.
Sept. 5, 1927

Dear Clark:

I have gone and gloated over your paintings for nearly three days now; after writing an inchoate rhapsody to Lovecraft, I decided to wait until I was in a less feverish state before acknowledging their receipt, but the longer I wait, the more their terrible and ineffable beauty becomes a part of me, inseparable from my thoughts and writing. From the tapestry I possess and the grotesques, and a few others that Lovecraft showed me, I had an idea what I might expect, but I was swept off my feet and carried away in what was, I think, the most ungovernable excitement I have yet had. I know that they were exhibited in Berkeley; you inform me that there were no purchasers; now that I have seen the paintings I can almost pity California if I were not so amazed at the total lack of cultural and aesthetic life, the artistic suicide, the dearth of appreciation of beauty, and that deadly, dry rot atmosphere in which no artist can thrive that you must know all too well. That any civilization, no matter how barbaric, degraded or decadent could lightly pass over such paintings as these is an incredible prostitution of the supreme gifts of expression which I in my most cynical summary of Man's beastly level have not believed him capable of. It is the worst and most significant indictment of contemporary civilization which I have found, that a people may pursue wealth and and [*sic*] scientific materialism is of secondary importance if the arts are not neglected; America has rotted to an aesthetic hell, an artistic morass, a mental quagmire has festered in, wallowed in, died in, and proudly extolled what is probably the lowest pit of mob mediocrity that any country as crediting itself with civilization has ever reached. It is excusable that an ape may scratch himself in the jungle, but picture a hundred and ten million people making that ape their god! Not in all the bye-paths of painting, not in the tedious and monotonous ranks of American, of English, of European painters have I found anything comparable with your work save, perhaps, Kay Nielsen, Harry Clarke, Wallace Smith, and Redon.[1] And none of these, though Nielsen came closest and Clarke next, has succeeded in tapping that strange and marvellous wonderland that I find in your pictures. They are magnificent with all the splendour and glory of the most utter lands of imagination and fable and with a weird and uncanny and superb feeling for colour and colour-contrasts such as I have sought in vain to find among painters of fame. Taprobana[2] is a lovely and unearthly exotic creation whose many odd colours and strange vegetation make it of phantasmal and haunting beauty. The "Desert Oasis" in its pure design and wondrous colouring is almost as perfect as "Taprobana." The black and the white tapestries, the "Dreamland", the "Coast of Saturn", in their sombre and cosmic and terrific implications of worlds that we know not and the imagination but faintly in its most alien flights of drug-arisen [?] wanderings are appalling. Your paintings are monstrous with sheer beauty and horror and wonder, transfigured into spectral supernal loveliness by your sorcerous use of elfin and eldritch and glittering and regally impressive or exquisite colour. They are vistas from Dreamlands and Shadowlands of Beauty and Nightmare and of morbid magnificence, touched with ecstasy, touched with terror, touched with a Lethean, Saturnian awe. Seldom does the imagination reach those remote abysses and supreme gulfs of twilight from which you have stolen so much wealth; and it is even more rarely that the imagination, if it can attain those greatest outposts, has control of the hand that will visualize what Memory briefly enjoyed. I can understand the long, laborious hours that saw the genesis of these paintings, the infinite patience, the endless pains that were required. Such things do not come into being instantaneously; there is patience written in every line of them, and beneath the surface glamour and glory I can read something of the toil; I know that writing drains away energy; and I have artist friends who tell me of the greater drain that the strain of composition imposes in even inferior work, and in the case of such paintings as yours where invention and colour and design and a unique and unheard-of originality are super-added, the strain must become shattering at times. I can hardly believe the testimony of my eyes in the case of originality alone. There are traces of oriental influence, especially in one Japanese-mask-like head in the "Hashish Dream", and in a kind of Indo-handling of the trees and decorative motifs in some of the landscapes; but of the influence of the likeliest artists—Beardsley, Redon, Ryder, Clarke, W. Smith, Rops, Nielsen—there is not a trace. This is a striking originality which is rare and almost unbelievable in this day of imitation and charlatanry. I took the drawing over to a couple of my artist friends, and they simply went wild over them, particularly those of the "Taprobana" group, whose colouring and unearthly beauty caught them.

If _____ of _____[s u]nknown are good to me this week, I shall be able to buy "Taprobana," or one of the group. I never before so bitterly regretted a lack of superfluous change as I do now; if I were in a position to, I would take the whole group. Perhaps I may be able to afford several of these sometime in the not-distant future; and if this becomes a certainty, I shall immediately procure those I especially desire if they are still unsold.

Did I tell you that the one regret of my life is a total inability to control a pen outline? If I could have painted, your own work is a perfect expression of the things I should have attempted. Writing is a poor substitute for the wealth and the splendour that can be put into form and colour. I suppose that the reason I am invariably unsatisfied by everything I write is the simple impossibility of putting a picture into words.

Though I can not write as I wish I could, though I can not paint at all, I am glad, at least, that I have the faculty of appreciation; and, for once in my life, the pictures to appreciate.

Donald

Notes

1. Kay Nielsen (1886–1957), Danish illustrator popular in the early 20th century; Harry Clarke (1889–1931), Irish stained-glass artist and book illustrator; Wallace Smith (1888–1937), American book illustrator, comic artist, author, and screenwriter. For Redon, see CAS to DW 22n1.

2. The name by which the ancient Greeks referred to Sri Lanka.

[49]   [CAS to DW] [ALS]

Auburn, Cal.,
Sept. 18th, 1927.

Dear Donald:

      I owe you my thanks for your poems, and for that supremely flattering and complimentary letter concerning my pictures. Forgive my delay in answering—I have been busy, in more ways than one.

I like a number of the poems—particularly some of the amatory ones, and several of the nightmare sonnets.[1] I envy your facility—not since your age have **I** been able to reel off any quantity of stuff at a time. I want to read these verses over again, and will then forward them to Long as per request.

Believe me, I appreciate what you say, and obviously feel, concerning the pictures. You are right concerning the labour that one can, and indeed must put into such work. There are times when I simply haven't the courage to attempt it, foreknowing, as I do, the cost in nerve-strain, the toll that it takes of eye and hand and brain. But even at that, I find the paintings easier to "do" than poetry.

I wish I could give you one or more of these pictures, but I don't feel able to do so at present, since I no longer have the time that I once had for making new ones. If you feel able to buy any of them, I won't "sting" you on the price.

Oddly enough, I have seen little of the work of any of the artists you name as having congenerate tendencies. Perhaps I have seen more of Nielsen than of the others; but have never encountered anything of Redon's till lately, and then not in colour. I was compared to him years and years ago by a Cleveland artist[2] (a friend of Loveman's) who thought my work superior. Harry Clarke I admire greatly, since finding (only a few months ago) some specimens reproduced in an art magazine, "The Studio."[3] Wallace Smith I know only by the simple drawing in De Casseres' "The Shadow-Eater." So you can see how little I owe to pictorial influences, apart from Oriental art, of which I have seen and studied a fair amount.

Perhaps I *may* yet achieve an exhibition in New York, since Bio de Casseres is still trying to get one for me. She is a woman of indomitable strength and energy—perhaps the most striking feminine personality that I have ever encountered. Out here, there is no hope: galleries are closing, and some of the best-known artists in the state are starving. S. F. becomes more hog-tied and hide-bound commercial every minute.

I've written nothing very recently. One needs the cream of one's energy for creative effort; and I've had to do some money-making (never mind what). Any way, it takes the edge off of me, and I'm not getting rich, either. Damn the U.S., and hurrah for Denmark, where worthy poets actually receive a salary from the state after they have given proof of their abilities!

Yours for the second coming of Casanova,

Clark

Notes

1. The latter being DW's *Sonnets of the Midnight Hours.*

2. William Sommer (1867–1949), American Modernist painter, watercolorist, and draftsman.

3. H. B. G., "An Exhibition by Three Book-Illustrators" [Alan Odle, John Austen, Harry Clarke], *Studio* No. 386 (15 May 1925): 260–63. This item, if it is the one CAS referred to, reproduced only Clarke's "Columbine" (p. 263).

[50] [DW to CAS] [ALS, private, water-damaged]

1152 Portland Ave.
St. Paul, Minn.
Sept. 22, 1927

Dear Clark:

Your welcome letter came an hour ago and was a great relief to me, who had been shellac[k]ing the same floor and steps I manicured several weeks ago.

I am glad if my enthusiasm for your work means anything to you. I sent the collection on to Lovecraft yesterday, after feasting on them again. HPL was becoming a trifle impatient, I fear, from my long retention. I should like to buy "Taprobana" and the "Desert Oasis", which I think I can pay for now. The Lord were good to me to the extent of yielding me enough cash to have Cook print me a book of poems; my expenses at the U. will be heavy this year, though ____ graduation fees of one sort or another and _____er ____ increase. I expect to break even on the [book]; if [so] this means I will have more money to buy _____ts in January. After "T." and the "D.O." _____ "Garden of Sheba", the "Den of the [Cockatrice]", _____ a couple of the tapestries and the _____ sent the group on to Lovecraft, you will _____ck our "T." and the "D.O.'" when they are return[ed] you ____ have the Eastern gang return them to me again [before] _____ on to you. On the whole, I favour this last plan _____ permit me to examine them all once more. I would [like] to buy a number of others—the "Dream of the Hashish-Eater", the "Coast of Saturn", and four or five of the untitled tapestries on white and black satin; but there is a limit to my purse, and I'll have to content myself with "Taprobana" and the "Desert Oasis" at present. From time to time I'll buy what I can if the pictures are still available and my "finances" merit the terms.

I wish you luck in getting a New York exhibition but the people I saw were a beastly rabble of foreigners, in general, and I'm not certain that aesthetic or artistic appreciation can be found anywhere in the U. S.

I have added both your poems & my fat group of others to my typescript, pilfering "Souvenance", partly because the poem is more original than _____ difficult translation. I still maintain that your Baudelaire is equal and better [than] existing translations.

I wish I could send you work of the artists I mention, but such books can't be taken from the art departments of Twin Cities libraries. Nielsen is my favourite in "East o' the Sun"[1] and a new book whose title escapes me.[2] Smith is perhaps better technically than Clarke, but I prefer Clarke for pure imagination. Smith was best in Hecht's "Fantazius Mallare" which has twelve full-page illustrations. Clarke in Poe with twenty-four black and whites and eight pages in colour. Clarke has done "Faustus", which isn't so good, and "The Year's at the Spring",[3] which has two or three fine plates in colour but some and a number of black & whites that are not exceptional. The Mpls. library has a very limited and expensive edition of Redon with all known drawings, engravings, and painting, which has some remarkable things in it. The Chicago Art Museum had an exhibition of nearly a hundred original prints when I was there __ June __ps I saw in N.Y. City. The Dauber & Pine shop see_____rted French editions. Vernon Hill I have seen _____ "Ballads Weird and Wonderful",[4] which is worth having. _____ before in _____ed ____tion in Phillip[s]'s _____ing for $3.69. I'd like to buy the _____ colour illustrations, "Ballads W[eird and Wonderful"] and "The Year's at the Spring". You _____ I warn you, they are all large, heavy _____ about as much in express charges as _____[.]

Substitute for Casanova in the gentleman's absence?

Donald

[P.S.] Glad you liked some of my poems. Will try to type the rest but may not have time. School opens Monday and I've had to be over there every day this week.

D. W.

Notes

1. A volume of tales edited by Peter Christen Asbjørnsen and Jørgen Engebretsen Moe.
2. Apparently *Hansel and Gretel and Other Stories by the Brothers Grimm* (1925). See CAS to DW 55.
3. Goethe's *Faust* and a poetry anthology edited by L. D'O. Walters.
4. By Richard Pearse Chope.

[51] [CAS to DW] [ALS]

Auburn, Cal.,
Sept. 26th, 1927

Dear Donald:

Your letter came yesterday. I had just mailed your poems to Long, as per the instructions you gave me some time ago. Pardon delay—I'm getting to be an awful slow-coach, in regard to some things. But I'll try to mend my ways henceforth.

I'll tell Lovecraft that the paintings are to be returned to you, when they have gone the customary rounds. Regarding price: I hardly know what to ask you. The two that you speak of buying—"Taprobana" and "The Desert Oasis"—were, I think, priced at $12.00 apiece in Berkeley. I'll be glad to cut this in half for you—which will be twelve dollars in all. "The Den of the Coc[k]atrice," by the way, was almost my own favourite among the group I sent you.

I made a new decorative yesterday using tube water-colours on a ground of India ink. The composition represents autumn shrubs and trees against a back-ground of cedars, and I am quite taken with the effect, which has a delicate fairy-like gorgeousness. I did the whole thing in six or seven hours, working with more speed and facility than is usual with me.

Yours, in haste,
Clark.

[52]   [DW to CAS] [ALS]

1152 Portland Ave.,
St. Paul, Minn.
Oct. 2, 1927

Dear Clark:

I am enclosing a money order for "Taprobana" and "The Desert Oasis." I feel guilty in taking the pictures at the price you make, which is much below their value. I would gladly pay their full worth if it were possible, but since I can't I can assure you that they would never find a more hospitable or congenial resting-place than my room. I have, however, made the m.o. for fifteen dollars; I haven't the pictures to verify my belief, but I think "Taprobana" was marked fifteen and "The Desert Oasis" twelve-fifty. I only hope that the pictures go the round without any catastrophes and come back to me safely. If they don't, I shall commit murder!

Some time I hope to see the new picture you mention. It must be an extremely interesting production both from technical and experimental standpoints. May your facility treble!

I am learning to trip the light, fantastic now. Since this will be my final year at the University, I have decided to enjoy myself with a minimum of study, and expect to go to "the most important of the social events"—the senior prom—and perhaps a couple of sorority formals. The idea of mingling to any extent with the hoi polloi gives me much inward amusement, though I am likely to be bored stiff at the functions.

Your preference of "The Den of the Cockatrice" is interesting; one of the artists to whom I showed the group preferred it to the others. It is one of those I hope to acquire later.

School has finally broken the prolonged period of writing which I began on my return. I am sorry, for I had been making good progress on my novels, and was well into the aesthetic adventure which will eventually contain an appreciation of your paintings. This was one reason why I kept the group so long and was so anxious to buy some now.

Cook seems to be working on my book though I haven't received the first proofs yet.

I have an extremely bad and extremely obnoxious cold which irritates me exceedingly. I studied rather late at the U. library last night, and, in a moment of gallantry, escorted a coed friend of mine home. It began to rain, and since I had no coat and they no umbrella, I waited for the rain to stop. I waited and waited and waited, and finally, at about half-past three, concluded that discretion was much better than procrastination and departed. I got home about half-past four or a quarter of five, wet, tired, and with an incipient cold.

On the whole, I am not so certain that substituting for Casanova is all it's cracked up to be!

[vertical and ornamented] A S E V E R D O N A L D

[53]   [CAS to DW] [ALS]

Auburn, Cal.,
Oct. 8th, 1927.

Dear Donald:

Many thanks for the welcome money-order. I have just heard from Lovecraft, who is also enthusiastic about the pictures, and am writing him that they are all to be returned to you after they have gone the rounds.

I have done three new ones on a black ground, but find myself at a standstill just now, through brain-fag, boredom, disgust, and a general sense of the infinite ineffable futility of everything. Also, I had two teeth pulled the other day, and have been suffering inquisitional tortures ever since the dope died out of my jaw. Every nerve seems to have turned up for a satanic concert.

I'm eager to see your book, when it comes out. Hope it will *épater*[1] all the bourgeoisie of St. Paul.

If you feel tempted to try the Casanova stuff, remember Huneker's advice. "A cool brain and a wicked heart."[2] Otherwise, the female will get the best of it—and of you.

As ever,
Clark.

Notes

1. To startle or shock out of complacency, conventionality.
2. From the dedication of Huneker's autobiography, *Steeplejack* 1.v.

[54]   [DW to CAS] [ALS]

1152 Portland Ave.,
St. Paul, Minn.
Oct. 16, 1927

Dear Clark:

My commiserations be with you on your dental difficulties; and my anathema on you for mentioning a subject whose correction I have been procrastinating for six or eight months!

To pass to a more pleasant topic, I hope your loss of interest in pictorial work is only temporary; I should hate to believe that you would make no further use of your power. Which reminds me, I have just acquired "Hansel and Gretel" with Kay Nielsen's marvellous and strangely lovely designs. I fear that I shall always be in a state of penury as long as a bookstore is within my reach.

I don't think you need to worry much about my success as a modern Casanova. I can not endure women unless they are beautiful, and I have never seen one who was beautiful. I can not imagine a more pleasant paradise than one inhabited only by maids of surpassing loveliness; but by the same token, I can not conceive of a more impossible paradise. At one time or another, I have idealized three women; but they all lacked something and seemed to have a mutual desire to prove themselves anything but perfect.

Cook hasn't yet sent me the first proofs of my book; hence it probably won't be out until New Year's. When it does appear, I shall of course be glad to send you a copy. It does not contain a number of poems that I prefer, and contains several which I don't like. This is because various ones have appeared in college magazines, and their inclusion in the book is a concession to those who liked them, since more people connected with the U. than not are likely to be purchasers.

[page missing?]

particularly desire to break even on this, for if I do, it will enable me to finance [a second] _____.

Has Long acknowledged receipt of the poems? I haven't heard from him for a month and a half.

Don't you think I'm a splendid artist? Thank you.

D W.

[55] [CAS to DW] [ALS]

Auburn, Cal.,
Nov. 9th, 1927

Dear Donald:

I've been in Berkeley for the past three weeks (two weeks longer than I intended to stay) and left orders at home that no mail was to be forwarded. Last night, when I returned to Auburn, I found your letter awaiting me, in company with letters from Lovecraft, Dwyer, and De Casseres.

No, I have not lost interest in pictorial art. Can't remember what I wrote that would lead you to infer that I had, even temporarily. I am planning to execute some more water-colours as soon as possible. At present, I am in a most abominable state of brain-fag and nerve-exhaustion, and am trying to pull my scattered wits and demoralized faculties together.

While in Berkeley, I saw at the public library a volume of Andersen's fairy tales illustrated by Harry Clarke, and three volumes (Andersen, Grimm, and Hansel and Gretel) by Kay Nielsen. I was greatly taken by the Nielsen pictures, on first inspection; but, after much study and comparison, I found myself preferring those of Harry Clarke; beside their unfailing richness and decadent complexity of colour and design, many of the Nielsens appear thin and cold, with a quality that reminds me of faded porcelains. However, I must admit that the best ones are really unsurpassable for fantasy and delicate colouring . . . I saw also much admirable work by Rackham and Dulac.¹

I think you are wise to eschew women. Would that I could!

Here is a Baudelaire that I may not have sent you.

As ever,

Clark.

Notes

1. Arthur Rackham (1867–1939), British book illustrator; Edmund Dulac (1882–1953), French illustrator who worked mostly in England.

[56]   [CAS to DW] [ALS]

Auburn, Cal.,
Dec. 10th, 1927.

Dear Donald:

I was glad to hear from you, as always. I agree with you about the last Baudelaire and the poem to G. S.¹ The misanthropy does lower the poetic tone, in the latter, and I'd leave it out, if I were writing it now. I hope you'll find something to your fancy in the enclosed verses. Several people have praised the Verlaine highly.

Miss Lee sent me a consignment of Nov. Overlands; but I have not yet received the Dec. issue. Perhaps there has been some delay in getting it out.

I hope your book will be ready soon. At Lovecraft's suggestion, I am writing to Cook to sound him out on the proposition of issuing a little volume for me. I can dig up forty or fifty poems—some of which, at least, are quite good.

Kay Nielsen's *best* plates are certainly of supreme and inimitable value; but in many others, I seem to detect a certain thinness and coldness. Clarke, I feel, has a surer hand—or a more sustained inspiration. However, a man should be judged by his best work, so doubtless you are right in feeling an equal admiration for Nielsen. I, too, have an increasing preference for pure beauty over horror.

It's raining to-day—a cold, bleak, bitter rain that is almost sleet. I loathe such weather, and am praying for something more clement—at least, around the holidays. I have certain projects—or designs—and bad weather won't assist them.

Your account of Miss Millay is decidedly diverting.[2] The hose and the carpet must have presented a Huysmans-like effect—a "Camaieu in Red!"[3] . . . I can't help wondering if she wore bloomers to match.

As ever,

Clark.

Notes

1. "To George Sterling: A Valediction."

2. CAS refers to the American poet Edna St. Vincent Millay (1892–1950). An unsigned article, "Recent Poetry," *Current Literature* 53, No. 4 (October 1912): 473, compared the budding careers of Millay and CAS, wondering which of the two would become a famous poet. In 1936 she collaborated on a translation of Baudelaire (see RHB to DW 25).

3. J.-K. Huysmans, "Camay in Red" (tr. Stuart Merrill) in *Pastels in Prose* (New York: Harper & Brothers, 1890).

[57]   [CAS to DW] [ALS]

Jan. 17th, 1928.

Dear Donald:

As usual, my correspondence is in arrears. But I've been absolutely engulfed, swallowed up, and consumed since the holidays. It would take Casanova to cope with my present situation! I['ve] done no work, excepting some literal prose-translations of "Les Fleurs du Mal." It seems to me that an absolutely faithful rendering of this sort might be of use and interest to people who can't read the original.

I have not yet heard from Cook. Hope he was not floored by my suggestion. I await your book with tremendous interest; and trust that a perfect job will be made of it.

The weather here has been simply damnable, for California; we had about ten days of fog, from New Year['s] onward; and now we're having a period of bitter cold, with frost and ice every morning. Lafcadio Hearn says somewhere that "cold shrivels up the little wings of dreams."[1] I agree with him. It shrivels everything up, as far as I am concerned.

Morton's criticism of my pictures was diverting![2] I derive immense amusement from that sort of thing.

I've made four trips to the dentist and must make some more next month.

Au revoir, epistolarily speaking.

As ever,

Clark.

Notes

1. "Cold compels painful notions of solidity; cold sharpens the delusion of personali-

ty; cold quickens egotism; cold numbs thought, and shrivels up the little wings of dreams." *Gleanings in Buddha Fields* 87.

2. See HPL to DW (19 December 1927):

> *James Ferdinand Morton:* [with his inimitable air of long-suffering patience]
>
> Well, these drawings are no worse than the things he expected us to praise last year!

See *Letters with Donald Wandrei* 189 for HPL's equally comic renderings of the gang's reactions.

[58] [CAS to DW] [ALS]

> Auburn, Cal.,
> Feb. 9th, 1928.

Dear Donald:

    I should have acknowledged the pictures and your letter before this: certainly, as a correspondent, I'm getting to be more and more of a slow-coach.

    Cook professes himself financially unable to bring out a volume for me at the moment. I'm practically broke myself, with no very immediate prospect of laying my talons on anything in the form of currency.

    I've gone on with the literal prose-versions of "Les Fleurs du Mal," and must have at least seventy of them drafted. The ideal way would be to publish them in the same volume with a poetical version. Prose is the **only** way to render every precise shade of the meaning and thought of the original.

    I've seen a few of Alastair's[1] drawings; certainly, they are fascinating. I seem to have read somewhere that he lives in an old castle (or is it a hunting-lodge?) in the heart of the Black Forest.

    Not much news. I've made a new painting that you would probably like.

    Why so misogynistic? Probably, like all idealists, you expect, or **have** expected, too much from women. Moderate your expectations, and you may find the ladies quite amusing.

    If your book is suppressed, you may become famous! Also, copies might be bootlegged at $20.00 per! Cheer up! Sweet are the uses of Comstockery![2]

> As ever,
> Clark.

Notes

1. Pseudonym of Hans Henning Otto Harry Freiherr von Voigt (1887–1969), author of *Fifty Drawings* (New York: Knopf, 1925).

2. Anthony Comstock (1844–1915), secretary of the New York Society for the Suppression of Vice, conducted an extensive campaign to censor materials he considered indecent and obscene, including birth control information.

[59]   [CAS to DW] [ALS]

Auburn, Cal.,
March 8th, 1928.

Dear Donald:

I will send your poems on to Lovecraft in a day or two. I like many of them; as usual, I find myself preferring the weird and horrible ones. The prose epitaph is very striking, and the pictures in that little poem about the cypress-swamp are unforgettable. And you certainly know how to write sonnets.[1]

I've gone on with my prose Baudelaire, doing a little every day, and have now roughly drafted about two-thirds of the poems in "Les Fleurs." Some are probably done, and I'll enclose a few more specimens. "Weird Tales" is going to run three in a group: "Une Charogne", "Les Sept Viellards" and "L'Irreparable." Personally, I don't see why the six suppressed poems attract-ed the attention of the censors any more than certain others that "got past". Most of the six are really beautiful, excepting the rather prolix and tiresome poem on Lesbos. "Femmes Damnées" is really marvellous; I have not at-tempted a version of it yet.

There's no news with me—at least, none that is good. My mother is in failing health, and there seems to be nothing ahead but desperate poverty and debts. Apparently I'll be driven to take a steady "job" of some kind, providing I can get one.

I hope your book has turned up by this time. Cook, I gather, is really snowed under with financial deficits and worries.

Remember, in reading my Baudelaires, that I have not tried to add any-thing to them, but have merely sought to render the exact sense into correct and fairly rhythmic English. The result should be something of a novelty,—no one has done it before, as far as I know. All the verse translations are more or less emasculated, enfeebled, and lacking in the peculiar supple and sensory vigor of the original.

As ever,
Clark.

P.S. I have two or three new original poems—will send them in my next.

Notes

1. Probably "An Epitaph on Jupiter," "The Cypress-Bog," and various *Sonnets of the Midnight Hours*.

[60]   [CAS to DW] [ALS]

Auburn, Cal.,
Apr. 13th, 1928.

Dear Donald:

Thanks for what you say about the Baudelaires. Here are some more of them, including several of "Piéces [*sic*] Condamnés." I have almost finished my draft of the book—there are only three or four left to tackle.

I enclose also one of the poems that "Weird Tales" accepted. If there were only a number of magazines like "W. T.", I might possibly make some kind of a living.

I sent some of my French verses to "Revue des Deux Mondes", and received a courteous and encouraging letter from the editor, who said that they showed "original inspiration and a profound knowledge of the language." It's more encouragement than I'd be likely to receive from "Harper's" or the "Century."

Lovecraft tells me that Cook has been very ill. I hope "Ecstasy" will come through in time, and that you'll be able to dispose of enough copies to pay expenses, at least. I could publish three books, one of verse, one of epigrams, and a sizable selection of Baudelaires, if I had the wherewithal. There is a possibility that some regular publisher may be interested in the Baudelaires.

I'd have written before, but life was quite exacting and absorbing for several weeks. Now, I've nothing better to do than work—damn the luck! And I can't even find anything remunerative in that line.

As ever,
Clark.

[61]   [CAS to DW] [ALS]

Auburn, Cal.,
Apr. 20th, 1928.

Dear Donald:

Many, many thanks for your volume, which should be a source of pride to both yourself and Cook. It is beautifully presented; and as is usual, the poems impress me as being even better in print than in typescript. I like in particular "Ecstasy," "On Some Drawings," "Sanctity and Sin," and "Valerian," by whose dedication I feel highly honoured. I do hope the sale will re-imburse you for the expense of publication.

I wrote you not long ago, enclosing some more Baudelaires. Have just finished my draft of "Les Fleurs", all but the poems in decadent Latin,[1] which I am unable to read. Of course, a lot of these are sorely in need of revision.

Did I mention that two of my paintings on black cloth, done about the same time as the one I gave you, have been on exhibition at the Independent Show in New York? These pictures, it seems, have attracted the favourable attention of two visiting art-critics from France; and I am in receipt of letters from two Parisian magazines, "Les Artistes D'Aujourd[']hui," and "Revue du Vrai et du Beau," asking for information concerning my artistic aims and aspirations—also, for any clippings of press-notices, photographic reproductions of paintings, etc, with which I may be able to furnish them. These critics, M. Henri de Montal-Faubele, and M. Comte de Chabrier, have signified their intention of writing articles upon me and my work—surely an honour which is not likely to be accorded to all the exhibitors at the Independent Show, which, I understand, is not taken seriously by New York critics. Recognition of this sort is truly significant, and may open the way to almost anything.

I hope you'll write before long, and send me some more poems. There's no question in my mind that you have unusual gifts and potentialities as a poet.

As ever,

Clark

Notes

1. "LXII. *Franciscæ meæ laudes.*"

[62]   [CAS to DW] [ALS]

Auburn, Cal.,
Aug. 26th, 1928.

Dear Donald:

I suppose you think that I have either forgotten you, or dropped out of existence. Neither conjecture, however, would be correct, no matter how much circumstantial evidence there may be to support it. I have merely been submerged in non-artistic pursuits all summer; and my correspondence, as well as painting and literature, has gone by the board. Now with leisure, I am trying to pick up the threads of what seems almost like another life; and I hope you will forgive me and return good for evil by writing me a letter before the second Deluge.

My main intention and endeavour, just now, is the writing of a few short stories, in a weird, fantastic vein. One, "The Last Incantation of Malygris,"[1] which I am just beginning, deals with an old sorcerer who tries to evoke the dead sweetheart of his youth, with disastrous results. Also, I shall try to finish my revision of the Baudelaire translations.

Hope you have some new poems or prose pieces to send me. You have a world of promise held before you; and the reception given your book was certainly encouraging, all things considered.

"Les Artist[e]s D'Aujourd[']hui" has published its little critique on my contributions to the Independent show.[2] A copy will come your way presently.

I received a card (signed by yourself, Lovecraft, and Long) giving your New York address, but have either lost or mislaid it. So I'm addressing this to the St. Paul number.

    Best wishes.

As ever,

Clark.

Notes

1. CAS actually wrote two separate tales with the same character: "The Last Incantation" (October 1929) and "The Death of Malygris" (c. May 1933).
2. Henri de Montal-Faubelle, "Clark Ashton Smith," *Les Artistes d'Aujourd'hui* (1 August 1928): 17. CAS translated this review for a news article, "Paintings by Auburn Poet," *AJ* (20 November 1941): 5.

[63]   [CAS to DW] [ALS]

Auburn, Calif.

Oct. 21st, 1928

Dear Donald:

    I found your letter awaiting me on my return last week from Berkeley, where I visited for nearly a month. It was good to hear from you, and to learn that you are so ambitious and so full of fine literary projects.

    As for myself, there is little enough to report at present. I am now starting to overhaul and re-type my Baudelaires, with the intention of preparing them for possible book-publication. I have had no time or energy, so far, for original literary work. I made seven new paintings in September (you would like some of these, particularly the three on a black ground) and have left them on display, together with some old work, at an art-store in Oakland.

    Good luck with the publishers! I haven't even tried anyone with "Incantations", but may sometime muster up sufficient courage to send it to Pascal Covici, of Chicago. Just at present, I don't even feel like expending the postage, since my last round of dissipation in the Bay region has left me practically "broke"!

    While in Berkeley, I saw a copy of Poe's "Tales of Mystery and Imagination" with the illustrations by Harry Clarke. They impress me as the best Poe designs I have yet encountered. The ones in colour, especially, are full of true Poesque horror—he seems to catch the very tints of psychic decomposition, morbidity, fear, and death.

    Here's wishing you all manner of good luck. And remember me to the "gang." I have just written to Lovecraft, who is certainly faithful and patient with my epistolary irregularities and short-comings. I've owed him a letter for nearly two months. I liked his "Dunwich Horror", which is truly Lovecraftian.

    Tell Long that "The Space-Eaters" was **great.**

As ever,

Clark.

[64]   [CAS to DW] [ALS]

Auburn, Cal.,
Nov. 26th, 1928.

Dear Donald:

I was very glad to hear from you again, but am sorry that you've been having, as you put it, "a devil of a time." Work, or the necessity of work—at least, anything aside from art,—is certainly a curse.

There's little enough news with me, as usual. I have done considerable writing of late—have started out with the industrious intention of completing all my odds and ends, including three or four prose fantasies that I have begun and abandoned at divers times. Also, I'm working on my prose Baudelaire, and hope to have it in some sort of shape by the end of the year.

I haven't taken any time for painting, of late. Some day, I'll loan you a lot more of my work. When I was in San Francisco last October, I procured a piece of Chinese silk, of the kind used by Oriental artists, and am planning to use it when the happy combination of leisure and inspiration presents itself.

I enclose a miscellany of verse—also, a prose-poem which you may like. "Weird Tales" has just accepted a prose-fantasy entitled "Sadastor," which was one of the odds-and-ends begun years ago and finished recently. The next one that I plan to finish is a story based on the effects of hashish.[1]

My best regards to the gang, and here's hoping that you will find something both tolerable and remunerative in the way of work.

As ever,

Clark.

[P.S.] Don't mention publishers to me!! *Anathema maranatha!* Carramba! [*sic*] *Jehannun kow chi!!!* (Probably I'm mis[s]pelling the Hindustani malediction, which I've never seen in print.)

Your idea for a pub. firm that would publish only literature is gorgeous. But you should be a multi-millionaire to begin with.

Notes

1. "In a Hashish-Dream" (fragment).

[65]   [CAS to DW] [ALS]

Auburn, Calif.
March 20th, 1929

Dear Donald:

As usual, I am in arrears—and I had honestly meant to answer your letter before this.

I think that a period in Carmel might be an interesting and worth-while experience for you. The cost of living is moderate, the scenery is full of varied beauty and rugged sublimity, and—if you cared for such—you could have the society of people whose aspirations, at least, are more or less artistic. Personally I prefer scenery that is unpopulated even by artists—but that is a prejudice, which I don't recommend to others.

As for **my** plans—well, in the present state of my affairs, emotions, sensations, fatigues, desires and ennuis, I find it almost impossible to formulate or, at least, adhere to any. I have written a few poems (one or two of which I'll enclose) and have put my new volume of verse, which I have entitled "The Jasmine Girdle and Other Poems,"[1] in the hands of a N.Y. literary agent,[2] who thinks she might inveigle some publisher into bringing it out.

I can well understand how N.Y. impresses you—since to me, **any** city, any crowded place, partakes too much of the nature of Baudelaire's "cauchemar multiforme et sans trêve."[3]

Remorse seizes me when I think of all the poems, prose-poems and stories that I **should** have written. I begin to suspect in myself some fatal deficiency of will or energy—or of both. But perhaps it is a hopeful sign that I begin to blame myself rather than circumstances.

Write when you feel inclined.

As ever, your friend,
Clark.

[P.S.] Did I send you "Nyctalops?"

Notes

1. Although the book was announced as forthcoming in 1929, it never appeared; however, there is a section in *SP* titled "The Jasmine Girdle."
2. Grace Aird.
3. "Le Gouffre," l. 18: "a nightmare multiform and without truce."

[66]   [DW to CAS] [ALS, private]

14 Morningside Ave.,
New York, N.Y.
May 11, 1929

Dear Clark:

From a bad correspondent I have degenerated to something quite beyond the limits of any well-ordered encyclopedia to a point where apologies were mere utterances devoid of special significance. I have been reckless of days, time, future, and most other things. The past fortnight I've been in but one evening. Early next month I return to Minnesota for a vacation.

The gang met and passed on. The two gatherings were great and I much regretted that you were not present—you would, I think, have found the members a strange and interesting group with their common bond but individual eccentricities. Yet most of them have done slight original writing in recent months—Lovecraft has been kept busy by revision work, Long by hack efforts in attempt to make a living income, Talman by his reportorial duties, Loveman by indigence, McNeill by his moving and illness.[1] My Muse has sadly departed for more responsive soil, I begin to think; I've acquired such a damned philosophy of fatalism, opportunism, and indifference that the result is futilitarian.

What luck have you had? I'm thinking particularly of your verse ms. which you placed in an agent's hands. I've made no such efforts myself, though I vaguely plan another private venture in the near future.

Lovecraft showed me the French sonnet and translation you sent him. You write it like a native—I think your command remarkable for the short time you've spent learning the tongue. Luck to all your ventures——

Don

Notes

1. Wilfred Blanch Talman (1904–1986) and Everett McNeil (1862–1929) were members of the Kalem Club, along with the others.

[67]   [CAS to DW] [ALS]

June 7th, 1929.

Dear Donald:

You needn't apologize for not writing oftener. I'm an utterly impossible correspondent, anyway. I scarcely write to anyone any more, since I am chronically pie-eyed from physical fatigue and lack of sleep.

Here is another French poem, with a fairly literal English version appended, which I did in one of my rare hours of leisure.

I'd certainly like to have met the "gang." . . . Some day, maybe . . .

It's a terrible pity that everyone is so incapacitated for artistic effort by lack of time, money, etc. I'm in the same glorious fix, and have some other troubles to boot, which are too damnable and disgusting to even talk about.

Good luck to you. And please don't think that the brevity of this indicates any lack of interest or friendship. I'm really so tired that I can hardly fit words together.

As ever,
Clark.

[68]   [CAS to DW] [ALS]

Auburn, Cal.,
Sept. 17th, 1929.

Dear Donald:

I was indeed glad to hear from you, and I applaud your actions and resolutions. Success to that "story of age-old horror" whereat you hint![1]

My literary agent, Miss Aird,[2] is sinisterly non-committal—I have vainly asked her for a report on my book. Porca madonna![3] I'll be as old and dusty as Rameses before there's any action, if I continue to depend on her.

I've had some moments of inspiration since I wrote you last. Probably "Shadows" and "Ougabalys" (enclosed herewith) will be as much to your taste as any of my recent productions. Some of the best are in French, and I'll send you copies of them later. I'm tackling some French magazines—"La Muse Francaise," ["]Revue de l'Amérique Latine," ["]La Revue Francaise," etc. "La Revue des Deux Mondes" wrote me a letter of praise, with a few helpful minor criticisms. I have hopes of "landing" something sooner or later.

I was in the mountains for two weeks, late in August and early in Sept. A glorious camping-trip! I climbed a 9000 foot peak, among other things. Of course, there are higher ones; but the prospect was tremendous.

Give my regards to Long when you see him.

As ever, your friend,

CAS [ornamented]

Notes

1. DW's description for his novel in progress, *Dead Titans, Waken!*
2. Grace Aird, based in New York City.
3. A blasphemous insult to Holy Mark: *Slut Madonna!*

[69]   [DW to CAS] [ALS]

1152 Portland Ave.

St. Paul, Minn.

Jan. 17, 1930

Dear Clark:

If this note does nothing else, it will at least inform you of my continued existence. As usual, I have been studying like a fiend, for some post-graduate courses I am taking, and have written some, but not bales, of new verse. I am ready to take a year off and do nothing but eat, sleep, loaf, and write; but I fear I shall lie in readiness a long, long time before that idea is anywhere near fruition!

These cold days, with the thermometer down to twenty and twenty-five below, they are irksome and unpleasant; and I contemplate California with more of warm interest each week. I shall make a strenuous effort to visit there this summer, or failing that, to attend somehow or other one of the California universities next year.

Weird Tales took some more verses of mine;[1]—I note the appearance of several CAS items in recent issues.[2] Have you been productive lately? Or had anything to relieve the tedium of existence? I hear nothing from the Easterners—probably because I am so poor a correspondent—except Derleth, who seems well on the way to fortune and fame of a sort as a concoctor of detective yarns. I envy him his prolific brain and facile pen. I am inclined to believe that a certain type of intellectual—to use an abused word—attains a kind of paradoxical pleasure in throwing sops to Mammon and hoi polloi.

Let me know what has been happening to you when you have opportunity and leisure to write. Hope I shall see you this year—

D W.

Notes

1. "Marmora" and "The Worm-King."
2. "Nyctalops" (October), "The Nightmare Tarn" (November), "Fantaisie d'Antan" (December), "Ougabalys" (January), and "Shadows" (February).

[70]   [CAS to DW] [ALS]

Auburn, Cal.,
Jan. 24th, 1930

Dear Donald:

I was indeed glad to hear from you; and, since I have a leisure moment which may not be repeated very soon, am going to answer your letter with unprecedented promptness.

The news that you may come to California next summer is certainly good. If you do, you must visit me and remain a long while if you can endure the primitive accom[m]odations.

You will perhaps be surprised to learn that I have fulfilled my ancient threat, and have plunged into the writing of fantastic fiction on a grand scale. Since the middle of last September, I have completed ten stories, two of them of novelette proportions. Also, I have eight or ten briefer things, of prose-poem length and style. "Weird Tales" has accepted five stories, including a novelette, "The Monster of the Prophecy", which deals with a starving and suicidally-minded poet who is taken to a world of Antares by an Antarean scientist who has a little game of his own to play, involving the fulfillment of an ancient prophecy as to the appearance at a certain time and place of an unheard-of monster with two arms, two legs, two eyes, and a pale skin. Apart from the gorgeous fantasy, the tale satirizes nearly everything, from sex to science. I've gotten a huge kick out of writing these stories; the chief fly in my amber is, that Wright has rejected my best "weird", "The Tale of Satampra Zeiros," which describes a semi-liquescent monster that could ooze through more than one aperture at the same time.

I hope you'll send me some of your new verses. I think "Ougabalys" and "Shadows", in "Weird Tales", are about the most recent that I have done.

Twenty-five below zero is simply unimaginable to me—twenty-five **above** is bad enough as far as I am concerned.

I see Derleth's work in "W. T." quite often—I don't know his detective stories. I doubt if I could really do hack-work myself—a pseudo-scientific fantasy, "The Metamorphosis of the World," is about the nearest I have come to it. I am now beginning a yarn about three mutineers on a space-flier, who are put off to shift for themselves on some unknown world in Andromeda. If I proffer any "sops to Mammon and hoi polloi", they'll have a squirt of hydrocyanic acid concealed in them, in the form of satire. It would delight me to "put over" that sort of thing.

How about the weird romance that you were beginning? You have a great gift for imaginative fiction—I've never forgotten some of the stories you once sent me.

As ever,

Clark.

[71]   [DW to CAS] [TLS]

1152 Portland Ave.,

St. Paul, Minn.

March 28, 1930.

Dear Clark:

First, pardon the typewriter, though I suppose it does have at least the grace of greater legibility than that curious hash I am pleased to call my handwriting. And second, do not indulge in too great anathema at my omissions as a correspondent. This business of acquiring a Ph. D. is quite as laborious and time-taking as it is fabled to be.

I was delighted to hear from you; and I hope indeed I shall arrive in Auburn this summer, and inflict myself on you for a time. Your offer was exceedingly kind; and I should like nothing better than to spend an entire summer up in the mountains, providing of course that I can scrape together enough money to account for essentials of existence. I want relief from cities and university life—quiet and open spaces; a spot where I can live leisurely and write. I expect to finish this summer the weird-romance I began in the east;[1] the story is pretty well outlined in my mind, and I think I could finish it in a month under proper conditions. At any rate, the mere completing of a novel ought to teach me a good many tricks, if nothing else. The poetic vein seems to have run out again for the time being; and my present wish is to finish this novel, and to start another which is more or less hackwork but has possibilities of selling. The placing of one novel, if so fortunate an event should come to pass, would induce me, I think, to let the scholastic life slide and gamble on writing for a couple of years. I have never really given it a thorough try as a possible bread-winner; and hackwork, if I can do it, at least offers leisure to do the things I really wish to. The older I become, the more I realize how life is little more than a continual compromise between things desired and things required.

It is good news that you are making a success of short stories; may the gods continue to assist you and favor you with considerable more fortune than they have been willing to grant in the past. I continue to await the appearance of another of your books; poetry or prose—I have a natural preference for the first, but either would relieve the aridity of current publications.

Spring is coming at last; and it is the more pleasant here for the relief from winter and gray days; but I was never meant to be an Eskimo, and I have often thought that the California climate and scenery would be far more to my taste, either in the mountains or along the sea-shore. There is always the possibility, of course, that my trip may not materialize; Lady Luck has taught me to count on nothing until it actually materializes, and I have found that those who count on nothing can never be disappointed. But present indications are that I will arrive; and heaven knows I shall assist them in pointing westward! Perhaps I may hitch-hike; but there is a possibility I may drive out with friends, or a remoter possibility that I may borrow my brother's ford [*sic*] for a month and waver along.

There is a poetry contest I shall enter, and which I would suggest your entering also. Full details may be had from the Harbor Press, 142 E. 32nd St., New York City. The prize is $300 for a manuscript of one or several poems to make not more than fifty printed pages; open to poets who have had no books published, unless such were at their own expense; royalties in addition to the prize to be paid on all copies sold after the first thousand. The judges are the president of Smith College, the bibliographer of the N.Y. Public Library, and three others; hence I think there will be more impartiality, less favoritism of free verse, mor[e] recognition of genuine poetry, than has been the case with most recent contests.[2] The Harbor Press is a small company, but two of its publications were on the list of the Fifty Best books (typography and format) of last year. Which means that the winning manuscript will, for something of a rarity, have an appropriate and perhaps distinguished appearance.

From the Eastern gang, I have not heard in a long while, nor does it appear that Cook has yet printed the book he planned to make of one of Lovecraft's horror-stories.[3] I dropped Cook a line last week but have not yet heard from him; and Derleth, whom I intended to visit last fall, I could not because of the burden of university work. Thus goes it! I hope the summer produces more to my inclination.

D. W.

Notes

1. The novel, *Dead Titans, Waken!*, was published as *The Web of Easter Island*.
2. The 1930 prize winner was *Horns in Velvet*, by Joan Ramsay (1902–?).
3. See CAS to RHB 10n3.

[72] [CAS to DW] [ALS]

Auburn, Cal.,
June 4th, 1930.

Dear Donald:

I had meant to answer your letter long before this—but I guess you know my erratic qualities as a correspondent.

The best news in your letter was that you might really come to California. And I'm certainly interested in your novel. There is undoubtedly a public for fantastic fiction; and literary form, such as you could achieve, is no drawback. Lovecraft says he has been approached by Simon and Schuster, of New York, who want him to write a weird novel.[1]

I've done a lot of new prose, including a forty-page interplanetary novelette, "Marooned in Andromeda." Wright continues to buy my stuff, and recently took one of my best, "The Uncharted Isle." "Murder in the Fourth Dimension" was taken by "Amazing Detective Tales."

I liked your fantasy in the current "W. T."[2] My "Sadastor," in the same issue, is marred by an atrocious misprint, "wens" for "webs."

Thanks for the tip about the Harbor Press contest; but I fear I'm not eligible, since two of my books were not published at my own expense. I'm trying my new book, "The Jasmine Girdle," on a few eastern firms. But I've almost ceased to think of myself as a poet.

Here's hoping your trip materializes. I'll certainly be glad to see you, and you'll be welcome to the somewhat primitive accom[m]odations which I can offer.

As ever,
Clark.

Notes

1. The publisher had turned down HPL's stories, and HPL never wrote or submitted any novel he had on hand. Simon and Schuster also rejected *The Outsider and Others,* as did Doubleday-Doran, Farrar and Rinehart, and Scribner's.
2. "The Green Flame."

[73] [CAS to DW] [ALS]

Auburn, Cal.,
Oct. 9th, 1930.

Dear Donald:

I was very glad to receive your letter. But what an everlasting shame that you should have had, and still have, so much illness! My one trouble and occasional sicknesses seem trifling in comparison.

Many thanks for the copy of "The Minnesota Quarterly" containing your sonnets[1] and the other poems which you sent me. I like all of these poems—

in fact, I am very much pleased and impressed by them. All of the sonnets are admirable, in their ease, grace, and melody.

I am sorry you could not come to California this summer. I was in the high mountains for ten days in August. You would love it there—also, you would like the country around Auburn . . . the autumn, too, is my own especial season; and everything is about perfect now, as far as I am concerned. Of course, much if not all of the autumn color around here is in the fruit orchards, but it is very lovely and gorgeous . . . Let's hope for better luck next year—also that you will finish your novel, and find a ready publisher in the meanwhile.

Who is Audrey Johnson? I think her drawings are quite remarkable—the decoration for your sonnets is about the best thing I have seen in ages.[2] And I like the Baudelaire illustration too. I shall be vastly interested to see photographs of some of your brother's work, if they are successful. I have not done any pictures myself in aeons, apart from three or four that I made between last Christmas and New Year's Day.

I shall look forward to your story in the next issue of W. T. Your poem[3] was one of the few bright features in the last issue—certainly most of the stories were pretty punk.

Wright has been a good customer for me—even though he has rejected some of my best work! On counting up, I find that he has accepted in the last year no less then thirteen tales and five poems—two of the poems, for use in "Oriental Stories", his new magazine![4] Two sizable yarns, "A Rendezvous in Averoigne", and "The Immeasurable Horror", have "landed" during the past month. I have also been doing some work for the Gernsback publication, "Wonder Stories", and the October issue contained an interstellar novelette of mine, "Marooned in Andromeda." The editor has suggested a series of such tales; and the next one, "The Red World of Polaris", should be out next month or the month after. Another tale, "Murder in the Fourth Dimension", appeared in the October "Amazing Detective Tales." I have not written any poetry this year and have the feeling that my vein is at least temporarily exhausted. But there seems to be no limit to the prose, some of which I write with as much facility as if it were being dictated to me! It may seem a bold project to make a living from fantastic fiction of a high literary type, but I believe it can be done. In fact, I shall have to do it—or else take to ditch-digging. I have no other alternative, since I am not fitted for business or any of the professions.

Lovecraft writes to me often; and I have been re-borrowing all of his stories to read. They are almost all that I **can** read in present-day fiction. I have completely sworn off on the realistic school, and can't even read Anatole France any more. In the name of Hecate, Medusa and Proserpine, please hurry up with your weird novel. I may do one myself, alternating the chapters with writing shorts and novelettes. In that way, it shouldn't be so much of a strain.

Heaven forfend those operations at which you hint. And write when you feel in the mood.

As ever,

Clark

[P.S.] I will send you a carbon of something or other before long.

Notes

1. "Dead Fruit of the Fugitive Years: Ten Sonnets," *Minnesota Quarterly* 7, No. 2 (Winter 1929): 27–31.
2. Johnson designed the dust jacket for DW's *The Web of Easter Island.*
3. "The Cypress-Bog."
4. *Oriental Stories* (1930–32; retitled *Magic Carpet Magazine,* 1933–34) was a companion magazine to *WT* focusing on tales of Oriental adventure.

[74]   [CAS to DW] [ALS]

Auburn, Cal.

Nov. 18th, 1930.

Dear Donald:

I am sending you under separate cover two copies of "Ebony and Crystal", and must absolutely insist that you do not pay for either of them. You are more than entitled to them.

Your letter was good reading, and I am indeed glad to hear of your recovered health. The worst thing about physical disability is that it too often hinders or impairs one's intellectual or creative capacities. I have always found it harder to work, and the results have often been less satisfactory, at times when I was more or less under the weather.

I was pleased by the excerpt from your novel which appeared in the last W. T., and thought it very well done.[1] I hope you will complete the whole story soon. Surely there should be a publisher for it.

I'm glad you liked "Medusa" and the other tales. "Medusa" is a favorite with me. It has just been returned with a personal letter by "Ghost Stories", which held it for six weeks; and I am now submitting it to Wright, with the prayerful hope that it may reach him in one of his saner intervals. Though he has taken much of my best work, he has also rejected several stories that were equally good, such as "Satampra Zeiros", "The Door to Saturn", "The Willow Landscape", "The Epiphany of Death", and "A Night in Malnéant."[2]

I'll send you some new work before long. Have just finished two short Orientales, "The Ghoul", and "A Tale of Sir John Maundeville," both of which are weird and even gruesome. I'll give you my extra carbon of the latter, if it seems to stand the test.

I'll be greatly interested to see your brother's work in the Quarterly— also, any drawings by Audrey Johnson, who, judging from your description, must be a remarkable person as well as a good artist. You are lucky to know so many people with congenial tastes. I, like Lovecraft, am pretty well isolated in that regard, though I have ceased to mind it very greatly.

Derleth is certainly talented, and I am amazed at his youth and accomplishments. Of some work which he sent me, I liked the non-weird material best: "The Early Years" seemed to be permeated with the freshness and joy—and also the mysterious ache—of youth itself.[3] The style is appropriate here, in its simplicity and seeming artlessness; but I think it is very hard, if not impossible, to write an effective ghost story in an every-day style. When one is creating an atmosphere of weirdness, ordinary locutions, sentence-rhythms, etc., are likely to produce a let-down, except as used in dialogue. I think the trouble with most of the yarns in "Weird Tales" is this lack of distinctive or appropriate writing. There are many good ideas, wholly or partly spoiled by commonplace wording, which would do well enough in a story by normal events.

We have had an unusually heavy rain, followed by frost and weather of sparkling clarity. I worked outdoors a good deal during the summer and early autumn. It isn't so feasible now,—but the air is perfect for a brisk walk.

Maybe you would like the Machenesque "Satyr", which I enclose herewith. You can show it to Derleth, if you wish, before returning it.

As ever,

Clark.

Notes

1. I.e., "Something from Above."
2. Of these, Wright later published "The Tale of Satampra Zeiros" and "A Night in Malnéant." *WT* published "The Epiphany of Death" under another editor.
3. "The Early Years" (ms., Place of Hawks, AWD's residence) was not published but probably reworked as *Evening in Spring.*

[75]   [CAS to DW] [ALS]

Auburn, Cal.,
Jan. 18th, 1931.

Dear Donald:

It was good to receive your letter and card and the copy of the Quarterly. If I have not acknowledged them before, it was not through forgetfulness.

The best news in your letter was regarding the projected book of poems, to which I am looking forward with eagerness. I like your idea for the binding; and the book will be sumptuously illustrated if the drawings are as good as the design for "Effluvia."[1] This latter impressed me as a fine piece of work; and I see no reason why your brother shouldn't become a formidable rival for Harry Clarke. My own pictorial as well as poetic ambitions seem to have merged with my prose aspirations for the time being.

I hope your check for "Something from Above" has materialized before this. W. T. has been about two months behind on payments since the starting of "Oriental Stories"—before that, the checks came promptly on publication. By the way, have you heard the latest from Wright—that W. T. will return to a monthly basis after three issues as a bi-monthly? This is certainly wise—as you say, neither the writers nor the readers will care for the bi-m. idea. Wright also tells me that he may have to go to the hospital for two months, for treatment. I am sorry to hear this. Personally—though a lot of people slam him, and though he has rejected some of my best stuff—I think Wright has maintained a pretty fair level in W. T., which is certainly far beyond other pulp-wood magazines in its literary standards. Also, the new magazine, "Oriental Stories", is far superior to others of its kind, and is very attractively gotten up. I could wish that the covers of W. T. were more of the same type as those on O. S.

I've sent work to "Astounding Stories," but have had it rejected as "too literary," or "lacking in action."[2] This magazine seems to want nothing but super-heroic deeds of derring-do, carnage on a grand scale, etc. My scientific stuff seems to fit in better with the policy of "Wonder Stories"—it isn't technical enough for "Amazing Stories." By the way, "Argosy" and "Excitement"[3] (the latter a Street & Smith publication) use a certain amount of material in the fantastic scientific vein; so there is really a fair range of markets for such stories. Exciting action seems to be the main requirement, except with "Amazing."

I am glad you liked the last consignment of my yarns. Derleth is to pass on some more stuff to you—"The Door to Saturn", which is one of my own pets, and a recent horror story, "The Return of Helman Carnby", which will come via H. P. Lovecraft. I have just finished a longish tale, "The City of the Singing Flame", which you may see later, if it seems good enough.

All of last month, and well into the present one, I was laid up with a vile and ridiculous malady—whooping-cough! The thing was no joke; but I managed to work most of the time in spite of it.

I don't envy you your proctoring! But certainly there must be an element of humor in college life—that professorial injunction to sum up Greek philosophy in four pages is truly funny. One would need the leisure and patience of a medieval scholiast to do the job adequately.

Good luck with "The Mystic Magazine!"[4] Have you ever tried "Ghost Stories" with supernatural fiction? It is immensely inferior to W. T. in its standards, unfortunately. The public for the weird, as Lovecraft observed some time ago in one of his letters, is divided between the extremely plebeian and the ultra-aristocratic. I fear that "Ghost Stories" prefers to appeal entirely to the former element.[5]

How about your novel? I must try something of book-length. The way to do it would be to alternate the chapters with the writing of "shorts"—in this way, one should obviate a lot of strain.

Here's to your volume of verse—I'll drink the toast in some home-made anisette that a French friend brought me. I wish you were here to drink it too.

As ever,

Clark.

Notes

1. *Minnesota Quarterly* 8 No. 1 (Fall 1930) contains HW's frontispiece "Effluvia" (6) and his story "Effluvia: An Exceptional Fable" (23–29).

2. *Astounding Stories* began publication in January 1930 under the editorship of Harry Bates (1930–33) as a magazine devoted chiefly to science fiction but with the occasional tale of the weird or supernatural.

3. Initially *Sea Stories* (1922–30), then *Excitement* (1930–31), and finally *College Stories* 1931–32).

4. *Mystic Magazine* was a short-lived pulp magazine, edited by AWD, that published five issues (November 1930–April 1931); the contents focused mostly on the occult.

5. *Ghost Stories* (1926–32) was a pulp magazine that generally published stories of a "true confession" type.

[76]   [CAS to DW] [ALS]

Auburn, Cal.,
March 24th, 1931.

Dear Donald:

Tempus fugit—as the wise have had occasion to note in more than one clime and era—and good intentions do the same. Honestly, I had meant to write long before this.

It was good news that my tales were so much to your taste. I have, however, re-written the ending of "Helman Carnby." In the new version, the secretary sees merely the shadow of the headless, re-united lich—not the monstrosity itself. When he finally enters the room, there is nothing but a *double* heap of human fragments, some fresh and some mouldy. "Ghost Stories" thought the yarn "too horrific"—the editor told me very gravely that "the reactions of our staff-readers showed plainly that you have sinned in this respect." I hope Wright won't be so asinine when he gets around to the tale. "The City of the Singing Flame" I have worked off on "Wonder Stories," as science fiction. It will be out in June, I believe.

I hope you have had a chance to indulge the fictional impulse of which you spoke—also, that your book of verse is coming on as per schedule. I am certainly looking forward to it.

Not much news here. The spring flowers have been very precocious—everything is out weeks ahead of their usual time. You would like the California foothills at this season.

I have been grinding away—mostly scientifiction, or something in that neighborhood. One long, purely fantastic tale, "The Testament of Atham-maus"—I'll show you the typescript some time, if Wright doesn't use it.

Your novel should be great stuff, from the sample of it that W. T. published. So far, I haven't started any ideas that seemed to demand very lengthy treatment. But I can see the advantages of a book-length story. My longest yarn to date—"A Captivity in Serpens"—ran to 57 pages.

Have you read the ghost stories of M. R. James? Doubtless you have. Lovecraft has loaned me two of his books.[1] They are certainly a distinct and highly competent addition to the literature of the fantasmal and macabre.

I note that Harold Hersey is to start a new magazine of scientifiction—"Miracle Stories and Science Fantasy", or some such god-forsaken name.[2] What amuses me, in magazines of this type, is the way the readers lap it up under the pretense of scientific credibility. Apart from their smattering of laboratory lingo some of the tales in "Astounding Stories" remind me of the delirious antics of Mickey Mouse.

As ever,

Clark.

Notes

1. *Ghost-Stories of an Antiquary* and *A Warning to the Curious*.
2. Only two issues of *Miracle Science and Fantasy Stories* (April/May and July 1931) appeared.

[77]   [CAS to DW] [ALS]

Auburn, Cal.,
April 14th, 1931.

Dear Donald:

I was delighted to receive your new book, and have read the poems through several times. All of them are excellent; and "Dark Odyssey" was a good choice for the title.[1] I like the sombre and plangent sonorities of this poem. Alone of anything that I have read in aeons, your volume took me back to the world of lyric urgencies and poignancies. More than ever, it made me aware of a profound kinship.

Your brother's drawings are admirable.[2] I was particularly arrested by the powerful and haunting design of the frontispiece. The printers are to be commended for their work, too. Are you sending out copies for review? If so, I trust that the book will receive some decent notices, and see no reason why it shouldn't.

Precious little news with me, of late. I have been confining myself to fantasies with a scientifictional basis. It is interesting to note how much of the fairy-tale element one can "put over" with a perfunctory attention to scientific credibility. I have worked in some double-edged ironies too. I think I mentioned the acceptance of "The City of the Singing Flame" by "Wonder Stories." The same magazine has recently taken a 57 page interstellar novelette, which will appear under the title of "The Amazing Planet." I am now sending in a story—"The Letter from Mohaun Los"—which combines the motifs of time-travelling and inter-cosmic transit. The hero goes a million years ahead in abstract time, but forgets the space-factor; and in the meanwhile the earth and the solar system have been moving away from him in space. He finally lands on another planet, which intersects the former position of the earth.

Have you heard of the new weird magazine—not yet named[3]—for which Harry Bates of "Astounding Stories" is now accepting material? Mystery and terror are to be stressed, according to Bates. Two cents per word and up on acceptance is certainly tempting.

Wright was afraid to take "Helman Carnby,"—thought it might shock his Pollyanna public. I am beginning to think the tale must be pretty good— other people have termed it "inexcusable."

You will probably receive a story of mine to read before long.

As ever,

Clark

Notes

1. DW inscribed the book "For Clark Ashton Smith—who, rare among mortals, possesses the two-fold gift—Donald Wandrei, April 5, 1931."
2. HW had five illustrations in *Dark Odyssey*.
3. *Strange Tales of Mystery and Terror.*

[78]   [CAS to DW] [TLS]

Auburn, Cal.

Aug. 7th, 1931.

Dear Donald:

I was heartily glad to hear from you. It was about time, methinks. It is good news that your novel is so far advanced; and I look forward to seeing the completed result with keen interest. Also, I want emphatically to see the carbons of the two shorts you mention, and hope you will send them on soon.

Nothing worthy of scare-heads in the way of news at this end. I have been turning out prose at about the usual rate; and one or two carbons of new tales will reach you in due process of time. "The Holiness of Azédarac," which you liked, was taken by Wright some time ago.

Here is a list of my published and accepted stories in other mediums than in W.T., for the present year. "An Adventure in Futurity" (somewhat hackney-ish time-travelling stuff) appeared in Wonder Stories for April; and "The City of the Singing Flame" in the July number of the same. "The Amazing Planet," a pretty fair novelette of interstellar adventure, is out in the summer issue of Wonder Stories Quarterly, now on sale. "The Satyr" appeared in the July "La

Paree Stories" (high-class medium, eh, what?)[1] and "The Willow Landscape" in the May "Philippine Magazine," published in far-off Manila. "Helman Carnby," re-titled "The Return of the Sorcerer," will adorn the first issue of "Strange Tales," the new Clayton magazine, which will hit the stands on Aug. 14th.[2] "The Martian," a piece of superfine hackwork done from a prize-winning plot by one E. M. Johnston of Ontario, will come out in the Fall Wonder Stories Quarterly, Sept. 15th. Those are all that I know of at present; though it seems probable that my sequel to "The City of the Singing Flame," entitled "Beyond the Singing Flame," will appear some time during the autumn in Wonder Stories. It has not yet been reported on; and the fate of "The Door to Saturn," now being held by Harry Bates of "Strange Tales", is somewhat in doubt. Bates wants to buy the story; but the final choice is exercised by Clayton, the publisher, who has already crabbed the sale of at least one story for me. I am out of spare copies of all published tales, or I would be glad to send you some. Probably the only way to get back numbers is to write to the publishers.

We had some excitement around here, early in July, in the shape of a two-days' forest fire. Somewhat dramatically, it interrupted the writing of my sequel to "The Singing Flame." Fighting it was a herculean and homeric task—it was like some dreadful thousand-headed hydra. It came to within three feet of our cabin, with a strong wind behind it!

I enjoyed "At the Mountains of Madness" tremendously, and agree with you that it is one of Lovecraft's best. That description of the onrushing shoggoth! My god! The tale is infinitely better than Poe's "Arthur Gordon Pym." I understand that Wright, in one of his lunatic lapses, has declined it. Then he prints the Edmond Hamilton drivel, and the Kipling–Burroughs hash by Kline! Of all the double-barred and triple-dyed and quintuple-plated idiocy! Certainly he has turned down some of my best things too—"The Door to Saturn" and "A Tale of Sir John Maundeville" being notable instances, not to mention "Helman Carnby." It will be a josh if "Strange Tales" should take the first-mentioned. The rate of payment on "Carnby" was exactly double what it would have received from Wright.

No, I haven't done any new pictures or written any verse. Some time, maybe, I'll try doing an illustration for one of my stories. It couldn't be worse than Senf.[3] "The City of the Singing Flame" had a really excellent black and white illustration by Paul—also a gaudy cover design by the same artist. Marchioni's drawing for "The Amazing Planet" is better than M's average. But Paul is much the best of the scientifictional artists. Wesso is often pretty good—his drawings in "Astounding" are quite often better than the stuff they illustrate.[4]

Write me soon.

As ever,

Clark.

P.S. Have I mentioned Wright's final acceptance of "The Testament of

Athammaus", a month after he had declined it? "Satampra Zeiros" (November issue) will be my next yarn in W.T.

Notes

1. *La Paree Stories* (1930–38) was considered a "saucy" pulp magazine, with elements of the risqué, sometimes in a Parisian setting.
2. William Clayton, the publisher of many pulp magazines from westerns to science fiction.
3. The *WT* artist Curtis Charles Senf (1873–1949).
4. Marco Enrico "Mark" Marchioni (1901–1987); Frank Rudolph Paul (1884–1963); Hans Waldemar Wessolowski (1893–1947), known as "Wesso."

[79]   [CAS to DW] [TLS]

Auburn, Cal.
Aug. 18th, 1931.

Dear Donald:

Here is your story, "The Lives of Alfred Kramer," which Lovecraft forwarded to me. I enjoyed reading it greatly, but agree with H.P.L., that it would be improved by simplifying the narrative. Also, I believe you could make it into something far more tremendous if you could secure a suggestion of unity in the dream-memories of Kramer—perhaps some dim, amorphous horror, taking many forms and embodiments, but recurrently recognized as being the same, which has followed him through all his ancestral lives, and which, eventually, he is forced to confront in its primordial lair as he returns on the track of memory. I wish, too, that you could suggest a mental devolution in Kramer, keeping pace with his physical atavism; but this may be rather difficult. Anyway, it's a great idea; and the ending which you have is quite tremendous.

No news worth chronicling since I wrote you the other day. You should receive ere long, if it has not already come, the sequel to "The Singing Flame." This is, by all odds, my best recent story. I haven't had any editorial reports of late. Harry Bates seems to be holding two or three yarns for further consideration. I have four new yarns under way, but haven't done much except loaf for the past week.

Let me hear from you soon. And send along the other story you spoke of. I am short on imaginative reading-matter—never can get hold of enough at a time to last me very long.

By the way, the next time you write to Farnsworth Wright, it would be a good idea to express regret at his refusal of "The Mountains of Madness." I, and some others, are going to do this. It might make him reconsider his damfool decision, if enough people write in.

Let me hear from you soon.

As ever,
Clark

[80] [CAS to DW] [ALS]

Auburn, Cal.
Aug. 29th, 1931.

Dear Donald:

I liked your last story, "The Tree-Men of M'bwa", [*sic*] very much. Bates or Wright ought to buy it. Let me know if you are submitting it to Wright—I'd give it an enthusiastic send-off in my next letter to him.

Bates has taken "The Door to Saturn" for "Strange Tales"—the wicked humor seems to have scored a hit.

As ever,
Clark.

[81] [CAS to DW] [ALS]

Auburn, Cal.
Sept. 14th, 1931

Dear Donald:

I'm sorry that "The Tree-Men of M'bwa" didn't land with Bates, for it would surely have been an adornment to S. T. I trust that Wright will grab it. He will, if it finds him in a semi-lucid interval.

I'll probably be able to send you a "Wonder Stories" with "The City of the Singing Flame," since I have an extra circulating in the neighborhood. The sequel, "Beyond the Singing Flame," will appear next month, coincidentally with "Satampra" in W. T.

My own phenomenal luck (I can't call it anything else) seems to continue. I may or may not have told you that Bates took "The Door to Saturn" and is seriously considering a revised copy of "The Hunters from Beyond." "The Planet Entity" (which I wrote from a prize plot) is out in the Fall "Wonder Stories Quarterly."

"The Vaults of Yoh-Vombis" will reach you before long, to be forwarded to H. P. L. I have several semi-scientifictional ideas to develop—"The Cairn,"[1] and "The Eternal World," in especial, both of which seem quite original, and will permit of a note of cosmic poetry.

I hope you will go on with your novel and some more short weirds. Rejections are disheartening, but they don't necessarily mean anything. I did eight yarns in a row last fall, which have so far failed to sell. Since then, nearly everything has landed!

Wright will have to reconsider "At the Mountains of Madness," with all the protests that are going forward! I know of at least four or five![2]

As ever,
Clark.

Notes

1. I.e., "The Secret of the Cairn."

2. Wright did not reconsider his rejection of *At the Mountains of Madness,* and HPL never resubmitted the story to him.

[82]   [DW to CAS] [ALS]

1152 Portland Ave.
St. Paul, Minn.
Sept. 18, 1931

Dear Clark:

In another envelope I am returning "Beyond the Singing Flame." I think I must have been spoiled by the original story; I liked the continuation, but would have liked it a great deal more, I feel, had I not been so impressed by "The City of the Singing Flame." I am delighted with your continued success; almost as much as if it were my own. It is richly deserved, and I sincerely hope that it will continue unbroken.

Things have been going very badly for me; so badly that I have written scarcely any letters for fear that they might be too moody. My closest friend here won a Rhodes Scholarship and leaves tomorrow for Oxford. Aside from that, another friend of many years standing, the only girl I cared for, and my own brother, all three united to play the most contemptible trick I've ever known against me, using my wholehearted friendship as the lever to double-cross me.[1] I am leaving home a week from tomorrow to room somewhere in Minneapolis, but my mail can be addressed here as I shall return every week or two to visit my mother and father. I have been pretty much broken up by the thing, and have learned the bitter lesson never again to let anyone be close enough to hurt me. Since I haven't any money, I am forced to sell my lovely illustrated books to obtain some; and the loss of each one will be like a drop of blood.

I sent out a number of mss. this week, but have no report on any. Wright holds "When the Fire-Creatures Came" and "The Tree Men of M'Bwa"; The Atlantic "Early Harvest", "Summer Roads", and "To a Friendship Broken"; Scribner's my six-sonnet sequence, "After Farewell"; Collier's a piffle story, "A Midsummer Knight."[2] The revised "Lives of Alfred Kramer" will go to Wright next week, "Moon-Magic" to Harper's. I am beginning work on one weird and one non-weird story. The novel is temporarily laid aside. A volume of poetry will be ready to start going the rounds next week, under the tentative symbolic title, "The Roaring of the Sea",[3] taken from an old ballad stanza.

> "For forty days and forty nights
> He waded red blood to the knee;
> And he saw neither sun nor moon
> But heard the roaring of the sea."[4]

I am not satisfied with any of a dozen or so titles that I have been considering.

As ever,
Donald

Notes

1. DW apparently refers to Hjalmar Björnson and Barbara Fawcett Craigie, whom DW incorporated under different names in his autobiographical novel *Invisible Sun* (begun September 1932).
2. The last five items mentioned appear to be nonextant.
3. Also nonextant.
4. "Thomas the Rhymer": "Oh they rade on, and farther on, / And they waded through rivers aboon the knee, / And they saw neither sun nor moon, / But they heard the roaring of the sea."

[83]   [CAS to DW] [ALS]

Auburn, Cal.
Oct. 7th, 1931.

Dear Donald:

I received your letter, and the carbon of "Beyond the Singing Flame" some time ago. Glad you liked the story, which is now in print, in the new smooth-paper "Wonder Stories." I'm still chasing a printed copy of the first "Singing Flame" yarn for you.

I trust you'll have an acceptance or two from Wright. I don't see how he could pass up "The Tree-Men of M'bwa." It's high time for him to be reporting on two tales of mine, "The Maker of Gargoyles" and "The Vaults of Yoh-Vombis," which were sent in last month. Bates has been holding up "Hunters from Beyond" (revised version) from everlasting to everlasting.[1] My newest completed yarn, "The Eternal World," has gone to the Gernsback Magazines. It deals with a time-traveller who shot himself clean out of the time-space continuum into eternity! I shall now write two or three weird shorts, "The Demon of the Flower," "The Nameless Offspring," etc., and then start work on a full-length novelette which I have plotted pretty thoroughly.

I'm damn sorry about the personal double crossing at which you hint. I've about come to the conclusion myself that human beings are better at a distance. I had a dose of mean, petty tattle the other day, from some one of whom I have been fond. Gossip is one of the things I can't stand—nothing disillusions me so much with people as to find that they are willing to lend an ear to invidious personalities and repeat them.

"The Roaring of the Sun" isn't a bad title for a book of verse; but probably you can find a better one. Good luck with publishers.

I don't think I saw "When the Fire-Creatures Came". Have you a carbon you could loan me? I like the title.

As ever, your friend,
Clark.

Notes

1. Ps. 90.2: "Before the mountains were brought forth, or ever thou hadst formed the earth and the world, even from everlasting to everlasting, thou *art* God."

[84]   [DW to CAS] [TLS]

[University of Minnesota stationery]
Nov. 18 [1931]

Dear Clark—

Herewith two of Derleth's recent work.

How are you prospering at what? I have written nothing new—am working on the next to last chapter of Dead Titans Waken [*sic*] which will be done before New Year's running to about 65,000 words. Do you want to see it in ms? It'll probably cost a young fortune to send it around, he said encouragingly!

Bates has held the "Raiders" six weeks, Wonder Stories "The Fire Creatures" for five. I am stupefied by their speed.

Shoot along any new shorts of your own—or poetry. I've written little verse recently, except for a sonnet group, which is non-imaginative.

As ever, & in haste,
Donald W.

[85]   [CAS to DW] [ALS]

Auburn, Calif.
Nov. 21st, 1931.

Dear Donald:

I liked your "Raiders of the Universes", particularly the idea of atomic shrinking. Hope you can place the story to advantage. I was glad to hear, some time ago, through August, that Wright had some good sense in taking "The Tree-Men of M'bwa."

Our weather has been very wintry—heavy rains, and to-day a morning of blue crystal, with ice and frost, and a north-east wind blowing from the snow-bound Sierras. Pretty bleak and boreal for the citrus belt—

"The land where bloom the lemon trees
And darkly gleam the golden oranges."[1]

Bates has just taken the least original of my recent yarns—"The Hunters from Beyond"—and has two better ones—"The Demon of the Flower" and "The Nameless Offspring"—under advisement. Wright accepted "The Vaults of Yoh-Vombis" and "Medusa" some time ago; and Gernsback has recently taken "The Eternal World;" a super-scientific that you might like.

How about those new stories of August's?

As ever, Clark.

Notes

1. James Elroy Flecker, "Mignon" (from Goethe), *Collected Poems* (New York: Alfred A. Knopf, 1921), 35 (ll. 1–2). The actual reading of l. 1 is "Knowest thou the land where bloom the lemon trees."

[86]   [CAS to DW] [TLS]

Auburn, Calif.

Nov. 22nd, 1931.

Dear Donald:

I got August Derleth's mss., with your note, just after I had mailed you a line.

Glad to know that "Dead Titans Waken" is so near completion. I trust that some publisher will accept it, either promptly or eventually. I'd surely like to see the Ms, if you are sending it around.

Your scientific tales are evidently being considered carefully by Bates and David Lasser:[1] six weeks is particularly long for B. to hold anything. Your "Raiders" ought to be o.k. for "Astounding Stories."

Here is a new short, which you can ship along to Lovecraft at leisure. I am sending it to Wright, since Bates is evidently not very partial to stuff under four thousand words—two of my tales having been turned down solely for their brevity.

You may have seen "The Nameless Offspring" by now.

As ever,

Clark

Notes

1. David Lasser (1902–1996) was an editor (1929–33) at *Wonder Stories*.

[87]   [DW to CAS] [ALS]

1152 Portland Ave.

St. Paul, Minn.

Dec. 22, 1931

Dear Clark:

"The Weird of Avoosl Wuthoqquan" is extremely well-done; and its atmospheric bizarrerie, I think, is neatly and ironically capped by the casually cannibalistic conclusion. I hope Wright will see the light of day when it reaches his hands.

You will receive my "Dead Titans Waken" about New Year's. I have two weeks of vacation before the winter school quarter begins, and am now completing the novel. It will be a great load off my mind when the last page is done; as novels go, it is not long; but I have been writing at odd intervals on it for a period of nearly three years.

Bates finally took my "Raiders of the Universes", after holding it for two months and a half, but says I won't receive a check till January. At least three months from the sending to the receiving—quite a bit different, I should say, from their vaunted payment on acceptance and "report within a week." At any rate, it begins to look as if I would reach *Europe* in 1932 after all. There is no certainty, of course, that my novel will be published, or if it is, when it will be; but aside from it, I think I'll be able to scrape together enough money for four to six months abroad.

We've been having crazy weather—damp, rainy, cool days of around forty degrees, instead of the usual snow and blizzards and zero cold. But then it was like this all last winter. I wonder if a change is coming about in the climates? And if so, why?

Best holiday greetings for a happy Christmas and a New Year full of as much, or more, creative and financial success as this dying year brought you.

As ever,
Donald

[88]   [CAS to DW] [ALS]

Auburn, Cal.
Jan. 31st, 1932.

Dear Donald:

I'm looking forward eagerly to your novel, which H. P. says will come in my direction presently. Here's to a speedy landing with some good publisher. I was glad to hear that "Raiders of the Universes" had been taken for Astounding Stories.

The weather here has been a round of storms, snow, hail, rain,—every goddam form in which terrestrial atmospheric moisture can be precipitated. There's a heavy, blustering, wind-blown rain at present. It's good weather for writing, anyhow, and I have reeled off about 25,000 words since the beginning of the year. One 10,000 word yarn, "The Immortals of Mercury", I am trying to land with Astounding. I have also done, at Bates' suggestion, a naturalistic horror story describing the agonies of a man who is **twice** buried alive—the second premature interment ending in death by slow asphyxiation.[1] Wright has accepted "The Weird of Avoosl Wuthoqquan", which you liked; and also "The Empire of the Necromancers", which you may have seen by this time. I guess I told you that "The Nameless Offspring" had been bought for "Strange Tales."

Your "Tree-Men of M'bwa" was the best tale in the Feb. W. T.

I am now doing a horror called "The Seed from the Sepulcher," describing a malignant plant-growth that takes root in a man's head, issues antler-like from his skull, burgeons through his eyes, etc; and trellises all his bones with its roots, while he *still lives* in a fashion.

Yours for the epiphany of Satan,

Clark.

P.S. Have you sent any stuff to Carl Swanson, Washburn, North Dakota, who is planning to issue a small mag. of weird and science fiction?[2] He has taken some of my unsold stuff, as well as Lovecraft's. Hope something will come of it.

Notes

1. "The Second Interment."
2. Swanson's *Galaxy* never appeared.

[89]   [CAS to DW] [TLS]

Auburn, Cal.
Feb. 17th, 1932.

Dear Donald:

Herewith is the ms. of H.P.L.'s "The Shadow over Innsmouth,["] which I have enjoyed greatly. It is a consummate piece of shudder-evoking atmosphere; and my only criticism is that even more could readily be made of the story.

I am also sending a new fantasy of my own, Ubbo-Sathla, whose ideation may remind you a little of your own tale, Alfred Kramer. The main object of Ubbo-Sathla was to achieve a profound and manifold dissolution of what is known as reality—which, come to think of it, is the animus of nearly all my tales, more or less.

Your novel ought to come any day. I'll read and "report" promptly when it does come. I hope the European trip will materialize.

As ever,

Clark

[90]   [CAS to DW] [TLS]

Auburn, Cal.
March 1st, 1932.

Dear Donald:

Your novel came o.k., and I have read it with immense pleasure. The plot seems all right to me, and I do not see that it calls for any structural modifications. My only suggestion is, that the wording might be touched up in places, in the earlier chapters. The later chapters are superior in style, it seems to me—especially where they are written in the first person. The tale is full of imaginative ideas; and some of the descriptions of strange phenomena—the changeability of the pitted image, etc.—might stand considerable amplification.

I'll send the ms. on in a few days, but would like to re-read portions of it first.

I'm glad you liked Lovecraft's new story and my recent Mss. "The Shadow over Innsmouth" certainly has a most pervasive atmosphere—I can still feel and smell it! I certainly wish H. P. would pitch in and do a lot of new work—he couldn't write enough to suit me!

I'm pegging away at some scientific junk. I think I mentioned writing a horror tale dealing with premature burial. This yarn has been definitely accepted for "Strange Tales;" and Bates has also given me a favorable report on "The Seed from the Sepulcher," which seems to stand a good chance of being taken. I am trying to unload a scientifictional novelette on Wright.

Here's to the placing of your novel. Have you thought of trying it on Wright for a four-part serial? I see no reason at all why he wouldn't take it.

As ever,

Clark

[91]   [DW to CAS] [TLS]

[E. P. Dutton & Co. stationery]
1152 Portland Ave.
St. Paul, Minn.
April 2, 1932

Dear Clark:

"The Double Shadow" is swell! as a friend of mine would say. In its poetic handling it reminds me of that same strange atmosphere that made "Augusthes"[1] and "The Envoys" favorites with me among your previous prose & poetry.

Recently I haven't had much luck. Bates & Wright both returned "A Sea Change", & Bates rejected two scientific shorts. At present Wright & Bates each hold one ms., but I expect them to come back. I have begun trying my hand at the wholly non-weird, non-scientific for financial reasons; Collier's now has the first two products of my experiment, with little likelihood that either will be taken.

The novel appears to have been lost in transit. It was returned by Simon & Schuster on March 7, but has not arrived, & no one seems able to discover its whereabouts. I haven't the forty dollars or so that it would require to hire a typist, & I haven't the time or energy to do it all over again from the carbon. Nerts. It may still turn up, but the chances seem rather small.

After much watching of second-hand book-stalls, I obtained both your "City of the Singing Flame" and "Beyond the Singing Flame." Felicitations are in order!

Lovecraft tells me the Swanson venture has flopped. I'm sorry for that, though I had suspicions to the extent that I did not send the man anything of mine. It's unfortunate for I think more competition would be highly desirable with regard to Messrs. Bates & Wright.

As ever
Donald

Notes

1. A character in the prose poem "The Shadows."

[92]   [CAS to DW] [TLS]

Auburn, Cal.
Apr. 6th, 1932.

Dear Donald:

I like A Sea-Change very well, since the idea is excellent. I've no criticisms to offer, except that you might touch up a few minor points of style and phrasing to preserve the eighteenth-century congruity a little more. The tale should be readily salable.

I returned the ms. of your novel the other day. Have you tried it on any one since Harpers? I think they were an unlikely choice—there are other firms—Dutton's, Macmillan, Simon & Schuster, etc, that would be much more probable. I strongly advise serial publication in W.T., if Wright will accept the story. Even if he holds it for a year, you'll receive some monetary returns as quickly—or more quickly—than you would from a book-publisher.

My own grist of fiction goes on grinding itself about as usual. The Double Shadow, which you will perhaps have seen by now, is the most demoniac of my recent tales. It has already acquired a rejection from Wright. My other late stuff has been mainly scientific. One tale, The Plutonian Drug, I am submitting to Amazing Stories. I am going to begin a new weird to-day, but have not decided on the plot. No poetry of late. An old lyric, On a Chinese Vase, will appear in the Spring Oriental Stories, according to Wright. The Maker of Gargoyles, re-revised, was accepted by Wright some time ago, and will appear in the August W.T. The Invisible City comes out in the June Wonder Stories; and The Immortals of Mercury will be issued as a separate booklet by Gernsback.

My best, as ever,
Clark

[93]   [CAS to DW] [TLS]

Auburn, Cal.
April 14th, 1932.

Dear Donald:

I was horribly sorry to learn that the ms. of your novel turned up missing in transit, and hope that it may have arrived after all. If I had gotten your letter a day sooner, I should have insured the carbon before mailing it to you. I trust that this reached you safely. By the way, did you receive a copy of the March, 1932 Wonder Stories, containing my The Eternal World? I sent you a copy some time back; but since you haven't mentioned receiving it, I've begun to wonder if it went the way of your novel.

I liked "A Sea Change" quite well, as I doubtless told you in my last. I am surprised that it didn't sell. Good luck with all your tales, non-weird as well as the others. It's a good idea to cultivate more than one branch of writing, if you can. My own half-hearted experiments at the non-fantastic have been my poorest sellers, so far: the only ones that sold were orientales.

Yes, I too am sorry that Swanson's magazine couldn't get started. I still think that it might be made to go, on a modest basis, if he could only get sufficient publicity. By the way, have you seen the new pseudo-scientific publications, Science Fiction, and The Time Traveler?[1] I had an invitation to contribute to the former some time back, but have not yet submitted anything, since the editor wants only short, fast action stories. I have sent for a sample copy of The Time Traveler. Lovecraft speaks of a new weird magazine, Weird Whispers, which I haven't seen. It sounds like some cheap spiritualistic proposition.[2]

No word from editors lately, except Wright, who fired back The Double Shadow on the plea that his readers wouldn't care for it. It has now gone, not very hopefully, to Bates, who still holds The Seed from the Sepulcher. Wright is holding my satiric scientifictional novelette, The Letter from Mohaun Los, and also a new short, The Supernumerary Corpse. The Plutonian Drug, a scientific fantasy, has been submitted to Amazing. I haven't completed anything else of late, since I have had considerable out-door work to do, in preparation for the coming forest-fire season. I have plotted a long novelette or two-part serial, The Master of Destruction, among other things, and hope to get at it before the onset of summer.

I am glad The Double Shadow pleased you. This tale is a particular favorite with me.

You'll probably receive another of my mss. presently. I can't make up my mind that The Supernumerary Corpse is worth shipping around in carbon. It will be just like Wright to buy the damned thing after rejecting a first rate piece like The Double Shadow.

All best wishes and regards, as ever,
Clark.

Notes

1. *Science Fiction* was a fanzine edited by Jerome Siegel (1914–1996), then of Cleveland. Five issues appeared from October 1932 to 1933. Siegel was later the co-creator of Superman. The *Time Traveller* was a fan magazine edited by Allen Glasser (1908–1971). Nine issues appeared from January 1932 to January 1933. CAS did not appear in either magazine.

2. "Weird Whispers" was in fact only a department in *The Gentlewoman*, published by

W. J. Thompson Co. (see *Dawnward Spire, Lonely Hill* 361). *Science Fiction Digest* (August 1933) reported that the magazine paid $2 per "short short ghoststory" (p. 8).

[94]   [CAS to DW] [TLS]

May 4th, 1932

Dear Donald:

I was very glad to hear that your novel had turned up finally—the loss of all that work would have been appalling. I hope it will have better luck with the next publisher.

Let me know if you can't get the March Wonder Stories. I still have a spare copy, and will clip out my yarn, "The Eternal World," and mail it to you in an envelope if you haven't already secured it. I rather think you might like this story.

I am glad that Wright took "The Destroying Horde," and hope that Bates will accept the yarn he has been holding. I have just had some rather discouraging news from Bates: Clayton has just instructed him to issue Astounding as a bi-monthly, and Strange Tales as a quarterly, until further notice. In the meanwhile, my tales, "The Seed from the Sepulcher" and "The Double Shadow," have not yet been definitely reported on by B.

Wright recently took a new short, "The Supernumerary Corpse"—and also "Ubbo-Sathla," which I re-submitted to him. H. P. had raked him over about the rejection of the latter.

I have just finished a new medieval yarn, "The Colossus of Ylourgne," which ran to 15,000 words. Do you want to see the carbon? It is about the most horrific of my tales dealing with the mythical province of Averoigne. I have plotted three others—which, in addition to those already written (six, I think, in all) will be enough for a volume.

We have been having heavy rains, daily thunder-storms, etc.—freakish weather for this season in California.

Your projected voyage sounds altogether magnific. *Bonne fortune!*

As ever, Clark.

[95]   [CAS to DW] [TLS]

Auburn, Cal.
Sept. 1st, 1932.

Dear Donald:

I was glad to get your letter from the den of iniquity and the modern lair of the Whore of Babylon. Too bad the Grand Tour has fallen through; but I think you would like California, if you can make it this winter. I certainly hope you can.

I trust you have been able to resume work on the items at which you hint. *Bonne fortune* with them. My own work has gone on about as usual, except that I have been writing even more copiously this past summer. The bulk of it will sell sooner or later, revised, unrevised, or re-revised. My 1931 output has been pretty well cleaned up—only three tales now unsold out of twenty. Of recent work, I think The Isle of the Torturers is perhaps the best. Wright took it, for a wonder. I've just finished a new Martian horror tale, The Eidolon of the Blind—a sort of running-mate for The Vaults of Yoh-Vombis. It is equally cruel and monstrous.

Probably some quiet place like Laguna, on the coast near Los Angeles, would suit you. A cabin there shouldn't be very expensive. I imagine there are lots of other places, though I have no recent personal knowledge of any of them.

E. Hoffman[n] Price says that he may come through California this fall. Maybe I'll meet some of my fellow weird tailors yet!

Congratulations on having the cover of the last Astounding.[1] Bates says the magazine is changing its policy a little—less of the stock adventure element, and more science and bizarrerie. Wonder Tales is also making a change, chiefly in the restriction of length. They want swift-moving tales under 10,000 words now.

Yours ever,
Clark.

Notes

1. "Raiders of the Universes" by "Wesso."

[96]   [DW to CAS] [TLS]

84 Horatio St.,
New York, N.Y.
Oct. 31, 1932

Dear Clark:

A month of freedom in my own studio-apartment has convinced me of what I used to believe—that, if I were alone, and free from worries for three or four months, I could accomplish an extraordinary amount of work. Well, since October 1, when I moved in, I have written six new stories, begun a seventh, and added three sections to my second novel.[1] I intend to concentrate on the novel during November and December, with excellent chances of completing it by New Year's at the pace I am going.

Your "Second Interment" is a fine piece of craftsmanship, one of the best tales you have yet spun. Derleth raised a question about insoluble problems of technique involved in such a presentation, but I answered with the simple assertion that certain types of potential or actual experience can not be handled at all except by such methods as were employed in your story; and of course, where the question is one of to have or not to have, the affirmative wins.

I am sorry that Strange Tales is now a thing of the past. They had nothing of mine on hand, but Belknap Long had had a story accepted and scheduled when the decision to suspend publication was made. Too bad. I hope you were not similarly unfortunate, though I know that at least half-a-dozen writers of weird tales lost an expected income. I only hope that Wright manages to survive the depression. For that matter, I believe that S.T.'s policies were not of the best for getting and holding circulation. "Murgunstrumm", for instance, is sheer and unconvincing tripe of a kind which I was quite unable to read through.[2]

Have you had any trouble dealing with the Gernsbach [*sic*] outfit? I have never bothered with them, because of their low pay and low standards, but Belknap says they ran a story of his more than three years ago for which he has never been paid, and concerning which all letters of his go unanswered.[3]

I spent an enjoyable week with Lovecraft in Providence—doubtless you received the inevitable card. Unfavorable criticisms and rejections from Wright appear to have discouraged him a great deal, to the point where he threatens to do no more writing for some time, if ever again. Aside from that unhappy information, we talked much shop, and explored various byeways [*sic*] of Providence, and recalled the days of '27. The city celebrated my arrival with the worst flood in its history, and it was a tremendous downpour—seven inches of rain in less than a day.

What luck lately? And what are your plans for the Winter?

As ever,

Donald

[P.S.] Lovecraft and I had a discussion, but could not remember, how or why I first got in touch with you, or whether it preceded or followed my becoming acquainted with the gang. I remember hearing of *Ebony and Crystal* which caused me to send for a copy, which I believe was the beginning; but where on earth did I find out about *Ebony and Crystal?*   D W.

Notes

1. I.e., *Invisible Sun.*
2. By Hugh B. Cave (*Strange Tales of Mystery and Terror,* January 1933).
3. "The Thought-Materializer" (*Science Wonder Quarterly,* Spring 1930).

[97]   [CAS to DW] [TLS]

Auburn, Cal.,
Nov. 10th, 1932.

Dear Donald:

It is not at all surprising that you find seclusion favorable to work. All other things being equal, concentration is far more easily achieved and maintained if there are no interruptions. I know how easily the chain is broken in my case. I am glad to hear that you have succeeded in finishing so much new work, and hope sincerely that a moiety of it can be placed to advantage. Your Alfred Kramer certainly held its place in the last W.T.

Thanks for your favorable opinion of The Last [*sic*] Interment. I doubt if much more could have been done with the subject, and feel that the method employed was the only feasible one. The tale was written to order, as I may have told you, and it is almost the only instance where I have done anything good under such conditions.

The failure of S.T. sent much of my prospective income glimmering, since Bates had three tales of mine on hand for use, with prices totaling five hundred dollars, and would probably have accepted some new stuff shortly. I have resold one of the unutilized tales, The Colossus of Ylourgne, to Wright at $150.00, but cannot persuade him that The Double Shadow, my best weird, would appeal substantially to his readers.[1] He has, however, accepted a fair amount of stuff lately: A Vintage from Atlantis, The Ice-Demon, and Genius Loci, in addition to the medieval novelette above mentioned. He is also holding my continuation of Beckford's unfinished Third Episode of Vathek (written at Lovecraft's suggestion) and may print the whole yarn as a sort of necromantic collaboration. I hope so at any rate.

I have recently had my first acceptance from Amazing Stories—The Plutonian Drug. Unluckily, they are overstocked, and won't be able to print it for quite a while. As to Wonder Stories, I am somewhat in a quandary. I can recommend the mag. for ultra-prompt publication of material; but they seem to make up for it on the payment end. They have, so far, paid for seven of my stories at ¾ of a cent per word, but are in arrears on the last five or six, and protest their inability to pay at present together with their anxiety to do so. I don't know whether to gamble any more stuff on them or not, since I more than suspect that they are capable of sharp dealing. My worst apprehension is that old Hugo may pull another bankruptcy stunt, as he did with Amazing Stories several years back. Undoubtedly the magazine—Wonder Stories—is having a hard time just at present. Their treatment of Belknap is pretty raw, I'd say. The chief reason that I've had anything to do with them is, that Gernsback has had the perspicacity to print some of my more out-of-the-way stuff which no one else would touch. And I have had, after all, about five hundred bucks out of the old highbinder.

I, too, can't remember just how you came to hear of Ebony and Crystal and write me for a copy. But your first letter is somewhere in the depths of my gargantuan litter of papers and epistles; and if I come across it some day, I'll let you know.

As ever,

Clark

(over)

P.S. I haven't any plans except work, work and more work. The financial crimps outlined in my letter have to [be] straightened out if possible, or so much as possible. I am trying to do some stuff for Astounding, but find the adventure twist peculiarly difficult and unsympathetic.

C.

Notes

1. *WT* finally published the story six years later.

[98]   [CAS to DW] [ANS, printed Christmas card]

[c. 24 December 1932]

[with / friendly / wishes]

Dear Donald:
      happy landings!

Clark—

[99]   [DW to CAS] [TLS]

84 Horatio St.,
New York, N.Y.
May 24, 1933

Dear Clark:
      The difficulty of making both ends meet has been too acute and present recently to permit of much letter-writing. The failure of STRANGE TALES and ASTOUNDING STORIES,[1] followed by the bank holiday and the freezing of the WEIRD TALES bank, has been costly to the extent of completely knocking the bottom out of my alleged finances. I suppose that you too have not been paid for recent stories in WEIRD TALES. Wright continues to think the bank will re-open soon, and has accepted a new yarn of mine, THE LADY IN GRAY, but I shall be less skeptical when the checks arrive.

Of late, I have taken to the writing of mystery and detective fiction. That type and that group of magazines seem to be about the only class which hasn't been seriously restricted by the depression. I have four or five stories out now, some of which have remained away for six weeks, leading me to mild hopes, but one can count on nothing these days. And editors are becoming infernally lackadaisical about reporting on tales. I had one story with a certain timely appeal which I submitted to BLUE BOOK[2] with a request that they act as promptly as possible. Their answer was to return it—at the end of nearly seven weeks. I am gradually compiling my own black list of unreliable and slow magazines, though it seems a bit like cutting off one's nose, etc., these days!

Of more serious work, particularly the third novel and my first two plays, which I plan next, I haven't been able to do anything. They must wait until the immediate present is taken care of.

Aside from these economic matters, I have been enjoying life greatly, meeting quantities of people, establishing friendships here and there, getting into all sorts of scrapes and escapades, and encountering fantastic adventures that would read like a continuation of Alice in Wonderland. Belknap Long has dropped in occasionally; of all things, he has been writing for the children's magazines, though with little success thus far, I believe. Lovecraft has not been in town since his holiday visit; for that matter, I owe him a letter too; his own financial condition—like everybody else's—is, I gather, nothing to be excited about. Kirk I have seen more frequently than the rest of the gang; largely because I've been reading books from his rental library. He and his wife and the recent infant are managing to flourish, if not quite a la Morgan.

What of yourself? And your recent work? Have you met with any success? Or have you abandoned everything except the weird? And did WON-DER STORIES come through with the checks owing [*sic*] you?

> Best wishes, as ever.
> Donald.

Notes

1. *Astounding Stories,* published by the Clayton Publishing Co., folded with the March 1933 issue. It was then purchased by Street & Smith and began publication with the October 1933 issue.
2. *Blue Book* (1905–75) was a long-running mainstream magazine that published a wide range of material and paid high rates.

[100] [CAS to DW] [TLS]

> Auburn, Calif.,
> June 7th, 1933.

Dear Donald:

It was good to hear from you again. I had wondered how you were faring in Babylon, and am glad to know that you are having an enjoyable time even though so many magazine markets have gone up the flume.

My own existence continues as usual, though with more unprofitable work, worry, and less remuneration than of yore. Gernsback is apparently waiting for the full tide of inflation, and the fall of the dollar to German mark values, before paying his debts; and W.T. owes me for four stories, counting Genius Loci in the current issue. Well, I hope that Fletcher bank will unfreeze before Styx, Acheron, Cocytus and Phlegethon[1] are frozen to the bottom.

You are lucky to be able to write detective tales, if you can sell them. I may try something of the sort, though I am handicapped by a growing distaste for everything but the ultra-fantastic. My work for the present year is nearly all weird—and Wright, confound him, has turned down some of the best items, on the plea that they are too poetic for his precious readers.

I am, by the way, printing six of my best tales in a pamphlet to sell at 25¢ per copy, and will send you one as soon as I get the edition from the printer. It's a gamble; but the thing should be easier to sell than a volume of verse, even though times are hard. I enclose a prospectus, which you might show to anyone who would be interested.

Much of the past month has been given to housecleaning, the making of firebreaks, and other necessary but tedious and unprofitable occupations. Also, I've had to oversee in person the printing of The Double Shadow. Publishing your own work is a laborious and exasperating business; and now I've got the marketing of the damned thing. The enterprise will hardly enrich me, even if I sell the entire thousand of the edition.

I have acquired a portable Underwood, and am beginning to like the machine, though I doubt if it will have the durability of my old Remington. The latter, however, was beginning to give out; and it was hard to get a clear impression with the worn type.

Good luck with all your stories. I liked the last one in W.T.[2]

A girl-friend of mine from Auburn, Miss Helen Sully, is planning a trip east this summer. She wants to meet you, and I am giving her your address. I'd greatly appreciate any little courtesy that you might show her, such as a visit to the Roerich Museum or the Metropolitan. She will not expect you to spend money on her, and would like also to meet Loveman, Kirk and Long, if this is feasible. I wish I could come too; but, with my obligations, etc, etc, I could almost as readily manage a rocket-trip to Mars.

Yours, in memory of John Dee,[3]

Clark.

Remember me to the gang.

Notes

1. Four of the five rivers in the Greek underworld, the fifth being Lethe.

2. "Spawn of the Sea."

3. John Dee (1527–1608/1609), English mathematician, astronomer, astrologer, and occult philosopher. In his "History of the 'Necronomicon'" (1927), HPL stated that Dee translated the "Necronomicon," but that that version was "never printed and exists only in fragments recovered from the original manuscript."

[101] [CAS to DW] [TLS]

Auburn, Cal.,
June 15th, 1933.

Dear Donald:

My friend, Miss Helen Sully, concerning whom I wrote you the other day, is to arrive in New York via the Panama Canal, on The President

Wilson, a Dollar Line freighter, July 15th. She will be in New York only about three days, and then, as part of a continental tour, will go on to spend a day in Providence, R.I.

If it is not too much to ask, and is not putting you to an excessive inconvenience, I wonder if you could meet her at the pier? She does not know anyone in New York, and it would take away the chill of landing in a strange place if a mutual friend could welcome her. I'd appreciate it as a great personal favour if you can manage this. Please let me know as soon as possible, since she will leave Auburn in about two weeks.

Miss Sully is of medium height, slender, blue-eyed and with light-brown hair. I think you will enjoy meeting her.

I hope you have received The Double Shadow by now. It is too soon to tell much about the salability of the pamphlet; but I have sold about 60 copies so far, and have given away nearly 40. This leaves me only 900 more to dispose of!

Here's wishing you unlimited sales.

Yours ever,

Clark.

Did I mention how much I enjoyed The Fire Vampires?

[102] [CAS to DW] [TLS]

Auburn, Cal.,

June 28th, 1933.

Dear Donald:

Your role of squire and knight will be greatly appreciated, I assure you, both by me and by Miss Sully and her family. I do not think you should have any difficulty in identifying each other at the pier. I am communicating your personal description to Helen. She, on her part, will wear a yellow California poppy (paper) on her hat. Also, I am enclosing two snapshots in which she figures, indicated by the arrows. I am the gent in these pictures; and Miss Sully's mother and younger sister, Marion, are the other participants. The one including all four was taken during a camping-trip in the Sierras. You will note my dual personality, one picture showing a French scalawag and the other an Oriental adept or necromancer.

Helen is about your age, I think—in the middle twenties. She is a talented musician, with a taste for the classic—Brahms, Beethoven, Bach, etc. She teaches music and drawing in the local grammar school.* Art museums, etc, will be exactly in her line. Also, she will be glad to meet unusual and interesting people of any age and intellectual type, particularly the members of the gang. Her stay in N.Y. will be pretty brief—three days at most—since she is

---

*Her instruments are violin, viola, and piano. She draws and paints prettily—has done charming water-colors.

now planning two days in Providence, where I am committing her to the cic-eronage of H. P.[1] This will be part of an extensive continental tour, including Quebec and other Canadian points.

The Sullys (mother and two sisters) are friends of long standing, and are the only people of cultivation that I know here in Auburn. Without them, my life would be pretty arid on the human side. I am not a good mixer, and frankly prefer solitude to the average sort of company.

I hope you can make use of the enclosure. I have the impression that I owe you a far larger amount, and would send more if my own finances were not so much in arrear[s].

I am glad The Double Shadow holds up on re-reading. In some ways, it is my own favourite among all my tales. But King Euvoran and The Maze of the Enchanter are not far behind in their respective classes.

I don't know how much of the low-down you will get on me from Hel-en. Possibly—I am not sure—she will represent me as a combination of Krishnamurti,[2] St. Francis & the Sphinx. For your own information, I might add that such aspects, if discernible even to the most illuded vision, are but the vizards of Petronius, Faunus and Diabolus.

Beaucoup des acceptances et des *pazoors!*[3]

As ever,

Clark.

[P.S.] You can return the snapshots at leisure—no hurry.

Notes

1. A *cicerone* is a guide who gives information about antiquities and places of interest to sightseers. In Providence, Sully stayed at the boarding house just behind HPL's residence.
2. Jiddu Krishnamurti (1895–1986), Indian philosopher who at this time was attracted to theosophy. He had been residing in California since 1922.
3. The *pazoor* is a monetary unit in CAS's Hyperborea.

[103] [CAS to DW] [TLS]

Auburn, Cal.,

Aug. 6th, 1933.

Dear Donald:

I felt sure you would like Helen, and think that you did won-ders in helping to make her N.Y. sojourn a success. Your epic letter is certain-ly eloquent of a good time enjoyed by every one. Helen's progress, as I foresaw, has been a triumphal one; and I only wish I could have been present. Her mother, sister and I speak often of your marvellous goodness and kind-ness. I don't see how you did it, under the circumstances. You seem to have beaten my record for going without sleep!

Your job sounds interesting, and I hope that it has been worth while. Don't worry about returning the paltry enclosure that I sent you. I am not yet bankrupt, and can always dig up a little dough somewhere if necessary.

The last three months have been uncommonly slack for me, as far as writing is concerned. There have been too many other things including my father's illness, to break up my time. But I have sold two recent yarns to Wright: The Flower-Women and The Death of Malygris, both of which he rejected at the first submission. Evidently he liked them better when I retyped them on my new Underwood.

I am glad to hear your good opinion of The Double Shadow collection, and await your further comments with great interest. The D.S. is my own favourite; then, in order, The Maze of The Enchanter and A Night in Malneant. The pamphlet continues to sell slowly, and I have now worked off close to 250 copies. I have, however, given up any hope of making a little money on it. The cost of advertising, etc, added to the expense of printing, is too great.[1] Also, it has involved me in considerable correspondence—which means time and postage-stamps.

I hope that you will soon receive a check from Wright for Spawn of The Sea. My story, The Ice-Demon, in the preceding number, was paid for some time ago, but I have not yet received payment for The Beast of Averoigne, in the issue with your story. Wright has ten of my yarns on hand for publication, and will use A Vintage from Atlantis in September, The Seed from the Sepulcher in Oct., and The Holiness of Azederac in Nov.

I have several partly written tales on hand, and others that will have to be re-written before I can sell them. The House of Haon-Dor and The Witchcraft of Ulua are two that I hope to finish ere long. The last-named is an erotic nightmare, and deals with a youth who had spurned a young witch and was bedevilled by her with various disagreeable sendings. He found amorous corpses in his bed, and was persecuted by peculiar succubi.

By the way, here is the circular of a new "fan" magazine, The Fantasy Fan, which will print (without payment) a few brief tales, either weird or scientifictional. Lovecraft and I have given the editor some material. If you have any good short shorts (the shorter the better) that you can't sell, I suggest that it would do no harm to get in touch with him.

I wrote a poem some time ago—the first in three years!—and will hunt up a copy to enclose with this. The composition of the poem, by the way, was interrupted by the arrival of a rattlesnake that had crawled close to my outdoor writing-table before I perceived it! I had to kill the snake, though it seemed a pity to snub his social inclinations in a manner so decided. This year has been a phenomenal one for rattlers, since my father had killed one not long before in one of his chicken-yards, after it had struck down a broiler; and the whole neighborhood is full of yarns about their incursions. Previous to this, we had not seen one on the ranch for many years.

I hope you can make, sooner or later, that promised trip to California. I can offer you a bed, and food, for as long as you care to stay with us, and anything that I can do will be yours to command.

It is a high honour to have Ebony and Crystal bracketed with The Hill of Dreams and Urn-Burial.[2] The former I read many years ago (unfortunately I do not own it) and liked greatly. The Urn Burial is one of my favourite pieces of prose—or poetry. In regard to Machen, my present preference is for some of his shorter stories, such as The White People, The Novel of the Black Seal, and The Novel of the White Powder, which I consider unexcelled in literature. But perhaps, if I were to re-read The Hill of Dreams now, I might prefer it to these.

> Yours ever,
>
> Clark

[P.S.] My thanks to Belknap and his family also, for their kindnesses to Helen.

Yes, I have heard that Gernsback has a doubtful reputation in matters of payment. Though I disapprove strongly of the Hitler regime, I think that it might be administered, not unjustifiably, on a Jewish gyp and literary sweatshop Keeper such as H. G. I have a suspicion that he may may [*sic*] try another of his bankruptcy stunts before long. I have the address of a lawyer in N.Y. who is said to be good at collecting money from backward publishers and shall at least try holding the threat of legal action over Gernsback.

Notes

1. CAS published four advertisements in *WT* and several fanzines, in addition to a printed circular.
2. Arthur Machen, *The Hill of Dreams,* and Sir Thomas Browne, *Hydriotaphia: Urn Burial; or, A Discourse of the Sepulchral Urns Lately Found in Norfolk* (1658), the first part of a two-part work that concludes with *The Garden of Cyrus.*

[104] [DW to CAS] [TLS]

> 84 Horatio St.,
> New York, N.Y.
> Aug. 20, 1933

Dear Clark:

Inclosed are the two snaps which I neglected to return sooner.

Still rushed, but I'm taking time for a short note to let you know, if you haven't already heard, that ASTOUNDING STORIES is being revived under the editorship of Desmond Hall at the Street & Smith publications, 79 Sevent[h] Ave., N.Y.C. They received, accepted, bought, and paid for a story of mine in the phenomenal speed of three days from start to finish. They want the weird note predominating, with a minor scientific background, woman interest or love element preferable, realistic characters, action but not melodrama, and good writing above all means. If you have anything good on hand, it would do no harm to try it or them on Mr. Hall.

Your long letter was welcomed with eager eyes. I shall make a better reply to it as soon as I'm not quite so busy. My job has been extended week to week, and meanwhile, I am supposed to be doing a story per month for the new A.S. With my new camera, photographic inclinations, sporadic social sorties, and the occasional arrival of out-of-town friends, I am certainly burning the candle at both ends, the middle, and the sides! Any day now I'm likely to expire in an incandescence of full living.

Best wishes on making the new A.S., and for a happy solution of your own problems. More anon, and I hope soon.

Donald

[105] [CAS to DW] [ANS][1]

[Postmarked Auburn, Cal.,
28 August 1933]
Aug. 28th, 1933

Dear Donald: Your note received. Thanks for tip about requirements of A. S., and congratulations on your sale. Wright has recently accepted my *The Flower Women* and *The Death of Malygris*. Am now writing *The IX Chapter of Eibon!*[2]

Expect to see H. shortly. Picture on back is her school-house.

Yours, Clark.

Notes

1. *Front:* Auburn-Union—Grammar-School. Auburn, Calif. 4099.
2. I.e., "The Coming of the White Worm."

[106] [CAS to DW] [ANS]

[Postmarked Auburn, Cal.,
date unclear—August or September 1933]

Dear Donald: Your kindness to Helen has been vastly appreciated, and I enjoyed more than I can express your wonderful account of her visit in N.Y. I felt sure that you would like her.

I hope to write you a letter before long, but I am absolutely floored and swamped just at present with a thousand things, including my father's illness. My writing seems to have gone by the board lately.

Good luck to you—and a million thanks. The inclosure in my letter was not to be returned.

Yours, Clark.

[107] [DW to CAS] [ANS, printed Christmas card]

[c. 20 December 1933]

[TO GREET YOU

MERRY CHRISTMAS
HAPPY NEW YEAR]

Dear Clark—

Some day I shall write letters again, when the terrific pace of recent months has lessened. My position during the day and my writing by night, to say nothing of photographing and friends, recreations and soirees and arts, leave me seldom a free hour. I hope all is well with you, and that the holidays are productive of pleasant memories for the year past, and prophetic of even greater successes in the forthcoming year. May 1934 see the meeting of you, and Helen, and me.

Donald

[108] [DW to CAS] [TLS]

[LOCKHART
INTERNATIONAL • INCORPORATED
CHANIN BUILDING
NEW YORK]

Jan. 9, 1934

Dear Clark:

How have you been faring? It seems like months since I last heard from you, though HPL quoted extracts from a letter received during his stay here. It was a pleasure to see him again, in spite of the fact that extraordinary demands upon my time entailed by the simultaneous arrival of half-a-dozen friends from out of town made it impossible to see nearly as much of him as I wished to. But I took advantage of the occasion to make some photographs of him and of Belknap. I've not had time to develope [*sic*] and print them yet, but when I do, and if the results are at all satisfactory, I shall see that you have copies.

Life has been continually hectic ever since Miss Sully's visit. My family were here for a month, and my brother has settled here more or less permanently. Incidentally, I photographed his batiks and am going to photograph his pen-and-inks, copies of which I believe would interest you greatly. My temporary position of last July still continues, except for a five-week lapse, and appears to show some signs of permanency. I like the work which involves unexpected and broadly varied duties. Evenings I've been spending much time on stories for Hall of A.S., as you doubtless may have gathered. Piling photography, amusements, friends, and general activities on top of these has led me to wish for alter egos or dual selves, but instead, I shall probably perish in a blaze of spectacular hecticity about the time I'm thirty.

One of the editors of Science Fiction Digest dropped in a couple of weeks ago with a copy of a 1911 Black Cat in which I was startled to find a story by you. I forget the title, but it was set in India, and rather totally different from the nature of your later things.

I am glad to see you appearing regularly in W.T. W. still owes me half the check for a story published in the Feb. '33 issue,[1] which suggests that I might get paid for The Lady in Gray by Jan. '35. Oh well. I'll have to curtail my interests somewhere for I'm not able to devote any time to serious work as things stand now.

A.S. has gone science fiction entirely, the weird element being abandoned by reader request. Hall is looking for science hooked up with social, political, and economic satire or general trends right now. S. & S. pay promptly.

Did you ever do anything about collecting from Gernsback? Hall has a lawyer friend, Nat Schachner[2]—the same one who writes science fiction— whom he says is good at getting payments. Suggest you communicate with him through Hall, if you haven't already taken action.

Let me know how you are prospering—successfully, I hope, and my best wishes for a supreme year.

> Donald.

Notes

1. "The Fire Vampires."
2. The science fiction writer Nat[haniel] Schachner (1895–1955) was trained as a lawyer.

[109] [DW to CAS] [ALS]

Jan. 12, 1934

Dear Clark—

Herewith the prints of F.B.L., H.P.L., and D.W. F.B.L. looks much swarthier than he is, because he was seated farthest from the light.[1]

Working harder than ever on my third novel. I think it will develope [*sic*] as a modern analogue to, but not an imitation of, *Moll Flanders*. It is based on the life-histories of several women I've known, and interests me because it is my first major attempt to deal objectively with a phase of contemporary life. I doubt whether it would appeal to you, but am enjoying greatly the writing of it.[2] However, my recent labors brought on my recurrent irritation, conjunctivitis, otherwise known as pink-eye, which has caused me a lot of trouble today.

How are you faring?

> As ever,
>
> Donald

Notes

1. See HPL, *Selected Letters* 2.329 (facing).
2. It does not appear that any portions of this novel (title unknown) survive.

[110] [CAS to DW] [TLS]

Auburn, Cal.,
Jan. 23rd, 1934.

Dear Donald:

I was glad to receive your recent letter, and note enclosing the pictures of yourself, Long, and H.P.L. The pictures seem very life-like, and I shall indeed prize them, both for the photography and the subjects.

Your program sounds like a fast and furious one. You seem to have the inside track with Astounding! Congratulations on the numerous landings. I am glad, too, that your job has turned out satisfactorily.

Not much news here. Apart from fiction-writing, I have recently turned out one or two poems, and have also (at Wright's request) been illustrating some of my own yarns for W.T. I hope Wright will let me do a design for a recently submitted poem also.[1]

That early yarn in Black Cat (it must have been either The Mahout or The Rajah and the Tiger—the only ones that I landed with this magazine) was nothing much to crow about. It does evince, however, the enormous interest which I felt in things Oriental during my teens. I wrote ream after ream of such stuff (most of it, luckily, unpublished)[2] between the ages of thirteen and sixteen, under a mélange [*sic*] of influences ranging from the Arabian Nights to Kipling, with Lallah Rookh[3] and Beckford's Vathek included. Two or three of the shorter yarns appeared in the Overland Monthly.[4] Then, for some unfathomable reason, I switched suddenly and entirely to verse, and did not think seriously again of fiction-writing till the summer of 1929.

I didn't know that Schachner was a lawyer. Thanks for suggesting him as a legal intermediary in the Gernsback matter. Not being in actual dire need of the money, and disliking the unpleasantness of legal action, I have deferred doing anything about it. Hornig, the editor, seemed to think I had a good chance of getting some of the arrears this Christmas; but said arrears have not yet materialized. Some time, if you can do so conveniently, I wish you'd get me the low-down on Gernsback; that is to say, whether he is paying any of his authors voluntarily, and is in a position to loosen up without feeling the pinch. If he is really in straits it would make a difference in my attitude. If he is not, then assuredly the blighter ought to pay.

I am rather sorry that Astounding has gone wholly scientifictional: that type of story doesn't come so naturally to me as the weird, nor do I do it so well. However, I mean to concoct something that will suit Hall's requirements.

We often speak of you at the Sullys. Hope you can manage a trip out this way in the not far distant future.

Here is a snapshot—myself and Mrs. Sully—which you can keep. You can keep also the enclosed grotesques.

Best wishes for 1934! As ever,

Clark

[P.S.] I'd like very much to see some photographs of your brother's work. H.P.L. mentioned it in terms of the highest praise in his last letter.

Notes

1. "In Slumber." It was not illustrated.
2. CAS's juvenile novels *The Black Diamonds* (2002) and *The Sword of Zagan* (2004) are now published, but much of his juvenile short fiction remains unpublished.
3. A long poem by Thomas Moore.
4. "The Ghost of Mohammed Din" and "The Malay Krise."

[111] [DW to CAS] [TLS]

84 Horatio St.,
New York City
Feb. 20, 1934

Dear Clark:

I was delighted to receive both the print of yourself and the new grotesques. They are welcome additions to my collection of Klark-Ash Toniana, to use HPL's coinage. Have you been doing much in the graphic arts recently, or are all your efforts devoted to stories now?

My job ran out again a couple of weeks ago, but will resume when the company obtains new business. I'm not sure that I want it back or will take it. For one thing, I've opened up another market and am selling mystery as well as science fiction. Also, I'm on the verge of opening still another market. Thus my hands and time are pretty well filled with pot-boilers, sufficient to keep my finances going, and still allowing some leisure for work on my serious interests. The present line-up is exactly what I want, and I shall do everything to preserve it, unless all magazines fold up.

Inclosed are the first prints of my brother's drawings, which you may keep. They are not very successful, unfortunately. The original drawings are done with a wide variety of colored inks, which make it difficult to render all the tones true in photographs. Also, you will notice what seems to be a blur on one or two of them. That is a photographic result of the fact that a fresh bottle of ink was started at that point, or that the ink was applied some days subsequently to the other parts of the drawing. No difference is visible to the eye, but the camera records a variation either in the ink's chemical content, or in its having dried over a period shorter than the rest of the drawing. For this reason, I doubt whether it will be possible to obtain perfect negatives that entirely reproduce the pictures. However, they will serve to indicate the nature of Howard's work. The originals vary in size from three by five inches, to 24 by 30. A majority are black and white, but some are extraordinarily rich and varied in color. "The Witches' Sabbath", for instance, is a somber study in deep purples, leprous olives, bloody reds, and decayed greens. I shall send other prints later, including his batiks.

I thought for awhile, immediately after the Lockhart position suspended, that I would return to St. Paul for a visit, and then possibly continue to California. I should like that journey very greatly, but deem it wiser to postpone my plans for the time being, in order to cultivate and capitalize my new markets, while I'm on the spot.

The weather has been terrible. It alternates between the coldest in history here, heavy snows, thaws, rain, and slush, warm winds, and biting blasts of sub-zero frigidity. Yesterday morning was spring-like, warm, and sunny. In the afternoon it turned cloudy, damp, and rained hard. By night, snow fell forming a fine thick coat of slush. Today is freezing with a blanket of white over the city. I wouldn't be surprised if tomorrow brought a dust-storm, followed by a heat-wave and tornados. Phooey.

If I were you, I would drive hard after Gernsback. Some of his authors who protested HAVE BEEN PAID. It seems to be a case of compelling him to shell out.

Well, best wishes and all success with the yarns. I hope to descend on California later in the year.

Donald

[112] [CAS to DW] [TLS]

Auburn, Cal.
March 24th, 1934.

Dear Donald:

I had honestly meant to acknowledge your letter and the pictures aeons before this; but in these swift-flowing "latter years" my time-sense illudes me, and a month seems no more than a week or a day.

The prints of your brother's drawings are fascinating, though I realize the difficulty of reproducing various tones of ink in a photograph. A large reading glass helped considerably to bring them out. They attest enormous imagination and linear dexterity. My favourite is The Sorcerer's Workshop. I also like very much The Top of the Island, which has a haunting charm. The colouring of The Witch's Sabbat, from your description, must possess a gorgeous and sullen morbidity.

Commiserations on the weather during the winter. From all accounts, the eastern and northern parts of the U.S. were afflicted with the rigours of an incipient Ice Age. California, on the other hand, has had an uncommonly mild and open season. In fact, it is too mild—there has been almost no rain since the beginning of March, and the grasses are already turning sere in spots.

Thanks for the tip about Gernsback. I have started some high-pressure dunning.

Congratulations on the various markets you have opened. I enjoy your tales in Astounding. This magazine, it would seem, is going strong. The editorial policy doesn't favour my best qualities, but I must try to do some work for it. Latterly, I have grown a little disgusted with science fiction and its fans. The paradoxical bellyaching of certain readers against weirdness and fantasy is too much for me.[1] Literary quality too is thrown away on them, which is another discouraging factor.

No, I haven't much time for pictorial work. I am about to make my fourth illustration for Weird Tales, to accompany my novelette, The Colossus of Ylourgne, in June issue.[2] If and when I have the needful leisure, I shall do some more paintings.

Helen spoke of receiving a fine letter from you the other day. I do hope your western trip will materialize.

As ever,

Clark

Notes

1. As chronicled in "The Boiling Point" (*FF,* September 1933–February 1934), which contained reader responses to Forrest J Ackerman's charge that CAS's "The Dweller in the Gulf" (published in *Wonder Stories,* March 1933, as "The Dweller in Martian Depths") was unworthy of being published in a science fiction magazine. HPL, RHB, and many others sent heated replies rebutting Ackerman's contentions.

2. The other three stories illustrated were "The Weaver in the Vault," "The Charnel God," and "The Death of Malygris."

[113] [DW to CAS] [ANS][1]

[Postmarked Montreal, Canada,
3 October 1934]

Dear Clark:

The woods are flaming. You would love the Hudson, the Adirondacks, & Montreal at this time of year.

I shall be leaving for California about the end of October.

Donald

Notes

1. *Front:* Scene at Westmount Park Mountreal [*sic*], Canada.

[114] [CAS to DW] [TLS]

Auburn, Calif.
Oct. 16th, 1934.

Dear Donald:

Your card from Montreal, which came some time ago, was a poignant reminder—not to say reproach—and made me realize the unconscionable lapse in our correspondence. Because of a multiplying of tedious chores, and a somewhat rundown condition of health, with lack of energy and pep, letter-writing has been difficult for me during the past few months and I have often deferred or neglected wholly the answering of correspondence. You must contrive to forgive me, and understand that the delay was not due to forgetfulness.

The announcement on your card is great news, and I hope fervently that the projected trip to California will materialize. In many ways, the country should be at its best in November. We have just had a fairly heavy rain—the first of the season—but prolonged storms are unlikely in the fall. The orchard leaves are late in turning but will doubtless offer an aerial wealth of gold, amber, red and purple for weeks after Hallowe'en. I trust that you can visit us, and hope you won't mind the primitive pioneer accom[m]odations.

Thanks for the tip which you have me [*sic*] some time back anent Desmond Hall's requirements. I began during the summer a story intended for submission to Astounding; but, alas, have not yet finished it. My work is sadly in arrears; and, apart from illustrations for two of my forthcoming yarns in W.T.,[1] the past month has been barren.

I have followed your stories in Astounding, always with interest. The magazine, it strikes me, is an improvement on its Clayton avatar: at least, there are fewer stories with formula plots, and more stress on ideas. Certainly it offers a first-rate market; and I must try to revive my one-time interest in the writing of science fiction. The idiotic criticisms of a certain class of readers have disgusted me deeply; but one should remember that the unimaginative and the literal-minded are always with us. However, it is a mystery why they should read anything that avowedly partakes of fantasy.

Through the offices of Miss Ione Weber, a New York attorney, I have finally compelled Gernsback to shell out some of his arrears, and he has promised to pay the balance in trade acceptances at 75 per month. Miss Weber certainly must be good![2]

Congratulations on your various and numerous sales! I envy your ability to write mystery fiction as well as weird and scientific stories.

I made a little wine during the summer, and have also laid in some excellent California sherry. Here's hoping that we'll drink a libation together ere long!

As ever,

Clark

Notes

1. "The Seven Geases" and "Xeethra."
2. Ione Weber, the lawyer CAS hired to help collect a sum of nearly $1,000 owed him by *Wonder Stories*.

[115] [DW to CAS] [TLS]

> 1152 Portland Ave.,
> St. Paul, Minn.
> Oct. 20, 1934

Dear Clark:

Another stage in my Odysseys begins the first week or so in November, when I roam westward after completing a novelette that I am now working on. I will reach California at long last, and spend a week or two before taking a boat back to New York. I write with only a mild grain of salt, since I have planned before to go west, but complications always rose. Now the finances are all right, the time is available, and I see nothing to prevent my going. Presumably I should weave my way into Auburn around the 15th.

There is much that I could write about, but I will save it for delivery in person.

> As ever,
> Donald

[116] [CAS to DW] [TLS]

> Auburn, Cal.
> Oct. 27th, 1934.

Dear Donald:

I was glad indeed to receive your note from St. Paul, confirming the Montreal card. It certainly sounds as if you were coming; and we are all rejoicing in anticipation of your visit.

I wrote to you some time ago at the Horatio St. address, but Helen seems to think that you have abandoned these lodgings. Anyway, I hope the letter has been forwarded. If not, the loss will scarcely prove irreparable, since the letter contained nothing of any great moment.

Good luck to the novelette! and a double health to Odysseus!

> As ever,
> Clark.

P.S. I have gotten part of the Gernsback arrears, and have been promised the remainder in monthly instalments. 15 per cent goes to the lawyer, Miss Weber; and I am inclined to think that she has earned it!

[117] [CAS to DW] [ANS, printed Christmas card]

[mid-December 1934]

[Christmas greetings
and every good wish for a bright and
happy New Year]

Dear Donald: To the usual wishes of the season, I'll add my hopes for your speedy return to California during the coming year.

As ever, Clark.

[118] [DW to CAS] [TLS]

155 West 10th St., N.Y.C.
Jan. 11, 1934 [i.e., 1935]

Dear Clark:

The holidays, seeing old friends, taking care of out-of-town friends here for the holidays, hunting for an apartment, getting settled, and turning out a couple of stories are some of the complications that have made life pretty hectic ever since I arrived, and which may explain why I've had practically no time to catch up on correspondence.

The California trip lingers in memory as one of the most delightful vacations I ever had. Neither you nor the Sullys could have done more to make my visit an unmitigated delight; and my only regret is that I could not have remained in California for a considerably longer time, at least all winter. I will be back there, whenever possible, and next time I shall plan for a prolonged stay.

As it turns out, my return here came at a highly strategic moment. Hall left Street & Smith a week ago, and is no longer connected with Astounding Stories. I immediately went over and talked to Tremaine, who says he does not plan any radical changes in editorial policy, but is thinking of trying to establish a better balance between science and action especially in the novelettes. That isn't very definite, and probably the contents of the magazine will continue to be about as they are at present. I will send you any further information that may develope. [*sic*]

I presume that by now you have received the joint greetings of the gang which we wrote at a perfectly grand session at Belknap's when Lovecraft was here. It was turned over to Loveman, who said he wanted to mail a letter of his own to you along with it. Meetings of the gang are always a bit dizzy; Lovecraft and Morton alone have phenomenal memories and access to immense reserves of erudition; Talman is going in heavily for photography and New England antiquarianism; Belknap generally indulges in flights into the philosophical theory and pragmatic working out of social orders; Kleiner and Leeds go in for the poetic and li[t]erary phases of the conversation; Barlow is an absolute monomaniac for everything concerning the weird in literature and art; Loveman has a special affinity for classical Greek civilization and other highly developed cultures of the same historical period; with the result that after a few hours, I usually feel as if I had picked up a decade in education and several Ph.D.'s by the way. This last time I maintained a policy of refusing to be drawn into controversial issues; at that, I got brain fatigue merely from trying to keep up with what was going on; it's no small feat to try to extract the gist from four or five equally intense discussions going on simultaneously among four or five groups.

We—Long, Lovecraft, Barlow, my brother, and I—had another splendid evening at Loveman's apartment in Brooklyn. Sam showed us some of his prizes—Mayan figurines, a Greek head in Parian marble, a small Egyptian statue, an African primitive, etc. The Mayan pieces are particularly exciting, they are so damned extra-terrestrial and suggestive of nothing that ever had anything to do with Mother Earth or the peoples thereof. But most of the evening we devoted to looking at Sam's immense collection of your drawings, water-colors, and grotesques. Barlow was positively ill with envy, and made a pest of himself by trying to beg, borrow, or buy one or all of them until Loveman patiently but flatly stated, "But Barlow, these are personal gifts from a very dear friend of mine." And even that did not phase [*sic*] Barlow. I can admire the fervor of such hero-worship, but I wish to heaven it were accompanied by a little tact.

Loveman is looking much better than he did when I last saw him, this summer. At that time, he was thin and run-down, but now he seems much healthier and more at peace with the world. Belknap told me he had been thinking of a California trip this winter, though it now seems rather nebulous; but Loveman is decidedly interested in taking a vacation to Auburn, and asked me innumerable questions about the town, the scenery, the climate, accom[m]odations, etc. I certainly have become America's prize booster for Auburn and the pleasures thereof. I hope Loveman does go out; you would find him both congenial and highly interesting, though, like almost everyone in whom the love of things artistic or the creative power burns, he has his moments of moodiness.

My regards to your parents; and my best wishes to you for an enviably prosperous New Year.

As ever,
Donald

[119] [CAS to DW] [ANS][1]

[Postmarked Auburn, Cal.,
11 January 1935]

Dear Donald: I received the round robin from the gang some time ago, and now have your highly welcome letter, which I shall answer soon. I was very glad, too, to receive Sam's letter. Your visit here is a frequent theme of pleasant and admiring reminiscence, and we all hope for a speedy repetition with no exigence of an early departure. I certainly hope, also, that Sam can come to California where a hearty welcome awaits him. Wishing you the best for 1935, as ever, Clark.

Notes

1. *Front:* A California Sunset.

[120] [CAS to DW] [TLS]

> Auburn, Cal.,
> Feb. 28th, 1935.

Dear Donald:

My unconscionable delay in writing must be laid to a number of causes, chief of which has been the difficulty of snatching enough leisure for a really adequate letter. I have been grinding away steadily at some new stories, and, with my slowness of composition and frequent recasting, it has been hard to make any headway without putting in from four to six hours per day on the labor. This, in addition to a multitude of chores, etc., has made anything else almost impossible. Letters have piled up to a most appalling extent: but yours can simply not be neglected any longer.

I am glad indeed that your California trip has proved so fruitful in pleasant memories. Certainly it was a most memorable and agreeable occasion, or series of occasions, for me. I shall never forget the charm of our evenings at the Sullys, and your visits to the cabin. Here's hoping that it will all be repeated at some early date—the earlier the better. Perhaps, when you come again, I shall have better accom[m]odations to offer, since I am hoping to build a sort of workshop for myself this spring, and if the building materializes, shall equip it with a couch, etc., for the use of guests.

The New Year sessions at Long's and Loveman's apartments must have been great! I enjoyed prodigiously the imposing round robin from the gang. I can imagine the diversity of erudite conversations or dissertations that must have been going on, with so many specialists present! Sometime—I don't know just when—I may be able to join in on one of those conclaves.

I'll be glad of any fresh tips about Tremaine's policy anent Astounding. So far I haven't done any new science fiction, but will start some new items this month. I have turned out several weirds, including The Treader of the Dust, Necromancy in Naat and The Black Abbot of Puthuum. The two last-named items are longish additions to my Zothique series. Wright surprised me by taking The Treader of the Dust offhand, without revision or re-submission. The last quarter of Necromancy in Naat, however, will have to be rewritten according to the specifications of the satrap (Damn!!....******) I have also done a few poems, and may enclose one of them with this. You would laugh, I dare say, at my methods of story-composition: my usual procedure is to scribble a rough draft of several paragraphs in pencil, and then work these up with more detail and literary finish on the machine. Then I draft a few more paragraphs, etc. The typed pages, I might add, are often recast two or three times. I don't imagine that many writers for the pulps pursue such methods. 1000 or 1200 words is a big day's work for me.

Have you done anything with your play? From Helen's account of your letters to her, I judge you have been caught in an increasingly hectic round of work.

My copy of the De Givry volume came a day or two after your departure.[1] It is certainly a valuable acquisition; though one needs a magnifying glass to get the full beauty of some of the illustrations! I have recently purchased M. Summer's [*sic*] anthology, Best Ghost Stories, which you have probably seen.[2] If you have'nt, [*sic*] I can certainly recommend it, since it contains much material that is not commonly met with. I do very little reading, however, but have gone through the late issues of W.T., which seem rather pediculous not to say downright lousy. I wish that Miss Moore would write a new story (hope this observation doesn't stamp me as a member of the feline tribe!)

The aspect of Auburn and the surrounding hills is quite vernal now, since fruit blossoms, acacias, japanese quince, and numerous wild flowers are all in evidence. We have had much rain, but comparatively little cold weather, and no snow whatever. There were heavy snows in the Sierras, but these seem to be melting away prematurely.

How about poetry? I hope your resolution will change. Anyway, I'd like to see a large collection of your poems in print. That last evening, when you read a number of them to us, was perhaps the best and most memorable occasion of all!

My parents join me in the kindest of regards and good wishes. I hope you'll overlook my apparent remissness, and write me when the leisure offers and the spirit moves.

> Yours ever,
>
> Clark.

My regards to your brother, to Long, Loveman, and others of the gang.
   Blast this pen!***!!

Notes

1. See Bibliography under Grillot de Givry.
2. Montague Summers edited no such book. Possibly CAS meant *Victorian Ghost Stories* (1933).

[121] [CAS to DW] [TLS]

Auburn, Cal.,
June 24th, 1935.

Dear Donald:

I was glad to hear from you again, but sorry to learn of your recent illness. Here's hoping that your health and other circumstances will permit of whatever work—plays, fiction or anything else—that you wish to do.

I seem to have lost all track of my own correspondence, and don't know
whether or not I have written you since my mother's breakdown in March. Her
condition is one of settled feebleness, together with seriously impaired eyesight.
My father hasn't been so very much better than she; and for months I ran a
hospital, cooking, nursing, serving meals in bed, etc. Writing of any sort has
been difficult under the circumstances; and to make matters worse, my nerves
are now beginning to wear ragged from the strain and from certain superadded
infelicities. To quote the vulgar adage, it's a great life if you don't weaken.

Your The Destroying Horde in W.T. certainly shone by contrast with most
of the other work in that issue. Wright, either through impaired judgement or a
mistaken idea of what his readers want, seems to have undertaken the ruining
of the magazine. Everyone that I know, almost, has severely criticized the recent numbers. Most of the stuff he runs is plain mediocre, and lacks even the
crude kick that an occasional yarn in Dime Mystery or Horror Stories attains.

Lovecraft has just written me from Florida, where he is again visiting
young Barlow.[1] The milieu seems to agree with him. I have also heard lately
from Derleth and Jacobi. The latter wanted your new address, and I shall give
it to him when I write.

Some day, when we meet again, I may be able to throw some light on
certain matters that have mystified and perhaps wounded you. The Study of
Woman is certainly a fearful and wonderful branch of biologic science. However, it is only fair to say—and well to know—that women don't all fall under
the same classification. As Lafcadio Hearn says somewhere, they differ amaz-
ingly and diabolically.[2] Also—contrary to the common idea—they are often
too damned easy to understand. Where men, especially artists, make the mis-
take, is in crediting them with all sorts of things that simply aren't there as a
rule. Most of them are hardboiled and practical at bottom, as few men, even
the most commercial, ever are. Also, they are more prone to petty snobbery,
and are swayed to an unbelievable degree by such details as the cut of a man's
hair, the way in which he tips the waiter, or helps them out of a car. They are
worshippers of success, who fling themselves in regiments and cohorts at the
head of the recognized genius but scorn the one who has still to make his way
through obloquy and hardship.

Of course, all this is generalization, and shouldn't be taken as bearing on
a particular case. The girl in question is remarkable, and undoubtedly superior
to most of her sex. She has been brought up with standards which, I some-

times think, no man will ever be able to meet. The one who could meet them would have to possess a combination of old-time chivalry with modern savoir faire. He would speak and write little of himself, much of the girl and her interests, and *would never show offense or hurt* under any circumstances. His attitude would be *cheerful, patient, modest,* what is called *"manly"* at all times and under all conditions. He would assume that all misunderstandings were his fault; that **he** was to blame in some way for any coldness or unfavorable reactions toward him. He would demand nothing, would make her feel that he was devoted without dramatizing his emotions or using language too high-flown and exaggerated. Here, as in all cases where more than mere gallantry is the object, the advice of Stendhal might well be followed, when he says that the art of love consists in expressing precisely the emotion felt, at the time it is felt, without abuse of superlatives or of any falsifying locution. . . . But of course, I don't know what your feelings are. If your affections are seriously engaged, it would do no harm to write a letter along the general lines indicated. But if you do this, for Christ's sake don't ever hint that *I* gave you any tips or advice. Avoid, above all things, either the complaining or the supplicative attitudes. I have been through the mill and know whereof I speak—even though I'm not always able to put my Lotharian wisdom into operation. But maybe you could profit by it. Anyway, I believe the attempt would strengthen you. Giving up the battle in love at the first reverse is bad psychology; and many an apparent defeat has been turned into a victory at the end by good generalship. A woman's disfavor isn't necessarily final. To become personal, I've had my face slapped, and have been loved to death an hour afterward by the slapper. Little things like that shouldn't be taken seriously in regard to such elemental perversities as the phenomena of sex. Hate and love, disgust and desire,* belong to the same spectrum and shade into each other through a thousand semitones.

Well, I hope that all this doesn't bore you. I've had it on my mind for a long time.

To return to literary matters, I fear that I have little news. I'm trying to cook up some fiction that will sell for cash, and have had to take time out for vomiting between periods, thus slowing my progress nearly to a standstill.

Apart from that, I've experimented recently with carving, and have done some small heads and figures, mostly grotesque, in such materials as steatite and dinosaur bone. I should have lived in the Middle Ages and carved gargoyles; or else have made the idols of some barbaric tribe! In either role, I might have had the success that seems to elude me under present conditions.

Yours for the grail of blood and Malmsey,[3] and the black debaucheries of the Sabbat,

Clark

---

*It's a nice art to turn the first into the second. "Can do", as the Chinese say.

Notes

1. HPL had visited RHB at his home near DeLand, FL, from 9 June to 18 August 1935.
2. See *Life and Letters* 2.25: "Never was there a huger stupidity than the observation that 'all women are in one respect alike.' On the contrary, in that one respect they differ infinitely, inexplicably, diabolically, fantastically."
3. A strong, sweet white wine imported from Greece and the eastern Mediterranean islands.

[122] [DW, HPL, and Frank Belknap Long to CAS] [ANS, JHL]¹

[Postmarked New York, N.Y.,
7 September 1935]

Clark—Will write you letter soon. Hope ill-health in your family has now turned to a brighter picture. H P L visiting me, a perfect guest, and the essence of phenomenal health after his long sojourn in Florida. Needless to say, however, he did *not* accompany me to this bar, where I am sipping a beer! ......
As ever ..... Donald

I'm glad young Melmoth exculpates Grandpa from the suspicion of having patronised the bar above which he sleeps.* Having a delightful time seeing all the gang—though the north seems anomalously chilly & barren after the tropics. Visited all the Poe shrines in Richmond, & had a day in Washington & a morning in Philadelphia. Hope all is improving in Averoigne! ¶ Yrs for the Black Pillar—Ech Pi El

*I'm not ashamed to confess that I think it an excellent bar.
Greetings
F B L Jr.

Notes

1. *Front:* Julius'—New York's Oldest Bar.

[123] [DW to CAS] [ANS]¹

[Postmarked New York, N.Y.,
21 September 1935]
Saturday.

Dear Clark—
My brother is getting married on Tuesday, whereafter I move out of my present quarters and resume residence at 88 Horatio St. No work accomplished in over a month, as result of visitors, impending matrimony, apartment hunting, et cetera. H P L stayed for about two weeks, a memorable visit which

ought to have been perfected by your own presence. At my new quarters, I am going into seclusion for at least a month, in the hope that by 1936 I will have my 1934 schedule completed. Best wishes and regards for your parents.

Donald

Notes

1. *Front:* Blank.

[124] [CAS to DW] [ANS, printed Christmas card]

[mid-December 1935]

[Greetings / for the / Holiday / Season
And / Best Wishes / for the / New Year]

Dear Donald: I'll write soon and at length. Yrs, in the name of Tescatlipoca,[1]

Clark.

Notes

1. In the Aztec religion, Tezcatlipoca is the "Smoking Mirror"—the god of the night sky, the god of time. With his opposite, Quetzalcoatl, he created the world.

[125] [DW to CAS] [TLS]

88 Horatio St.,
New York, N.Y.
Jan. 7, 1936

Dear Clark:

Greetings, and may the new year be infinitely more happy than the last, and the fates generous to you in all the ways that you wish.

I've just returned from a month's visit to St. Paul to visit my parents for the holidays, and to find out what snow and cold weather were like. I got my fill of the latter—it snowed every single day that I was home, and the temperatures ranged from zero to 15 below. I enjoy that dry cold and those ineffably lovely snowdrifts for short periods, but I think I can do with warmer climes now for another few years.

Lovecraft arrived in New York the same day that I returned. There have naturally been several sessions and reunions, all of which though highly satisfactory would have been completed by your presence. Loveman asked me if I thought you had any interest in visiting New York, and I informed him that I believed you would relish the experience depending on whether the gods favored and fostered it. Sam still has his dream of going to California but of course he's now hard at work getting his mail-order book business launched and under way. I understand that the venture is developing satisfactorily.

Lovecraft looked extremely well, and presented an unexpected picture of health in view of the fact that winter has come and that cold weather is worse than anathema to him. I think that the two sales to ASTOUNDING STORIES late last year[1] were also highly beneficial to his general spirits. Long has turned into an industrious little one-man factory, finishing, polishing, and delivering a story about every two weeks. Most of his recent sales have been to the THRILLING group, of which Leo Margulies is the managing editor.[2]

The year started off well for me, with a check from ARGOSY for the second novelette they've purchased from me, one from CLUES–DETECTIVE for another in the Ivy Frost series, and a 50% payment from WEIRD TALES for a story published last June.[3] Incidentally, both AMAZING STORIES and WONDER are in shaky condition. As you probably know, both have skipped issues recently, and with their extremely low circulations—21,000 and 17,000 respectively—it would not be surprising if they folded up by spring. There are rumors of new magazines to appear in the science fiction field, but nothing definite has come to my knowledge. ASTOUNDING STORIES almost never uses weird material now, but would be very hospitable to anything in the vein of "The City of the Singing Flame". That story, by the way, lingers in my memory as your masterpiece to date in the field of imaginative prose.

My brother, under the nom-de-plume H. W. Guernsey, continues to appear regularly in DETECTIVE FICTION WEEKLY.[4] That market has proved so dependable for him that he has not written a weird or scientific story in close to a year.

While Lovecraft was here, he, Long, and I paid a visit to the Hayden Planetarium, which provided one spectacular impression. The illusion of the night skies is perfect; and each time that the lecturer mentioned a particular galaxy or star, a white arrow leaped out on the dome to indicate the subject of discussion. It was as though, if one looked at the actual skies and said, "There is Antares", a flaming arrow would cleave the Milky Way and single Antares out of the multitude. Not in a long while has anything so gripped my imagination as that simple but fascinating device.

As I began, so I close—with best wishes for a brilliantly successful and prosperous new year.

Ever,
Donald

Notes

1. *At the Mountains of Madness* and "The Shadow out of Time" (the latter facilitated by DW).

2. Leo Margulies (1900–1975) edited numerous pulp magazines, including *Startling Stories* and *Thrilling Wonder Stories*, the latter in collaboration with Mort Weisinger (1915–1978).

3. "The Witch-Makers" (the purchase was "The Monster from Nowhere"), "Giants in

the Valley" or "Bone Crusher," and "The Destroying Horde."
4. HW's detective stories are gathered in *The Last Pin*.

[126] [CAS to DW] [TLS]

Auburn, Calif.,
March 6th, 1936.

Dear Donald:

This letter has already been written many times, in thought. My infernal procrastination, which seems to have extended itself to everything and everyone, is alone to blame for the fact that I have not written it on paper.

I was glad to hear from you in January, and to know that the year has started well for you in respect to sales. I do hope you have survived the period of prolonged and Hyperborean rigors from which the East has suffered. Here, the temperatures have been milder than usual, with diluvial rains and piled-up snows on the Sierras. March, so far, is warm and almost cloudless. I'll soon be able to do all my work out of doors, if such weather keeps up.

Astounding has certainly become a more promising market than I thought it would be. The magazine is distinguishing itself by the publication of At the Mountains of Madness. I am glad that Lovecraft's recent sales proved so beneficial to his spirits and morals, and trust that he will turn out much new work. I am meditating some more yarns in the general style of The City of the Singing Flame, and will start them as soon as I have cleaned up several unfinished odds and ends. Writing, which I now attempt daily, is still damnably hard for me; but I know from past experience that habit and regular practice are three-fourths of the battle. Discouragement, grief, worry, and, more than this, the total disorganizing of my time-schedule, simply put me out of commission for a long while—that is to say, as a story-writer.

I was delighted to receive Loveman's volume of poems a few days ago. I am glad his new book business promises well. Sooner, or later (unless I decide on a one-way trip to Acheron in the meanwhile!) I shall descend upon New York with a few bales of paintings and trunkfuls of sculptures. When that day comes, I trust we can all foregather and quaff Amontillado till the milk-wagons come in!

Re my sculptures: I believe you will see a small loan-exhibit of these before long, and shall be vastly interested to learn how they impress you. I have done them at odd moments during the past year, and have sold a few locally at rather trifling prices. Many people seem to like them better than my drawings. I intend to make you a gift of one presently: perhaps I shall try my hand at carving the Red Brain or one of the Tree-Men of M'bwa!

I have it in mind to make a few small imaginative oil-paintings this spring, if I can snatch the time. Future finances, however, make it advisable for me to do as much fiction-writing as I can. I may take a fling at some [of] the cashpaying weird and horror markets; though the cheapness and luridity of their standards fail to inveigle me.

Yours, in the elder Faith,
Clark

P.S. The enclosed drawing was done from one of my carvings.

[127] [DW to CAS] [TLS]

88 Horatio St.,
New York, N.Y.
June [*sic*] 29, 1936[1]

Dear Clark:

     For a long time I've been intending to write you, and couldn't for various reasons, but now that I've received the sculptures from Sam, I can't delay any longer.

     To begin with, I report that the lot as it came into my hands consists of fifteen (15) pieces, all in excellent condition except number ten (10), which has been fractured into a number of pieces and glued together again. It may have been that way when you sent it out, or it may have gotten that way en route. Not knowing when or where you sent it first, I of course can't tell. I simply record the state of the shipment as it came into and as it will leave my hands.

     I am sending it on to Lovecraft, with instructions to return it to me when he is finished with it. I want it sent back to me because my brother Howard, now out of town, will be back in a couple of weeks, and I am most anxious to have him examine the group. He will be deeply interested. If you can spare the time, therefore, I wish you would drop me a postcard letting me know whether the shipment is then to be returned to you, or whether it is to go elsewhere.

     The entire group fired my imagination. I like them so much that I want to buy one. Incidentally, my sister-in-law Connie was fascinated by the floral pendant, marked no. 6, and I believe there is a good chance that Howard will buy it for her. Getting back to my own desire, I particularly liked no. 7, the happily smirking orange-red chap with a pronounced Joosh nose; no. 11, the wicked little tadpole-worm; and no. 12, that twilight dweller midway between the fish and the human kingdoms. My choice will probably be no. 12, but I wish you would quote the prices on all four (6, 7, 11, & 12. And I hope my descriptions are sufficiently close so that you can identify the ones I mean.) And no. 13 too—the scaly monster with the incredibly dreadful and vacantly idiotic face. (I can see that I'm going to have the devil's own choice trying to make up my mind which one I want most!)

     How long does it take to carve each unit? And what tools do you use? And do you fit your imagination to the raw shape of the rock, or carve the rock to a preconceived form? How are your other creative faculties working? Or have you adopted an interlude upon stories and poems?

With regard to stories, it would be well worth sending any that are of a more or less scientific nature to ASTOUNDING STORIES or THRILLING WONDER STORIES. This latter, the former WONDER STORIES, has just appeared on the stands as a bi-monthly edited by Leo Margulies at 22 West 48th St. Payment is one cent a word upon acceptance. I haven't had time to read the issue, but Mort Weisinger, who is the sub-editor for the magazine, dropped in a couple of weeks ago, and I gathered the impression that they wanted two varieties of tales—the kind that emphasizes action and adventure; and the kind that emphasizes idea. In either case, send on anything you have. You'll find them much better to deal with than that Soandso Gernsback.

The past year, even before my brother's wedding,[2] has been a hard one on me. The longest, most consistent, and most cumulative run of bad luck and tough breaks of my life thus far wore me out. A severe cold. A case of flu. Another of stomache [*sic*] dysentery. Two plagues of bugs that descended on my former apartment. A bad case of poisoning from inhaling carbolic fumes of the fumigant. Sudden evacuation of the apartment and moving to another. Another siege with flu, during which I was delirious and marooned for two days. An overwhelming nausea and general poisoning that resulted when the mechanical refrigerator in my new studio broke down and I inhaled a mixture of carbon dioxide and illuminating gas for five hours without realizing it. And the grand climax ten days ago when the Greyhound bus in which my sister-in-law was returning from St. Paul crashed in the third of a series of connected accidents, killed one person, injured seventeen, and gave her concussion of the brain. Since then my time has largely been spent as a sort of nurse, errand man, jack-of-all-trades, and aide-at-large. Until my brother gets back I suppose the program will continue. My plans have been shot to pieces, my novels and plays are a vague memory of the remote past, even my potboilers have been few and far between, and I scarcely recall that I once was developing photography as my second hobby. And somewhere among my vanished correspondence lie the fragments of friendships that I have been long out of touch with. It's about time that life favored me with some of her happier slings and less pointed arrows.

I hope that all is well with you, and that your own troubles are lightening. Incidentally, Helen has an identic double in New York. I've run into her several times around the Village, though not for several months now. The double has a nice big Rolls.

Friends just dropped in.

Ever,

Donald

Notes

1. DW to CAS 133 indicates his sister-in-law's accident occurred in late May. It seems

DW should have written *May* 29.

2. Howard married Connie Comstock 24 September 1935.

[128] [CAS to DW] [TLS]

Auburn, Calif.,
June 23rd, 1936.

Dear Donald:

I was glad to get your letter, and damnably sorry that you have had a run of such infernal and pestilential luck. Here's hoping for a lighter admixture of lead in the future's dice.

My own circumstances remain substantially unchanged; but at least, so far, I have escaped any incapacitating illness. My father's condition has been somewhat worsened of late.

Re the carvings: I am greatly pleased to learn that you like them so well. It is hard to set prices on such work: and any that I have asked so far have been no more than a bare wage for time and labor spent. The pendant, no. 6, which I call Proserpine's Flower, could go at $2.00; no. 7., The Goblin, and no. 11, The Primal Eft, at $2.50 apiece. No. 12, the fish-god Dagon, and no. 13., The Harpy, which I really consider the gems of that collection, I am pricing at $4.00 each. No. 10, The Venerian, was broken and pieced together long before I sent it East; and for my taste, at least, the dilapidation is actually an improvement, since it helps out the impression of exotic fabulous antiquity that I aimed at in this piece. It is hard to say just how much time I have given to any one carving, since most of the work is done at odd moments and therefore distributed, in nearly every case, over several days or perhaps a week. When I am not too tired, I often work for an hour or two in the evening; and the rest is done in the intervals of cooking, housework, errand-running, nursing, wood-chopping, etc., etc, etc. The system seems to lend itself to sculpture; but not, unfortunately, to writing. Literature, as far as I am concerned, requires a hell of a lot more concentration than the manual arts of carving and painting; or, properly, it calls for a different and far more exacting *kind* of concentration.

I enclose a list of titles corresponding to the numbers on the 15 carvings. It is often arbitrary, and perhaps useless, to name a particular piece; but in some cases, I think the names help. After you are through with the collection and have shown it to Howard, you can forward it to R. H. Barlow, B[o]x 88, De Land, Fla. Barlow, at his leisure, will return it to me.

Recently, at the prompting of a local art gallery director, I have done a few pictures. Eight or nine of them are fantastic scenes in colored crayon, and I believe them the best work I have so far made in that medium. Perhaps, later, I may have a double exhibition of carvings and pictures. My newest sculptures are slightly larger than those in the collection sent East. As to tools, I use anything that will dig, chip or cut: knives, chisels, files, and even, on some of the heavier pieces, an old ax-blade! The finishing is done with emery-cloth and fine sandpaper.

I trust your sister-in-law will suffer no lasting ill-effects from her accident. Really, you seem to have incurred the most abominable piling-up of disasters, illnesses and tough breaks that I have heard of for a long time. I thought that old [*sic*] Man Disaster was camping pretty persistently on my trail; but now I begin to feel like an amateur in misfortune. When your luck turns, it should turn with grand momentum!

Yours ever, Clark

[P.S.] Thanks for tip concerning the new W. S.

[Enclosure:]

List of Carvings.

1. The Black Dog of Commoriom
2. Nameless Entity
3. Hyperborean Cat-Goddess
4. Aurignacienne
5. Proserpine
6. Proserpine's Flower
7. The Goblin
8. Reptile-Man
9. Entity from Algol
10. The Venerian
11. The Primal Eft
12. Dagon
13. The Harpy
14. Death-God of Poseidonis
15. St. Anthony

[129] [DW to CAS] [ALS]

88 Horatio St.,
New York, N.Y.
July 15, 1936

Dear Clark—

The sculptures are still in my hands but I shall ship them on to H P L this week. My brother returned and, as I expected, found them as exciting as I did. He thinks the Dagon the best in the group.

I tried photographing them, with not very good results. Here is a set of prints which you can keep. I'll send you a better set later if possible.

I am buying the Dagon. Howard is buying Proserpine's Flower for Connie to wear. We think your prices are too low, so we are doubling them, and will send you $12.00 for the two items. Money order will be in my next letter.

In haste,
Donald

[130] [CAS to DW] [TLS]

Auburn, Calif.,
Aug. 16th, 1936.

Dear Donald:

I had meant to acknowledge weeks and weeks ago your note of July 15th, enclosing the photographs; and should surely have done so had it not been for a daily round of superadded duties plus the infernal heat and a crushing fatigue. Just at present I am breathing a little easier and am not covering quite so many leagues daily on my rheumatic ankle.

I want to thank you many, many times for the photos, which strike me as being superb. In fact, it is hard to see how they could be better. The two of Dagon are magnificent, and the Harpy, Goblin and others all came out well too.

Helen tells me that you may visit California this winter. I certainly hope that you will come and can spend some time with me. The cabin, and Indian Ridge, are at your disposal. I think you will like many of my sculptures: nearly a hundred are on hand at present, some of greater size and weight than any in the small Eastern exhibit.

I shall like to think of Dagon in your possession. Later, I shall present you with something that I have in mind to make when a suitable piece of material presents itself.

My best to you and Howard. As ever, your friend,

Clark

[131] [CAS to DW] [TLS]

Auburn, Calif.,
Sept. 7th, 1936.

Dear Donald:

Thanks, muchly, for the welcome money order, which came some time ago. I'd have acknowledged it sooner, but have been waiting to hear some word of the carvings from Lovecraft. No word has yet arrived from him, so I won't delay any longer. Perhaps he has been away on a tour: certainly this seems the readiest explanation, in view of his usual promptness.

Congratulations on the sale of your horror story to Esquire,[1] which ought to afford a prime market. I shall watch for the appearance of the tale. Glad that Lady Fortune is showing the less seamy side of her feminine nature. The jade is certainly full of tricks; but not all of them are dirty. I guess indifference is the best policy in treating with her: as Keats says of Fame, "Then, if she likes it, she will follow you."[2]

Paul Winchell's portrait of you sounds very interesting.[3] I hope you will let me see a photograph of it sometime.

I got a huge amount of diversion from your yarn in the last Astounding. It was beautifully worked out, from premises which, after all, were no more fantastic than most of the stock premises in science fiction. What I particularly liked was the cosmic consciousness part, which somehow made me think of Li Po's line: "A full gallon, and nature and I are one."[4]

I enclose a new poem which I am rather inclined to like. Am working on a new story of Zothique, Alkahest, which goes very slowly, partly because of a broken-up schedule, and partly because of my rustiness. Apparently the only way I can get time to write anymore, is to let everything else slide; and you would be quite astounded at the mess which results from this procedure.

My best to you, always. May the checks increase, like the tribe of Abou Ben Adhem![5]

Yrs, under the seal of Sixtystone,[6]
Clark.

P.S. Potable (and potent) Burgundy can now be obtained in Auburn at 50¢ per gal.

Notes

1. "The Eye and the Finger."
2. "On Fame," l. 14.
3. Paul Winchell (1903–1972) was a teacher at the Minneapolis School of Art. His portrait of DW shows DW holding CAS's sculpture "Dagon" in his right hand. See p. 159.
4. Arthur Waley (1889–1966), *The Poet Li Po: A.D. 701–762* (London: East and West, 1919), 26.
5. Ibrahim ibn Adham (c. 718–c. 782), a prominent of the early ascetic Sufi saint. As king, before he became an ascetic, he was said to have 16,000 wives.
6. An allusion to "Novel of the Black Seal" by Arthur Machen.

[132] [CAS to DW] [TLS]

Auburn, Calif.,
Nov. 17th, 1936.

Dear Donald:

As usual, I seem to be damnably and hopelessly in arrears on correspondence, and am sorry that I have not answered your last before this.

I note your story in the current Esquire, and shall buy a copy the next time I visit the new[s]stand. I read the opening, which is fine.

I am glad that Song of the Necromancer pleased you so well, since I too felt that it is one of my best things. It is, however, the only lyric that I have written in an indigo moon. Wright accepted it by return mail.

Yes, I heard from Lovecraft, some time ago, and received the sculptures back from him. He seems, in his way, to have been as badly swamped as I am with various and multitudinous accumulations but is apparently having better luck at digging out from under. I was delighted to read The Haunter of the Dark in print, and found it, as one often does, even better than in ms.

Ina Coolbrith, concerning whom you inquire, died some years ago after a long life. Her poetic career began back in the Bret Harte period; and during her latter years she was poet laureate of California.[1] I had the pleasure of meeting her in 1927, a year or two before her death: a lovable soul, still bright and unquenched by the infirmities that had gathered upon her.

I hope you were able to get a satisfactory photograph of Winchell's portrait. I'd appreciate seeing the photo, if you have a copy to lend.

I haven't any news that is really worthy of headlines but have received some sort of local encouragement regarding the sculptures. My friend Harry Noyes Pratt, poet, and director of the Crocker Art Gallery in Sacramento, came up to see them a couple of days ago and was evidently much impressed.[2] He will give me a showing at the gallery after the first of the year—which, at least, can do no harm. He also expressed the opinion that they could be sold through high-class novelty stores but advised me that my best way of making money would be to turn them out in plaster or terra cotta casts that could be sold cheaply. I am going to experiment a little with mould-making and hope that I can get satisfactory reproductions of some of the pieces best adapted to this purpose. Incidentally, I have done some new things that you would like, including a grotesque "armless Venus" and a sizable statuette (11 inches high) showing a hoofed monstrosity with two serpent-like tentacles issuing between eyes and mouth. One tentacle is looped on the creature's body, its four-fingered hand clasping the swollen side of a pendulous and asymmetrical belly; the other tentacle droops down with its hand reposing on the right hoof. I have christened it Cthulhu's Child and am sure that Lovecraft would be delighted with the conception. Pratt, to my surprise, admired it greatly and took several snapshots of the thing.

I'll send you something presently, as a gift. Yours, for sales unlimited,

Clark

Notes

1. Ina Coolbrith (1841–1928), American poet, writer, librarian, and a prominent figure in the San Francisco Bay Area literary community. She was the first California poet laureate and the first poet laureate of any American state. At a meeting of the Berkeley League of American Pen Women at her home on 5 May 1927, CAS's poems were read and discussed. CAS met her in 1927, so perhaps he was in attendance.

2. Harry Noyes Pratt (1879–1944), poet, editor of the *Overland Monthly*, and director of the Crocker Art Gallery.

[133] [DW to CAS] [TLS]

1152 Portland Ave.,
St. Paul, Minn.
Dec. 8, 1936

Dear Clark:

Since I last wrote you, I have aged tremendously. My older brother and wife[1] have sponsored a black-haired girl that looks like Conan's counterpart. I tell you, becoming an uncle adds a generation to one's burden of years. Don't be surprised if the next picture you see of me shows distinctly white hair.

I seem to be budding out in quite a number of periodicals, being currently represented in ESQUIRE, CLUES–DETECTIVE, and THRILLING WONDER. Next month BLACK MASK,[2] and thereafter ESQUIRE again, and somewhere along the way WEIRD TALES with a thoroughly nasty little horror story that I finally broke down and let Wright have.[3] The first story in ESQUIRE seems to have curdled the blood of quite a large section of the American public, judging from direct reactions. The second one, "The Painted Mirror" is less chilling, more in the fantastic vein.

Winchell has not yet taken the portrait of me to his home studio, and until he does, I can't photograph it. The canvas reposes in the Minneapolis Art Institute's storeroom, where Acts of God are necessary in order to disturb it. I haven't even seen it since the day it was finished.

I am much happier these days. The long run of devilish misfortunes that plagued me constantly during the last year and a half in New York came to an end when I returned to St. Paul. My work is proceeding at a steady pace to my full satisfaction. I have the feeling now that this will be a splendid year, perhaps to compensate for the ill-fated hoodoo-ridden witch-cursed nightmare that lasted from the dawn of 1935 to the middle of 1936. My brother's wife, by the way, only two weeks ago was finally permitted to return to work after the bus accident that occurred late in May. The Greyhound Lines made a settlement out of court which, after paying all medical and hospital and other expenses, will still enable the eastern Wandrei menage to subsist for a year or two. Which is one way that I hope I never make any money.

I've been doing work of a different sort the past few days. It was snowing when I got up Saturday morning, but I shovelled the walks which were heavily covered. It kept on snowing, and after lunch I shovelled our sidewalks again. It kept on snowing, and after dinner I shovelled the walks. It kept on snowing, and at midnight I decided, WHAT THE HELL, DONALD, YOU CAN'T BEAT NATURE, so I went to bed. I got up Sunday with some callouses the size of igloos on my hands, and the walks were covered with deep, hard-packed, wind-furrowed drifts, so I shovelled the walks. Yesterday it was snowing again, but I cleverly waited till late afternoon and a lull, before shovelling the walks. The air had a stinging bite. When I was through, I looked at the thermometer and noted to my consternation that the temperature was 16 below zero. That is the coldest that it has been within living memory here so early in the season. Today is much warmer, the temperature having risen to a pleasant zero. By all the signs and tokens, this winter will exceed in severity last year's all-time record-breaking siege of polar sub-temperatures. Just imagine 30 consecutive days in which the thermometer never registered higher than -6, and hovered around -36, and be glad that you are in California.

> Ever,
> Donald

[Wedne]sday morning—snowing again.
> **NUTS!**
> D. W.

Notes

1. David Guernsey Wandrei (1906–1959), married to Agnes Anne Niemic (1911–1988).
2. "The Eye and the Finger" (*Esquire*), "Killer's Bait" (*Clues Detective*), "Black Fog" (*Thrilling Wonder*), and "The Rod and the Staff" (*Black Mask*). "The Painted Mirror" did not appear in *Esquire* until May.
3. "Uneasy Lie the Drowned."

[134] [CAS to DW] [ANS, printed Christmas card]

[mid-December 1936]
> [Joy to you at Christmas—
> Happiness to you always.]

Dear Donald:
> Will write soon. Yrs for the grand midwinter Sabbat,
> Clark.

[135] [CAS to DW] [TLS]

> Auburn, Calif.,
> March 23rd, 1937.

Dear Donald:
> The news of Lovecraft's death, which I received last Saturday from his Providence friend, Harry Brobst, has left me deeply saddened and depressed.[1] I had known, through a previous letter from Brobst, earlier in the month, that he was quite ill; but the fatal termination came nevertheless as a great shock. In his last letter to me (Feb. 5th) Lovecraft had spoken of suffering from indigestion and general weakness. Brobst spoke of his illness as being due to some gastro-intestinal trouble of long standing. Perhaps you will have learned more than the few meager details that are known to me.

It is all too melancholy, and stirs one to a black rebellion against the demoniac destinies that have the ordering of such things. One of the things I had most eagerly looked forward to was the future time when I might meet Lovecraft:[2] and, now, if ever I should reach Providence I shall be able to do nothing more than lay some futile wreath on his tomb. For myriads of others, I know, the loss will be equally great.

I am horrified to note the date of your last letter and infer that I haven't yet answered it. For justification I can at least plead a paucity of anything worth writing about. The weather has been execrable—a disgrace to the so-called citrus belt; and I am still about half frozen. Have about given up my sculpture, casting, etc., for the time being, and am concentrating on fiction. Two shorts are finished, one of which Wright will no doubt buy.

I think that Esquire distinguished itself by publishing *The Eye and the Finger*—a great and unforgettable story. Has *The Painted Mirror* appeared yet? I must look for it.

Well—here's hoping that the present year will more than make up for any past hoodoos and other malefice.

Yours, as ever,
Clark

P.S. I'll mail you some casts in a few days.

Notes

1. Harry K. Brobst (1909–2011), a psychiatric nurse who moved to Providence in 1932 and thereafter spent much time with HPL.
2. See "To Howard Phillips Lovecraft," written 31 March:

> For, even upon
> This lonely western hill of Averoigne
> Thy flesh had never visited,
> I meet some wise and sentient wraith of thee,
> Some undeparting presence, gracious and august. (ll. 31–35)

[136] [CAS to DW] [TLS]

Auburn, Calif.,
Apr. 3rd, 1937.

Dear Donald:

I can readily understand how HPL's death has affected you, since even to me, who knew him only through prolonged correspondence, the loss is a staggering and grievous one. Other deaths in the past have brought sorrow to me (2 women friends, Sterling, my mother) and one can't compare degrees of grief. What one feels in HPL's case is necessarily unique; for the man himself was incomparable, and in all ways extraordinary. There never was, and never will be, anyone to take his place either in life or literature.

The irony of your writing to Lovecraft on the day of his death[1] is something that I can almost match with the enclosed poem. In his last letter to me Lovecraft copied a fine complimentary sonnet which he had recently addressed to me. When I received that sonnet, I little dreamed that my answer to the tribute would take the form of an elegiac ode. My poem is poor and meager enough; but perhaps he would have liked some of its lines, which carry on the literary play-spirit that often marked our correspondence.[2]

I am glad the posthumous volume is to be sponsored by you and Derleth.[3] As to the letters, I believe that a collection of them would establish Lovecraft as one of the supreme masters of that latterly neglected art. Many of those that he wrote me (sometimes running to 6, 8 or more sheets) are unique mélanges [*sic*] of erudition, fancy, criticism, humor, personalia, scenic description, etc., and no doubt those to more intimate friends must surpass them. I agree with you heartily that they complement the genius shown in his tales. I am starting to get together in one box the letters I have (the correspondence began about 1920)[4] and if you need any specimens or passages, will be glad to type them. Derleth had already written me when your letter came.

I mailed you four of my casts yesterday: Eibon the Sorcerer, Janus-Faced Demon, Tsathoggua, and The Dog of Commoriom. You may remember the original of the last-named, which was in the loan collection seen by you, Loveman, Lovecraft and others. I am shelving sculpture entirely for the present, and concentrating on fiction. Wright has taken a recent tale of Zothique, *The Death of Ilalotha,* and I am preparing others for submission to W.T. and to cash markets. Also, I have written two or three poems. Work is slow under the circumstances; but at least I can do a little. I believe the sculptures will get a break sooner or later; but, for one reason and another, things seem hung up for the present in that quarter.

My fervent best wishes for the success of your play-writing; also, for the projected sojourn in California. Weather here has been execrable this year; but maybe it's only the sunspots! I don't remember a worse winter. However, it doesn't seem to have done me any harm, since my weight is back to normal for the first time in years; and my energy (though far from rivalling that of A.W.D.!) is beginning to return.

Re that theory about an artist's growth being linked with or rooted in his native soil: probably it depends a great deal on the type of mind or temperament possessed by the artist; that is to say, whether he reacts realistically *upon* his environment or romantically *against* it. However, maybe it could be argued that there is an indirect debt in the latter case as well as a direct one in the former. Poe, who reflected nothing of America in his writings, may have owed to America something of the reverse impulse that drove him so far into fantasy and sheer creation. Lovecraft is essentially different from Poe, combining as he does both local realism and cosmic fantasy. I, though not incapable of realism, am plainly more of the Poe order. Derleth, I would venture to say, is more thoroughly and positively identified with his native milieu even than Lovecraft, and feels no need of transdimensional dreams or flights into the vasts of antiquity and cosmic space. Perhaps, too, he draws from the soil his astounding electric vitality, like Antaeus in the myth.

Write when you have leisure and inclination.

As always,

Clark.

Notes

1. DW had written HPL on 17 March, not 15 March.
2. HPL included the poem "To Clark Ashton Smith, Esq., . . ." in his last surviving letter to CAS (postmarked 5 February 1937). CAS wrote the elegy "To Howard Phillips Lovecraft" on 31 March 1937.
3. *The Outsider and Others.*
4. It began with HPL's first letter to CAS of 12 August 1922, from Cleveland, where he had learned of *The Star-Treader and Other Poems* from Samuel Loveman, a friend of both. CAS had begun the task of typing selections from HPL's letters, but overwhelmed by the task, he turned his letters over to Arkham House for transcription. Of 160 letters, 130 are transcribed (usually in highly truncated form) in the Arkham House Transcripts. The letters published in *Selected Letters* were edited even further. *Dawnward Spire, Lonely Hill* contains their joint correspondence, using entire letters from ms. when possible.

[137] [DW to CAS] [TLS]

1152 Portland Ave.,
St. Paul, Minn.
April 19, 1937

Dear Clark:

I have just returned from a week's visit in Sauk City with August W. Derleth, as the climax of a month of furious activity. If my nerves in their present state were conjoined with Augie's hyperactive tummy, the result would be something to startle even Believe-It-Or-Not Bob Ripley. When the news of Lovecraft's death came, I had just begun a new Ivy Frost story[1] of 16,000 words, which had to be done before I went to Sauk City. At the same time, Mother, bless her soul, took a notion to get the spring cleaning done, so I started a quick cross-fire of correspondence with Augie to establish our Lovecraft posthumous publication before the Barlow pest became a menace. To the tune of vacuum-cleaners and dismantled rooms and clouds of dust and thumpety-banging of furniture, I whacked the keys of my typewriter with a fiendish determination to drown out all other sounds. By some miracle of perseverance I completed the novelette on the day that the housecleaners returned to their den in the sub-nethermost regions of hell. Last [week?] I gathered together the things I thought

I would need, and after having worked all night and morning, finishing the story, started out Monday afternoon in a driving rain and a state of frenzy for Sauk City. I didn't arrive till half after midnight, and had forgotten where Augie's house was, and prowled around town like the ghost of Hamlet until I located some of the natives in their obscure retreats who gave me good misdirection that enabled me to find Augie three blocks away after another half-hour stretch.

He has put on weight since I last saw him, and now presents somewhat the appearance of a formidable grizzly at about 210 pounds of volcanic energy that erupts like a dozen Krakatoas. Augie has thus far written as much as he did all last year, and I am firmly convinced that in the event of his untimely demise, 100,000,000 words will perish. We stayed in talking till about two-thirty and rose at eight to drive on to Milwaukee, where we looked up Lovecraft's friend of more than two decades, Moe, and collected from him an immense quantity of letters, poems, and miscellany. We also looked up Bloch, who says he may go to California soon, and obtained more letters from him. We drove back to Sauk City the same day, and on the following kited off north to Appleton where we stayed overnight with Galpin the prodigal, whom I had never met, and his wife. Galpin and I became fast friends virtually upon sight, partly I am sure because we are such striking similarities in general physique and nervous energies, Galpin coming within a quarter inch of my six feet two and three-quarters and nearly at my constant weight of 137. A whole swarm of people moved in during the evening, but I was content to sit back and let them all buzz with Augie. The Galpins went to extraordinary lengths to serve dinner with all the trimmings they could find in the 1880 period of his new novel, and successfully. Such is fame, though nothing appears to dent Augie's colossal ego and his well-nigh dictatorial attitude. They are not offensive—I merely cite them as subsidiary phenomena accompanying Augustus Imperator. Thursday noon we had a farewell dinner with the Galpins, and drove back to Sauk City. We were set to drive to Chicago Friday, but Augie couldn't take it and begged off, which secretly gave me much glee since Augie doesn't drive and I who had undergone the strain of piloting a Plym[outh] for 700 miles at 40 and over up to that point really should have been the one to weaken. We spent Friday starting in on the letters, and I cleared two or three minor groups of correspondence out of the way by copying them. Saturday much the same, with a cursory run through the voluminous Moe material,[2] more copying, a trip across the hills with Augie in the afternoon, a number of Derlethian friends in for dinner, and final discussion of plans during the evening. Sunday morning I started the trek home, drove through high winds, dust, and rain squalls, and reached St. Paul safely in later afternoon. My legs still ache from the strain of driving over a thousand miles without relief, and all this activity of the past month was carried on under the additional hindrance of a severe cold. The thousand on the Plym probably took a thousand days off my life. Oh well, eheu fugaces, sic transit, and O tempora.

Your elegy to HPL is very fine, far above the other memorials in prose and verse that I have thus far seen. The four casts likewise arrived in perfect condition, and needless to say, I am delighted to have them. They now surround the Dagon like a brood of extra-galactic familiars waiting the summoning call of Cthulhu. Congratulations on the sale to W.T.,[3] and I hope it is followed by many others. Even more, I hope you can establish favorable relations with a market that pays spot cash. I would suggest a try at ASTOUNDING, though, as you are no doubt aware, it has changed the critical policy and now goes in exclusively for science fiction. THRILLING WONDER[4] also wants science, but it seems to be aimed at the six-year-old mind for the most part, with exceptions in favor of wellknown names. At least they too pay cash on acceptance.

Yes indeed, the desire for financial success is the second major motivation behind my recent entrance to the field of playwriting,[5] the primary reason being simply an ever-expanding range of interests that has taken me through poetry, short stories, long stories, novels, and now, logically, plays and the drama. I suppose the next development will be motion-picture scenarios, but that's probably several years in the offing. If I had plenty of cash resources, Augie and I could forget the labor of typing involved with the HPL material, could hire a fleet of stenos to do all the copying, could treat recalcitrant publishers with a high hand and publish the volumes in the distinguished format that they merit. Ah well, 'tis a noble dream, and perhaps errant fate will some day redeem her worser self by a few rectifying plums. Or will she?

I mentioned the Barlow menace. Heaven knows what imp of perversity induced HPL to name that unbearable pest his literary executor. I can understand it to a degree, HPL having received his first full physical well-being during his long stay with the Barlows in Florida, and the youngster being an unquestioned devotee of weird literature. But there my understanding ends, for it has taken us three weeks to get one corrected ms.—"At The Mountains Of Madness"—(HPL left corrected copies of all his tales, all of which Barlow walked off with)[6] from that b————. At this rate it will take us a year to get all the corrected versions. Furthermore, Barlow, who lives in Kansas City now and who returned from the east by way of Chicago, couldn't be bothered going a hundred miles out of his way so that Derleth and I could examine in toto the Lovecraft material and make the necessary selections at one meeting. Barlow's sole interest seems to be to put everything into his private files and to leave it there, and Lovecraft's friends be damned and the public be damned and who the hell cares if it's published or not. I am probably exaggerating the case to some degree, but Augie and I are pretty burned up about the half-hearted co-operation we're getting from that animated wart. For goodness' sake, Clark, I hope that you yourself, when the time comes, will make a better choice than HPL did and name some library to guard and preserve your mss. If Derleth and I succeed in establishing the name of HPL among a wider audience through book publication, we are going to donate our own Lovecraft mss. & material to a library, probably Brown University,[7] [to] form the nucleus of a Lovecraft collection in his beloved New England and upon the campus adjoining his residence, and then see if we can't shame the Barlow Unprintable into disgorging his personal loot into the safekeeping of more distinguished hands. It is a mystery to me why HPL passed up Long and Loveman who were friends of long standing, especially Belknap who appears to have been his favorite protegee. [*sic*]

I hope you don't mind my letting off steam in this fashion. As Augie remarked, each man is harried by time in his own way, and to experience delays dependent upon the whim and inclination of an irresponsible brat is provoking beyond words.

As we have outlined our work, it will require years to complete[. W]e intend to see first through publication THE OUTSIDER, containing the bulk of his tales. The second volume will include the [less]er [ta]les and prose miscellany (except SUPERNATURAL HORROR IN LITERATURE which will form an appendix to THE OUTSIDER). The poetry will comprise the third [volume] while the fourth and as many are necessary will be de[vot]ed to letters.[8] In case it is nece[ssa]ry for us to finance publication, the basic plan will be slightly modified and the work will be issued in three thick volumes. Sauk City is our headquarters, because my share in the undertaking will involve much travelling, as you may have guessed. I am going to New York in the middle of May to see all Lovecraft's group of friends there, and to continue with the collection of letters, mss., and any other available data, after which I visit Providence and Mrs. Gamwell.[9]

While I was [at] Sauk City, Augustus Imperator read me parts [of a lett]er he had received from you, in which you made a statement [regard]ing your intention of leaving California.[10] Is that an imminent prospect or a plan of procedure? Have you some definite goal in mind? The statement naturally interests me a great deal. Are you going to carry out your oft-expressed wish to visit the east? And is it to be a vacation, an extended change of scene, or a permanent removal?

May the improvement in your health continue, and may chance favor you with some of her more extravagant graces with less reluctance than the old harridan usually displays. Write me when you have a brief interval to spare from your own work. And so to copying my HPL letters to send on to Derleth, whereafter an article that I will try to place in the magazines. Peaks of endeavor lie ahead, life is fantastically crowded, but not dull, not dull.

   Always,

    Donald

[Enclosure?]

[Photograph of painting of DW. On back:]
    Oil Painting by Paul H. Winchell,
    Sept., 1936

Clark—Do you recognise "Dagon"? Paul calls the painting "The Voice", but my father named it "Portrait of a Communist With Bomb."
    Donald

(Photo courtesy John Hay Library)

Notes

1. Possibly "A Beetle or a Fox" (*Clues Detective Stories,* June 1937) or "Skeletons, Inc.," (*Clues Detective Stories,* August 1937).
2. The correspondence between HPL and Maurice W. Moe (1882–1940), including various round-robin letters, extended from 1914 to HPL's death.

3. Probably "The Death of Ilalotha."

4. It published three stories by CAS.

5. In his final letter to HPL, DW speaks of working on a play entitled *Love to Murder.* It appears to be nonextant.

6. HPL granted RHB possession of his manuscripts and other matter, as spelled out in "Instructions in Case of Decease" (1936).

7. The John Hay Library of Brown University houses the HPL papers, thanks to RHB, who donated HPL's mss. and letters to Brown along with other materials. DW's letters from HPL were not donated to the library but purchased by it (along with the mss. of DW's novels *Dead Titans, Waken!* and *Invisible Sun* and his set of the Arkham House transcripts) after his death. AWD's letters from HPL reside at the Wisconsin Historical Society. Neither donated any significant HPL material.

8. There was no third or fourth volume, per se. *Beyond the Wall of Sleep* contained only thirty poems, although Arkham House later published a *Collected Poems* (1961) with forty-seven. *The Ancient Track* contains virtually all HPL's verse. Although a single large volume of letters was envisioned, Arkham House issued five volumes in a more conventional format between 1965 and 1976. The Hippocampus Press editions comprise twenty-five volumes (excluding letters to R. H. Barlow).

9. Annie E. P. Gamwell (1866–1941), HPL's surviving aunt.

10. See *Eccentric, Impractical Devils,* 257–58 (14 April 1937). See also his letters to RHB herein.

[138] [CAS to DW] [TLS]

Auburn, Calif.,
May 17th, 1937.

Dear Donald:

I'd have written before this, but have had considerable outdoor labour to do in the effort to ensure some sort of protection against the annually growing fire-menace. The work has tired me, and I haven't felt fit for much after a few hours of it. Owing to the unusually wet and long winter, there was a terrific crop of weeds, poison-oak and other newly grown brush to contend with. We still have many cool and cloudy days, with occasional sprinkles of rain; and this will retard a little the drying-up process.

You and August have certainly assumed a tremendous undertaking, and obviously won't be able to complete it in a day or even a year. I hope the Outsider volume will receive some approximation of justice from reviewers. Apart from HPL's legion of admirers among pulp readers, there should surely be a response from the public that cares for Dunsany, De la Mare, Blackwood, James, etc.

Barlow's delays in turning over mss. must have been provoking. As to HPL's choice of B. for executor, I believe it can very readily be explained. I do not believe it occurred to HPL that there was any prospect of his work being brought out by a professional publishing firm; and from this angle he would have felt that he was imposing a thankless and futile task on Belknap,

Loveman, or any of the older friends. On the other hand, he would have felt that Barlow, with ambitions toward the establishment of a fine private press, might some day be in a position to print his work. This sounds logical to me. Certainly the choice shouldn't be taken as a slight to Belknap or others: HPL could only have thought that he was sparing them an embarrassment.

As to my own mss., I doubt if their postmortem disposition would matter greatly. Most of the work (poems and stories) worth preserving is already in print, in some form or other; and if any one ever wished to print a memorial volume, or volumes, they could be gotten together from books and magazines. It is true that I have made a few slight revisions in some of my earlier poems. Ten poems from The Star-Treader are being reprinted in booklet[1] form by a young admirer (Cla[i]re P. Beck) in Lakeport Co.; and I revised some of these a little—the most extensive changes being in Song of a Comet. I have in my desk a revised copy of The Hashish-Eater. Most of the changes in this were made to vary the cadence of the blank verse. Also, I have a few unpublished poems, including some erotica that would insure suppression of any volume containing them! These are all in my desk, together with carbons of all stories either published or unpublished. However, my end doesn't seem very imminent, and I'll try to work out a plan of disposition in the meanwhile. Your suggestion of a library might be good if I could think of one likely to appreciate the honor.

A more serious problem, with me, would be the disposal of my carvings and paintings. These I regard as an essential part of my contribution, and I think that they round out and express much that is not expressed in my writings. But sometimes I fear that the people who will appreciate and understand them fully are still in the cradle—or in the genes of their future parents!

Winchell's portrait of you is indeed interesting; but, off-hand, I found it easier to recognize Dagon. However, mere physical likeness is sometimes the least important element in a picture. This portrait grows on one with repeated study, and is certainly a striking and memorable work. Your father's title is amusing but I think "anarchist" would be better than "communist." There's a world of difference: I wouldn't mind calling myself an anarchist—that is to say, an absolute individualist: but I can't stomach the Marxian stuff. Bobsky Barlovich, in a recent letter, inquired if I was open to conversion; but I must say that he and Belknap are welcome to my share of collectivist cabbage soup. I have no faith whatever in any of these isms, even though I am unable to hold a brief for the existing system. From all indications, the net result of the spreading class-struggle will be the complete downfall and demolishment of western civilization. However, the eventual return to barbarism should be a good thing for the survivors, since barbarism is the natural and healthy state of man. It would seem that the more "civilized" he becomes the rottener he becomes. Human beings have, in my opinion, demonstrated more and more their utter unfitness to use advanced machinery and control the forces of nature.

August was apparently rather shocked when I spoke of intending to quit California. No doubt he would have been even more shocked if I had told him my full intention—which is to leave the U.S.A. when my present responsibilities are over. I haven't made any definite plans; but such plans are not important, since, varying the title of Baudelaire's prose poem, I shall take as my motto "Anywhere out of America."[2] There are many reasons—too many to list here. One is that I don't wish to be killed by the country that killed Poe, Lovecraft and A. P. Ryder.[3] I'd rather perish at the hands of cannibals, or the fangs of cobras or wild dogs, than be done to death over a course of years by the Boe[o]tians[4] of this republic. I believe that my life-expectation (normally a long one, if heredity means anything) has already been shortened many years by hardship and neglect. The last two years have been terrible ones; and it would seem that the worst is still to come. But I hope to live through it and escape.

The best of fortune with your plays or with anything else you choose to write. I am getting back to my own work after a hiatus due to the brush-burning, etc. I am submitting a recent short to Esquire, and intend to keep after them till I land something. Your tale in the last issue was excellent, and it is plain that the magazine is open to well-written fantasy.

I enclose a recent poem that Wright accepted; also, a new Baudelaire version.[5] The Baudelaire is a nice depiction of what the artist or poet often receives at the hands of an idealized female.

Yours ever, Clark.

(over)

P.S. I make a new carving occasionally. Wish you could see the piece I have cut for a bookend—a coal-black thing that is half human and half bat. There is also Yuckla, the roly poly god of mirth from Zothique; and a wild-looking Ancient One whose legs droop down into squirming wattles.

Notes

1. As *Nero and Other Poems*.
2. I.e., "N'Importe où hors du monde," usually translated as "Anywhere out of This World."
3. Albert Pinkham Ryder (1847–1917), American painter best known for his poetic and moody allegorical works and seascapes.
4. The Athenians portrayed the inhabitants of the province of Boeotia, which included great authors like Pindar, Hesiod, and Plutarch, as proverbially dull and incapable of appreciating music or poetry. Boeotia came to be proverbial for the stupidity of its inhabitants.
5. "Farewell to Eros" and "Outlanders" appeared in the June 1938 issue.

[139] [DW to CAS] [TLS; unavailable]

42 Perry St., New York, N.Y.
26 September 1938

[Roy A. Squires[1] to Kenneth W. Faig, Jr., 27 April 1972 (ms., JHL):]

[. . .] I can flash a beam of light onto the estrangement of RHB from CAS (although, until you mentioned it, I believe I had not known that such had occurred). I have here a letter from Donald Wandrei to Smith [. . .] which I stole from the archives. My purpose in doing so will become apparent—though I might better have destroyed it (the letter, of course). At any rate, I took it for purposes of censorship. [. . .]

The substance (?) of this 4-page typewritten letter is that Barlow and Beck called on Mrs. Gamwell soon after HPL's death and stole books and other papers. Ironically, Wandrei discovered that when he and Derleth visited with Mrs. Gamwell for a similar purpose, I infer. And Wandrei even admits that Barlow took with him a paper naming him HPL's literary executor and heir to his books etc.—after Mrs. Gamwell had selected her choices of things to keep.

Perhaps you can help out here: "it is well known in fandom that Barlow was named by HPL as heir to his papers. Well known, yes, but I do not know of a valid source for the thought."[2]

At any rate, my feeling is that Barlow did only that which HPL had given him permission to do. And Wandrei's letter was written with the purpose of warning Smith against Beck. This letter is vicious: not only in its quite mistaken charges, but also in its intemperate, downright actionable language. [. . .]

Notes

1. Roy A. Squires (1920-1988) was a major and influential science fiction fan, collector, book dealer and small press publisher. He acquired CAS's papers after his death and slowly sold them over the years, including HPL's letters to CAS. At the time of CAS's death, the two were working on CAS's last book, *The Hill of Dionysus*.

2. RHB mentioned to AWD (c. 22 March 1937) that HPL had appointed him his executor and names HPL's "Instructions in Case of Decease." HW learned of HPL's document from Frank Belknap Long around the same time. So AWD, HW, and DW all knew full well that HPL had instructed RHB to handle his books and papers. (DW also suggested to CAS that Beck and RHB would next be coming for his mss.) As late as November 1942, HW and Samuel Loveman were still seething about the matter—even though Arkham House had by then issued two books of HPL material—with RHB's assistance and cooperation—and Larry Farsaci even contemplated duplicating the "Instructions" for RHB, so that he could prove HPL had in fact appointed RHB his executor. AWD had heard that HPL had not actually divorced (as was the case) and was of the mind that HPL's still-living wife could nullify HPL's instructions. DW contacted the Phillips family lawyer to try to take action against RHB, but when the lawyer received RHB's testimony, he advised DW to drop the matter.

[140] [CAS to DW] [TLS]

Auburn, Calif.,
Sept. 30th, 1938.

Dear Donald:

I received your letter last night, and must reply immediately even though briefly, since the matters of which you write are serious and grave to the last degree.

Knowing you as I have known you all these years, I cannot but believe that you have incontrovertible reasons for what you say. I am, frankly, not unprepared for the revelation of Barlow's rascality. What shocks and astounds me, however, is the thought that Beck, who, from what I have seen of him, struck me as being an honest, somewhat naive and dreamy youth, should be implicated in such scullduggery. [*sic*] Isn't there a chance that he has been used as a sort of cat'spaw by Barlow, and does not realize the moral obliquity involved in taking from Mrs. Gamwell the books, magazines and other matter that would be of such value to her in her present need?

The whole business finds me in a very awkward situation, since I had consented to the issuing of a small edition of my unpublished verse volume, Incantations, by the Beck brothers. It is, in fact, possible that work has already been begun on this project by Groo Beck. Even though I believe most publishers, even some of the major ones, to be more or less crooked, I do not relish the idea of having the book brought out by people who could, knowingly, be guilty of such turpitude as you have indicated. Have you any suggestions as to what could be done? Since Groo Beck has my consent to the publication of Incantations in a letter, I fear that I could do nothing legally if the Becks wanted to be ugly and hold me to my promise. I believe that I shall try to get the ms. back on the plea of checking it over and making alterations and changes; but they, or Barlow, may possess transcripts.

As to the looting of my own collection, in the case of my sudden and early demise (which seems damned unlikely for such a tough bird as I have grown to be) you can, I think, set your mind at rest. Not long after my father's death, I wrote out a holographic will bequeathing all books, mss., pictures and other art objects to my long-beloved friend, Mrs. Sully.[1] She would take immediate charge in case anything happened to me. (She has, by the way, expressed repeatedly her suspicions of Barlow, and an antipathy toward him, and was in no way surprised when I read your letter to her last night.[)]

I should write more at length, but have little time, since I am preparing for a week-end in the Sierras with the Sullys. I shall, by the way, take the precaution of placing my holograph *immediately* in G. S.'s hands. It will be safer with her than here in the cabin.

I hope fervently that Scribner's will bring out H.P.'s book.[2]

Please write as quickly as possible, if you can suggest anything anent the Beck proposition.

As ever,

Clark

P.S. A group of my carvings is on permanent display at Gump's,[3] in S.F. Five pieces have already been sold, and much interest and admiration aroused.

[P.P.S.] My very best wishes and highest hopes for the success of your play-writing—as well as everything else that you do, or wish to do!

Notes

1. See *Eccentric, Impractical Devils* 309 (9 May 1942) for a later will.
2. DW and AWD had tried to shop the ms. of *The Outsider and Others* with mainstream publishers, but all rejected it, so they founded Arkham House to publish the book.
3. S & G Gump was founded in San Francisco in 1861 as a mirror and frame shop by Solomon Gump and his brother, Gustav, but later sold moldings, gilded cornices, and European artwork to the nouveau riche following the California Gold Rush. The store eventually carried exotic rugs, porcelains, silks, bronzes, and jades imported from Japan and China.

[141] [DW to CAS] [TLS]

42 Perry St.,

New York, N.Y.

Oct. 2, 1938

Dear Clark:

Like yourself, I have been inclined to give Beck the benefit of the doubt. It is an undeniable fact that he has been sending to Mrs. Gamwell the small profits from his publication of HPL's Notebook. But the hurdle I can't get over is the fact that I first met him about three weeks before the trip that Derleth and I made to Providence. I met him at Sam Loveman's place, and remarked then that Derleth would be in town and would visit Providence—I had not, until the last moment, known whether I could find time to accompany Derleth. On the night before we went to Providence, there was a meeting of the HPL group at Frank Long's in honor of Derleth—Sam Loveman, James F. Morton, Arthur Leeds, Rheinhardt Kleiner,[1] my brother Howard, and others were present, including Beck. Both Derleth and I talked independently to Beck, as also did Sam. I told Beck that Derleth and I were driving up the next day to examine the Lovecraft files, and he remarked that he had just returned from Providence. I asked him if he had spent much time there, to which he replied, "Over a week." I said that that was quite an extended stay, and he dismissed the subject by casually agreeing.

When Derleth and I reached Providence and discovered what had happened, one of August's first remarks was in reference to Beck's failure to tell us that our trip would be largely a waste of time, since there was nothing left to examine. And when I returned to New York and talked the matter over with Sam, he made an almost identical comment. Beck had apparently seen Sam two or three times, trying to get the loan of all his collection of your work. Now, much as I would like to give Beck all benefit of doubt, and to assume that he acted unwittingly upon simple instructions from Barlow, I am still unable to see why, knowing the facts of our projected trip to Providence, he should have withheld the facts of his trip from us. His actions seem to me to make him a co-conspirator by silence with Barlow.

The whole affair has been disgusting. Actually, I suppose, as nearly as I can estimate on the basis of the typed list of his weird collection which HPL fortunately left, and as nearly as I was able to determine missing items during the couple of hours at our disposal, the total of approximately a hundred books and the complete file of WEIRD TALES and all files of other magazines that Barlow took have a cash market value of around $250. That is not a large sum, but in Mrs. Gamwell's reduced circumstances, it would represent a modest living for about six months. Barlow knew that. He was fully aware of her very meager livelihood; and if Beck did not know it in advance, I can not see how he could have spent a week in Providence without becoming acutely aware of the fact. Furthermore, since Beck himself apparently lives on a slim margin, and since he planned to meet Derleth, and since he knew that Derleth was driving east and on to Providence, it seems more than strange that Beck lighted out for Providence and cleared everything out, whereas he might have waited and gotten a free lift to Providence.

As for the INCANTATIONS which Beck is planning to publish, I am not at all sure that I can give any adequate comment or suggestions. I would rather see your poems in print than not; but printing from amateur and small private presses generally weighs against the possibility of an established firm issuing the same work. I am inclined to say that, if Beck and Barlow will return at least the books and magazines to Mrs. Gamwell, in their entirety, the publication might be allowed to proceed. But if they refuse, the HPL group ought to have no further dealings with them in the future.

Mrs. Gamwell's own attitude in her letters to me has been that she is too old to carry on a protracted battle, and that she would rather put up with her loss than do anything about it. But I am going to make every effort to see that she has the return of property rightfully hers. From a strict legal viewpoint, Barlow has every right to the material, since Mrs. Gamwell was the sole heir. And as my lawyer informed me, she could give it away or destroy it or do anything she wished with it, since it was entirely hers. But she had no knowledge whatsoever of the value of the material taken; she didn't know what was taken; and she placed an implicit confidence in Barlow simply because he was a friend of HPL. She realizes now that she has been grossly taken advantage of; but the damage is done.

Because of the hurricane, I have had difficulty in communicating with Mrs. Gamwell. I received her last letter yesterday, and will take it to my lawyer tomorrow, though I am fairly sure that there is no action he will recommend except exerting upon Barlow and Beck such moral pressure as the HPL group can bring to bear.

I think your suggestion is a good one: first to recover the ms. of INCANTATIONS for revision; and then to hold it pending what action Beck and Barlow take upon restoring part of the HPL loot to Mrs. Gamwell. So far as I know, Beck could do nothing legally if you change your mind about publication. An author's consent, given for good cause, can also be withdrawn for good cause, and has been done in numerous instances. I'll try to find out more about that from either the Dramatists' Guild lawyer, or Mr. Fleischer, the lawyer whom I have been seeing, and who is an authority upon literary affairs. I will write you again, very likely within two days, and report on my conference.

It is a relief to know that the bars are up against the possibility of Barlow repeating his shabby performance with other members of the HPL circle, principally you and Sam Loveman, though the scoundrel on numerous occasions has been trying to worm parts of our respective collections from both my brother and me. Both Howard and I were suspicious of him from the day we met him several years ago, and repeatedly expressed our convictions to HPL.

I hope you had an ideal week-end. Some day I shall return to California for a much longer visit, when I have a car and can explore whatever picturesque, out-of-the-way spots I desire. This winter, however, will be a trying one. I'm tired of the endless woodpulp grind, and have been working for months on a seven-day basis in order to cast the plays into the hoppers of the gods.

As ever, Donald

[P.S.] I was glad to hear of the exhibit in S.F. But your explorations in sculpture raise an interesting problem on how to present your collected works—photographic reproduction has never been very satisfactory, and three-dimensional printing has not yet been evolved!

D

Notes

1. DW continually spelled Rheinhart Kleiner's name incorrectly in HPL's *Selected Letters* as "Reinhardt."

[142] [CAS to DW] [TLS]

Auburn, Calif.,
Dec. 10th, 1938.

Dear Donald:

I fear that I have become the most remiss and neglectful of

correspondents. Here, at long last (I *should* have returned them weeks—or is it months?—ago) are the various documents relating to the Barlow affair that were marked for return to you. Of late, I have been sojourning so much in the realms of myth, fable, and fantasy, and have had so much of my wildest and most exotic poetry coming to life before me, that I lose all track of terrestrial time. A recent poem, WIZARD'S LOVE, which I enclose, may suggest a little of what I cannot write, or even tell verbally, in prose.

As to l'affaire Barlow: the ms. of Incantations was duly returned to me on my demand, and I am of course holding it permanently. I have not written to the Beck–Barlow outfit, and have no intention of communicating with them, or replying to any possible communications of theirs. Barlow wrote me a card some days ago, saying that they were now ready to begin work on the book. This card I consigned to the stove. I hope sincerely that neither Barlow nor Beck will try to see me in person. If they do, it is probable that I shall run them off the ranch with an old fencing-rapier (a quite formidable-looking object) that was presented to me by the girl for whom I wrote WIZARD'S LOVE. During the recent quail-hunting season, I went around the place with the rapier stuck in my belt, singing bawdy songs or chanting the Dies Irae; and quail-hunters soon began to give it a wide berth!

I hope things are well with you, and that all your literary projects are coming on as per program. As for mine, I think there will soon be more to tell than in years past. At present, I am compelling Wright to buy some of the stories that he has previously refused; these with very minor revisions or excisions. The Double Shadow will appear in the next issue of W.T.

A number of carvings have been added to my display at Gump's; and a few of my paintings and drawings are now being shown there. It is amusing to recall that that [*sic*] I visited G.'s in 1927 with some of these same paintings and tried vainly to interest the art-director in them. The same director received me with deference when I walked into the store during a recent visit in the Bay region. I am sure that he had no recollection of my former visit, or of having seen the pictures before. Life is full of such drolleries; and they seem to multiply as one gets older.

Apart from that, life has become much pleasanter for me than of yore: one reason being a tremendous improvement in my health. I now look ten or fifteen years younger than I did during your visit here in 1934, and have developed the figure of a Greek athlete—152 pounds of iron muscle. And my 46th birthday is imminent next month!

My best wishes to you, and to all the N.Y. gang, for a happy holiday season. Mine, I hope, will be spent in the demesne of paganry, with fauns and Bacchantes for co-celebrants!

Yours affectionately,
Clark

[143] [CAS to DW] [TLS]

Auburn, Calif.,
July 25th, 1941.

Dear Donald:

  I have been intending to write you for ages; my good intentions in that regard being, I dare say, not the least and lightest of the paving-stones that I have contributed to a subjacent region hardly necessary to name. But I will spare you any banal apologies. My correspondence in general has been neglected or procrastinated . . . and the story behind the neglect is one that can be hinted only in poetry.

  Poetry, indeed, has been the bulk (?) of my literary production recently; since, though plotting many tales, I have left most of them still unwritten. I'll enclose a few recent pieces with this. The sonnet, *Swine and Azaleas,* was written from a description given me by Mrs. Sully, who, in a lonely Sierran meadow, had come upon two huge black swine sniffing the wild azalea blossoms: truly, a startling and incongruous picture. Since the sonnet was hardly poetry anyway, I couldn't resist ending it with a crack at the modernist crew. But I like better such things as *Resurrection, Bond, Silent Hour,* etc.

  Many strange things have happened since I last wrote you: not the least strange being the erection of a Catholic nunnery (a novitiate) on the old fruit-ranch facing my hill-top! Stranger still, I had a job for several weeks last fall, mixing cement, etc, for the concreting of a well recently sunk on the novitiate property! It was the hardest kind of work, but well worth while from the standpoint of experience. I became very tough and strong doing it. The head well-digger and concreter was a German who professes to be a full-fledged Buddhist lama! Some crew for a nunnery well, with the inclusion of a pagan like me! I hear that the well isn't yielding enough water.

  August wrote me not long ago about the plan to bring out a volume of my best shorts if his own book makes expenses.[1] I'll certainly be delighted if the plan should materialize.

  I had hoped to come east this year, in company with two Californian friends who are now in Passaic, N.J. But the plan fell through for lack of cash which, however, may be available later on. If you are in New York at any early date, I'd very much like to have you meet these friends. They are Mr. and Mrs. Eric W. Barker; their present address is 34 Randolph St., Passaic. Eric is a poet whose work has been highly praised by John Cowper Powys; his wife, Madelynne, is a talented dancer and sculptress.

  I hope you'll return good for evil by writing me soon.

As ever,
Clark

Notes

1. CAS, *Out of Space and Time;* AWD, *Someone in the Dark.*

[144] [CAS to DW] [TLS]

Auburn, Cal,
Oct. 29th, 1941.

Donald: I wish to hell you'd write me: surely you aren't silly enough to be offended by my long but personally meaningless silence.

Note enclosed dance program. The dancer inspired my recent W.T. poem, *Witch-Dance.* Her *Witches' Sabbath* is something that no weirdist can possibly afford to miss. It's the thrill of a whole lifetime for such as you and I. She has the makings of another Martha Graham if given one quarter of a chance. Sans manager, alone except for her poet-husband, against a multitude of obstacles and difficulties, she is trying to put herself over in a huge and strange city.

I don't know whether or not you are in N.Y. If in N[.]Y., attend if possible: otherwise shoot the program to someone who might be interested.

I'm getting the biggest boom of my lifetime, and will shortly rival August in production. Apart from that I'm setting up publicly as sorcerer, mesmerist, psychoanalyst, and fortune-teller. I have the stuff and will put sendings on people if they don't behave.

Please don't think me crazy: I was never saner in my life.

Pardon haste: I'm writing num[b]erless air-mail letters.

Yours,

Clark

[145] [DW to CAS] [TLS]

1152 Portland Ave.,
St. Paul, Minn.
Jan. 18, 1942

Dear Clark:

By degrees I am emerging from the various wreckage of the past couple of years and beginning to impose some sort of orderly pattern on my life again. I certainly owe you apologies for the long delay in answering your two letters of last summer and fall, but hope that I have not permanently been consigned to the lair of Ubbo[-]Sathla.

I sent the dance-program to my brother in New York but, as luck would have it, his wife was having a baby that week, which was bad timing by Connie for she used to be a dancer herself and is deeply interested in the modern dance. They gave the program to some friends of theirs whom I don't know, hence I still have no idea of the impression that the recital made. I will certainly pay her a visit if I reach New York this year, and hope that any such visit will coincide with another recital. A few months ago, the chances looked excellent for my spending some time in both Washington and New York, but now the prospects appear most unlikely. For one thing, I am in the 28 to 35 draft classification, and expect to be summoned into military service any day. For another, my father who has chronic heart trouble has had several serious attacks the past year, the most recent being over the holidays. I feel it an obligation to remain here until the Army makes up its mind.

As a matter of fact, I thought for a long time in 1941 that I had greatly offended you, because of a long letter I wrote you a year ago about this same time; but judging by your recent letter that epistle of a year ago must have gone astray somewhere. It's of no especial importance now, since its subject has been pretty well covered by correspondence between you and Derleth, and the plans for the book are well under way.

In that letter of a year ago I wrote that Derleth and I were thinking of publishing an anthology of all your stories, or all your poems, or both, eventually, similar to what we did for HPL. Events of the year—the steady approach of war, looming paper shortages, the liability of both Derleth and I to military service, and so on—made us decide to rush our plans and try to issue a selection of your best tales while there was still time. This you know, of course.

But in the earlier letter—and this is what I thought might have offended you—I had inquired how you would feel, or whether you would care, about making Derleth and me, collectively or separately, your literary *executor*. As your own lawyer can explain to you better than I, this has nothing to do with property rights or inheritance, and is something quite separate and apart from them. It would simply be the right to *control* any posthumous publications or writings of yours, the right of access to manuscripts, notes, diaries, stories, poems, etc., published or unpublished, and the right to arrange for their publication. Such an executorship of course would require that periodic accounts be rendered to your legitimate heir or heirs. What Derleth and I intended was that we should not again face any such dirty work as we ran into in the case of the Lovecraft estate and the little Barlow rat.

If you have someone else in mind, or if you know someone closer to California who is fully reliable and honest, then there would be no particular reason in making Derleth and me literary executors, since we are half-way across the continent. It doesn't matter much who you choose, so long as it's somebody you can depend on to get action.

I have just finished reading over every single story of yours in my files in connection with the projected OUT OF SPACE AND TIME; I don't have a complete file, but the bulk of your stories—all of *Weird Tales* and *Strange Tales*, a sprinkling of *Fantasy Magazine, Wonder Stories, Wonder Stories Quarterly, Amazing Detective Tales, Magic Carpet Magazine*, and *The Double Shadow*. Oddly enough, I picked out 19 stories as outstanding, the same number as on your list, and 13 of these were your own choices. My list goes: THE UNCHARTED ISLE, A VOYAGE

TO SFANOMOE, THE TALE OF SATAMPRA ZEIROS, THE MONSTER OF THE PROPHECY, THE WEIRD OF AVOOSL WUTHOQQUAN, THE TESTAMENT OF ATHAMMAUS, THE ISLE OF AFORGOMON, THE DEATH OF ILALOTHA, THE MAZE OF MAAL DWEB, THE DOUBLE SHADOW, A NIGHT IN MALNÉANT, THE DOOR TO SATURN, THE SECOND INTERMENT, THE CITY OF [THE] SINGING FLAME, and BEYOND THE SINGING FLAME. I have also suggested to August that, whatever the final list is, we use those two magnificent cosmic legends from *Ebony and Crystal,* FROM THE CRYPTS OF MEMORY and THE STATUES,[1] to close the book. This is partly because they are among the finest prose in all English-American literature, and partly because they would be new to the majority of magazine readers who would buy the volume.

When I was east with August late in 1940, someone—Frank Long?—said that Helen Sully had married and moved away from Auburn. I asked about this too in my missing letter, and sent congratulations and all best wishes if the rumor were true. I have often thought about Helen and wondered what she was doing. Indeed, I have often thought about Auburn and wanted to make another visit; though California must be changing radically under the impact of war and the avalanche of war industries. However, when I visit California again I want to have a car of my own to drive, and to delve into some of the more out-of-the-way parts of the state.

Your new poems are wonderfully lyrical.

A couple of plays that I was writing were both nullified by the outbreak of war. I recently sold another horror story to *Esquire*[2] which, I presume, will publish it in an early issue.

August writes that you are thinking of leaving Auburn, though he did not say whether this was just a temporary absence or a permanent departure that you had in mind. Well, it would be ironic if the Army called me, trained me, and shipped me out to the Coast just as you decamped for other regions.

At any rate, I hope that all goes well with you, and that this year is a good one in all respects, ample both in new creations and in abundant living—

As always,

Donald

Notes

1. DW means "The Shadows."
2. "It Will Grow on You."

[146] [DW to CAS] [ALS]

Co. G, 357th Int., Camp Barkeley, Texas   April 14, 1942

Dear Clark—

      This is merely to let you know that Uncle Whiskers is now pay-
ing my salary. I was inducted into the Army on March 20 and sent down here
a few days later. As it happened, I wound up in the hospital where I've been
for 10 days & will be for another ten or eleven. It is an isolation ward—I had
a touch of pneumonia.

      I asked for Intelligence service, but the Army is trying to make an infan-
tryman out of me. So far we've only had the very basic work—gymnastics,
close order drill and field drill, classes in rifle disassembly & reassembly, hand
signals for field use, how to take cover & concealment, and so on. We also
had daily hikes that began at 3 miles & got a little longer every day until, eventually, I suppose they will run to overnight trips of 25 miles with full equipment. We haven't had rifle practice yet, though last week we were issued 1917
model Enfields, a bolt-action five-shot .30 calibre weapon. They are only for
training—the new M-01 (Garand) is issued only to troops going into battle.

      This camp is a new one begun a year ago & not yet finished. It covers
miles & miles of ground—barracks, canteens, mess-halls, churches, post-
office, field house, 4 theaters, ordnance shop and machine repair shop,
6 powder magazines, rifle, artillery, and anti-tank ranges, immense hospital,
just everything. Right now there's a double epidemic of mumps & measles—
1,100 hospital cases out of 20,000 men. At full strength the camp can hold
from 30,000 to 45,000 men.

      The food is good & varied for the most part. We are quartered in box-
tents about 15 × 15, six men to a tent—not too cramped. My tent mates are
all southerners, & fortunately we're all congenial.

      But I shall never like this climate & country. We're in West Texas, about
150 miles west of Ft. Worth. The land is flat, except for a long, sharp escarp-
ment of hills about ten miles south that runs for forty or fifty miles east & west.
No trees, springs, lakes, or streams within a hundred miles. Soil is red clay &
red gravel, very poor, and there is a strong wind that blows day & night, whip-
ping a fine red dust like talc into eyes, mouth, food, clothing, bedding, wash-
bowls, everything. It's hot here already, & I'll bet we fry in summer.

      I doubt if I'll find much time to write. I'm doing a new horror story (did
you see my last one in the April ESQUIRE, "It Will Grow on You"?) here in
the hospital, but after that I don't expect to find time to write until my basic
training (13 weeks) is complete, & possibly not till the end of the war. I hope
for a furlough home late this summer, but that too probably depends on how
the spring & summer battles go.

      I suppose August has kept you informed of OUT OF SPACE AND

TIME. The ad is scheduled for the July WT, and we should have an estimate from the printer within a few weeks. My only regret is that we couldn't publish your complete tales, like HPL's (but dash it all, you haven't finished your complete tales yet!) Later on I'd like to publish your collected, complete poems—everything. They have never lost, & never will, their extraordinary hold on my imagination, and I know there must be hundreds if not thousands that I have never seen—either unpublished or published, in out of the way places that I missed.

What are you doing now? Working on the farm? (Ranch, I mean) Or writing? Or both? And are you still thinking of leaving Auburn? And if so when & where? If you do see to it that your priceless poems, stories, sculptures, paintings, are either well stored or safely taken care of. Best of luck, best of sales, best of new successes—

As ever, Donald

[147] [DW to CAS] [ALS]

Co "H", 413th Inf.,
Camp Adair, Oregon
Feb. 24, 1943

Dear Clark:

If you are still in Auburn, this is to let you know that I will be in that vicinity shortly after this reaches you. Unless some unforeseen emergency arises to prevent me, I am taking a three-day pass from March 1 to 3 inclusive. My regular week-end pass will let me depart from here Saturday at noon, Feb 27. There is a train at night that gets me into Sacramento at 6:00 p.m. Sunday. I have not yet checked the Greyhound bus schedule to see if I can catch an afternoon bus that will get me into Sacramento earlier Sunday afternoon, but I am inclined to believe that the train will be my best bet.

My rather beautiful girl-friend Muriel is now in Martinez, at 1315 Brown St., and that is my immediate destination. But the trip would be half a loss if I did not see you also. I had hoped to hear from Muriel today, so that I could give you a definite schedule. My intention was to stop at a hotel in Sacramento, and have you and Muriel join me there, since my time will be limited from Sunday night till Tuesday night, when I must start back for camp. If my plans are more definite before I depart Saturday, I will wire you. If I haven't heard from Muriel, I'll catch the connecting bus or train that leaves Sacramento around 7:30 and reaches Martinez about 9:00 p.m. Sunday. In that case I'll send you a wire from Martinez. I'll either leave Martinez early Tuesday morning in order to have time to see you at Sacramento, or it may be that you could join us at Martinez. All expenses are mine, incidentally, and there will be no cost to you except in time. I would enclose travel-money with this letter if I knew for sure you are still in Auburn. I would, indeed, like to see Auburn again, but it is doubtful if bus or train connections will be good enough for me to visit both Auburn and Martinez without spending the bulk of my time in transit, just riding. Anyway I want you and Muriel to meet. She's very young, only 20 or so, but has good tastes in poetry and music.

I do hope I shall see you. You will hear from me by wire.

I have just emerged from a three-weeks siege in the hospital. The trip should do me good.

With best wishes, and the hope that you are there, in the best super-Klark-Ash-Tonic form,

As ever

Donald

[148] [DW to CAS] [ANS]

[PACIFIC TELEGRAM]

Corvallis Oregon Feb 27 [19]43
[Postmarked 28 February 1943]

[TO] Clark Ashton Smith

Auburn California

Arriving by bus Sacramento one thirty Sunday afternoon
Donald Wandrei

[149] [DW to CAS] [ANS][1]

[Postmarked Camp Shelby, Miss.,
21 July 1943]

Cpl Donald Wandrei
Co H 259th Inf 65th Div
Cp Shelby Miss

U S Army

July 18, 1943

Dear Clark—New Orleans is perfectly fascinating, & I'm having a beautiful time in the Vieux Carre and along Canal St. This is my new station. I'll write you a letter soon, as I have intended doing ever since I saw you. The women here are astonishingly beautiful. I can't help feeling the spirit of HPL here—for the archaeological vistas, not the women!—Donald

Notes

1. *Front:* The Warrington House (Haunted House). New Orleans, La.

[150] [CAS to DW] [TLS]

Auburn, Calif.,
Aug. 13th, 1944.

Dear Donald:

I was delighted to get your letter, which was a little delayed in reaching me, since I am picking fruit at present (a somewhat fatiguing occupation) and don't go to the P.O. every day. Today, Sunday, is my first chance to sit down and write you: the letter, by air-mail, should reach you in care of August.

Derleth had already mentioned a plan for a selected volume of my poems, though with no definite time of publication, and I had planned to start working on as soon [it] as the fruit-season ends, which will be early in September. Needless to say, your project for a *complete* collection thrills and pleases me immensely; yet I am not sure that all the work in my published volumes, nor all the uncollected stuff, is worthy of such preservation. For instance, some of the nature lyrics in the Star-Treader seem a bit banal to my present taste. The compiling of the volume will take careful consideration. I doubt if it could run to the size of the Lovecraft omnibus; but it might run to 350 or 400 pages. Like August, I favor a regrouping in regard to general subject matter form, etc: the blank verse poems from the Star-Treader and Ebony and Crystal could be grouped together for the first section; then the odes; the shorter poems of fantasy and weirdness under some such subtitle as Incantations; the love poems to be grouped together as The Book of Eros. But, as you say, the book is still fluid and uncrystallized. It would be splendid if you could use a few of my paintings or drawings: I'll look over what I have with a tentative view to this purpose.

I have The Eye and the Finger, which I am enjoying vastly. The title story is new to me, and it is certainly a neat little horror. Gods! but you have an imagination! The ones I have read before seem even better on rereading in book form. Incidentally, I liked your preface too, and was pleased by the high mention you gave me.[1]

Re a preface for my poems. I'd be delighted to have one by you; and it seems to me that Sterling's brief foreword to Ebony and Crystal, and a short appreciation by Benjamin De Casseres (which runs to about two pages) could also be included to advantage.[2]

Yes, I think it will be best for me to do the typing: I don't even possess a printed copy of Sandalwood (I have a typescript made by Barlow!) and shall want to sift many piles of scattered mss. for some of the stuff to be included.

I've thought many times of our meeting in Sacramento, which was one of those unexpected episodes that do so much to take the staleness from existence. It prefaced a run of unusual Sundays for me: on the following Sunday I had an experience too beautiful and macabre to write about here; on the next, I stole rhododendrons for a girl out in Golden Gate Park.

I'll hunt for some poems to enclose with this.

As ever Clark

[P.S.] My best to August—I'll write him soon.

Life still has its surprises. A charming and unlooked-for brunette is lying close at hand, reading your book, as I write this.

Notes

1. "Like Lovecraft, but in his own individual genius, Smith has developed his conviction in the dark jewels of his otherworldly poetry, in the magical splendours of his tales" (x).
2. *SP* had no frontispiece. There was a single preface by Benjamin De Casseres, "Clark Ashton Smith, Emperor of Shadows," first published as a booklet by Futile Press. The "Ebony and Crystal" section of *SP* retains George Sterling's preface to that book.

[151] [CAS to DW] [TLS]

Auburn, Cal.,
Sept. 9th, 1944.

Dear Donald:

I finished fruit-picking last week and have started to assemble and retouch material for the typescript of my poems that you suggest. I think it a good idea myself, to get together everything that is not hopelessly mediocre, and have gone through immense piles of ancient mss. and even boxes of old letters for whatever I could retrieve. Many poems of The Star-Treader and Ebony and Crystal period are still missing (I think I told you once that I had destroyed a number of them in a mood of disgust) but I'll probably find enough to floor you and am even planning to include some parodies and satires on modernistic verse for variety. Also, it seems to me that a selection of my epigrams would add range to the published volume, following the prose poems.[1]

Here are two sonnets dating from 1912 (never published anywhere) which I have revised in part:

The Pursuer
Climbing from out what inframundane sea,
From nether lives by death long compassed round—
Sealed with the night of suns, forever bound
With frozen systems—comest thou to me,
Despair, whose darker name in memory
I know not—bringing from the dead profound,
With cerements and sepulchral purples wound,
The foulness of thine immortality?

O shape of loathlier horrors, here untold,
Have I not climbed secure from their abyss,
Those lower spheres, those limbos dire and old?

Thou tearest me beyond the hells of this,
Down chasms dreadful for the light of tears,
And ampler glooms alive with crawling fears!

TO THE SPIRIT OF SUBLIMITY[2]
I wane and weary: come, thou swifter One,
Clad in thine uttermost austerity,
With zones of night and flame and mystery
Sevenfold, and awful power to blind and stun
Beyond the bolted levin. Though Time, undone,
Abide not thy supreme epiphany,
Though Earth should fail to that ascendancy,
Come thou, and bear me to thy chosen sun.

Yea, in the fiery fastness of the star
That thine empyreal wings most often find,
Thy loftiest eyrie, lone in gulf and gloom,
Leave me and lose me, safe from wasting war
Of finite things unworthy, and resigned
To some deific ecstasy of doom.

All sorts of stuff has been coming to light, some of it highly erotic. But you
and I and August can decide what we want to print. We wouldn't want to
blow the dome from the Library of Congress! I think it will take me months
and months to do the typing, since I shall retouch many pieces as I go along.

Probably you and Derleth are right about the consolidating of various
critiques and appreciations into a single preface. As for the frontispiece, I
think it would be a good idea, when the time comes, if I were to loan you and
Derleth some of my paintings (the more exotic ones) from which a choice
could be made.

Type-paper is easily obtained in Auburn but I've had lousy luck with ribbons for my Underwood Portable. The one I'm using is o.k.—but it was procured for me by a "fan" in the armed forces.[3]

I suppose my book will be out shortly, and I'll send you an inscribed copy as
soon as possible. I'm going to San Francisco next week—the weather here has
been hotter than the underside of Astarte's girdle, and I feel like sticking my
nose into an ocean fog. Also, I want to keep check on the ladies of the harem.
Among other things, I'm dated for a Chinese dinner with the visitor that I mentioned in my last. She and I certainly had ourselves a time after I had finished my
letter to you! One of our little stunts was bathing in an irrigation ditch, sans everything but our shoes, by starlight! The rest, however, can be told only in poetry.

As ever,
Clark

Notes

1. *SP* contained no epigrams or prose poems.
2. Published as "To the Daemon of Sublimity."
3. I.e., Rah Hoffman.

[152] [DW to CAS] [TLS]

1152 Portland Ave.,
St. Paul 5, Minn.
March 14, 1946

Dear Clark:

One of my old friends, Audrey Johnson Brunet, and rather a good artist in her own right, says that she met you two or three years ago during an exhibit at Sacramento. Small world. I'm hoping to have her do one of the Arkham House jackets.

Derleth and I are still eagerly awaiting the poetry collection, which will be scheduled for publication as quickly as we receive it. I may go down to Sauk City again late next month for one of our periodic meetings. As you probably know, my revised and vastly improved SONNETS OF THE MIDNIGHT HOURS will appear in the forthcoming anthology of weird verse,[1] and a revision of my old novel, re-titled THE WEB OF EASTER ISLAND, is slated for next year. Currently I'm working on a new novel, tentatively titled POSSESSION, which looks very promising. Apparently never completed and now non-extant. It's in the field of fantasy and horror, but is somewhat different from other tales of mine, and could have an appeal wider than its specialized field.

The winter has been a most trying one, for I was laid up much of the time with a skin infection inherited from Europe which developed a far more serious secondary infection that sent me out to the VA hospital. They were very stubborn in responding to treatment, but are much improved now, and will, I expect, be entirely gone in another two or three weeks. At least I can be grateful that I came out of the war with nothing worse.

Are you in Auburn now? Writing any new poems or tales? Or still engaged in war work in the coastal cities? What is new, interesting, or current?

I've been trying to find a cabin or cottage on one of the Minnesota lakes to which I could retire for as much of the spring, summer, and fall as I wished and work as hard as I please free from interruptions, but it's a poor year to be looking. Real estate is scarce and prices high. What is offered is mostly year-round residences, or resort developments, whereas I want something secluded and wild, away from the maddening crowds. I won't feel too disappointed if I don't find what I want.

Let me hear from you, when you've time. As ever,
Donald

Notes

1. *Dark of the Moon,* ed. August Derleth.

[153] [DW to CAS] [TLS]

1152 Portland Ave.,
St. Paul 5, Minn.
Oct. 2, 1946

Dear Clark:

If this reaches you, I would very much like to hear from you—where you are and what you are doing. I've written several times since my exit from the Army a year ago, but perhaps my letters haven't reached you. Derleth says he had word several months ago, and thought you had left Auburn, but couldn't remember where. At any rate, we both are quite anxious to know if you've been able to make any progress on the collected poems, which happens to be a special, pet project of mine for Arkham House.

After I got Derleth's note, it occurred to me that perhaps you have continued working at some war job that does not give you the time to prepare the book, and possibly keeps you away from Auburn for such prolonged periods that you have not access to the files material.

In this connection, I have a couple of alternative suggestions to make, if they would be of any help in advancing the project. One possibility would be for you, on your next stay in Auburn, simply to bundle up everything that contains a line of your poetry, typescripts, manuscripts, magazines, anything, everything, and ship the whole works to me. I'll run off a complete and exact typescript in 3 copies, and return the whole works together with 2 of the typed copies to you. Then it should be a fairly easy matter for you to go through the typed sheets, strike out any poem you don't want, make as many and as extensive changes as you wish. One corrected copy you would keep, and send the other to me for re-typing to prepare the final copy for the book. This final copy would again be sent to you for any last changes or corrections.

This sounds, perhaps, a trifle complicated, but actually should involve no more work on your part than simply wrapping and mailing or shipping by express a parcel, and later a few evenings editing the typewritten copies to your satisfaction.

The second alternative would be for me to make a trip to Auburn and do the work on the spot. This also I am in position to do if it would be more satisfactory to you, since I realize that probably many of your poems exist in single copies only which might be irretrievably lost in the unlikely event that anything happened to the shipment. My memory of Auburn has grown rather hazy with the years. Let me know if it has a hotel—I suppose it has—and what is more important, whether it's as jammed as those in larger cities. If you would prefer that I take care of the typing on the spot, I'd likely need a couple of weeks or so.

In any case, I would be delighted to hear from you; and I hope all the tidings are good.

I spent a wonderfully happy summer at a cottage I bought on a trout-stream in wild and secluded country in Wisconsin. It was doubly fortunate for me, since we had, and are still having, the worst polio epidemic ever recorded here.

As ever,

Donald

[154] [CAS to DW] [TLS]

Auburn, Cal.,

Oct. 8th, 1946.

Dear Donald:

I am sorry to have been such a dilatory correspondent. But I have had it in mind to write you dozens of times. No doubt I have become the world's worst correspondent—in direct contrast to Lovecraft, who was easily the best!

I have not been away from Auburn for any long periods but have done a certain amount of seasonal agricultural work, which of course can, or could have been, classed as essential war work. My last two bouts of it were unusually fatiguing and I am only now beginning to recover a little energy and ambition.

Some of my delay with the preparation of the poems has been due to revisory labors: I wanted to make as many improvements as possible before starting the final typing. Also, repeated search has failed to uncover the mss. of many early efforts, which may have been destroyed in spite of my impression that copies still existed. I have given up any present hope of finding them and am now starting the final typing of the opus. With any luck, and in spite of my chronic eyestrain, I should have it finished, or nearly finished, by the end of the year.

I have decided against regrouping the poems according to type and subject, which might, particularly in the case of the love-lyrics, lead to a certain impression of monotony. The French translations, however, can best be grouped together; also the various prose-poems, which can come most fittingly at the volume's end. What I shall do, mostly, is to preserve a rough chronological order: the Star-Treader poems first, followed by a few unpublished items written a[t]the same time or a little later; then Ebony and Crystal, with unpublished items belonging in the same group, etc., etc.

You are more than generous to suggest undertaking the typing yourself! Some [of] the earlier mss. (not typewritten) are palimpsests that would baffle any but the perpetrator! Anyway, you are doing enough (and I think sometimes, in my disillusionment, more than enough) in publishing the volume.

I am glad that you had such a happy summer in idyllic surroundings. I had a pleas[a]nt two weeks sojourn on the coast in April, spending part of the time with Helen and her husband and bonny infant in Berkeley, part with friends in San Francisco, and winding up with a weekend at Carmel and Pt. Lobos. Since then, poverty has confined me to my somewhat arid native heath.

Here is a recent snap that you may like to have, taken with my youngest girl friend.

Faithfully,

Clark

[Enclosure: Photograph of CAS and child (Helen Sully's?).]

[155] [DW to CAS] [TLS] [fire-damaged on right margin]

1152 Portland Ave.,

St. Paul 5, Minn.

June 27, 1948

Time of the Angled Extension of the Dweller in the Vortex of Dzö

Dear Klarkash-Ton:

At long last, after more than a year of perusal, I have finished my [editing] of the Lovecraft letters, and tomorrow will send the remaining typescript _____ to Derleth. He in turn will have to eliminate some of my choices, for I ma[_____] everything that I wanted to see published if there was all the money in the [world?] available. Since there isn't, Derleth must reduce my selections to publishi[_____] reason. This has been in truth a labor of love, for just as your poems and [stories?] formed the peak of emotional and esthetic exaltation in my life, so the Lov[ecraft] letters represented the peak of intellectual liberation. It was, indeed, with [a] feeling of most poignant regret that I read the last sentence of the last let[ter] and left the infinite range of a mighty mind. The publication of the Lovecraft letters was the original goal of Arkham House, toward which all other Arkham House volumes were, as it were, mere groundwork. But irrespective of publicat[ion] I count myself among the most fortunate of living men, in having one of the o[nly] two typescripts of the bulk of the Lovecraft letters. It will be out of my po[ssession?] for a number of months, until the typist has re-copied the selections marked [for] publication, but will then be returned to me. At that time, if you have any interest in reading letters to other correspondents, I will be most happy to s[end] any or all of such volumes as you may care to read on to you—and I may add th[at] you are the only other mortal to whom I would relinquish them. They are a fabu[lous] and inexhaustible mine of ideas, concepts, rationalism, esthetics, knowledge, humor, fantasy, comment, appraisal, speculative inquiry, data, and fancy—all [_____] rich amplitude of a fetterless and fearless mind. I have been raving about Lov[ecraft's] letters for years, just as I have chanted the praise of your own magnificent cosmic imaginings to many an indifferent cold and occasionally responsive lis[tener.] Truly I believe that Lovecraft's reputation may rest more on his letters than o[n] his tales.

But my first discovery—and that through mention of you by Lovecraft i[n] the WEIRD TALES Eyrie more than two decades ago—in the field of cosmic mindedn[ess—] was EBONY AND CRYSTAL and subsequent Klarkash-Tonic splendors of poem and prose and color and line. As Lovecraft looked back across the years to his discovery [of] Dunsany, so I look back to the reading of Clark Ashton Smith as the magical ape[x] of literary enjoyment, the utmost flowering of that incredibly rare human gift [of] cosmic perception which I have wished so often I possessed in higher degree myse[lf.] For me, ARKHAM HOUSE will have existed for a dual purpose: the Lovecraft letters and the collected Smith poems, each of which volumes will be a publication uniqu[e] in its field and designed above all for my constant enrichment of cosmic travell[ing.] I hope that other mortals follow, but if they do not, the more fools they.

Thus, I am very interested indeed in finding out how you are progressing in the preparation of your collected poems. I hope that you are well along with them, for I look forward with the most intense anticipation to the reading of the typescript. Derleth and I have talked over the general problem of typography and format, but decided it would be useless to make any decisions until we had the typescript on hand and could take it up with the printers.

You were very nearly the recipient of an extended visit from me this year—and may yet be so beset next winter! An aunt of mine offered for sale her re-built 1938 De Soto for $700, and, having sold my cottage on the Willow this spring, I was greatly tempted to buy the car and drive to California. This was to be, and will be if I go in the fall or winter, no pleasure trip, but primarily a search to find a place for permanent settlement. My mother who spent a month with relatives in Los Angeles in February of 1947 would like to move west; and I myself would like a place of my own if one could be found at something le[ss than] the current inflated prices. My original thought had been to drive west, [_____] different communities, and if I found anything satisfactory to settle and [have my] own things shipped on; or if nothing proved available, to sell the car in [_____] and fly to New York. My aunt still has the car. However, I will under pre[ssure to] leave soon for New York, to finish some commitments I made, which will be [_____] by October or November.

I have been expecting the page proofs any day of my novel THE WEB OF [EASTER] ISLAND—the same which you saw in the early '30's but completely re-written [and] very greatly improved. I will, of course, send you a copy when the book is r[eady] in late July or August. This brings me to another point. When THE EYE AND THE FINGER was published in 1944, I received two bundles of 5 copies each at Camp Shelby, Mississippi, and mailed them out to friends including you. This past winter, in New York, I learned to my complete consternation that no less than t[wo?] of the recipients never received their copies. Although the book is out of print, I had half-a-dozen copies left and replaced the lost volumes. Now, I would like [to] know if you too failed to receive a copy, for if so I still have 3 left and will gladly send one on. I am convinced that one entire batch of the original 5 may [have] somehow got destroyed near Camp Shelby, perhaps in an army post-office fire or baggage-car wreck or something of the sort.

The household here had two unusual additions during my years in the Army, in the aristocratic personages of two stately Persian cats. These felidae are large and long-haired, and beautiful to behold. One is a solid and lustrous oyster-grey, the other an equally solid and richly resplendent black, a black so intense that in sunlight it seems to take on an undertone of the darkest red imaginable. They speak but little, having super-mundane means of communication that scorn such un-cosmic and primitive modes of interchange as speech. They ought to bear names as distinguished as their royal appearances, something of the order of Haroun Al Raschid and Afreet. Instead, my unimaginative sister,[1] with an Olympian disdain of the appropriateness of things, has saddled these princely felidae with the incongruously Hibernian appellations, PETE and MIKE!!! Shades of Shuleima! Shantih, Shantih, Shantih! Shards of Shamballah! By the way—what is the origin of the Shamballah myth-cycle? Lovecraft alludes to it frequently in his letters but never to its source. I gather only that it derives from some branch of Theosophy.

It was a pleasure to see TO THE CHIMERA reprinted in the September WEIRD TALES which I got today—but a curse on the typesetter who pluralized "desire" and converted "below thee fading" into the hash of "blow thee fading". Indeed, after your own proof-reading of your collected poems I shall proof-read them myself, in the hope of achieving that rarest of all printing products—an errorless book. I almost succeeded when I proof-read Lovecraft's THE OUTSIDER, but a single misprint escaped me.

I have begun a new novel of cosmic fantasy, which I am sure will be much superior to THE WEB and which I hope is at least half as good in the writing as in the conception. It is an idea that has haunted me for years, the story of a man who falls in love with what seems to be a woman of unusual beauty, and his gradually mounting terror and cosmic dispersal as he discovers that the woman-body is simply a temporary form assumed by an infinitely higher and more cosmically complex form of life the true nature of which he never discovers. This idea of intimate human contact with something totally non-human and cosmically alien for some reason produces in me an emotion of profound horror, as deep in its way as Lovecraft's horror of the Antarctic and cold. I've had two different titles for this brain-buster, POSSESSION and THE STRANGER IN THIS BODY. I'm not sure which will win out—

perhaps neither if I dream up a title I like better.

I hope that this letter finds you in the best of health and in the process of creating new marvels for my enjoyment.

As ever,

Prinn Von Drei

[P.S.] [Don']t know which of my alter egos I shall adopt—[the ob]vious "Don Juan", the current Germanicized [____]ich, or some other eventual new cabalistic combination!

Von Drei

Notes

1. Jeannette Alberta Wandrei (1913–1972).

[156] [CAS to DW] [TLS]

6666th autumnal equinox of the black yuga.[1]

[17 October 1948]

Dear Donald:

If you had received all the letters I have intended to write, you would be in possession of a sizable file of correspondence by now!

It was certainly good news to hear that you had finished the editing of the Lovecraft letters. I can well realize the monumental scope of this labor of devotion, and the fabulous and inestimable riches uncovered by it. I can never quite accustom myself to the strangeness, and the sense of irremediable loss, in no longer receiving letters that were to me, as well as to you and others, a stimulus without parallel. Indeed, I shall be most grateful to read some of the volumes if you will loan them to me at your convenience; and am inclined to leave the choice to you.

As for my poems, the remaining labor is largely one of assembling and typing and should not take so long if I could only settle down to it. The heaviest revision, some of it including the partial or entire recasting of poems, has been on the Star-Treader group and certain unpublished pieces of the same or a slightly posterior date. These are all typed in triplicate. Revision of old work is a hellish task; but I hope that I have salvaged some poems which, in their original form, were too inferior or uneven. For instance, take the new octave of a sonnet in The Star-Treader, called The Unrevealed,[2] in which only one line remains as originally written:

> What close prenatal palls occlude from us
> Once-prevalent Signs, once-rampant arms! How straight
> The sunless road, suspended, separate,

That leads from death to birth. Not luminous
With lodestar, or with star calamitous,
The past is closed as by the night-black spate
Of planet-gulfing seas—its keyless gate
Lost in Avernian shadows cavernous.

The revisions on later work are comparatively slight and minor, apart from my Baudelaire translations, some of which I have retouched considerably. There must be around forty of these in all. I enclose one of the more exotic Fleurs, Sed non Satiata, which has cost me a lot of trouble.

I have made a few changes in The Hashish-Eater, designed mainly to vary the cadence of the blank verse. And there are three new stanzas for The Nereid to be inserted preceding the last stanza:

The berylline pallors of her face
Illume the kingdom of the drowned.
In her the love that none has found
The unflowering rapture, folded grace,

Await some lover strayed and lone,
Some god misled, who shall not come
Though the decrescent seas lie dumb
And sunken in their wells of stone.

But nevermore of him, perchance,
Her enigmatic musings are—
Whose purpling tresses float afar
In grottoes of the last romance.

There is a considerable mass of uncollected material which has accumulated subsequent to Sandalwood, and I shall try to start typing this shortly, leaving the pages unnumbered (as I have done with the earlier poems) until the entire typescript is finished. It will fall into three main sections; one, Incantations, including most of my later weird and fantastic poems, as well as miscellaneous material; and the other two, The Jasmine Girdle and The Hill of Dionysus, being sequences of love-poems, many of which are in themselves more or less touched with strangeness and fantasy. I have too a few satires, travesties on modernism, vers libre, etc, of which I enclose the most recent specimens, Surrealist Sonnet and Sonnet for the Psychoanalysts. There are also some poems in French, two or three of which seem correct enough in diction, grammar, etc., for possible inclusion.

I hope you will like some of the enclosures—a rather motley lot. Such recent lyrics as Calenture and Some Blind Eidolon strike me as being probably among my best. The experiments in haiku, the so-called "one-breath" Japanese form, seem to have evoked rather various reactions in those who have read them; some thinking the form too fragmentary, too exotic for domestication in English. However, I believe that others, such as Amy Lowell and John Gould Fletcher, have experimented with it. Personally I like the form, into which almost any sort of single impression or image can be distilled.[3]

Anyway, I am anxious to finish the typing of all this material and get it into your hands; and wish the task were further advanced. The last two years, however, have been rather hellish ones for me, since I have had almost no money to live on, and have been stone broke for weeks at a time. Oct. 1947 was the worst period, and I'm hoping that I can somehow avert another quite as bad.

Anent some of the things in your letter. I *did* receive The Eye and the Finger, and thought I had thanked you for it years ago. The book is one of the most highly prized items in my shelf of Arkham House publications. I certainly enjoyed re-reading The Web of Easter Island, and think you have improved marvellously on the ms. that you showed me so many years back. It was a pleasure to review the book for The Arkham Sampler.

Your idea for a new novel of cosmic fantasy is what the late H. S. Whitehead would have called a "honey-cooler," and strikes me as having infinite possibilities. I wonder if the old ecclesiastical word *energumen,* meaning a possessed person, would appeal to you as a title, or part of a title.

I imagine that Lovecraft derived his information about Shamballah from E. Hoffmann Price, who in turn probably drew the data from Blavatsky or some other theosophical authority. I have some notes that Price gave me, in which Shamballah is mentioned:

"The word came from Shamballah, the Holy City, to destroy Atlantis 850,000 years ago, and overthrow the Lords of the Dark Face. The divine race of Aarab escaped the catastrophe, and in Al Yemen they reared the mighty Himyar palaces, with prodigious bulks, uncounted domes."

S. is supposed to exist, invisible, somewhere in the Gobi desert. It was, I seem to remember, built by the Lords of the Flame who came down from Venus. In it is kept the Book of Dzyan, older than the world.

I hope fervently that you do come to California this fall or winter. Prices are horribly inflated here; but perhaps a place of settlement could be found.

Yours, under the seal of Dagon and all the Ashtaroth,
KlarKash-Ton

Notes

1. In Hindu philosophy, a *yuga* is an epoch or era referring to a cycle of four ages.

2. The poem appeared in *SP* as "The Unremembered." The original lines in *ST* (57) are as follows:

How dense the glooms of Death, impervious
To aught of old memorial light! How strait

The sunless road, suspended, separate,
That leads to later birth! Untremulous
With any secret morn of stars, to us
    The Past is closed as with division great
    Of planet-girdling seas—unknown its gate,
Beyond the mouths of shadows cavernous.

3. In the late 1940s, CAS assisted Kenneth Yasuda (1914–2002) of Auburn, the Japanese-American translator and scholar, render Japanese haiku in English. CAS himself wrote more than 100 haiku, many of which he included in *SP* under the title "Experiments in Haiku," a subset of which was titled "Distillations."

[157] [CAS to DW] [TLS]

Auburn, Calif.,
Oct. 20th, 1949.

Temps du haut marée de la mer noire en le Saturne[1]

Mon cher Donald:
        I have just finished the typing of all the poems that seem possible for inclusion in my volume. The pile of triplicate pages, which I have yet to sort out, number and index, is about seven inches deep. I'm certainly breathing a huge sigh of relief, since typing alone—not to mention all the brain-curdling problems of revision I have more or less solved—is a tedious task for me. But I've stuck at it day after day for several months, practically going broke in the process. The blasted financial angle alone has kept me from finishing it years ago.
    Not knowing whether you are in St. Paul, New York, or elsewhere, I am uncertain where to send your typescript, but will no doubt have it ready to ship by the time I hear from you. Have you given up the idea of coming to California? I had somehow hoped that you might turn up in Auburn during the past year.
    When you get the poems, you will note that they are grouped mainly, though not entirely, in chronological order. The translations, a small anthology in themselves, follow Sandalwood, thus occupying about the middle of the book; but some of them have been done quite recently. Incantations, which follows the translations, is a melange including work from 1925 up to the present. The more personal love poems (with a few exceptions) are grouped at the end in the two small collections, The Jasmine Girdle and The Hill of Dionysus. Some of my miscellaneous erotica, and other odds and ends, I have listed as translations from the French of one Christophe des Laurières (an old and privately used pseudonym of mine.)[2] Also, you will find occasional poems of my own in French scattered through the volume, and am wondering if you know any French scholar who could overhaul them for possible flaws. If

you and August decide to use any of them, I could provide literal translations to accompany them or be added in an appendix.

When I get this book off my hands, I believe I'll be able to finish up some of the various fiction that I have started or plotted.

With affectionate regards, as always,

Clark

Notes

1. "Time of the high tide of the black sea in Saturn."
2. There are 22 items in *SP* attributed to des Laurières.

[158] [DW to CAS] [TLS]

% E. R. Morton,
32 Schermerhorn St.,
Brooklyn 2, N.Y.
Nov. 17, 1949

Seventh Vortex of the Dimensional Prism of 'Q'x

Hour of the Extension of the Absolute

Dear Klark-Ash-Ton:

Your letter caught up with me about three weeks ago, but I have been in a state of flux to say the least, and must apologize not only for not writing sooner, but for being so long-overdue in not replying to a previous letter. Briefly, I've been working on a play which I finally finished early last month. It's in the hands of an agent now. I also had a lease on an apartment in the Village which expired toward the end of October, and I then moved over to the above address staying temporarily with some old friends. Next Sunday night I am flying to St. Paul to spend Thanksgiving with my mother and to take care of some small business matters. About the middle of December I will return here, and stay with the Mortons long enough to find what I hope will be a sub-let till April, at which time I expect to return to Minnesota, and later in the year get started at long last toward California. Getting involved in the play was the main factor in the postponement of my plans, though I have also heard not very cheerful reports on the housing problem in California.

I am delighted to hear that the Collected Poems are ready, and I look forward indeed to perusing them with infinite pleasure. I think you may as well address them to 1152 Portland Ave., St. Paul 5, Minn. They ought to arrive while I am there. Since I will do the proof-reading, probably the original copy should go to me, that being the copy that will also go to the printers. The duplicate can go to Derleth; or if it will make things any simpler, you can send both copies to 1152 Portland, since I will be stopping off at Sauk City on my way back to New York, and can take Augie's copy along with me.

The inclosures were read, of course, with the same delight as always; I like best MORS and THE WHISPER OF THE WORM. I have always found it hard to make a choice among your poems, since all of them have for me a special kind of magic that I have never found elsewhere.

Yes, it will be a simple matter to have a French scholar authenticate the French poems, either through my old contacts at the U. of Minnesota, or Augie's at the U. of Wisconsin. We have no intention of omitting anything, by the way, the whole point being to print the collected poems as you want them.

I myself am thoroughly tired of New York and the confinement of life-in-a-rabbit-warren. I want and need a more open and leisurely kind of living than is possible here, and I still believe that California is more likely to give me that kind of living than any other part of the country. I hope to find something within sight and sound of the ocean, which has always fascinated me. My only purpose in coming back to New York for a few months this winter is to find out whether anything will happen with the play, and to make some contacts in television which may be useful if I end up anywhere in the Los Angeles area. I also expect to do some magazine short stories, in fields of more general interest than any thing I've tried in the past. But 1950 in my calendar is marked California.

The best of luck on your new fiction, which I anticipate reading as the tales appear. In the meantime, when the Collected Poems arrive, I shall revel in more splendors than ever existed in time or space.

With affectionate regards,

as always,

Donald

[159]   [CAS to DW] [TLS]

Auburn, Calif.,

Nov. 22nd, 1949.

Dear Donaldius:

I was glad to get your letter, and am certainly anticipating your eventual arrival in California. Your idea of settling in sight of the sea accords with my own tastes: I have long wished that I could afford to live on the coast, preferably either in Marin County, north of the Bay, or in the Monterey section. I don't know Southern California, but believe it is more congested than the Superior portion of the state. There are plenty of places to rent in the inland section where I live; and I doubt if it would be too difficult to obtain one on the Marin coast of the peninsula south of San Francisco. I expect to spend Christmas in San Francisco, and will make inquiries.

Here's wishing you the best of fortune with your play. Have you done anything with the fantastic novel that you outlined to me some time back? I hope that I can sometime muster enough sustained energy to finish The Infernal Star, of which I wrote about 12,000 words some years ago. It should run to a long novelette or short novel. Another opus that I have rather vaguely planned is The Scarlet Succubus,[1] an erotic fantasy of Zothique, which will concern the curious happenings that ensued the breaking of a vial in which the Succubus, a spirit of unearthly and exorbitant luxury, had been imprisoned by the saint Yos Ebni;[2] said vial having been sacriliegiously [*sic*] stolen at the prompting of a mischievous wizard from the urn containing the sacred ashes of the saint, by a libertine and a gay lady looking for some novel mode of amusement. Thereafter the moral corruption of Zothi[q]ue begins to exceed all carnal limits and assumes ultramundane forms and colors! This tale was suggested by Balzac's The Succubus (in The Droll Stories) but will not bear too much resemblance to that remarkable opus.

I'll send the poems on (both first and second copies) as soon as I have drawn up a table of contents and rectified an error of paging in the carbon, caused by the accidental insertion of an extra sheet. Have you ever numbered the pages of a typescript by *hand?* It took me hours to do the job! Counting the separate title pages, etc., the book runs to 393 pages, double-spaced and continuously typed. I've included a brief appreciation by Benjamin DeCasseres, as well as the Sterling preface to Ebony and Crystal; but would be delighted if you and August were to add a brief foreword. DeCasseres errs at one point, it seems to me, when he says that there is "no variation" in my poems. In fact, there is so much variation, from first to last, that I see no reason why the book should not appeal, at least in part, to almost any lover of classic English poetry. The extreme modernists, of course, will disregard it; and you will note that I have inserted (in Incantations) a small group of bitter satires and parodies on the more cryptic and sordid excesses of modernistic writing.

As to printing *everything,* I did not really expect, when I typed these poems, that all of them would see print, but merely wished to afford a wide choice for selection. It would not hurt my feelings if some of the slighter lyrics were omitted; possibly, also, one or two of the poems listed as translations from Christophe des Laurières (an old and privately used pseudonym of mine) are too frankly erotic for general circulation. I refer in particular to the sonnet Concupiscence, of which Sterling said that Baudelaire "would have given an eyetooth to have written it;" which shows, I think, that G.S. did not understand Baudelaire very well. Verlaine or Pierre Louys might have written such a sonnet; but not the author of Les Fleurs du Mal, whose sensuality is *never* simple and pagan but is usually complicated by a curious medievalism not far removed from the viewpoint of a St. Anthony. At this point I might say that I think my poetry (apart from certain macabre and exotic elements) has very little real resemblance to that of Baudelaire; in fact, the underlying viewpoint, if not the technique, has more in common with Poe and Verlaine. I have written perhaps one poem (Some Blind Eidolon, p. 305) which contains or even implies a moral idea; whereas B. was obsessed by the idea of original sin and "the abject wickedness of man." However, if my poetry stands for anything, it does stand for the absolute freedom of the human imagination, and implies a profound revolt against current standards, not only in literature but in life.

When you compare my typescript with the volumes already published, you will note numerous alterations, ranging from the substitution (or in some cases omission) of adjectives to the recasting of entire passages or the insertion of fresh ones as in Song of a Comet and Ode on Imagination. There are comparatively few revisions in Ebony and Crystal; but one sonnet (The Mirrors of Beauty) has been partially recast to vary and enrich the imagery; and The Medusa of Despair even more extensively rewritten to embody what seems to me a subtler and profounder conception—that is, of despair as a dynamic rather than merely negative energy. Hence such lines as "Thy visage carven from the heart long dead / Of some white, frozen star" are replaced by "Thy face / Lethal as are the pale young suns in space," and the Medusa becomes a recommended substitute for "the flameless Furies" embraced by the dark gods. If you should ever publish a variorum edition of my poems, you will certainly have abundant material! However, if you think I have erred in any of my changes, please tell me so: I have merely followed my own instinct which is, I fear, one that can never be wholly satisfied anyway.

Such changes as I have made in The Hashish-Eater (apart from the addition of new lines in the passage beginning "I am page / To an emperor who reigns ten thousand years") are designed mainly to vary the cadence of the blank verse.

You will note some omissions of published poems, many of which are due to the fact that I have not so far been able to bring the poems in question up to the standard I have set. Also, some unfinished and fragmentary pieces have been typed for possible use. Fragments are often more suggestive than completed poems. As a matter of fact, such a poem as The Saturnienne is merely the first part of what I had originally planned as a much longer composition.

You will perhaps be surprised by some of my experimentations, such as the cinquains[3] and *haiku* which form the last section of Incantations. I owe my interest in the latter form to a young Japanese poet (a native of this locality) who brought me a manuscript volume of haiku (translations from Japanese originals) several years ago, for criticism and advice. This poet, Kenneth Yasuda, has since had a volume of such work brought out by Knopf with an appreciative preface by John Gould Fletcher. Though the form has been little used by English-writing poets (Fletcher himself and Amy Lowell are, I believe, about the only ones who have employed it) I believe that it deserves domestication. The form is designed to present a single picture or image in the compass of not more than eighteen or nineteen syllables, and the Japanese rules for its composition are very strict, involving the verbal equivalent of actual pictorial perspective—that is to say, the object nearest to the imaginary spectator must be mentioned first, and others in order of recession! (I fear that I have sometimes violated this rule!)

Apart from the group entitled Strange Miniatures, most of my haiku have been drawn from personal impressions and experience, and form what is really my main contribution to "regional poetry." They have provoked widely varied reactions from readers, some being wildly enthusiastic and one or two (such as Stanton Coblentz)[4] considering the form too fragmentary and exotic for English poetry. One curious thing is, that they have been hailed with delight by comparatively unlettered readers. What fascinates me is the emotional and imaginative suggestion, the overtones that can sometimes be concentrated in so brief a compass. One of my own favorites is Night of Miletus:

> "When I saw you dance
> Milesian roses swayed in the wind
> Of a lost romance."

This bit, for me, has a double element of evocation, since, apart from suggesting the lost and naughty Tales of Miletus, it also symbolizes a personal romance . . . But of course, symbolism is a wide open field; and Christ knows *what* symbols will eventually be deduced from my writings by variously imaginative readers. I've already heard of some that are pretty fantastic.

As to French poems, I have tried not to overload the book with such experiments, of which I have a number. There are eight in all; the first being a French rendering of Alexandrines, and following this poem in the revised Ebony and Crystal. Paysage Paien is a partial parap[h]rase of my English poem, Fantasie D'Antan, which Derleth used in his anthology Dark of the Moon. Une Vie Spectrale (one of the best, I think) is similar to the English poem Revenant, which it follows in Incantations. Two of the poems, Au Bord du Léthé, and L'espoir du Néant were overhauled many years ago by Alfred Galpin, Jr., a fine French scholar with whom I am now out of touch. I adapted his suggestions as to verbal and metrical changes. Probably any further changes necessary will narrow down to the use of a few conjunctions and prepositions; though there is one bad rhyme, "perdus" and "doux", in Paysage Paien, which would no doubt make a Parnassian howl. Incidentally, French rhyming is a curious business: accented endings such as boisé, fané, etc, don't constitute rhymes at all unless there is an identity of the consonant as well as the vowel. That is to say, boisé rhymes only with such words as pensé and fané with mené, etc., etc. The sounding of the mute e in French verse is very pleasing to me, and I regret sometimes that the English language ever departed from the old Chaucerian usage in this respect. Yeats made a noble effort to revive the accented e in past participles, which would certainly make for euphony and relieve many a consonantal plexus.

Well, I seem to have run to what journalists would call an "extra."

Here's wishing you a happy Thanksgiving. For once, I seem likely to spend mine alone, and will treat my old tom-cat, variously known as Senor Tigre, Monsieur Pied-Blanc, Bumbo, and Balls, with some canned fish. I fear some of these names would have shocked Lovecraft; on the other hand, they would hardly shock E. Hoffman[n] Price, who is also a redoubtable cat-lover.

With affectionate regards,

Clark (or)

Klark-ash Ton

Notes

1. This work was apparently never finished or even begun.
2. The late "sage and archimage" in "The Witchcraft of Ulua."
3. In *SP* the poems are instead labeled "Quintrains."
4. Stanton A. Coblentz (1896–1982), American writer, poet, and anthologist. He printed many poems by CAS in *Wings* and reprinted some in his anthologies *The Music Makers* (1945) and *Unseen Wings* (1949).

[160] [DW to CAS] [TLS]

1152 Portland Ave.,

St. Paul 5, Minn.

Dec. 1, 1949

Dear Clark:

That was an exceptionally interesting letter which I have read several times. I shall use it for reference and comparison when I receive the Collected Poems, which I look forward to perusing with unmitigated pleasure. What you say of your own poems naturally has a special value to me, and I am completely in agreement with you in your observations on poetry in general. The haiku form is not new to me—I first came across it many years ago when I read a book of translations called, if I remember, ORNAMENTS IN JADE, from the Chinese.[1] I did some further reading in translations from Japanese, and then by some curious process of westerly progression through the Orient I delved into Hindu poetry, Persian, Arabic, French translations from the Arabic, and thus eventually made the full circle back to English and American from which I had originally started! Indeed, not since the mid-30's have I read any non-English poetry except your own experiments in French. The haiku can be highly effective in several ways ranging from a cameo-like incisive clarity of imagery to shadowy adumbration of things and a haunting suggestion of elusive mystery. But the strict brevity of the form does make it in a sense only a single pipe compared with the full organ-range of say, THE HASHISH EATER.

Incidentally, while home I have been going through and rearranging old and accumulated files of correspondence, records, etc., among which are all the poems I have extracted from all your letters since 1926, the letters themselves being in a separate file. There are well over 100 of the poems, closer to

200 I should say at an off-hand calculation, and I shall use them too in comparison with your own Collection. If there are any that you have omitted and which I think ought to be included I will write and find out if you have any objections to their being so included.

I have indeed thought many times of a Variorum Edition of all your poems. I only hope I earn enough some day to carry out such an ambitious project. Whether my play will earn anything is problematical. At the moment, my agent, who thought it would make a better motion-picture than stage play, has sent it to his Hollywood affiliate who presumably is trying to make a direct sale of it to one of the producers.

I am returning to New York on Dec. 15, and will be staying for a few weeks anyway with an old friend, ℅ E. R. Morton, 32 Schermerhorn St., Brooklyn 2, N.Y. While I've long since had my fill of the east, I have some unfinished business to take care of, and want to make a number of editorial contacts and perhaps some television ones also, prior to pulling up stakes. My tentative schedule is to leave N.Y. for good about May 1, come back here and finish getting all my belongings in order, and perhaps in July or August start driving to the West. I have a great many relatives and several friends scattered from Spokane to San Diego and from Whitefish, Montana to Tucson. I would like to live in California for a year simply to determine whether I would want to live there permanently, before having my books and stuff sent on.

Where is the Marin peninsula? The California maps that I have are too small to show it. Is it hard by San Francisco, or farther down toward the Carmel vicinity? I had no definitive goal in mind, but I remember La Jolla most vividly as being a beautifully situated small town with marvellous rock formations along the beaches. The only other town I've seen like it, and it is, or was surprisingly similar when I last saw it, was Newport, Oregon, though the damp cold of Oregon coastal towns would, I fear, be more than I would care to endure in winter.

Anything you hear about rentals and housing will be deeply appreciated. Over the past couple of years I have from time to time bought the Sunday *San Francisco Chronicle, Los Angeles Times,* and *San Diego Union* for the Classified sections, but rentals were so far out of my reach—$100 a month and up— that I got discouraged. Then, too, friends who returned from winters in California gave a gloomy report even on veterans['] housing projects, with tales of outrageously-priced shacks at $10,000 and up—mostly up—many of which had begun to crack open and even to collapse the same year that they were built. Of course I realize that it is hard to get at the truth from a distance, and that I would probably need to be right there in order to explore all prospects. My principal reason for mentioning the L.A. vicinity was that I thought I might have better chances of earning a living in view of the concentration of both film studios and television and radio shows there. But I think I would be happy coming to rest at almost any point in California.

With affectionate regards, as always, Donaldius

Notes

1. DW confuses *Ornaments in Jade* (1924), a slim volume of prose poems by Arthur Machen, with Pih Yuh She Shoo, *Chinese Lyrics from the Book of Jade,* tr. by Judith Gautier as *Le livre de jade,* tr. James Whitall (London: Macdonald, 1919).

[161] [CAS to DW] [TLS]

Auburn, Calif.,
Dec. 10th 1949.

Dear Donaldius:

   Re your letter of the first: You are free to include any omitted items in your possession if you think them good enough. However, let me know *which* ones so that I can suggest their placing in the collection, and perhaps make emendations of text. I have a number of pieces that I was doubtful about.

  I await your reaction to the poems. Here is my latest experiment in French verse, which I believe to be tolerably correct in regard to diction and versification. Possibly, in one or two places, a different preposition, such as *à* instead of *en* would be preferable. I seem unable to get any expert advice hereabouts. A local French professor (retired) whom I consulted, was able to correct one error, but promptly followed this up by making *two* boners himself! Luckily, I was able to prove his errors. For instance, he insisted that *large* meant *long* in French. For this I can find absolutely no authority, either in dictionaries or in translations made by experts such as Lafcadio Hearn. The meaning of the word is broad, vast, or wide. Hearn translates a phrase in Fla[u]bert[']s Temptation of St. Anthony, "Des fleurs plus largs" as "vaster flowers;" and I had this phrase in mind when I wrote the line beginning "Des larges fleurs." I hope you can find a professor who appreciates French romantic writing, and has read Baudelaire, Verlaine and Mallarme as well as Victor Hugo. For some reason, I've never been able to work up much enthusiasm over Hugo, in spite of his many excellencies.[1]

  You will note that the first stanza of this poem, designed for repetition at the end, is highly elaborated in regard to alliteration and tone-color, sounds being repeated almost like musical notes. The idea embodied in the poem is one that has haunted me since early youth: back in 1913 I wrote some verses beginning:

> "In ultimate lone valleys evermore
> Immutable large purple blossoms bloom;
> Munificent unfading suns illume
> And amplest moons are perfect evermore."[2]

But the poem as a whole was far vaguer and more uneven than this "Camaieu in Red," which can be taken either as pure fantasy or as symbolizing the mental state of one who lives a detached and monotonous life, in an intellectual world unknown to those about him, and who steeps himself in the oblivion of gorgeous poetic imageries.

I hope your play goes over. I've wondered sometimes why producers of fantastic films have missed out on the spectacular possibilities of some of my tales, such as The Dark Eidolon and The Colossus of Ylourgne. It would be a help if I could ever make a little money.

Marin Co. is just *north* of San Francisco Bay. The peninsula to which I refer is the section lying immediately south of S. F. itself, and including Palo Alto, Redwood City, and Half Moon Bay, where Drake is said to have made a landing. I'll learn what I can about rentals when I see my friends, Eric and Madelynne Barker, with whom I expect to spend a hell-raising Christmas. Probably we'll have our dinner with Eric's mother, who lives near San Rafael, in Marin Co., in sight of Mt. Tamalpais.

Well, I guess this covers the ground for the moment.

Affectionately and fraternally,

Klarkash-Ton

[Enclosures: "Dans l'univers lointain" and "In a Distant Universe," on which CAS has written:] *amarante* is used in the sense of amaranthine color. I think the spelling *amaranthe* (preferable here) exists in French but can't find it in my Heath's Dictionary. I'm badly in need of a Larousse.

Notes

1. CAS, however, did translate a poem by Hugo: "The Wheel of Omphale" (in *CP* 3).
2. From an untitled poem (dated 12 December 1912) now titled "[In the Ultimate Valleys]" (*CP* 1).

[162] [DW to CAS] [TLS]

1152 Portland Ave.,

St. Paul 5, Minn.

Aug. 10, 1950

Dear Klarkash-Ton:

Since I last wrote, I returned to New York, finished up odds and ends there, and for the time being am here at the old hangout. I'll be here till the middle or end of October, when I will be heading for California, unless the Korean war gets to a point where gas is rationed.

My mother bought a new car, but the dealer offered such a small trade-in allowance for the old that she kept it. I told her I'd buy it myself for more than the dealer offered ($338). It's a 1941 Plymouth, that easily ought to be good for much more than a trip to California. I've been looking at the real estate listings in the Sunday San Francisco, Los Angeles, and San Diego papers from time to time, and notice that much more is available than a year or two ago. I like San Francisco as probably the most beautiful city I've ever seen, but for climate and nearness to ocean beaches I think I still prefer smaller places like La Jolla, Laguna, and Carmel. At any rate, I want to look them all over, and see if I can find some approximately ideal spot where I would be perfectly happy to live. San Francisco also seems to be the tightest city as far as housing is concerned, with very little available even now.

Of course I would drive through Auburn, or if you happen to be away I would stop off wherever you were. As it looks now, it would probably be the early part of November before I reached your vicinity, but I will let you know more definitely well ahead of time.

I did not stop to see Derleth en route from N.Y.—I flew home—but from correspondence I gather that book sales of Arkham House are down as is the case with most publishers. The projected *Letters* of Lovecraft is far behind schedule, though of course the immense typing problem is partly responsible. The volume will probably precede your own collected poems, though I regard the poems as a publication of equal importance with *The Outsider.* It will be one of the things to talk about in detail when I see you, since I'll probably have the typescript with me.

In New York I became a member of the Hydra Club, a loosely organized group of persons interested in various aspects of fantasy and science-fiction: writers, artists, editors, critics, scientists, fans, etc. I was fortunate in meeting Ray Bradbury during a business trip he made to N.Y., and I shall certainly look him up also in California. By a curious coincidence, he is a friend of the Curtis Harrington at the University of California at L.A. who is making an experimental art film of my story, *The Eye and the Finger.* This is under the direction of Kenneth MacGowan's Department of Theater Arts. The film ought to be finished by now, and I certainly am anxious to see it when I'm in the L.A. vicinity. It's on 16 mm. film.[1]

I hope this finds all well with you and with the felidae. My sister's two Persians, one jet-black and the other pearl-grey, are flourishing in their eighth year, and more active than usual at this time because of a remarkably cool summer. A curious happening has given us an accurate clue to their nocturnal perambulations. My sister has been repeatedly developing mild poison-ivy swellings on her arms. There is no poison-ivy anywhere on our block. But about two and a half blocks away from here is a railway tracks [*sic*] at the bottom of an embankment where poison-ivy grows. My sister, who is extremely sensitive to the stuff, is undoubtedly getting it by proxy from the cats' fur. The Persians have such long, thick fur that they are probably immune, as these handsome and princely creatures ought to be.

As ever,

Donald

Notes

1. The film, if completed, is apparently nonextant. Gene Curtis Harrington (1926–2007) was a film and television director who focused on experimental films and horror films early in his career. Kenneth MacGowan (1888–1963) was a film producer who in 1947 became the first chair of the Department of Theater Arts at UCLA.

[163] [DW to CAS] [TLS] [fire-damaged]

>1152 Portland Ave.,
>St. Paul 5, Minn.
>Nov. 1, 1950

Dear Klark-Ash-Ton:
>Unless there should be some unforeseeable development, I leave here on Nov. 10 and drive first to Sauk City to spend the Armistice Day week-end with Derleth. I leave Sauk City on Monday, the 13th, and should arrive in Auburn by the following week-end. The distance from Sauk City is just over 2,000 miles, and if I average 350 to 400 miles a day, I would arrive in Auburn late Friday or Saturday, the 17th or 18th.

>Needless to Say, [*sic*] I look forward with vast pl[easure] to seeing you again. I shall arrive with suitable [libation?] to Bacchus, to whom we must pay due homage as we in[tone] necromantic runes. Till then,

>>As ever,
>>Donald

[164] [DW to CAS] [TLS] [fire-damaged]

>1152 Portland Ave.,
>St. Paul 5, Minn.
>Nov. 8, 1950

[Dear Klark-A]sh-Ton:
>[The] inevitable has happened, and I won't be able [to leave] until Monday the 13th.

>[I bought] a brand-new 1950 high-compression engine [. . .], but have not yet got it back from the [garag]e to drive it around for a few days to break [. . .] it's working properly, before I take to [. . .]

>[. . .] Sauk City on Wed., the 15th, I should [. . . fo]llowing Mon. or Tues., the 20th or 21st. [. . .] more driving time than I had originally [. . .] engine can't be run at higher speed than [. . .] hour for the first 1,000 miles.

>[. . . un]less you hear from me again, the above is [. . .] and I look forward with the greatest anticipation [. . .] again in a car well-lubricated for human pleasures [. . .]nical needs.

As ever,

Donald

[165] [DW to CAS] [TLS]

1152 Portland Ave.,

St. Paul 5, Minn.

Nov. 12, 1950

Dear Klark-Ash-Ton:

There has been a slight additional delay at this end. I didn't get my car back from the garage until Thursday, and it must go back tomorrow for final adjustments and checkup. I have therefore scheduled my departure for Wednesday, Nov. 15. I will start west from Sauk City on Friday, the 17th. As closely as I can judge, I should be in Auburn Wednesday, the 22nd. However, we have already had the first snow here, in fact light snows for the past four days, and there is a real risk of my running into snowstorms in the Rockies that could delay me. Barring such intervention of the weather, however, I'll be seeing you in about 10 days.

I hope all is well with you.

As ever,

Donald

[166] [DW to CAS] [ANS]

[Postmarked North Platte, Nebr.,

Nov. 26, 1950.]

North Platte, Nebr., Nov. 17[?]

Dear Clark:

I'm on my way & ought to be in Auburn by Wed. night or early Thurs. morn. Snow here. If you haven't the nerve, I'd like to take you to Thanksgiving dinner. I forgot about that holiday when I made my plans. In Sauk City I had a short but pleasant visit with Derleth. I hope all goes well with you.

As ever,

Donald

[Front: Blank?]

[167] [DW to CAS] [TLS]

7760 Hollywood Blvd.,

Hollywood 46, Calif.

Dec. 13, 1950

Dear Klark-Ash-Ton:

I'm a little late in writing you my new address, but as you may imagine, I've been very busy getting settled and ready to operate. When I left you, I reached San Francisco without incident, spent the rest of the day with the Newtons, and stayed overnight on their spare cot. The drive to Los Angeles was farther than I had realized, and I ran into dense fog in the morning, so I stayed overnight at Santa Barbara, at a motel right on the beach. I got into Los Angeles about noon Sunday, and took the first apartment I looked at. It was in a good district, and within easy driving range of the various contacts I have and the people I wanted to see.

Since then, I've done the odds and ends of shopping I needed, got the basic groceries laid in, began establishing my contacts, and studied the map of the L.A. area and did enough driving to begin to be familiar with places and locations. It's all still quite new to me, but the novelty has begun to wear off. Actually, I like it so far very much, and I think I'll make out all right in Hollywood, in time. I had lunch with a friend in Beverly Hills, a few days ago, the first time I had occasion to drive out in that direction. Everything there is much newer and fancier than here in Hollywood, and I think that after a few months, when I am more familiar with the different areas of the city, and when I know more definitely how my writing, plans, and contacts develope, [*sic*] I'll probably settle down in Beverly Hills. But I'll be at this address for at least a few months, and I'll let you know before I move where I move.

You probably realized what an immense pleasure it was for me to see you again. My only regret was at the brevity of my stay, but I hope to make up for that the next time I am in Auburn, and that will be at an interval far shorter than the last gap between 1943 and 1950. I'll be delighted to see your poems, but I don't want you to use up precious hours making copies for me. I'd like to see your name on printed pages more often. I keep buying Weird Tales regularly, and it is always a disappointment when I don't come across a new tale of yours. I look at the science-fiction magazines too, though I seldom buy them unless they have stories by author-friends. With the markets so wide open and expanding, I certainly would like to see you ride the crest of the wave. I'd be doing it myself, except that motion-pictures appeal to me more at present, and I want to see how I fare with picture-scripts. I'm working now on a script, and I'll let you know how I make out. If you see Mrs. Sully, be sure to tell her how very sorry I am that she was not at home when we called. Perhaps we'll have better luck the next time.

As ever,

Donald

[On verso, in CAS's hand:]
   Dominium
      Isle of Saturn
         Shapes in the Sunset
            Don Quixote[1]

Notes

1. The poems appeared in *DC.*

[168] [DW to CAS] [TLS]

7760 Hollywood Blvd.,
Hollywood 46, Calif.
May 14, 1951

Dear Klark-Ash-Ton:

The new poems were a magical pleasure to me and, as always, it would be hard for me to single out any as my favorite where all are favorites. *The Dark Chateau* is splendid, but so is *Hesperian Fall,* and *Seeker,* and *Soliloquy in An Ebon Hall.* [*sic*] I sent *The Dead Will Cuckold You* on to Derleth, along with a note concerning a new volume of your recent poems, for you have certainly written enough of fine quality to make a separate volume. Getting out your COLLECTED POEMS is a real problem! As for Hollywood, *The Dead Will Cuckold You* is much too poetic and artistically imaginative. It is far over Hollywood's head, and probably over Karloff's[1] too.

I'm glad to hear about your new *Morthylla,* for while I've been getting *Weird Tales* regularly, the quality of the stories in it has been inferior for a long time. It's years since I've found in it a tale up to your standards, or HPL's.

The script I was working on is laid aside for the time being, by reason of my having developed a new collaboration with a new friend who lives at this same address, a man named Henry Barsha.[2] The convenience of being so close, of both of us having single status, of congenial temperaments, etc., have made this an ideal collaboration. We are about half-way into our screen play, but I will need to see it in complete rough draft before I can tell if it's good enough to sell. This is a story entirely of human characters and relationships, without any trace of fantasy or science-fiction, and up to now it interests me deeply. Henry hopes we can finish it in another month, but I think we'll be lucky if we do it in 2 more months. If I am ever to achieve any real kind of economic independence, I believe it is more likely to be accomplished here than anywhere else.

I'm sure I won't be doing any travelling, at least until Henry and I have finished our script. But Auburn has been on my mind often, and when I am next able to visit there again, I hope it can be with a little more leisure for me, and less pressure to get on to further destinations, as was the case last Thanksgiving.

I started a new science-fiction tale some months ago, and laid it aside also in order to develop the collaboration with Henry. I'll take up these other writings later on, but right now it seems more important to me to concentrate on the collaboration.

I'm inclosing a verse market list that I got for you weeks ago, then misplaced among other magazines. It is the best list that I know of, and I hope it

proves useful to you. May the shekels of Mammon flow back from the out-
pourings of the Muse!

Affectionately, as always,

Donald

Notes

1. Boris Karloff (stage name of William Henry Pratt, 1887–1969), English actor noted for roles in horror movies.

2. Little is known about Henry Barsha (b. 1901?), apparently the author of the novel *Corsicana!* (1959). He once appeared on *The Jack Paar Tonight Show* (28 January 1960).

[169] [DW to CAS] [ANS][1]

[Postmarked Sauk City, Wis.,
9 November 1955]
Sauk City, Wis. Nov. 9, 1955

Dear Clark:

August looks just like this photo & as you probably remember
him—Sandy & the baby looking at their best too. I'm visiting here a few days.
. . . When I return to St. Paul I'll write you in more detail & enclose the snapshots you sent of the new sculptures. I've been admiring the very large group
that August has in the upstairs studio. They are magnificent. I hope all prospers with you & your family. Ever, Donald

Notes

1. *Front:* August Derleth and Home. Sauk City, Wis.

[170] [DW to CAS] [TLS]

[ARKHAM HOUSE: PUBLISHERS
SAUK CITY, WISCONSIN]

[Postmarked Sauk City, Wis., 17 October 1957]

Dear Clark:

Forgive my long, long silence and neglect. August told me he'd
heard from you recently (I'm here visiting him this week before returning to
St. Paul) and that you wondered if I'd taken offense at something. Nothing
could be more remote and unlikely than that. But ever since my return from
California, there has been a continuous gloom in our house because of major
operations, costly and extended hospitalizations, and critical illnesses. My
brother, Howard, died in September of last year at only 46 and when he was
just entering the full flower of his fantastic genius in weird art. His passing
was such a shattering shock to me that I have been very slow to recover, and,

in fact, do not think that life will ever again continue on its previous plane. I have also had the immense task of putting his affairs in order, and of preparing his mss. for eventual book publications, and collecting his art works for an exhibition and possibly publication too.[1] But I have thought of you countless times and with many pangs and twinges of conscience—I still have color photos of your own sculptures to be returned as soon as I am back in St. Paul and can locate them. I hope that none of your creative art and writings or your files and library and correspondence were lost in the cabin fire. And I hope that all prospers with you and your wife and family. I am glad to know of your new book of poems[2]—I anticipate it keenly. I don't know of anyone who has enriched my imaginative life so opulently as you. Perhaps one day, when ill tidings and evil luck turn away from my door, I may have the pleasure of meeting your family[3] and seeing you in California again. As ever,

Donald

Notes

1. An edition announced for publication by Arkham House c. 1950, *Orson Is Here,* never appeared. Following AWD's death in July 1971, DW became editorial director at Arkham House. In that capacity, he issued a new Arkham House catalogue (1972), announcing forthcoming publications by HW: *Radial Symbolism: The Phenomenal Art of Howard Wandrei; Catalogue Index: The Complete Art of Howard Wandrei; The Diaries; Selected Letters,* and also *The Circle of the Pyramids* by DW and HW. HW's *Collected Mystery Tales I & II* and *Time Burial* appeared from Fedogan & Bremer under the titles *Time Burial* (1995), *The Last Pin* (1996), and *The Eerie Mr. Murphy* (2003).

2. *Spells and Philtres.*

3. CAS married Carol Jones Dorman on 10 November 1954, at which time CAS became the stepfather of three children.

R. H. Barlow

Letters: Clark Ashton Smith and R. H. Barlow

[1]   [CAS to RHB] [ALS, on RHB microfilm]

Auburn, California
June 8th, 1931

Dear Mr. Barlow:

   I thank you for your interest in my work, and your commendation of "The City of Singing Flame." Perhaps I can write a sequel to this story[1]—certainly there are possibilities for one. I like the tale about as well as anything I have written so far; but I hope to do better work.

Yours sincerely
Clark Ashton Smith

Notes

1. CAS did write "Beyond the Singing Flame" in August, perhaps at RHB's suggestion. He wrote "The City of the Singing Flame" in January.

[2]   [CAS to RHB] [ALS]

Auburn, Calif.
Sept. 1st, 1932.

Dear Mr. Barlow:

   I only wish I **did** know of some foreign fantastic magazines; but, as far as I can learn, there are none in existence. If you read the letter columns of Wonder Stories, Amazing, etc., you will note letters from British and other foreign readers saying that there are no periodicals of a corresponding type abroad; and it seems even less likely that there would be magazines devoted to the supernatural. It says a good deal for the U.S., that we do have a few mediums for fiction.

   You are more than kind to offer to type some of my work in exchange for the mss.,[1] and I thank you cordially. I may take up the offer, if I ever do anything of mine in legible long hand. I used to write out full preliminary ms. draughts of stories, but latterly have fallen into the habit of draughting them directly on the machine, or else working them up from rough and more or less incomplete notes in pencil.

   However, I have gone through a pile of old stuff, and have dug out the original scrawls of two of my Weird Tales contributions—"The Uncharted Isle" and "A Rendezvous in Averoigne." These you are welcome to have for your collection, with no "strings" whatever attached.

   Thanks for your praise of some of my recent tales. You may like The Isle of the Torturers, recently accepted by W.T.

Cordially yours,

Clark Ashton Smith

Notes

1. RHB had made the same offer the previous year to HPL. RHB's collections of HPL's and CAS's manuscripts constitute a large part of the HPL collection at the John Hay Library, Brown University (Providence, RI).

[3]   [RHB to CAS] [TLS]

[Envelope postmarked Fort Benning, Ga.,
14 September 1932]

Dear Mr. Smith:

Thanks very much for the two mss. I'll be glad to copy any anytime you want me to.

Thanks, too, about the information concerning fantastic magazines abroad. I feared there were none as the letter columns bore witness, but as there are 48,000 periodicals published monthly in the U.S. I thought there might be a similar number in Great Britain and perhaps all had not been seen by the letter writers.

After Clark Ashton Smith
(Copy by RHB)

In THE DOOR TO SATURN last winter you mentioned some headless beings. Are you aware that similar monstrosities were supposed to inhabit America before it was fully explored?[1]

I am sending a few pictures of mine (under separate cover): (I recently sent some to Lovecraft, who thought you might be interested.) I am enclosing sufficient postage to return them. I'd like, if it is not imposing on you too much, an honest opinion of them. I am an *amateur* artist and hope to someday be more! I admire your work greatly although I have seen little of it (mainly small water-colours & pencils.)

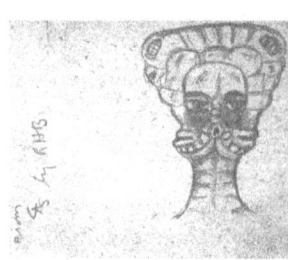

Thanks again for your kind letter!

Yours sincerely,

R. H. Barlow.

[Enclosure: three small drawings]

Notes

1. Sir Walter Raleigh (c. 1552–1618) provided an account of creatures resembling the Blemmyes of ancient mythology called *Ewaipanoma,* reported to have their eyes in their shoulders, and their mouths in the middle of their breasts. He claimed these beings lived in Guiana, in South America. CAS had made several sculptures of Blemmyes. See RHB to CAS 4 and 53.

[4]   [CAS to RHB] [ALS]

Auburn, Calif.
Sept. 30th, 1932.

Dear Mr. Barlow:

Your drawings are highly interesting; they show remarkable imaginative possibilities, and a genuine feeling for the demoniac and grotesque. The hellish green salamander in crayon (is it one of the primordial lizard-men?) and the hairless, gigantic, ravening monster—like a combination of sow and sewer-rat,—and Satan knows what else!—especially pleased me. Your defects are those of unmastered and imperfect technique; but by study and practise, you should be able to overcome them.

I enjoyed also the newspaper article, with the learned professor's admirable creations. Will return all your enclosures in a few days, and add one or two of my own grotesques,[1] for you to keep.

Of course, I can't absolutely swear that there are no fantastic periodicals abroad; but I have vainly tried to track down anything of the sort, through magazine lists, books on places to submit mss., and personal inquiry. Of course, some of the British magazines may publish, occasionally, a fantastic story or two. I have old copies of the Strand containing some of the short stories of H. G. Wells, and also of Gaston Leroux and others. I think one of the Leroux tales, about a man who gambled with the devil, was also published in W.T., two or three years back.[2]

I don't remember reading explicitly about the headless people that were supposed to inhabit America, but I knew that such creatures were widely fabled during the Middle Ages, as existing in unknown parts of the world. I have even seen pictures of them, reproduced from old beast-books; they were called blemmies (which suggested my name Bhlemphroims, in The Door to Saturn). Flaubert, in The Temptation of St. Anthony, brings in the Blemmy, as one of the innumerable strange monsters (creations of human myth and belief) which appear to Anthony in his delirium. The *Catoblepsas* [*sic*], which had a neck that lay on the ground "like a flaccid gut," was another menagerie item that came along at the same time.[3] Also there were the Nisnas,[4] who had one eye, one hand, one leg, etc, and "lived in their halves of houses with their halves of wives."

I'll remember your generous offer about typing, if it ever becomes practical to accept it. The trouble is, that I usually have to revise and rework my things so interminably. The real labor doesn't begin till I have made a typed copy. Certain pages—endings in particular—are sometimes re-written three or four times. But if crude mss. are of any interest to your collection I can give you some more of them without any obligation whatever. Often I destroy these; but probably there are many left among my miscellaneous papers.

> Cordially,
> Clark Ashton Smith

Notes

1. See *Grotesques and Fantastiques* for examples.
2. Gaston Leroux (1868–1927), "Letters of Fire" (*WT*, March 1930).
3. Flaubert described it as "A black buffalo with a pig's head, falling to the ground, and attached to his shoulders by a neck long, thin, and flaccid as an empty gut. [¶] He wallows flat upon the ground, and his feet entirely disappear beneath the enormous mane of coarse hair which covers his face." *The Temptation of St. Anthony* 252.
4. Or *Nasnas,* monstrous creatures (also known as the Monopod) of Arab folklore.

[5]   [CAS to RHB] [ALS]

> Auburn, Cal.
> Nov. 17th, 1932.

Dear Mr. Barlow:

Here are some old Mss. of mine—the original drafts of *The End of the Story* and *The Tale of Satampra Zeiros*. Later on, I'll give you a few others.

Glad you liked the drawings I enclosed. Yours were indeed interesting, and I hope you will go on and do more. You have the requisite imagination.

Carl Swanson, Washburn, North Dakota, who deals in second-hand fantastic magazines and books, might have the early issues of W.T. At least, I'm pretty sure that he would have, or be able to obtain, some of them for you.

The depression seems to be hitting the magazine world pretty badly—both Strange Tales and Astounding Stories are discontinued with the current issues. Tough luck. Bates had three of my stories in line for publication—and now I've had to take them back. One of them—*The Colossus of Ylourgne*—has been taken over by W.T.[1]

> Best wishes,   Cordially,
> Clark Ashton Smith

Notes

1. The others were "The Seed from the Sepulcher" and "The Double Shadow."

[6]   [RHB to CAS] [ALS]

7019 Ga. Ave, N.W.
Washington D.C.
November 30, 1932

Dear Mr. Smith:—

Thanks immensely for the Mss. drafts. I'll be thankful for any you care to send me. The cruder, the more interesting!

I am already in communication with Carl Swanson, but he has no WT as far back as I need.

Terribly sorry to hear STRANGE TALES has failed, although I rather expected it when they went bi-monthly.[1] It was a great magazine and infinitely better than its companion ASTOUNDING.

I intend to keep on drawing, though my eyes are a handicap. I'll send some more along in a while (drawings—not eyes!)

Incidentally, this is most presumpt[u]ous, but could you give me a rough idea or sketch for a book-plate? I have tried my best to find something distinctive and original, without avail. Something suggesting the weird and fanciful; as that is what composes my library. I'd appreciate it more than I could tell you if you'd dash off something in your spare time. The idea is the principal thing. What suggested it was the interwoven initials in your two drawings you gave me. I'm afraid I am an awful bother to even mention it. In fact, I *know* I am, but it'd be the envy of my bibliomaniac friends if you favoured me with it, and I'd be *eternally grateful*.

"Murray Leinster"—who's [*sic*] work you have doubtless read—is entering a law-suit against a major film company for "borrowing" his title *RED DUST*.[2] I don't think he has much chance.

The depression seems to have hit WONDER STORIES pretty hard, doesn't it?

Hoping to hear from you soon, and thanking you again for the mss, I am yours most sincerely, R H Barlow

P.S. I enclose postage you paid on Mss. RHB

Notes

1. *Strange Tales* began as a bimonthly magazine, its first four issues dated September 1931, November 1931, January 1932, and March 1932. Its remaining three issues came out even less frequently (June 1932, October 1932, January 1933).

2. Murray Leinster was the pseudonym of William Fitzgerald Jenkins (1896–1975), American science fiction writer. "The Red Dust" appeared in *Argosy All-Story Weekly* (2 April 1921). A film entitled *Red Dust* did appear around this time (MGM, 1932), directed by Victor Fleming and starring Clark Gable, Jean Harlow, and Gene Raymond. The film was adapted from a play of the same title (1928) by Wilson Collison.

[7]   [CAS to RHB] [TLS]

Auburn, Calif.
Dec. 13th, 1932.

Dear Mr. Barlow:

Here are some more Mss. One of them, The Holiness of
Azederác, [*sic*] is incomplete, since the latter part was done directly on the
machine. The tale will appear in W.T., and runs to 8000 words in all.

I have been laid up with a cold, and I diverted myself, the other day, by
trying to invent a bookplate design for you. I enclose the result, and hope you
won't think it too rotten. One could imagine a lot of fantastic things about
the man-beast with the bloodied horn, and the horned viper and poisonous-
looking desert plant that he is envisaging.

I suppose you have heard of Henry S. Whitehead's death.[1] Too bad. He
was one of the best living fantaisists.

I understand that a new scientific pulp, to sell at 5¢ on the stands, is to be
started before long, but haven't heard its name.

Probably a one-third or one-half reduction would be almost right for the
book-plate, if you were to have it reproduced. But you may want to draw it
over and vary it—the thing is only a suggestion, anyway.

Cordially,
Clark Ashton Smith

Notes

1. Whitehead died on 23 November.

[8]   [CAS to RHB] [TLS]

Auburn, Cal.
Feb. 8th, 1933.

Dear Mr. Barlow:

I fear the bookplate design wasn't very good. Drawing, with
me, seems to be more dependent on inspiration than either poetry or prose.
If you have it printed, though, you might send me a copy of it.

The Door to Saturn is one of my own favorites. I'll dig [up] some more
mss. anon, when I can find the time for the labor of disinterment.

I have published three books of verse in addition to Ebony and Crystal,
but fear that all of them are now out of print. Odes and Sonnets, however (an
expensive de luxe volume put out by the California Book Club) consisted partly
of reprints from my first book, The Star-Treader; and the other poems contained in it were consequently included in Ebony and Crystal. It is possible that
the Star-Treader might be obtained from the publisher, A. M. Robertson, 222
Stockton St., San Francisco, Cal., but it would probably cost about $3.00, since,

the last I heard, R. was putting up the price on the few that he had left. My fourth and last book, Sandalwood, seems to be wholly unobtainable.

My tale, The Dweller in the Gulf, published as Dweller in Martian Depths in the current Wonder Stories, has been atrociously garbled by a re-writing of the end—apparently done by a semi-illiterate office boy.[1] In the tale as I submitted it, no escape was possible for any of the three earth-men, since the Dweller was filling the **whole** of the narrow path ahead of them. Bellman met the same fate as the others. The tale is hopelessly ruined by this Hunnish butchery, and I am writing an indignant letter of protest to the editor. Apart from this, whole paragraphs of weird description and atmosphere were excised from the body of the tale. It is very doubtful if I shall publish anything more in Wonder Stories, apart from two tales that are now held for early publi-cation.[2] I can only hope and pray that these will escape similar mutilation.

Sincerely yours,
Clark Ashton Smith

Notes

1. For a complete discussion of the publication of "The Dweller in the Gulf," as well as presentation of both the corrected text and the mangled ending, see *The Dweller in the Gulf*, ed. Steve Behrends (part of *The Unexpurgated Clark Ashton Smith* series).
2. These were "The Light from Beyond" and "A Star-Change."

[9]   [CAS to RHB] [ANS]

Auburn, Cal.,
Feb. 19th, 1933.

My dear Mr. Barlow:

The tale by me, published in the current Wonder Stories as Dweller in Martian Depths, has suffered from editorial tinkering—the whole ending was re-written without my knowledge or consent, and was utterly ru-ined. If you have bought the tale, and care to send it to me, I'll correct the end-ing for you. Also, many paragraphs of description were ruthlessly excised!!

Yours—

Clark Ashton Smith

[10]   [CAS to RHB] [TLS]

Auburn, Calif.
March 15th, 1933.

Dear Mr. Barlow:

I have crossed out the interpolations (done by David Lass-er) in The Dweller in the Gulf, and have appended the original ending. I sup-pose the change was made to tone down the horror; but it seems pretty senseless even from that angle.

I am also sending you a late scribbled ms., The Weaver in the Vault, drafted very hastily and crudely on the backs of discarded sheets from various typescripts—even some that I did of the Weaver itself as I went along. Hope it will be of interest for your collection.

Yes, I knew George Sterling very well indeed—we were friends for many years. His poetry is grand stuff, but I suppose the volumes do come pretty high now. His Selected Poems, published by Macmillan,[1] could, I should think, be obtained more reasonably than the various original collections.

The current issue of Astounding is to be the last, I understand. It was beginning to show slight signs of improvement, I thought; but even at that, S.T. was leagues ahead of it. Yes, I've noticed the epidemic of weird movies. The only good one I have seen was Jekyll and Hyde. I missed The Mummy. The Isle of Lost Souls ought to be good.[2]

I wish you all kinds of luck with the completion and marketing of The Shunned House.[3] Put me down for a copy. I am, by the way, printing six of my own tales (unpublished in magazines) in a pamphlet to sell at 25¢. The title story, The Double Shadow, dealing with Atlantean magic, was to have appeared in S.T. I don't know when the thing will be ready—the local printers are slower than Mark Twain's leaded frog.[4] As to my previously published work, I wrote very little prose prior to the fall of 1929, apart from a lot of worthless juvenilia, done before the age of 18. Some of this got into the old Black Cat and the Overland Monthly, but I don't think it would be of any interest to you. My first published story of any value, The Abominations of Yondo, appeared in the Overland for April, 1926. After that, there was nothing, till The Ninth Skeleton in W.T., Aug. (or Sept.) 1928.

I agree with you about the covers on W.T. The current one, for Williamson's serial, is very find indeed; but the one before that was a positive disgrace.[5] As for my own tales, I guess I'll have to illustrate them sooner or later, in self-defense![6]

I have some esoteric data about the lost continents, etc, which is going the rounds from E. H. Price. Price has now instructed me to send it to Robert E. Howard, who will forward it to you. It is very interesting. Re occultism, did you know that the existence of the planet Pluto (and also the tenth planet, now postulated by astronomers) was known to Oriental adepts long before its telescopic discovery?

Cordially yours,
Clark Ashton Smith

Notes

1. The publisher was Henry Holt.

2. *Dr. Jekyll and Mr. Hyde* (Paramount, 1932), directed by Rouben Mamoulian; starring Fredric March, Miriam Hopkins, and Rose Hobart. *The Mummy* (Universal, 1932), directed by Karl Freund; starring Boris Karloff, Zita Johann, and David Manners. *The Island of Lost Souls* (Paramount, 1933), directed by Erle C. Kenton; starring Charles Laughton, Richard Arlen, and Bela Lugosi. Based on *The Island of Dr. Moreau* by H. G. Wells.

3. HPL's *The Shunned House* was set in type and printed in 1928 by W. Paul Cook's Recluse Press, but the sheets were not bound. In 1933, Walter J. Coates of the Driftwind Press intended to bind the sheets but never did so. RHB acquired 115 copies in 1934 and 150 more in 1935 but bound only a few. (He did not intend to print it [CAS to RHB 13].) The sheets RHB obtained were eventually bound and distributed by Arkham House in 1959–61.

4. In "The Celebrated Jumping Frog of Calaveras County" (1865).

5. J. Allen St. John did the cover illustration for Jack Williamson's "Golden Blood," *WT* (April 1933). Margaret Brundage did the illustration for Seabury Quinn's "The Thing in the Fog" the previous month.

6. CAS illustrated seven of his own stories for *WT*.

[11]   [CAS to RHB] [TLS]

Auburn, Calif.
Mar. 20th, 1933.

My dear Mr. Barlow:

I received your letter of the 14th, also copy of the Dweller in the Gulf for correction, to-day. But before this, you will have received from me a corrected copy of the story—the reason being, that someone else wanted the same revision done, and the copy arrived a day or two after your previous letter. The address was printed, the postmark blurred and there was nothing to indicate the sender's identity—so I assumed that it was you! I guess you can keep that copy, and I'll fix up the other person with yours.

I don't think I have ever seen Broken Mirrors, which you speak of as being by Wandrei and others.[1] Why not write to Wandrei? His address, at latest hearing, was 84 Horatio St., New York.

The earthquake was not perceptible in this part of California.[2] It was sharply localized, and I don't think that Pasadena was badly shaken. Some scientist, however, has predicted that this disturbance is merely the precursor of the real earthquake!

The Star-Treader appeared when I was nineteen. I wrote practically no prose during my twenties and early thirties—in fact, I was verging on thirty-seven when I began fiction-writing with any seriousness and assiduity. But there's no reason at all why you or anyone else would have to wait for middle-age before turning out meritorious work. Too bad about your eyes—I have enough trouble with my own to sympathize.

Of course, I'll be glad to inscribe the Star-Treader for you.

Cordially yrs,
Clark Ashton Smith

Notes

1. See Bibliography under Donald Wandrei (Books).
2. A succession of earthquakes occurred on 10 March in Southern California, killing 123 people and injuring 4,150.

[12] [RHB to CAS] [TLS]

April 10[, 1933]

Dear Mr. Smith:—
        Thanks very much for the inscribing of STAR TREADER; also corrections. I've been trying to write you for two weeks, but have been feeling like the wreck of the Hesperus[1]—so didn't get about it. My many-times-accursed eyes have been troubling me much; I have a beautiful cold, and in short, (as in THREE MEN IN A BOAT[2]—"I *haven't* got Housemaid's Knee—everything but.["])
        Thanks, also for the DWELLER and mss., both of which I appreciate.
        Incidentally, I am compiling a LETTERS of Henry S. Whitehead,[3] which I hope to issue for his friends. Would you have any for inclusion? All contributors will be presented with a copy of the final product.
        Hope your pamphlet gets eventually printed—I'll be in the market for one. SHUNNED HOUSE has momentarily lagged, but I trust I'll manage it in time.
        I'll write more later—that is, if I survive!
                Yours,
                R. H. Barlow

Notes

1. "The Wreck of the *Hesperus*," a narrative poem by Henry Wadsworth Longfellow, first published in *Ballads and Other Poems* (1842), is a story presenting the tragic consequences of a sea captain's pride.
2. A comic travelogue (1899) by Jerome K. Jerome (1859–1927).
3. In March 1933 RHB conceived the idea to publish extracts of Whitehead's letters in a small volume entitled *Caneviniana* (see RHB to CAS 23n1). He cut some stencils, but the booklet was never completed, although Paul Freehafer ran some of the letters in *The Letters of Henry S. Whitehead* (FAPA, n.d. [December 1942]). AWD asked RHB to write the introduction to Whitehead's *Jumbee and Other Uncanny Tales* (1944), perhaps prompted by RHB's "A Checklist of the Published Weird Stories of Henry S. Whitehead" in *Leaves* No. 2 (1938).

[13]   [CAS to RHB] [TLS]

Auburn, Calif.
May 31st, 1933.

Dear Mr. Barlow:

I am sorry you have been unwell, and have had so much trouble with your eyesight. Life is enough of a bore and a bother even when the physical mechanism runs smoothly.

So far, in running hastily through my accumulation of letters, I have been able to locate only one communication from Dr. Whitehead; and this, as you will note, was written by an amanuensis during a period of illness. You are welcome to use it for your book if you find it of interest. It was written to me apropos of the praise I had given to one of his stories (The Passing of a God) in The Eyrie.[1] I may have another note somewhere, and also a card written jointly by Whitehead and Lovecraft; but these I cannot find.

Yes, I have much Sterling material, in the form of letters and auto-graphed volumes.[2] I have been getting the letters together lately—they were scattered through a score of boxes. They cover a long period of years—1911 to within a fortnight of his death in the fall of 1926. I seem to have given away most of the Sterling manuscripts that I once had—that is to say, those in longhand,—but possess many typed and signed copies of poems.

My pamphlet of stories has been endlessly delayed. The job is being done in a one-horse newspaper office. But they'll have to finish it sometime, if only to get the type out of the way! I enclose a prospectus. Thanks for the order—I'll be glad to send you one as soon as it is ready.

Too bad there was a hitch—or a catch—in regard to your printing of The Shunned House. I had looked forward to seeing the story again.

I commiserate you on the ordeal of moving. I have been cleaning house, etc. for weeks, which is almost as bad. An incredible amount of old papers, magazines, etc.; had accumulated, and I simply had to move out a few truck-loads of them, so as to effect a little more gangway. Also, I have put my bookshelves in order for the first time in years.

With all best wishes and regards, as ever,
Yours,
Clark Ashton Smith

Notes

1. "Passing of a God" appeared in *WT* (January 1931). CAS's letter praising the for-mer appeared in "The Eyrie," *WT* 17, No. 2 (February–March 1931): 154 ("*The Pass-ing of a God* is one of the most sheerly original tales I have ever seen in your pages. The idea was one that required careful handling—only a good writer could have done it acceptably"). CAS also wrote a letter praising Whitehead's "The Tree-Men" (*WT,* February–March 1931); it appeared in *WT* 17, No. 3 (April–May 1931): 297.

2. Roy A. Squires offered for sale CAS's inscribed copies of GS's *Ode on the Opening of*

the Panama-Pacific International Exposition: San Francisco, February 1915 (1915), *The Caged Eagle and Other Poems* (1916), and *Rosamund* (1920). CAS owned many other of GS's books and also received 209 letters from GS.

[14]   [CAS to RHB] [TLS]

> Auburn, Calif.
> Aug. 6th, 1933.

Dear Mr. Barlow:

I had been meaning to answer your letter for some time past; also, to mail you, in a flat package, another copy of The Double Shadow to indemnify you for the one that got crushed in transit. I'll try to get the book off in a day or two. If you like, you can remit the postage on it sometime.

I have not yet located any more Whitehead letters. There are such vast quantities of correspondence lying around here in an unassorted [*sic*] condition, that it means no end of research to locate anything that is more than a few months old. Let's hope you will be able to carry out your plan for printing the letters you have. No, I don't think that I shall print a Sterling collection. So many of the letters are complimentary to my work, that it would seem like a self-advertising stunt if I were to bring them out. Also, I have not, at present, either the means or the time to embark on another publishing venture. The Double Shadow has brought me enough grief in the form of work, worry and expense.

A friend once read me some enjoyable chapters from A. A. Milne; but apart from that, I am not familiar with his books.[1]

I rather enjoyed King Kong,[2] which came to Auburn some time ago. But I seldom attend movies, and, as a rule, am disappointed in the few that I do see.

The last three months have been pretty slack with me, as far as writing is concerned. A multitude of other things, mainly flat and unprofitable, seem to have intervened. Also, my father has been unwell. I have, however, recently sold two new stories to Wright: The Flower-Women and the Death of Malygris.

Have you seen The Fantasy Fan? I enclose a circular describing it. Lovecraft and I are both contributing some stories to future numbers.

Too bad that conditions are so inharmonious for you. The only defense is too make up your mind that you won't take anything seriously. Also, make an effort to concentrate on something abstract, and to view the irritating conditions in a sort of cosmic perspective that will cause them to dwindle into triviality. Well, I can see that you don't think much of the practicality of my advice; but believe me, the mere endeavor to see things in this way will help if you keep it up.

The spirit photograph is good—I am sure Conan Doyle would have accepted it as proof of an authentic materialization![3] I return it herewith.

Here is a note from Sterling that you might like to add to your collection.[4] I can well afford to spare it.

A little excitement here lately—we have killed two rattlesnakes on the ranch during the past month. One of them had crawled within a yard of the outdoor table where I was writing, before I noticed it. The critters are certainly sociable—I hear of their invading streets and pavements and porches around Auburn; and an acquaintance of mine says that he has one living in his barn!

All best wishes, and hopes that this will find you in a less depressed mood.

Yours cordially,

Clark Ashton Smith

[P.S.] Sorry I can't identify the quotation about the moonbeam that turned to worms.[5]

Notes

1. A[lan] A[lexander] Milne (1882–1956) was a popular British author, best known for his books about the fictional anthropomorphic teddy bear Winnie-the-Pooh. He also wrote a celebrated detective novel, *The Red House Mystery* (1922).

2. *King Kong* (RKO, 1933), directed by Merian C. Cooper and Ernest B. Schoedsack; starring Fay Wray, Robert Armstrong, and Bruce Cabot.

3. A photograph that captures images of ghosts and other spiritual entities, especially in ghost hunting. Such photographs emerged in the late 19th century, and Sir Arthur Conan Doyle was a notable proponent of them.

4. GS to CAS, 10 June 1912 (postcard); ms., JHL. In *The Shadow of the Unattained* 51.

5. In *A Free Soul* (1931), a movie starring Norma Shearer, Lionel Barrymore, Clark Gable, and Leslie Howard, Shearer's character says, when commenting on the disintegration of a once-happy relationship with the character played by Clark Gable: "And suddenly the moonbeams turned to worms . . . and crawled away."

[15]   [CAS to RHB] [TLS]

Auburn, Calif.

Sept 19th, 1933.

Dear Ar-Éch-Bei:

I have exhumed the unanswered letters of the past month or six weeks (filed in a peach-box on my outdoor table) and am answering them all in one fell swoop. Yours comes early in the list.

Glad my advice was not so remiss and remote from the point. Even major annoyances are not so important if one can see them in a sort of macrocosmic perspective—which is the only way to regard them. Anyway, I hope that your father is better.[1]

So you too have been bumping off some specimens of the crotalus horridus![2] I admire your resolution in skinning one of them and tanning the hide, but I lack the fervor to emulate you.

As to book-collecting, I have some first and old editions, but doubtless lack the true bibliophilic ardour, since I buy books mainly for their contents, and am now specializing wholly on items of the weird and fantastic. And with the present financial outlook, I am buying very few indeed even of those. My last purchase was the Collected Ghost Stories of M. R. James, all in one volume. James is a growing favourite with me, and I admire his tales more as I reread and analyze them. I have recently written a brief article on him, which will be published in The Fantasy Fan.[3] I saw Eliphas Levi's History of Magic listed at $5.00 in a catalogue which came recently, and would like to buy it, but hesitate over the expenditure. One highly prized item which I possess is Montague Summers' monograph on The Vampire.[4] I wonder if Quinn hadn't been reading that when he cooked up his yarn about the penanggalan in the last W.T.[5] Confound Quinn—he has botched something on which I had an eye myself.

Re Cabell:[6] I esteem him as a remarkable stylist, but do not admire and relish his type of fantasy nearly as much as I did ten years ago. Too many allegories and double meanings; and since I have lost most of my interest in mundane sophistication, I am easily bored by such obvious though inverted didacticisms. Satire, in my opinion, contrary to that of my friend Benj. DeCasseres, is far from being the highest form of art. As Lovecraft once remarked in a letter, if one laughs too persistently at things, it might come to seem that they were worth laughing at.[7]

No, I never met Bierce—he passed out of the American (and, no doubt, the mundane) scene not long after the beginning of my acquaintance with Sterling. I could have met him, one occasion, and have often kicked myself since that I did not stretch my leave and do so.[8]

If I ever visit S.F. again, I may be able to pick up a copy of Odes and Sonnets for you. A friend of mine procured one there last summer.

I have written a story, The Coming of the White Worm, which purports to be a rendering (from the Old French of Gaspard du Nord) of Chapter IX of The Book of Eibon. Wright, by the way, turned down my recent The Witchcraft of Ulua as being too sexy for the pure and virginal pages of W.T. In view of his covers, he certainly is [not] a stickler for consistency. Anyhow, the tale was far more macabre than risque.

I'll see what I can dig up in the way of enclosures. Thanks for the interesting cut of your house.

Yours, under the black onyx seal of Azathoth,[9]
Klarkash-Ton

[P.S.] You might like the enclosed card from De Casseres (acknowledging The Double Shadow) for your autographic collection.[10]

Notes

1. E. D. Barlow, a lieutenant-colonel of the army, retired "because of failing health." Before making his trip to De Land in 1934 to visit RHB, HPL was concerned that his presence "might disturb him [RHB's father] & increase his depression to have a stranger—& a far from breezy & exuberant stranger at that—butting in on him" (HPL to RHB, 10 April 1934; *O Fortunate Floridian* 127).

2. *Crotalus horridus,* the timber (or banded) rattlesnake, common in the Eastern U.S., but not in RHB's milieu.

3. "The Weird Work of M. R. James."

4. *The Vampire: His Kith and Kin.* Summers also wrote *The Vampire in Europe.*

5. Seabury Quinn, "The Malay Horror" (*WT,* September 1933). See CAS to AWD, 7 June 1932 (*Eccentric, Impractical Devils* 121): "In going over [Summers's] book, I was struck by the charming Malay creation, the penanggalan—a vampiric human head with esophagus and stomach sac still attached, that flies around at night seeking victims. Christ, what a specter! Have you ever heard of a story being written about it?"

6. James Branch Cabell (1879–1958), American author of fantasy fiction and belles lettres, whose work is ironic and satirical, and thus quite unlike the work of *WT* authors.

7. HPL to CAS, 9 August 1926: "Nothing in the universe matters very much, & to laugh habitually at any one set of things seems almost to imply that they are worth laughing at" (*Dawnward Spire* 109).

8. Bierce spent the summer of 1912 in California (he had been living in Washington, DC, since December 1899), arriving in Oakland on 26 June, leaving to spend time in Lake Tahoe (1–17 July), and returning to Oakland.

9. The "blind idiot god" of HPL's pseudomythological pantheon.

10. Benjamin De Casseres to CAS, 16 June 1933 (ms., JHL).

[16]   [CAS to RHB] [TLS]

Auburn, Calif.
Oct. 4th, 1933.

Dear Ar-Éch-Bei:

Herewith is my carbon of the allegedly lubricious and salacious The Witchcraft of Ulua, concerning which you inquired. There seems to be no likelihood of magazine or other publication for it at present. You can send it on at your convenience to Lovecraft.

Your youth is nothing against you—rather the converse, I should say. I hope you will not lose your taste for fantasy, as some people do when the myopia of middle-age creeps upon them. It is no sign of breadth or enlarged outlook, as some of the victims are prone to maintain.

That storm must have been exciting. We seldom ever have anything in the nature of a high wind here, since this country is ringed with mountains, and the force of the seawinds, etc, is more or less broken.

Glad you liked the sketches. Sometime, if I ever circulate a large bunch of my pictures again, I'll put you on the itinerary. Thanks for your invitation, which I shall assuredly accept if I ever make the Grand Tour. At present, on account of finances and the infirmity of my parents, I am absolutely tied down and can certainly be classed as a recluse.

Astounding Stories has just bought a tale of mine, The Demon of the Flower, which has gone begging for two years. Editorial tastes are certainly a gamble—I give it up. I hope Astounding will improve—some of the selections in the first S.&.S. issue seemed to betray editorial inexperience in the field of weird and bizarre material, since they were triter than cold mutton hash. But then, look at some of Wright's selections, such as the current vampire serial*******[1] The W.T. covers, I understand, are for circulation purposes—the sale always jumps up when there is a nude cutie or several on the front. You can draw your own inferences as to the intellectual level of the dear public.

As to Flagg,[2] I fear that he may be seriously ill. He has, I understand, tuberculosis, and was living in Arizona the last I heard.

I have written another Hyperborean tale, The Seven Geases, outrageously grotesque, sardonic and satiric. Bates would have grabbed it for S.T., but I don't know where it will find a berth with the present humourless crew of editors. By the way, though, I understand that the Strange Tales title has been bought by some one, and that the magazine will be revived. I certainly hope so.

Well, I guess that's all for the present. I have just batted off letters totalling well over two thousand words, and have not yet made a beginning on the day's fiction.

Hope you won[']t find Ulua too rotten from a story standpoint. I feel that it is well-written; and it gives a certain variant note to my series of tales dealing with Zothique.

Yrs, in the service of the Old Ones,
Klarkash-Ton

Notes

1. Hugh Davidson, "The Vampire Master" (*WT*, October 1933–January 1934).
2. Francis Flagg, pseudonym of George Henry Weiss (1898–1946), poet, pulp writer, and author of socialist tracts.

[17]   [CAS to RHB] [TLS]

Oct. 25th, 1933.

Ar-Éch-Bei,
Phlegethonian Envoy to Phlo-Ri-Dah:
Esteemed confrere:

I was pleased to learn that Ulua was neither too pediculous nor pudendal for your taste. As to Wright and his taboos, well, I give it up. I have re-submitted the tale to him with a slightly subtilized version of the temptation scene; and if he returns it this time, shall not bother to do anything further with the tale for commercial purposes.

A Southern Recluse Press[1] would be a grand idea, and of course I'll contribute something—either Ulua or some better tale. Hornig only uses very short stories in The Fantasy Fan; and my best things usually run upwards of 3000 words. As to Cook's arrangement, that, I believe, was "completely amateur." My advice to you, in regard to this printing project, is to publish a small edition that you can dispose of within a reasonable length of time, and to take any financial profit—if such should accrue—as an agreeable surprise. If I had published only 300 or 400 copies of The Double Shadow, I might at least have broken even on it by this time; but 1000 seems to have been a serious overestimate of the possible demand. Cash sales to date number somewhere around 250 or less; and new sales, even with my ad in W.T., are not drifting in very fast.

As to Flagg, I am not *sure* that he is seriously ill—merely conjectured this as a possible explanation of his non-appearance in magazines. The current Science Fiction Digest contains an article by him.[2] Some of his tales are quite passable, and far less stereotyped than the usual scientifiction. The Dancer in the Crystal and The Picture[3] were really fine.

Yes, The Seven Geases is the title; geases being the plural of geas,[4] a Celtic word meaning a magical compulsion that is laid upon someone to do something. Cabell uses it several times in Figures of Earth. Astounding still holds The S.G.; and I hope they will have the guts to publish it. They have also held The Coming of the White Worm, which Wright rejected pro tem as being too poetic, with the proviso that he would use it if times ever got better. Wright, by the way, has bought The Tomb-Spawn, a monstrous item belonging to my Zothique series; and he has also sprung a complete surprise by asking me to do an illustration for The Weaver in the Vault, which appears in January. I have finished and mailed the drawing, and hope it will pass the art board of WT.

My mother is laid up with a bad burn—result of pouring hot tea on her foot—and this unfortunate accident has thrown another monkey wrench into my literary programme. I am doctor, nurse, chief dish-washer and god knows what. Apropos of all this, I wonder if your offer about typing still holds? If it does, I wish you'd make me a typed copy of The Maze of the Enchanter from my booklet.[5] It is possible that I can sell the serial rights of this tale to Astounding Stories; and at any rate there is no harm in trying. You needn't bother about a carbon. Though I cannot give you a ms. copy of this tale (I don't believe there ever was one) I'll see that you don't lack for other Mss., autographic items, etc.

I note that a copy of my Odes and Sonnets is listed at $4.00 in the catalogue of the Holmes Book Co of Oakland, Cal. Do you want to pay this much for the item? If you do, let me know and I'll buy and autograph it for you. If I could get down to the Bay region in person, it is probable, or at least possible, that I could find a copy at $3.00. But, with present indications, it looks as if I were nailed to the mast.

Here are some drawings which I have made at night as exercises in pen-and-ink technique. I assure you that I was not thinking any invidious thoughts about the Hon. Franklin D. Roosevelt when I did the one of the gentleman with the choker of Kohinoors.[6]

Yrs, under the night-black seal of Thasaidon,[7]

Klarkash-Ton [stylized]

Notes

1. CAS alludes to W. Paul Cook's Recluse Press. RHB was very impressed by Cook's publications, and since he offered to take over the binding of HPL's *The Shunned House* (a stillborn project from the Recluse Press of 1928), HPL felt it appropriate to call his operation the Southern Recluse Press. RHB's few publications ultimately came out under the imprint of the Dragon-Fly Press.

2. Francis Flagg, "About 'Ardathia,'" *Science-Fiction Digest* 2, No. 3 (November 1933): 11f.

3. Francis Flagg, "The Dancer in Crystal" (*WT*, December 1929) and "The Picture" (*WT*, February–March 1931).

4. Farnsworth Wright dismissed the story as being merely "one geas after another."

5. The story was published in *DS*.

6. The Koh-i-noor ("Mountain of Light") is a large, celebrated diamond (108 carats) whose history can be traced back to 1304. In 1849 it was purchased by Great Britain and is now in the Queen Mother's crown.

7. Thasaidon is "lord of evil" in CAS's stories of Zothique.

[18]   [RHB to CAS] [TNS]

[Postmarked De Land, Fla.,
1 November 1933]
1 November

Dear KlarKashton:—

Surely I will type the MAZE OF THE ENCHANTER! Thanks for the sketches, I will write when I send the typescript.

Yours by Azathoth;

Ar Ech Bei

[19]   [CAS to RHB] [TLS]

Auburn, Calif.
Nov. 16th, 1933.

Ar-Ech-Bei
Master of the Phloridean Sabbat:
Dark and Formidable Frere:

Thanks for your trouble in typing The Maze of the

Enchanter. Hall, the sub-editor of that triply xxxed Astounding, now writes me that they are not buying any more weird fiction—only stories with "a definite scientific basis"—whatever that may be. Anyway, I'm glad to have the ms., which I'll put aside against the time when I am ready to tackle some book-publisher with a collection of my yarns. In return for your labour, I enclose a miscellany of scripts and autographic material—also, one or two drawings.

I suppose Forrest Ackerman and other laboratory-minded donkeys of the same breed have been braying their disapproval of the mild and tepid element of weirdness in some of the *Astounding* items. I fear, too, that the fantasy in Craw-ford's magazine[1] will get the same reception. These birds who are so hell-bent on realism and scientific verisimilitude should stick to the Scientific American, in which they will find no superstitions other than those of current materialism.

I saw, and rather liked, your first Annal of the Djinns in Fantasy Fan. I commiserate you on the misprints; my yarn had some bad ones too, such as *cetopahs* for *cenotaphs*.[2] Thanks for your defense of my stories against Acker-man.[3] That fellow needs a visitation from poltergeists equipped with sledge-hammers, to knock a little sense into his head; and a few blood-sucking oupires and penanggalans, and galloping cauchemars and Mourioches,[4] might help to broaden his outlook.

Congratulations on the sale to Unusual.[5] I hope this magazine will have some measure of success.

Between us, I should think we might work off an edition of 100 from the Southern Recluse Press. I can give you a lot of addresses; though the 250 sale of the D.S. doesn't mean 250 separate purchasers. One well-to-do friend in S.F. bought 20 copies, and a sprinkling of others gambled as much as a dollar apiece on the pamphlet. Also, many are bought locally, by people who were curious rather than appreciative. Of those who ordered the book by mail, in response to ad or circular, about five out of six were men; which goes to con-firm my impression that few women care for fantasy.

I wonder how it would appeal to you to print The Third Episode of Vathek,[6] which Beckford left unfinished and which I have continued and completed, adding about 4000 words to B.'s 13,000. The history of Zulkais and Kalilah is abundantly ironic as well as fantastic; and I have tried to carry on the special qualities and style of Beckford. I believe you will like the result. Lovecraft and others have praised my ending in the highest terms. Wright, too, was impressed by it, and said that he would use the Episode in W.T. if times ever got better. I'd like to have you print this, if it isn't too long. If the idea sounds interesting, I'll send you my continuation (I infer that you possess the Episodes).

Geases does have a phonetic connotation of ambiguity and bastardy. I can't find geas in any available dictionary. Possibly the Celtic plural would be geasa; but, anglicized, it would have to be geases or nothing.

I am glad the various mss. and drawings pleased you. Later you shall have others. As to Maze of the Enchanter, I didn't bother submitting it to

Astounding after Hall wrote me anent their new policy. I have, however, just received another letter from H. slightly qualifying the first. He wants me to try my hand at something of the semi-weird type, based perhaps on the mysteries of psychology, but now purely fantastic. The idea seems to be that an occasional tale of this sort might be swallowed by the pseudo-scientific fiends. Evil emanations, supernatural materializations, etc. are definitely "out." The only hopeful thing is that Hall does seem to feel a deficiency in the magazine as it stands at present. No denying that there's room for improvement— several light-years of room in fact.

I hope your illustrations will prove available for Unusual. I enjoyed the second Annal of the Jinns[7]—a charming vignette like the first. It seems to call for a Sime drawing.

The chief objection to Ackerman is that he represents an all too numerous type. He differs only in his degree of virulence from the average Science fiction [*sic*] addict.

The Geography of Witchcraft[8] is indeed a most learned and erudite tome. I dare say the gymnastics of the medieval Sabbat are not wholly sans parallel at the present time—in fact, that sort of business is well proselyted, either with or without the sanction of sorcery and Satanism.

Tabasco's principal vice at the present season, as far as I have had occasion to observe, is gastronomy. His cubic capacity is a practical proof of the fourth dimension. However, it's winter-time, and a boreal sort of winter at that. No doubt the activities of the Maltese Generalissimo will exhibit more diversity around Walpurgis Eve. As to the Chatte—well, so far, I have not detected any infantile mewlings under the cabin or in the woodshed. [9]

Yours for the sounding of the ultrageometric pits,

Klark-Ashton [vertical, ornamented]

Notes

1. William L. Crawford was planning two weird magazines, *Marvel Tales* and *Unusual Tales;* each ran for a few issues in 1934–35.

2. RHB's story was "The Black Tower," the first of ten installments of his annals, published in *FF* and the *Phantagraph,* now collected in *Eyes of the God.* CAS's story was "The Kingdom of the Worm."

3. See RHB's letter under "The Boiling Point" (*Dawnward Spire* 691). Ackerman had attacked CAS's "Dweller in the Martian Depths" as a horror story that had no place in a science fiction magazine, claiming "I could not find one redeeming feature about the story." The letters that fueled the lengthy controversy in *FF* are collected in *Dawnward Spire* 689–98.

4. An *oupire* is a vampire in Polish folklore. *Cauchemar* is French for "nightmare"; an incubus. A *mourioche* is a water-horse, a shapeshifter usually seen in the form of a yearling colt, pig, cow, or sheep, often with a pair of muscular arms. See CAS to RHB 15 regarding the *penanggalan.*

5. "The Experiment."

6. RHB published William Beckford's "The Story of the Princess Zulkais and the Prince Kalilah" in *Leaves* No. 1 (Summer 1937): 1–16, followed by CAS's "The Third Episode of Vathek" as "Conclusion to Wm. Beckford's Story of Princess Zulkais & Prince Kalilah," 17–24. CAS completed his conclusion to the story in September 1932.

7. "The Shadow from Above."

8. By Montague Summers.

9. One of CAS's cats, named General Thomaso Tabasco; *la chatte* was Simaetha.

[20]   [CAS to RHB] [ANS]

[Postmarked Auburn, Cal.,
17 November 1933]

Dear Ar-Éch-Bei:

This is by way of postscript to my letter of yesterday. I over-looked your query about Whitehead's correspondence. Nothing more has turned up; and I don't believe that I have any items of consequence anyway.

Hope you will like The Demon of the Flower in Dec. Astounding. Schachner's yarn is rather amusing,[1] but the rest of the issue is **down** to form.

Yrs, Klarkash-Ton.

Notes

1. Nat[haniel] Schachner (1895–1955), "Ancestral Voices" (*Astounding Stories,* December 1933).

[21]   [RHB to CAS] [TLS]

November 19th 1933

Dear Klar-Kashton;

I'm awfully sorry that the editor of the resuscitated Astounding was unwilling to take your excellent MAZE OF THE EN-CHANTER. What fools editors are. I hope that the drivelling of that wretched urchin Ackerman won't affect the prospective UNUSUAL, which has at least promise of being original. My personal opinion is that the afore-said Ackerman is of such an infantile mentality that he must either have things written down to his level or he can't comprehend them at all. There-fore, he does not appreciate imaginative literature, but demands the pseudo-scientific and frequently misleading technicalities of so many hack-writers.

A bibliophilic orgy was the result of your beneficence, and in momentary seriousness I thank you from the bottom of my small black heart! I prize the Sterlingiana very much,[1] thoroughly enjoyed the drawings, particularly the one that resembles the picture Blake drew (in the Victoria and Albert Muse-um, reproduced about 1927 in a large collection of hitherto unpublished work[2]) that purported to be a drawing from life of "The Soul of a Flea". It is highly curious that he made a first attempt on the edge of the paper, then he stated that the monster had closed its mouth, so he was forced to change its position! And of course, your Ms. are always treasured.

The things of mine that Hornig has were written some time ago, and are slightly mangled in publication. My forthcoming ones in UNUSUAL are—I think—a bit better.[3] Your tale was very clever.

I should like to issue your splendid ending to the 3rd Episode of Vathek (which Eich Pi El smuggled to me as a loan) and I shall take occasion to let you know I think it better than Beckford could do. There might be copyright difficulties, though, think you not, concerning the reprinting of the original? Of course, whatever I do will be necessarily limited, for my type is perforce hand-set and I'm rather a novice, likewise, I don't want to put anything out unless I have the best of materials. I need a few dollars more worth, and when they are acquired, I believe that the V. ending would be entirely satisfactory to print, (if you were not impatient). I think 100 copies ought to sell well, both to Beckfordiana collectors and your usual audience. What purchase price would you tentatively set? I'll have to have the binding done by a professional, which would be at minimum a quarter a copy. My main object in the Satyr Press (which I think I shall use unless the name is preempted,) is to produce things approximating the excellent typography of Cook at his Recluse, and publish a few of the finer tales of the confraternity. Those of an apogeotrophic[4] nature are favoured!

Sorry that the Odes & Sonnets was in dubious shape. I'll be patient, though, and rather have a perfect copy later than a battered one at present, the same applicable to Sandalwood.

I trust that your feminine cat is safely past the line of having innumerable feline bastards dashing about; and if your Tabasco chooses to misbehave, it's well-known "it's the woman who pays!" It is odd that all the crowd seems to have a fondness for cats, even if some, such as HPL cannot gratify it. Mine is named Doodlebug (!) and the newly acquired lady is originally titled Ladybug. The kittens have not made their debut as yet, but we have heard them. [Later— I repudiate that—they have—3 of 'em!] A friend of mine has one that answers occasionally to the name of Soho.

Glad that Ulua has been accepted, even if in adulterated version. The peculiar views held upon reputed aphrodisian literature amuses me. Some of the filthiest erotica written gets past, and then a story like Ulua is turned down. The style was the nicest part of the tale, being something almost Dunsanian.

Dear me! That Geography of Witchcraft (which I have not yet encountered) must be sumpin'! I daresay that medieval misbehavior was no more than that of today, and I suppose it had the added virtue of being *sanctified*. Yeah?

I tried a couple of frankly badly-drawn illustrations on the forthcoming Unusual, but fear rejection.

Yours by the ultra-terrestrial dwellers of Chas Fort,[5]
Ar-Ech-Bei [stylized]

P.S—I thought you might be interested in the loan of the enclosed—(written truthfully) by a friend of mine. An *actual* account of vudu stuff. The abominable spelling is due to inordinate carelessness of his, not illiteracy. I'll make you a copy later, if you desire it. HPL seemed very interested.

[Enclosure: two drawings; note on reverse of head] Dispose of as you see fit!—They'd fit the wastebasket, methinks.

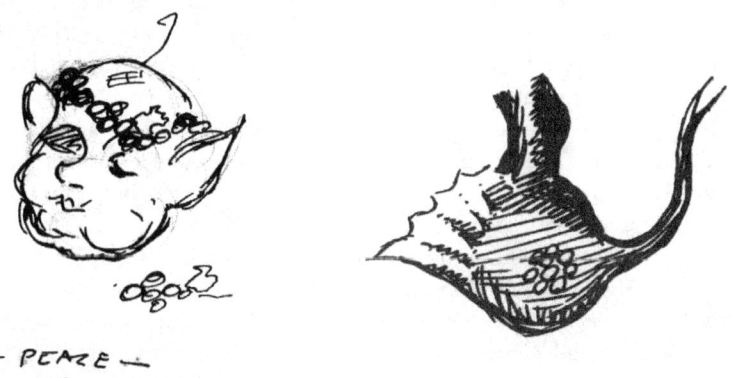

Notes

1. Presumably CAS sent to RHB the TMS of GS's "On Fifth Avenue" (*Munsey's*, February 1915) and the clipping of "The Voice of the Wheat" from *Overland Monthly* (April 1926). Both are now in the collection of HPL's papers at JHL.
2. *Pencil Drawings* (1927).
3. RHB had only one story in *Unusual Stories* (see CAS to RHB 19).
4. "Bending or turning away from the ground" (*OED*), by which RHB presumably meant antimundane or interplanetary.
5. Charles Fort (1874–1932), author of four collections of accounts of bizarre phenomena: *The Book of the Damned* (1919), *New Lands* (1923), *Lo!* (1931), and *Wild Talents* (1932).

[22]   [CAS to RHB] [TLS]

Auburn, Calif.
Dec. 5th, 1933.

Dear Ar-Éch-Bei:

The possible copyright angle of the 3rd Episode had occurred to me before. After completing my ending, I wrote to the publishers of the copy I had used (borrowed from Lovecraft) asking if there would be any objection to magazine publication of the opus. The letter came back to me unclaimed; so apparently the original publishers of the Abbey Classics[1]—I forget their name—have gone out of business. Lately I purchased a copy of the Episodes for my library, and note that it now bears the imprint of Chapman & Dodd, at 25 Denmark St., London. I suggest that you write to this firm about the matter. I see no reason why they should object, even if there is a copyright on Marzials' translation. Perhaps, in some future edition, they might even include my ending!

Anyway, I am glad you liked it so well; and I hope that you can eventually manage a small edition. As to selling-price, I should think that would be conditioned by the actual cost of publication per copy. My own practice, in regard to Ebony and Crystal, Sandalwood and The Double Shadow, has been to sell them at exactly double the net expense. Ebony and Crystal (originally priced at $2.00) cost me one buck per copy; Sandalwood cost $.50; and The D.S. .12½. Of course, this doesn't include advertising in magazines, circulars, etc. Oddly enough I cleared a dollar or two on my books of verse; but evidently I am sunk on the pamphlet of stories, which will take about fifty years to sell out at the current rate of expedition. Moral: don't bite off more bookpaper than the public will ingest. I can't advise you about a price on the 3rd Episode, but suggest that you leave yourself a good profit granting that the whole 100 sells. Then, if you don't sell all of them, or have too much extra overhead, you will at least break even. As I said before, I'll help you as much as I can in selling the Episode.

I sent The Seven Geases to Lovecraft not long ago, instructing him to forward it to you for reading. Wright, as I probably told you, declined the tale as being too plotless. Now, if you please, he writes me asking for another look at the ms! So, when you are done with it, you can send it on to the Chicago Satrap of magazine sorcery and weirddom. I hope sincerely that Pharnabosus will take it this time: For by all indications, I shall need the ensuant 75 pazoors. No doubt you will have heard that the Lovecraft–Price collaboration, Through the Gates of the Silver Key, has been reconsidered and accepted for W.T. The actual writing of this tale, according to Price, is about 99 & ¾ per cent Lovecraft.

Thanks for that vivid little account of the voodoo proceedings by your friend. I return the ms., but would greatly appreciate a copy of it sometime. I should think Hornig would be glad to run this in The Fantasy Fan.

Thanks too for the likeable snapshot. I'll reciprocate presently with some kind of alleged simulacrum of my own vulpine visage and borzoi figure.

I can't guarantee the condition of that Odes and Sonnets, so maybe we had better wait. I'll get one for you sooner or later. As to Sandalwood, it shouldn't cost you more than $1.00 or $1.50. Perhaps I can buy one back locally—I'll inquire when I have the time and opportunity.

I am relieved to learn that you and your banker-friend refrained from spearing the bystanders with anything sharper and more pernicious than paperclips. Such forbearance speaks well for your self-mastery and ability to resist the obsessive demonian influences of the autumnal sabbat.

As to your cat and his family affairs—well, it is notorious that cats will be cats. Mine, by judicious and skilful elimination, have been reduced in number to a black and ancient witch-cat, yclept Simaetha, the grandam of multitudes; and a swashbuckling Maltese tom, who answers to the name of General Tabasco. I am beginning to hope that the witch-cat is past the age of feline propagation. As to Tabasco and his doings in the neighbourhood at large— well that's his own business and his own risk.

Wright took the slightly revised Witchcraft of Ulua. You are damned well right about aretology[2]—the word itself is marked obsolete in my Webster, which is of no recent date either. If I'm not careful, the latter-day bigots of phallicism will lock me up in the Iron Maiden for such anaphrodisiacs as Ulua! By the way, don't undervalue this tale; I wouldn't have had the originality to write it a few years back.

I have been reading Montague Summers' erudite and curious tome, The Geography of Witchcraft, which I have newly acquired. My, my, such doings. Some of the goings-on in medieval nunneries were certainly er, exotic. My current W.T. yarn, Azédarac, is far from exaggerated, since bishops, canons, etc, have been historically charged with sorcery.

                    Yrs for the Alkahest,[3]
                    Klarkash-Ton [vertical, ornamented]

Notes

1. CAS refers to a reprint of *The Episodes of Vathek* by Simpkin, Marshall, Hamilton, Kent (c. 1929), part of the publisher's Abbey Classics series.
2. The part of moral philosophy that treats of virtue.
3. The "universal solvent" of the alchemists.

[23]   [RHB to CAS] [TLS]

                    December thirteen ? [, 1933]

Hon. KlarKashton; Watcher of the Tower of the Elder Ones; Seer of the translunar Mountains; Lord of Illusion; Ruler of all that is of consequence; Delineator of the Horrific; Inscrutable mystick vanguard, Thy majesty;

Perhaps as you suggest, the copyright on the 3rd E of V would be easily obtained. I'll enquire. I had another thought, after writing you, a small, evil thought. Since your ending is equivalent to perhaps one-third of the entire, why not just print it seperately [*sic*] in identical format as Abbey's ed, and buy up a few of the latter & bind them together? The A. Classics are knocked down to about thirty-five cents, remaindered, I have noticed, so that would eliminate the Hell of a Job of setting up the Beckford part again! Perhaps it is impractical, tho. At any rate, I shall surely endeavor to put out your excellent conclusion during the coming year if it is humanly possible. It would sell to Beckford collectors, also, I think. Awfully sorry your clever little pamphlet is financially a failure, but come! let us rejoice in the fact it is at any rate Art!

I was infinitely pleased with the S. G. which HPL sent me. I am forwarding it, as you request, to WT. That deprives me of the pleasure of being its possible sponsor, but at all indications I'll have a great deal else on my hands! Strange, of all the letters Canevin[1] wrote, I have located only half-a-hundred of sufficient interest to warrant publication; and of these only four are before 1930! Many destroyed theirs, including Wright, Baird, Bates, etc. But there are one or two real gems among the survivals.

I have before me the original typescript of Price's[2] and the holograph of HPL's of the S.K. sequel, and upon comparing them, the collaboration is most interestingly traced. P. wrote first, then L. revised, then they revised, as I understand it. In certain passages HPL has left the wording of the Peacock Sultan verbatim, but the ending and starting are in his own phraseology, and the whole thing bears more the impression of Randolph Carter rather than Malik Taus. But the nucleus was EHP. . . . . There is a place where my bibliomania is of particular interest, and I have to thank Price for the kindness in donating this pair of Mss. Was glad to hear from both ends of the line that it had been accepted for 140 *phrulder*—also, I trust you land your SG this time at 75 wolf-chasers![3]

I may possibly print the Vodu encounter in pamphlet; if not, I shall make you a typed copy in time. I think it is pretty well authenticated. HPL was quite interested.

I shall be very pleased to get your gelatined visage for my Rogues' Gallery, and trust mine own gives you no nightmares!

Sorry that Hall insists on the popular types of drivel for Art. Don't prostitute your art for commerce! Unless the Brobdi[n]gnagian Wicked Lupus necessitates such a deplorable move! I'll second the motion that AstSt needs improvement. It is a little bit better than its predecessor, but still is nothing to tear one's hair about.

I hear UNUSUAL will have to tone down a bit. Sorry.

Yes, I agree that it was not only in Medieval times that the surprising feats of the Geography of Witchcraft were practised, in fact, there is an astonishing preoccupation with aretoeology [*sic*] even now! . . . heard something with possibilities the other day; an Old Wife's Tale of a musical manifestation that ran up and down the piano scales twice, and then no apparent cause could be found upon nocturnal investigation! Page Chas. Fort!

Since I've successfully disposed of my Beloved Father for the time (he is at Kansas City, and I'm virtual Lord of the Realm) I have asked Price if he can't come over for the Xmas season, but fear he won't be able to.

Did you read the two DIARIES OF A PROVINCIAL LADY—Delafield?[4] Exceptionally amusing.

Trusting that you have an enjoyable Yuletide, with a few beneficent manifestations of banshees (or is there no such thing as a favorable banshee?)

In emulation of Munchausen,[5]

Signed in the absence of the Lord Mayor,

Ar-Ech-Bei

By the proboscis of Bacc[h]us.

Notes

1. An epithet for Henry S. Whitehead after a recurring character in his stories. In his introduction to *Jumbee and Other Uncanny Tales,* RHB wrote: "The character 'Gerald Canevin' is Whitehead himself, a harking back to the ancestral Caer-n'-Avon. 'I use the form "Canevin" because it is easily pronounced and is made up of "cane" and "vin," that is, cane-wine—RUM, the typical product of the West Indies'" (xi), the setting of many of Whitehead's stories.

2. Called "The Lord of Illusion," hence RHB's salutation.

3. *Phrulder* and *wolf-chaser* are coined equivalents of *dollars.* See "The Hoard of the Wizard-Beast": "No shining phrulder, as of old, lay stacked about the strongroom; and over empty coffers the sardonic spider wove webs of mocking design." To "keep the wolf from the door" is to have just enough money to avert starvation.

4. E. M. Delafield (pseud. of Edmée Elizabeth Monica de la Pasture, 1890–1943), *Diary of a Provincial Lady* (London: Macmillan, 1930) and *The Provincial Lady Goes Further* (London: Macmillan, 1932). There are two further volumes in the series: *The Provincial Lady in America* (1934) and *The Provincial Lady in Wartime* (1940).

5. The central character (based upon an actual figure) in *Baron Munchausen's Narratives of His Marvellous Travels and Campaigns in Russia* (1785) by Rudolf Erich Raspe, a collection of tall tales later expanded by other writers.

[24]   [RHB's printed Christmas card]

[Postmarked De Land, Fla.,
13 December 1933]

BY / THE /NINE /SATURNIAN / SATELLITES / OR / THE / SCALES / OF / GREAT / CTHULHU / OR / SOMETHING / SIMILAR / I / WISH / YOU / THE / USUAL / MERRY / CHRISTMAS / MCMXXXIII

Ar-Ech-Bei

[25]   [CAS to RHB] [TLS]

Dec. 30th, 1933.

Dear Ar-Éch-Bei:

Herewith the original of The City of the Singing Flame, which seems to have been batted off mainly on the old Remington, with liberally over-scrawled revisions in longhand. During the search for this, which involved going through vast piles of mss., I found the originals of some other stories which you might like to add to your collection, and am sending them along with The Singing Flame. The Epiphany of Death will appear in Hornig's magazinelet.[1]

I hope, and trust, that there will be no difficulty about obtaining the copyright on Marzials' translation of 3rd Episode. Your idea of buying up a number of the Abbey classics and binding in my termination of the Episode is certainly rather inveigling. It might be hard, though, to make a neat job out of the actual conjunction of sheets. Otherwise it sounds rather nifty.

Glad The 7 Gs was so much to your taste. I am rather partial to that opus myself. These grotesque and elaborate ironies come all too naturally to me, I fear. Incidentally, Wright bought the tale, though jewing me down on 5 of the anticipated 75 loupgarou exorcisers.

The originals of The Silver Key sequel must indeed form an interesting study in collaborative method. I found the tale an excellent one but was unable to detect more than a few paragraphs of Price's characteristic phrasing in the actual workmanship. Much of the ideation, though, was obviously his.

I'll have some copies of a good snapshot before long and will enclose one in my next.

I blew myself for a few books lately, in spite of poverty. Lewis Spence's The History of Atlantis, The Satyricon of Petronius (J. Lindsay's translation, with drawings by Norman Lindsay)[,] The Golden Asse of Apuleius (Bosschère illustrations) and The Mysteries and Secrets of Magic by one Thom[p]son (can't recall his lengthy initials) form the lineup. The last-named, ordered from a firm in Glasgow, has not yet arrived. The others are all worthwhile investments. Apart from this, I made myself a Christmas gift of sherry—my favourite tipple when I can't get arrack,[2] Benedictine, Chartreuse, apricot brandy or Sam[-]Shu![3] Beer, light wines (especially of the German type) and very sweet wines are not so much to my taste; and I detest gin and nearly all cocktails.

That haunted piano is surely a case either for Fort or Doyle. Some one should page them in the Elysian or Hadean meads. Apropos of funerealities, I note that R. W. Chambers has at last received The Yellow Sign. His King in Yellow was a great book.[4]

Hope you will like The Weaver in the Vault and its illustration.

Literally speaking, I am at present finishing some cold turkey.

Yours for tax-free liquor,

Klarkash-Ton

[P.S.] Thanks for the diverting sketches!

Notes

1. CAS dedicated the story to HPL.
2. *Arrack:* a strong alcoholic drink of the Middle East and Far East, distilled from fermented palm sap, rice, or molasses.
3. A Chinese alcoholic beverage, also known as *arak.*
4. Robert W. Chambers (b. 1865) died on 13 December. "The Yellow Sign" is a story in his collection *The King in Yellow* (1895).

[26]   [CAS to RHB] [TLS]

Feb. 11th, 1934.

Dear Ar-Éch-Bei:

I can't locate any mss. of The Hashish-Eater, in the strict Latinical sense of the word.[1] A carbon of the first typescript of the poem seems to be the best I can do for you; and this may be of some interest and value, since many alternative readings are scribbled on the margins. I guess the field of modern originals would be pretty narrow if you confined yourself entirely to handwritten stuff. It may be that I shall yet find the first ms. of the H.E. There are vast heaps of papers that I have not found time to go through. You shall have it if I ever do locate it. In the meanwhile, here are some other items, holographs and first typings. If I were a collector, I'd prize the ms. of The Monster of the Prophecy, which is still one of my favourite yarns. I'm including two or three old typings of poems that went into Sandalwood.

Glad you enjoyed The Ghoul. I had the Arabian Nights, rather than Vathek, in mind when I wrote it; and, at the time of writing (over three years ago) had not read the Episodes of V. Vathek itself, however, was one of my earliest enthusiasms; and I dare say that it left its mark. I wrote endless Oriental romances, about fire-worshippers, devil-worshippers and other gentlemen of that kidney, when I was fifteen.

I'll be grateful if you can do *anything*, at *any* time, with the 3rd Episode. If the thing sees print before Cocytus and Phlegethon freeze solid, I'll be satisfied.

I have enough new verse for a small volume, but, with fifty bucks still owing on The Double Shadow, I do not feel like sinking myself any deeper in the financial syrtis.[2] Damme if I'll print *anything* again, at my own expense.

Yes, the Satyricon was a good bargain. Did I mention acquiring Lewis Spence's The History of Atlantis? Though some of his arguments are a little far-fetched, S. makes out a pretty fair case, by circumstantial evidence, for the existence of a large continent in former ages between Europe, Africa and the Americas. He traces the witch-cults (so strikingly similar in Mexico and the Mediterranean countries) to Atlantis.

Oh, yes, here is a picture of myself—an enlargement from a snapshot that is considered good. The Dark Damsel is *not* my sweetheart.

That crack about drawings "reduced to the barest essentials" would apply equally well to Rops or Bosschère,[3] I imagine.

Thorne Smith sounds as if he might be rather diverting.[4] I have not read any of his books. The next time I do any buying, I shall acquire a Rabelais. R. is one of the most glaring omissions from my shelves.

I fear that I burned the few scribbled notes from which I wrote The 7 Gs on the typewriter. Wright, in a sense, has the original—the typed copy that *you* sent him. Of this I possess only one carbon, which I want for my files of story carbons.

I don't want to be irreverent; but Rosenbach and his museum are welcome to the Star-Spangled Bandanna. I could, however, utilize the 24,000 pazoors with considerable unction and ingenuity.[5]

Yes, Merritt is a broth of a boy. I admire his writings, and have really gotten more pleasure from them than from most of the so-called classics. I am glad that Ech-Pi-El had a chance to meet him.[6]

I hope that L. will make Florida this summer. Too bad you are marooned; but anyone with a taste for fine and recherché literature is likely to find himself in that predicament almost anywhere. At one time, it irked me considerably; but I seem to have grown case-hardened the last few years.

No, I do not correspond with Leinster or A. Hall.[7] Apart from Ech-Pi-El, Derleth, Wandrei, Carl Jacobi, E[.]H. Price and R.E. Howard seem to be my chief literary correspondents.

Good luck with your longish story. I liked the little skit about the cockney poll-parrot that strayed into the realms of Faerie.[8]

As to Woodstock,[9] I am not quite sure but have the impression it is either a nudist colony or a lunatic asylum. Unless the inhabitants of a literary colony are hand-picked, I'm afraid the place would have certain resemblances to both of the above-named institutions. Carmel (the only one that I know personally) was not so "hot" even in George Sterling's time; and I fear it is infinitely worse with the present crew. Maybe I'm a recreant; but I've grown to prefer plain hicks and bourgeoisie to a certain type of Bohemian studio-hound.

> Yrs for 25¢ hooch (25¢ per gal., demijohn included.)

As ever,

Klarkash-Ton

Notes

1. CAS refers to the fact that "mss." (manuscripts) is derived from two Latin words meaning "written by hand."

2. *Syrtis:* "Proper name of two large quicksands . . . off the northern coast of Africa; hence *gen.* A quicksand" (*OED*).

3. Felicien Rops (1833–1898), Belgian artist and printmaker. Jean de Bosschère

(1881–1953), French artist and illustrator.

4. American writer James Thorne Smith, Jr. (1892–1934) gained popularity for the humorous ghost novels *Topper* (1926) and *Topper Takes a Trip* (1932). He would die four months after this letter was written (20 June).

5. Abraham Simon Wolf Rosenbach (1876–1952), American collector, scholar, and seller of rare books and manuscripts, who parlayed his passion for books and manuscripts (much like RHB's) into a successful business, becoming the most famous dealer in rare books and manuscripts in the first half of the 20th century. He successfully bid $24,000 for the earliest draft of Francis Scott Key's "The Star-Spangled Banner."

6. HPL met A. Merritt in New York on 8 January 1934.

7. Austin Hall (1885?–1933), prolific pulp writer of western, fantasy, and science fiction tales.

8. Probably "The Sacred Bird," no. IV of *Annals of the Jinns.*

9. In *On Lovecraft and Life,* RHB writes of traveling to Lakeport, CA, in the winter of 1938–39 to visit Groo and Claire Beck, with the "intention [of founding] a sort of Transcendentalist colony of Woodstock, centering around a printing press. Fine hand-made books of exotic content" (20). The Byrdcliffe Arts Colony was founded in 1902 near Woodstock, NY. It is the oldest operating arts and crafts colony in America.

[27]   [RHB to CAS] [TLS]

Feb 21 1934

Dear Klar-Kashton:

It is most exciting to receive a package from you, for I can be certain that it will include some really significant bibliophilic treasure. You are ever so kind; and it is an inordinately pleasing thing to have periodic visitations from Santa (in your avatar). Each of the enclosures in your latest donation are carefully and neatly put away amidst my hoard, and it would be indeed hard to give precedence as to the merits of the items, for verily, they are all splendid. The carbon of the H.E., since apparently the earliest extant, has claim to vast importance (as well as very great interest. If the *original* should ever materialize I surely would like to be on the waiting list!) while the very long THE MONSTER OF THE PROPHECY is certainly adequately holographic, as well as being literarily conspicuous. But then, the short typescript of your rather early (from WT chronology) Last Incantation counts from *that* angle. And, of course, I was exceedingly pleased to add your picture to those on the wall of my chamber of horrors, Yoh-Vombis, wherein I keep my treasures.[1] Therefore, all I can do is to thank you most profusely.

I was glad to note that the Dark Damsel was not entanglingly affiliated with you. Such a procedure would be wholly too conventional to be feared from you! To my mind you ought to be extraordinarily erratic, mysterious, and generally conceded mad by the wondering populace. Of course, I may be fooled, but that is what I rather picture you as. Maybe I'm like the person Merritt told me of in a letter. ". . . . who tried for a year to meet me, and when the young lady did . . her eyes were stricken, and she gasped 'Oh, *you* never wrote the Moon Pool!' I tried to convince her that my clothes & flesh were but a misfit & that inside I was the lean, romantic, poetic and dark-visaged one she evidently had pictured me. But it was of no use. The dream was gone." (And he concluded). "Since then I have been more gun-shy than ever!"

I went on a mild orgy the other night—a real old county fair, with the Penny Arcade, the allegedly humorous crudities of the jig-show (that was particularly amusing). Five muscular old nigger wenches got up and whooped and did a few lewd contortions, at which the largely colored audience shouted in ecstasy every time one of the piquant ladies wiggled! Most amusing!) and all the other paraphernalia. The Penny Arcade, as is conventional, had only ten-year hack shows, invariably entitled such things as "Oh Boy!" "Oriental Nightclub,['] "The Sea-Nymph" (the latter apparently contained two unpleasant-looking women in a hosiery department!) and one hilarious Apache Dance, that I simply had to see twice. If one animates them regularly all sorts of strange motions take place. Oh, I was wicked! I even managed to get insulted by one of the barkers, so it was a regular evening. The pictorial portrayals on the outside of one of the sideshows would have interested you, I think, for the artist had ambitiously combined a frog with a girl, most peculiarly, to represent one attraction. Sometimes I almost covet those gaily tinted improbabilities, for they are certainly fantastic!

I believe you'd enjoy some of Thorne Smith, notably, TOPPER TAKES A TRIP, which, though a sequel to a not very animated original, is readily picked up with little confusion, and has a good deal of surprisingly expressive writing and both subtle and rank humor. The whole tale is such a mad-cap story that I for one have enjoyed it vastly.

I surely do hope that L. will visit me, and it looks rather probable at present. His erudition is practically limitless, and on every subject he seems very well informed. What's more, there is no pedantry in him that I can see—all he writes is extremely pertinent & interesting.

I don't begrudge the [$]24000 Star-Speckled Banana (in fact, privately, I won't care to give it room! Heretic?) but there was a Poe letter (at 1800 dollars!) recently sold that I wouldn't have objected too violently to having. Merritt is, as you say, a very fine writer, and L. tells me that there is a prospect of his dropping the pulp-market that had been impressed upon his style. I would welcome that.

Too bad that THE DOUBLE SHADOW isn't financially successful, but remember there is always a hope that it will ultimately pay. I would consider issuing further *poetry*, in time, if you wished, because that's not so much a nuisance to set up as is sheer text!

Wow! I'm doing a little plain & fancy smirking, for you say that the 7 G's is in Wright's possession, and for some obscure reason I had already done something odd. A vague prompting caused me to retain the initial page and make an identical and careful copy, so one page, at least, is in my possession!

Therefore, when I sent it on, page #1 was left in my hands. I still don't quite know why I did it, but I'm glad I *did.*

See the improvement made by using a new ribbon! I'm of such a stingy nature I lingered long with the old & almost illegible one!

I see, from the PUBLISHERS WEEKLY, that A. M. Robertson has quitted this sphere.[2] I wonder if he ever wrote upon his reminiscences of Sterling? They must have had a long and close acquaintanceship, I judge.

You mentioned corresponding with Carl Jacobi in reply to my query about Hall & Leinster. Now the name seems irritatingly elusive . . . can you tell me who the gentleman is? I'm rather curious because I can't place it.

I have odd ideas concerning unusual bookbinding materials, and I have determined if the holograph HASHISH-EATER should ever come into my possession, I shall have it bound with a backstrip of the venomous coral-snake, whose delicate and gay hide I managed to tan from a local specimen. They are rather infrequently encountered, and I think it would give an interesting effect.

I must cease from both scruples and haste.

Your by the Ship of Ishtar, Ar Éch Bei [stylized]

[P.S.] Periodically I apologize for my bad spelling . . . I never *was* very brilliant!

Notes

1. The "locked closet," named for CAS's story, in which RHB stored his books and magazines.
2. A. M. Robertson (1854?–1934), San Francisco bookseller and publisher who issued many of GS's poetry volumes and also CAS's *ST;* he died 12 February. Cf. *Publishers' Weekly* 125, No. 7 (17 February 1934): 771.

[28]   [CAS to RHB] [TLS]

Auburn, Calif.
Mar. 23rd, 1934.

Dear Ar-Éch-Bei:

You aren't the only one who clings to wan and ancient ribbons: it is only recently that I summoned up enough energy to install a fresh one on my portable. The result is certainly a lot easier on my own eyesight, not to mention that of the recipients.

I was glad to hear that you were pleased with the contents of the grab-bag envelope. I haven't yet located the holograph of The H.E., but probably shall sooner or later, since I doubt very much if I ever destroyed it. In the meanwhile, maybe you could utilize the original typed draft of The Willow Landscape. I enclose also a few drawings. You will get the full beauty of the pen-and-ink creation if, after scrutinizing it in the customary fashion, you turn it upside-down.

Re the personal equation: I seem to have gotten past the age of entanglements with damsels, dark or otherwise: at least, the liabilities are not lessened, and I trust that neither the Romeo nor the Casanova phase will recur. I guess your qualification, "generally considered mad by the populace," would apply alright; but I fear I am only fair-to-middling erratic and mysterious. Books and liquor are my chief vices: said liquor consisting of a nightly thimbleful of sherry or other California wine when I sit up reading.

That country fair must have been full of quaint divertis[s]ements. The combination of girl and frog on the poster you mention makes me think of The Moon Pool and the frog people. As for the nigger wenches, that reminds me of my current story, Xeethra, since the king in the story called up certain black performers whose limbs were "pied with amber."

I hope that H.P.L. can make the Florida trip. You are dead right about his erudition—he could rival Montague Summers as well as a whole corps of ordinary astronomers, chemists, mathematicians, geologists, archaeologists and other garden scientists.

Thanks for your intimation about the possible future issuing of some poetry. I could easily dig up a few verses if this became practicable.

You must have been psychic, to retain the first sheet of The 7 Gs. By the way, I am vastly impressed with your plans for the binding of the H. E. holograph. I'll dig up, exhume and disinter that ms. somehow, if it's possible.

Jacobi has contributed some very fine items to W.T. One, entitled Mive, was in the same issue with my The Monster of the Prophecy. Another, Revelations in Black, appeared in April, 1933. You will note a story by Jacobi is announced for the forthcoming issue of W.T.[1]

I don't believe that Robertson ever wrote up any of his reminiscences of Sterling or anyone else. The San Francisco newspaper obituaries quoted him as having said that if he did this he would have to tell the truth—and the truth would cause altogether too much of a ruction. At least, that was the gist, if not the literal wording.

I have been reading a book by M. P. Shiel, entitled Shapes in the Fire. Two of the first stories, Xélucha and Vaila, are gorgeously fantastic. I haven't read the rest as yet. Vaila, I am sure, is the first version of the yarn referred to as The House of Sounds in H.P.L.'s monograph on Supernatural Horror in Literature.[2] It is certainly great stuff.

Yours for the Kalends of *les boucs noirs*.[3]

Klarkash-Ton [ornamented]

[P.S.] I missed the Annals of the Jinns in current Fantasy Fan. Your last one was excellent. Was interested in the note on Wells' *Time Machine*.[4] I first read that story when I was visiting George Sterling in Carmel (1912). I remember indistinctly the grey binding and the sphinx-like device which you mention.

Notes

1. Carl Jacobi, "Mive" (*WT,* January 1932); "Revelations in Black" (*WT,* April 1933); "The Cane" (*WT,* April 1934).
2. HPL correctly identified "Vaila," in *Shapes in the Fire,* as an early version of "The House of Sounds" by M. P. Shiel.
3. "The black goats."
4. *Annals of the Jinns* resumed in May. The previous appearance was in February. CAS also refers to RHB's "The Time Machine: A Bibliographical Note" (see Appendix).

[29]   [RHB to CAS] [TLS]

[R. H. Barlow
Bibliomaniac]

29 Mars
1 9 3 3 [*sic*]
[w. envelope postmarked 8 April 1934]

Mon Cher Klar-Kashton;

Mon Francais est très mal, mais Je entendre votrè renvoi á le jour de homme de chévre, et applaudir.[1]

Likewise, I find myself wholly unable to sustain the undoubtedly ungrammatical sentence any longer. I probably got the gender of "day" wrong, at that.

I was of course pleased with the donations. Your little drawing of the double-faced gentleman was particularly good. I'd certainly like to see some of your oils someday, since you get such excellent work in small things, the others must be veritable masterpieces. And the ms. of THE WILLOW LANDSCAPE, a very good tale, too, which I enjoyed in The Double Shadow, was gratefully received. Tsk tsk! What an immoral ending! Seriously, tho, I really liked the story quite a bit. You're very kind, I'm sure. And I shall hope fervently that the original Hashish Eater will turn up someday to enter my tender clutches.

Was glad to hear you are unhampered sentimentally. Books are my unending vice. I don't care especially for the devotion to Dionysus, wine is about as far as I go. Remember, Socrates' morals were corrupted through beverage. More than his morals, I guess. I'm a damned fool concerning reading & similar sedentary occupations, for my cursed eyes never let me alone. Certain doctors have said if I'd be a little child of nature (fancy that!) for a few years, my sight would improve, but by the whiskers of Sathanas,[2] I can't stop the principal pleasure I derive from existence. Which all brings me, as I embark upon a new sheet, to enquire how you like my stationery? Home-products, inc.

My dear Papa (the old coot) will indubitably have to go back to the hospital soon, for he not only succeeds in making himself entirely miserable, but endeavors to communicate the feeling to everyone around him. I'm going to get him out by the time Ech Pi El makes his visit, which looks favourable right now. I do hope he'll come.

I have not read the current WT. I have to buy mine from the publisher, to obtain copies not unreadably disfigured.

Goodness! So Sterling had on his shelves the scarce and desirable first edition of the Time Machine! It took me some time to be able to get my own copy. What ever became of Sterling's library? A recent beautifully put-up catalogue of Penguin Bk Shop quoted something I want like Hell. Lilith, ltd. signed, with a page of the ms. in it.[3] But I haven't the money, and by the time I get it, the book will be sold, undoubtably. [*sic*] Same as the recent disappointment I had at Goodspeeds. The copy of the Last American that Mitchell gave to Jno. Kenderick [*sic*] Bangs, for twelve bucks. Well, with a frantic rush, I got an order off, not an hour after the catalogue came, and the damn thing was sold. Life is awful for a book-collector!

Were you responsible for Penguin sending the catalogue? If so, I'm sure I thank you. It is an excellent piece of work & includes some very desirable items.

Horning [*sic*] excludes me from both the current and next FF. Lack of space, says he. I don't much care, for he has a foul tale I did, in store, and the miasma will undoubtably [*sic*] scare off whoever has so far endured my gabble.

This printing process is slow work, but very grat[i]fying at times. I suppose I'll get Caneviniana out some day!

The only Shiel thing I've read (frank confession of ignorance) is THE PURPLE CLOUD, parts of which were masterful, and part of which was lousy. I've heard a great deal of THE HOUSE OF SOUNDS, and must get a copy some day.

I'm engaged in reading THE OLD WIVES TALE.[4] Have you ever read this splendid book? I never cared much for Bennett till I started this.

I hear the Monster of Loch Ness is reputedly cast up, dead, on the shores of France. A friend saw it in a newsreel. I wish I had! It fascinates me unutterably, and recalls Charles Fort to a vast degree.

I must cease.

> By the supernumerary digits of the Monster,
> And by the Palimpsest of Eibon,
> And by the Hammer of Thor
> As well as Mephisto's
> Whiskers, I subscribe
> Myself, Faithfully,
> Yours,
> Ar-Ech-Bei [stylized]

Notes

1. "My French is very bad, but I understand your reference to the day of the goat-man, and applaud." RHB's French is indeed very bad.
2. I.e., Satan. See the closing to this letter for another reference to Satan's whiskers.
3. The verse drama by George Sterling. RHB refers to the Book Club of California edition.
4. By Arnold Bennett.

[30]   [CAS to RHB] [TLS]

Auburn, Calif.
Apr. 30th, 1934.

Dear Ar-Éch-Bei:

To-night being Walpurgis Eve, I must delay no longer the acknowledgement and answering of your last epistle, duly received earlier in the month by the coven of Tsathoggua.[1] What to-night may bring forth I do not know and dare not surmise: so it were well to discharge my obligations while the opportunity remains!

Your rubricated stationery is quite fetching and effective.[2] Good work! I look forward with much interest to the volume of Caneviniana. I half wish that I had a printing outfit myself: but I lack both the time and the necessary pazoors for such divertis[s]ements.

From Éch-Pi-El's last card to me, written in Charleston, I rather surmise that he may be with you when this letter arrives. I wish I could join the conclave![3] Price is now in Oakland, and I hope he will visit Auburn ere long. When he does, we'll quaff a few libations to the gods of Averonia and the White Peacock, and (metaphorically) make fiery sacrifice of several editors in a wicker cage, ... *la manière des Druides*.[4]

I agree with you that books are an all-round satisfactory vice. As to liquor, I don't really enjoy it much after the first few drinks (three, four, five or seven, depending on modifying circumstances) Owing, no doubt, to some latent Puritanism, I dislike showing the effects of alcohol; and my efforts toward self-control have, in the past, given me the reputation of possessing a "hollow leg." Alone (as I usually am) I drink very little. Socrates, whom you mention, no doubt put away gallons to my glassfuls.

Sterling's library was sold some years ago (I can't recall the identity of the purchaser). He had the largest collection of modern verse, poetry and vers libre that I ever saw—many of the items, of course, being presentation copies. Yes, buying items from book-catalogues by mail is a precarious business, and the farther you live from the dealer, the more precarious it is. I have not yet received a book on sorcery and magic which I ordered last fall from Glasgow, Scotland. The dealer, John Smith, had sold the copy he possessed, but undertook to get me another if I would wait.

Wright has been very consistent of late in his rejections, having turned down three of my higher-class tales in succession. I enclose one of them, which you can show to Éch-Pi-El before returning to me. It is possible that the tale is a little overwrought; and I may, eventually, cut out the portions about the merman and the salamander.[5] I'd appreciate the opinions of yourself and Grandpa Theobald on this point. I enclose a newspaper picture of the creature that was cast up, dead, on the French coast. Evidently it was *not* the Loch Ness monster: the latter, according to a very recent newspaper item, has been seen and photographed by a noted London surgeon, who got four pictures showing a long neck and small head poised above a bulky body on the water's surface! Hoot mon! [']Tis a pity that Charles Fort is dead.[6] Biologists who have seen Dr. Wilson's photographs won't even hazard a guess as to what the monster is![7]

By the way, apropos of weird news items, I wonder if you have read about the dog which was asphyxiated some time ago by a scientist at the University of California, and then brought to life after being pronounced thoroughly dead. This canine Lazarus, at last reading, was still "alive" after fifteen days, and is able to eat, bark, wag its tail, etc. Its brain, however, seems to be impaired, and its actions and reflexes are the mechanical ones of a Zombi![8]

I am still looking for the H.E. holograph.

You can give Éch-Pi-El the clipping about Gibson, that feline Gargantua[9] or Anakim of Ulthar.

No, I haven't read the Old Wives' Tale. I once tackled something of Bennett's but found it unmanageable. Shiel is great stuff. Personally, I like nearly all of The Purple Cloud, though preferring the first half of the book to the last. The House of Sounds, even in the first version (I haven't seen the last) is a honeycooler.

Yrs, by the Black Meteorite of Mecca & the Well of Skelos,
Klarkash-Ton [vertical, ornamented]

Notes

1. The entity CAS introduced in "The Tale of Satampra Zeiros." HPL, on reading the TMS of the story, promptly incorporated references to Tsathoggua into "The Mound," a story he was revising for Zealia Bishop c. 1929–30. HPL's "The Whisperer in Darkness" contains the first reference to Tsathoggua in print. See RHB to CAS 36n6.

2. RHB's stationery was printed with red ink.

3. HPL visited RHB in Cassia (near De Land) from 2 May to 21 June.

4. [In] the manner of the Druids.

5. "The Last Hieroglyph." Variant early titles include "The Last Hieroglyph; or, In the Book of Agoma" and "In the Book of Vergama."

6. Fort (b. 1874) had died 3 May 1932.

7. Robert Kenneth Wilson, a London gynecologist, had taken a photograph showing the head and neck of the supposed Loch Ness monster, published in the *Daily Mail* on 21 April 1934.

8. Robert E. Cornish (1903–1963) conducted experiments on fox terriers (named Lazarus I, II, etc.) killed using a nitrogen gas mixture and left clinically dead for six to ten minutes before attempting to revive them. The *Berkeley Daily Gazette* reported that "he admits that the dog, more dead than alive, is decidedly not an ideal house dog but it appeared most likely that he would have to take the animal to the home of his parents." The films *The Man They Could Not Hang* (1939) and *The Man with Nine Lives* (1940) were inspired by his work.

9. At thirty-five pounds, "Gibson" was regarded the world's largest cat. He died in 1934.

[31]   [CAS to RHB] [Envelope only, postmarked Auburn, Calif., 1 May 1934]

[32]   [RHB and HPL to CAS] [TLS, Bancroft]

> [R. H. Barlow
> Bibliomaniac]
>
> May tenth 1934

Dear Klar-Kashton;

I find a number of matters in what might be termed my mind. First let me thank you very much for the clippings you sent, which were of extreme interest. I return them herewith, except for the picture of the French monster, which was marked obscurely "keep this", and which I presume I may retain, if the notation was intended for me. Of course, if you wish it, I shall send it back, but otherwise I'll appropriate the item for my files!

And next let me offer congratulation on the excellent tale IN THE BOOK OF VERGAMA,[1] which I gather from certain intimations in the text is intended to be one of a series. Or am I wrong! The tale was extremely clever & well-written. By all means leave it as it stands; don't delete the merman & salamander portions . . . they are emphatically all right.

I hope you were unmolested by the Horde of the Dark on Walpurgis Eve. It was relatively peaceful here, although strange shapes flew screeching through the gloom, and a great deal of blood was untidily left on the back stoop.

Thankee for the comment on my stationary! Éch-Pi-El recently assisted in the issuing of a second edition of the same. I don't know when I'll get Caneviniana done. I may even have to delay till my autumnal ocular quest . . . My eyes are behaving very badly.

And now for another subject. You of course know my vast admiration for your work, and I find myself with the precise sum of four dollars that is not involved in any of my frenzied finance. HPL tells me that Donald Wandrei bought several of your paintings a few years ago. I should like to have something a bit more representative of your drawings than the tiny pictures you have been so kind as to donate me, therefore, I enclose the four pazoors, and I'll leave it entirely up to you what to select. You know my tastes, I think. The only suggestion I should make would be that a *landscape* type would be more preferable, giving the celebrated klarkashtonic vegetation full play. The medium I shall also leave to you as long as it is in colour. Is this too much of an imposition? I'm sure I shall treasure immensely the result!

Sorry Wright has turned down your recent tales. That is all the more assurance they are good. And when my eyes get better, I really think I'll be able to issue further poetry of yours.

I think you might care to read THE METAL MONSTER, by Merritt?[2] Theobald says you have not entirely read it, so it will be sent on to you by Duane W. Rimel, with whom I believe you correspond. If you skip the first 7 pages, it becomes a magnificent tale. You may return it directly to me after as long reading as you wish.

And thanks for the sketch appended to our letter!

Enclosed is a clipping from HPL.

Have you access to a phonograph that would play homemade voice records? HPL & I are thinking of making such records & sending them to you, just for something or other. A person can correspond with another and yet never know the sound of his voice! We recently bethought ourselves of this, and wondered if the idea would amuse you.

Trust Price is able to visit you. I envy him the long voyage, and resulting encounter as well.

I shall surrender this letter to Theobald, with best wishes, and hoping I am not causing too much trouble with my purchase idea!

Therefore, I start a fresh sheet only to subscribe myself

Yours by the tentacles of Cthulhu,

Ar-E'ch-Bei [vertical, ornamented]

PS—Can you give me the dates of Overland containing Wandrei's article on you, and your article or poem on Sterling? . . . or as a matter of fact, any weird or general material aside from Sterling's poems which are more accessible?

Hail, Great Vergama! I'll add a line to the epistle of my young host, with his permission. Having a great time down here, and feeling 20 years younger! You ought to see the bas-relief plaque of Cthulhu that Barlow has just made—a marvellous thing, which precisely embodies my conception of Wilcox's dream-plaque in the story. He is also doing a splendid clay statuette of the elephant-god Ganesa (prototype of Sonny Belknap's Chaugnar) for good old Bill Lumley. It ought to send the old boy into ecstasies. I never realised what a sculptor Ar-E'ch-Bei is till I saw him at work on these specimens ¶ Edition of the Shunned House recently came from Cook,—you'll see a bound copy in the course of time. ¶ Had some trips to interesting antiquities—old Spanish sugar mill antedating 1763, old Franciscan mission (picturesque arched ruins) of 1696, site of old Turnbull plantation of 1768, &c. ¶ Have had some interesting rows on the lake—which we have named The Moon Pool. ¶ Ar-E'ch-Bei is enclosing his latest picture, which you can keep. Later we'll send you snaps—including one with a great coach-whip snake. This is Yig's favourite stamping-ground, & R H B has shot many of his children to use in binding books. Some of the local ophidians have magnificent skins. ¶ Duly recd. your card. Thanks! That old Indian surpasses even me for venerable years!

    Well—now to get this in the mail! Yrs in Iog-Sôtot's³ name—

E'ch-Pi-El

[P.S.] Iä! Shub-Niggurath! The Goat With a Thousand Young! Just got card from you & Sultan Malik at P.O.! Diabolic greetings to you both! Would that we might be present to swell the chorus of Eblis' praise!———E'ch-Pi-El

Just to be sociable I shall add a line of greeting.

RB

[P.P.S. (by HPL)] Your new story is magnificent. Take Ar-E'ch-Bei's advice, & don't cut anything out. ¶ Xeethra hasn't come yet. ¶ Have seen *Marvel Tales* at last. Not so bad for an amateur venture.

Notes

1. A variant title of "The Last Hieroglyph."
2. RHB had prepared a crudely bound copy of the *Argosy All-Story* serialization of Merritt's novel.
3. CAS's variant name of HPL's Yog-Sothoth.

[33]   [CAS to RHB] [TNS]

[Postmarked Auburn, Cal.,
18 May 1934]

Dear Ar-Éch-Bei: Rec'd joint letter from you & Ech-Pi-El, and will write at length in a day or two. Thanks for the 4 green papyri! I'll pick out a representative landscape in Lemuria or Sfanomoë, and mail it to you promptly, along with some mss. You & Theobaldus will be glad to know that I am not curtailing the Vergama story. On the contrary, I have done a longer version, detailing efforts of Nushain¹ to sidestep his guides and evade the destiny that will turn him into a cipher. The guides, ironically, twit him with a lack of faith in his own horoscopic vaticinations! Vergama also waxes sardonic.

    General Thomaso Tabasco sends his most military compliments to Doodlebug, & wishes him fortunate strategy in all excursions either amatory or commissarial. Yrs, by the black piled taper that Nushain stole from the unnamed giant sarcophagus.

Klarkash-Ton

Notes

1. Nushain the astrologer, in "The Last Hieroglyph."

[34]   [CAS to RHB] [TLS]

May 19th, 1934

Dear Ar-Éch-Bei: I mailed you this morning a representative landscape in water-colour, yclept Beyond Cathay,[1] and hope it will be satisfactory. Am throwing in a grotesque from the under side of the moon, also sending you original typescripts of The Devotee of Evil and Vaults of Yoh-Vombis. Letter will follow later. Just read and approved your Flower God in TFF.

Klarkash-Ton

P.S. Go ahead with the records!—I can commandeer a phonograph somewhere or sometime.

Notes

1. There is a poem of the same title in *EC*.

[35]   [CAS to RHB] [TLS]

Auburn, Calif.
May 21st, 1934.

Dear Ar-Éch-Bei:

By this time, you should have received my cards, the painting, and mss. I hope you will like the exotic landscape, Beyond Cathay, which has been singled out for admiration by most of the people who have seen it. The mss. may be of interest to you, as illustrating my rather toilsome method of working. If you compare The Devotee of Evil typescript with the printed story, you will find material alterations. Also, the first version of The Vaults of Yoh-Vombis is longer by about 1700 words, mainly descriptive, than the tale as it appeared in W.T. Wright demanded the excisions, which are all in the first part.

Thanks for the loan of The Metal Monster. I shall look forward to it, since I missed several instalments of the story as published in magazine form. It contains magnificent stuff.

I hope that Éch-Pi-El is still with you, and am writing him in your care. Wish I could look in on some of your sessions, via Brazen Horse or Arabian Nights carpet. Price's visit here was all too brief;[1] but since he is staying indefinitely in Oakland, little more than a hundred miles away, he will probably be able to come again before long. We nearly talked the clock around and paid visits to several of the gold mines in the neighbourhood apart from consuming a certain amount of liquid gold[.] (Our sessions however, were not nearly as alcoholic as you might have inferred from the joint card. We drank only a little of the Muscat brandy, having decided that said beverage was not all that it purported to be; and Price consumed the lion's share of the sherry without visible effect.)

I'm glad you liked Vergama. I think I told you that I had amplified and embroidered the tale somewhat. It will form the concluding item of my Zothique series, if this series should ever appear between book-covers.

I hope that you and Theobaldus have gone ahead with the phonograph records. Some friends of mine here in Auburn will gladly play them for me. I like the idea tremendously, and hope that you have chanted the rituals of R'lyeh[2] in antiphon as well as chorus.

My copy of The Overland containing Wandrei's article seems to have mislaid itself; but I think it was either November or December 1926. My article on Sterling, along with many other appreciations of S., was in Overland for March 1927. As to weird material, the Overland has never gone in for it much: my fantasy The Abominations of Yondo, which I believe you have, being the only example that I can recall in its pages. I heard that this tale evoked many loud, lugubrious and indignant howls from the readers.

Certain sounds, sights and odours—particularly odours—intruded themselves hereabouts on Walpurgis Eve; but it would seem there were no influences that could not be fended and driven away by the Medal of St. Benedict.[3] At least, *so far.* I am still alive and with no marks of invultuation, no obsessions or possessions other than those of my wonted devils.

Thanks for the likable snapshot. I'm damned sorry about your eyes, and hope the trouble will somehow ameliorate itself. Mine give me the deuce on occasion. Each of my line drawings for W.T. has given me a severe headache in consequence of the strain involved; and moving pictures are also a sure-fire cause of such headaches. I've about given up going to movies—which isn't a very serious deprivation.

Your drawing of Nushain and the salamander is quite spirited. In my new version, the salamander whacks Nushain into the flames with "flailings of his dragon-like tail," when Nushain tries to escape. There are some nice new episodes in the catacomb portion; the astrologer, passing with his guide through a vault where tapers of black pitch burn about an immense unlegended sarcophagus, steals one of the tapers and tries to return to the upper world. His exit, however, is barred in certain curious manners.

If certain editors persist in rejecting my stories, I shall perform to their detriment the fearful and dreaded Mass of St. Sécaire.[4]

Yrs. by the inkhorn of Eibon,

Klarkash-Ton

[P.S.] Keep all enclosures.

Notes

1. See E. Hoffmann Price, "Clark Ashton Smith: A Memoir," *TSS* 3–17.
2. The undersea city in the Pacific where HPL's Cthulhu is imprisoned.
3. Known as the "devil-chasing medal" (it bears the admonition *Vade retro satana,* or "Step back, Satan").
4. A form of the "Black Mass," a parody of the Roman Catholic Mass, notable for its unusual parody of the Eucharist. Described by James George Frazer in *The Golden Bough* (1890), Chapter IV: Magic and Religion.

[36]   [RHB to CAS] [TLS]

[R. H. Barlow
Bibliomaniac]

June 2 34

Dear Klarkash-Ton;

I was extremely pleased with BEYOND CATHAY—it is truly an excellent drawing and you made a good guess at the kind I desired. Only thing, I underpaid such fine work! Ah well; we paupers.

And thanks for the crayon, as well as the Ms. You neglected signing Yoh-Vombis, so I send it, with two pages of my dismembered RECLUSE,[1] which I'm trying to get signed by all contributors. Incidentally; I am *immensely* interested in the not-ever-completed #2 of THE RECLUSE. I understand from Cook that you were to have *The Passing of Aphrodite* in this number. I suppose this has never been issued elsewhere? Do you have any proof-sheets, (or have you ever had,) of this second issue? May I see a copy of the poem? And finally, have you the original manuscript? I'd be very much interested in any information you can give me on this number.[2]

Would you loan me as much as was done of THE FUGITIVES? HPL has aroused my interest on the subject, and I would like very much to see the work.[3]

L. read aloud THE COLOSSUS OF YLOURGNE to me, and I found the tale utterly delightful. It's one of your best, in my opinion. Really, I certainly enjoyed the story. And while I'm on the subject I'll brazenly ask if the manuscript is around? (that is a crude trick, putting my sentence & punctuation & questionmark that way, but it has a certain fetching Bohemian air!)[4]

Any news on the H-E. holograph? I do manage to bother you pretty well, don't I?

That FLOWER-GOD thing of mine was utterly, miasmatically, lousy. Hornig insisted on using it, though, or I'd have destroyed the damned thing. He was so *touching!* And that reminds me of a fact that somewhat surprised me. The article (signed by one D. McPhail) is nearly literally, (save for the wording of paragraph #1) an article *I* wrote last fall, on H. G. Wells & Machen.[5] I was startled to find I had acquired the pseudonym with no warning. Hornig is clever, no doubt!

Is Wright returning the originals to your WT drawings?

Your BEYOND CATHAY so interested me that I should like to know if I might borrow "on approval" a bale of your paintings, (for some of which I should hope to substitute green papyri) I'd take care of the expense to you in shipping, and the only danger you'd risk would be a possibility that I should refuse to return any! (Mania is a great asset to a collector.)

How many of yours has Wandrei? Long? Loveman?

Incidentally, *for goodness' sake don't let Price corrupt your literary ideals with contaminating "action-and-plot" elements!*

Do you intend to ever do any more of THE BOOK OF EIBON? I shall be glad to see The Coming Of The White Worm in published form, and trust that will be soon.

HPL and I have been copying out references to various angles of the azathothian mythology, and we'd like you to supplement & correct this rudimentary "Style-sheet" which we are preparing to keep people from making contradictions. Would you fix up the details of Tsathoggua's ancestry & actions? We've taken the liberty of fixing up his ancestry this way. If you have objections, will you correct?[6]

I've been only two weeks in the composition of this letter, so I'll conclude!

With renewed expressions of approval for the painting,

Yours by the supernumerary eyes of Wilbur Whately [*sic*],[7]

Ar-Ech-Bei

Notes

1. Presumably the pages of W. Paul Cook's *Recluse* containing CAS's "After Armageddon" and "Mists and Rains."

2. HPL had said that he had seen proofs of his story "The Strange High House in the Mist," printed for the second issue of *The Recluse*. See HPL to CAS (1 October 1927): "I am extremely glad to hear that you are sending Cook 'The Passing of Aphrodite', & hope he will accord it the place of honour in the *Recluse* which it deserves" (*Dawnward Spire* 144).

3. See CAS to DW 13n1.

4. RHB's practice was to put a space ahead of question marks and exclamation points.

5. "About H. G. Wells."

6. HPL to RHB, 25 June 1934 (*O Fortunate Floridian* 142): "I see that C A S is linking up his own Tsathogguan data with the legends in 'The Mound', so that a minimum of discrepancies will exist. I infer that he has sent you a full transcript from the Parchments of Pnom—which you will no doubt incorporate into your 'style sheet.'" In August, HPL complained to RHB that Hugh B. Cave, in a story published in *WT* ("The Isle of Dark Magic," August 1934) had wreaked havoc with the "style-sheet" by referring to Yuggoth as a "devil-god" instead of a place. See also CAS to RHB 39n2.

7. The more nearly human of the twin offspring of Lavinia Whateley and Yog-Sothoth in HPL's "The Dunwich Horror" (1928).

[37]   [CAS to RHB] [ANS]

[Postmarked Auburn, Cal.,
15 June 1934]

Dear Ar-Éch-Bei: Letter rec'd. Glad to know that *Beyond Cathay* didn't disappoint you. Will ship a lot of drawings for inspection in a few days. By the way, have you an express office at De Land? Mss. etc, could be sent much more reasonably by express than by mail. Will write shortly, when I have verified Tsathoggua's family affiliation and have located a few mss. Can give you 1st carbon of the *Passing of Aphrodite* when I have copied it. Wright has taken The Last Hieroglyph. Yrs, by the marking on Sixtystone,[1] Klarkash-Ton.

Notes

1. See CAS to DW 131n6.

[38]   [CAS to RHB] [ALS]

[15 June 1934]

Dear Ar-Éch-Bei:
               Herewith the holograph of my ending for Zulkais and Kahlilah, and the first typescripts of *The Double Shadow* and The Passing of Aphrodite. Also, the typescript of the original version of The Disinterment of Venus, which isn't much of a story in any of its phases. The last sheet is over-scrawled with notations for a later draft.
    I have found most of the holograph of the H.E., which is damnably battered. Will have another look for the missing leaves before I send it. I fear it will be an awkward thing to bind, on account of the large legal-size sheets. And I defy anyone to read such an execrable mess of pothooks and deletions!
    The drawings go forward to-day in a separate package. Hope you will like them.
          Yrs. by Mohammed's coffin
               Klarkash-Ton.

[Envelope postmarked Auburn, Cal., 15 June 1934.]

[39]   [CAS to RHB] [TLS]

Auburn, Calif.
June 16th, 1934.

Dear Ar-Éch-Bei:
               I have made up a package of drawings to loan you and will

mail it the first of the week. I might have done this before—in fact, I *should* have sent you a number so that you could make your own choice. Perhaps you would have preferred something else to Beyond Cathay. If you wish, you can make another selection. I am not setting prices on any of the drawings, since, in one sense, they are priceless; and, in selling them to a connoisseur, the tariff must be determined by what the aforesaid c. feels able to pay.

Your praise of The Colossus of Ylourgne is heartening. Others have commended the tale, so I begin to think that perhaps I have under-estimated it. So far, I haven't found any ms. of this story and I am inclined to think that I burned the preliminary scraps and notes from which I worked it up on the machine. I have, however, the first carbon of The Passing of Aphrodite (a prose poem) and shall send it on shortly. Also, I have located an item which you will like to have—the holograph of my continuation of the 3rd Episode of Vathek. I'll take another look for the H.E. holograph. As to The Disinterment of Venus, the copy held by Wright is the third or fourth revision of that pesky little opus. The cabin is littered with discarded versions of the damned thing. I'll see if I can find the original one. If there is an express office at De Land, I'll ship you a huge consignment of typescripts and holographs. First rate postage is too much of an extortion, in my opinion. I resent such robbery more, if possible, than the U.S. tax on liquors! Express rates, on the other hand, are reasonable enough.

No, I haven't any proof-sheets of the 2nd Recluse, and doubt if any were made. Too bad Cook was unable to continue the venture.

Wright hasn't returned any of the originals of my WT drawings. I may or may not have mentioned that he recently presented me with about a dozen originals of illustrations done for my earlier stories by Senf, Nelson, Doolin and Wilcox.[1] Some of them are better than the published reproductions; evidently the pulp paper is a chancy or mischancy medium for prints.

Hornig, it would seem, is possessed of various and versatile talents, especially in the journalistic line. I am not altogether surprised that he was able to furnish you with a hand-me-down pseudonym.

Re my drawings: Loveman, I would say, has by far the largest collection of them. God knows how many I gave him. He used to present me with whole shelves of books, and the drawings were the only return I could make. Wandrei purchased three or four of my landscapes. I don't believe that Long has anything, except, perhaps, a few of the grotesques. George Kirk, another of the "gang," bought 2 or 3 pictures when he visited me in 1920.[2] Other purchasers include Bio de Casseres and a New York Russian Jew (friend of De Casseres) whose name temporarily eludes me. This Jew has several of the best landscapes, done about the same time as Beyond Cathay.

Yes, I hope to continue The Book of Eibon. I am returning the "style-sheet"[3] with much details regarding Tsathoggua as I am at present able to furnish. Some of these have required much delving into the Parchments of Pnom (Pnom was the chief Hyperborean genealogist as well as a noted prophet);

and I am well aware that certain of my phonetic renderings from the Elder Script are debatable. You raise some interesting points with your questions. Azathoth, the primal nuclear chaos, reproduced of course only by fission; but its progeny, entering various outer systems, often took on attributes of androgynism or bi-sexuality. The androgynes, curiously, required no coadjutancy in the production of offspring; but their children were commonly, though not always, either male or female. Thus you will note a progressive trend toward biological complexity. Hziulquoigmnzhah, uncle of Tsathoggua, and Ghizghuth, T.'s father, were the *male* progeny of Cxaxukluth and the androgynous spawn of Azathoth. It is worthy of record, however, that Knygathin Zhaum, the half-breed Vormi, reverted to the most primitive ancestral characteristics following the stress of his numerous decapitations. I have yet to translate the dire and abominable legend telling how a certain doughty denizen of Commoriom (not Athammaus) returned to the city after its public evacuation and found that it was peopled most execrably and innumerably by the fissional spawn of Knygathin Zhaum, which retained no vestige of anything earthly.

Éch-Pi-El, I am sure can furnish much fuller data concerning the genesis of Tulu. It would seem, from the rather oblique references of Pnom, that Tulu was a cousin of Hziulquoigmnzhah but was somewhat closer to the Azathothian archetype than Hz. The latter god, together with Ghisghuth, was born of Cxaxukluth in a dark distant system. Cx. then came en famille to Yuggoth, the family already including Ghisghuth's [*sic*] wife, Zstylzhemgni, and the infant Tsathoggua (Cx., I may add, has most mercifully continued to sojourn in the glacial night of Yuggoth) Hz., who found his parent slightly uncongenial owing to Its cannibalistic habits, emigrated to Yaksh (Neptune) at an early age; but, wearying of the highly devout Yakshians, went on to Cykranosh,[4] in which he preceded his nephew Tsathoggua. Ts. and his parents lingered in Yuggoth, having penetrated certain deep caverns beyond the incursions of Cxaxukluth; but eventually Ts., leaving his parents behind, followed in the steps of Hz. Hz., a rather philosophic deity, was long worshipped by the quaint peoples of Cykranosh, but grew tired of their ex-votos even as of the Yakshians; and he had permanently retired from active life at the time of his encounter with Eibon as told in The Door to Saturn. No doubt he still resides in the columned cavern, and still quenches his thirst at the lake of liquid metal. A confirmed bachelor, and *sans* offspring.

I have filled out your sketch of Ts; and am returning it. My account of Ts's terrene advent can be reconciled with the references in The Mound. Ts, through another dimension than the known three, first entered the Earth by means of the lightless inner gulf of N'kai; and he lingered there for cycles. Later he established himself in caves nearer to the surface; and his cult thrived; but after the coming of the ice, he returned to N'kai. Much of his legend was forgotten or misunderstood; and thus, through a mythopoetic variation,

Gll'Hathaa-Ynn came to tell the Spaniard Zamarcona [*sic*][5] that only the images of Tsathoggua, and not the god himself, had emerged from the inner world.

Well, I hope all this will clear up a few obscure points and prevent future contradictions. Of course, owing to the infernal difficulty of reading and transliterating the Elder Script, it may be that I am in error regarding some of the references; and I shall willingly submit myself to the correction of a superior scholar, such as Éch-Pi-El.

Yrs, in the faith of Hzioulquoigmnzhah,

Klarkash-Ton

[Enclosure]

Genealogical Chart of the
ELDER GODS[6]

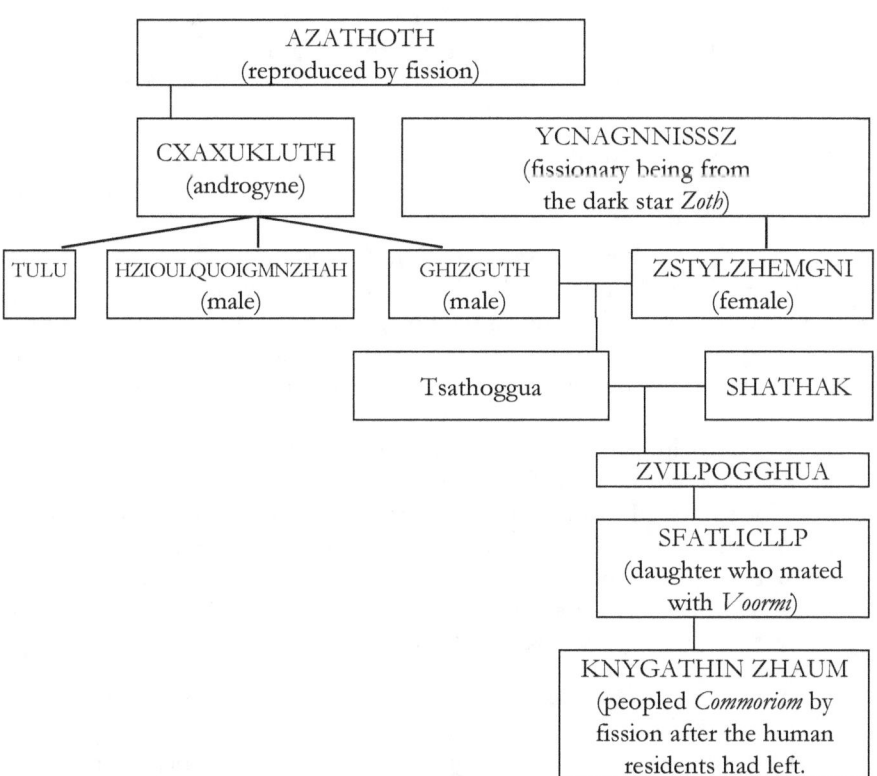

Notes

1. C. C. Senf (1873–1949), "The Immeasurable Horror" and "The Monster of the Prophecy"; T. Wyatt Nelson (1888–1973), "The Vaults of Yoh-Vombis" and "The Maker of Gargoyles"; Joseph Doolin (1896–1967), "The Tale of Satampra Zeiros";

and James M. Wilcox (1895–1958), "The Isle of the Torturers," "The Seed from the Sepulcher," and "The Ice Demon."

2. See the cover of *The Last Oblivion*. The first edition included two other prints in color within.

3. The following three paragraphs were printed in slightly revised form as "The Family Tree of the Gods" in the *Acolyte* (Summer 1944), with a "Genealogical Chart of the Elder Gods" devised by RHB. CAS's tongue-in-cheek "genealogy" draws links between his Tsathoggua and HPL's Azathoth and Tulu (Cthulhu). HPL himself jokingly made a similar chart, ostensibly for showing that Azathoth, Yog-Sothoth, and Shub-Niggurath were part of not only his own but also CAS's heritage (see HPL to James F. Morton, 27 April 1933; *Letters to James F Morton* [New York: Hippocampus Press, 2011], 317). Although both charts contain Azathoth, Cthulhu, and Tsathoggua, there is little similarity or linkage between them.

4. See RHB's drawing "On Cykranosh" (*Eyes of the God* 62), dated 30 July 1934.

5. I.e., Panfilo de Zamacona, the protagonist of "The Mound."

6. The chart, taken from the *Acolyte,* had been submitted to Rah Hoffmann.

[40]   [CAS to RHB] [TLS]

[late June 1934]

Dear Ar-Éch-Bei:

        I have autographed the pages from the Recluse and the opening of Yoh-Vombis, and have initialed the drawings you returned. Together with these, I am sending the holograph of the H.E. which, apparently, is still minus one sheet—the full draft of the opening. The present beginning, however, may interest you as a variorum—you will note that I rejected nearly all of it. I am also sending the holograph of The Ninth Skeleton, the first of my stories to appear in W.T., and the h. of The Abominations of Yondo. Also, a sheet of epigrams, which may amuse you.

        The picture of that clay deity is great! I hope to see one of its companion; and I shall prize a photo of Éch-Pi-El, if he has one taken at De Land, as he spoke of intending to do.[1]

Yrs by the Unutterable Name, in great haste,
Klarkash-Ton

Notes

1. The clay deity was Cthulhu, its companion Ganesha. It was during this trip to Florida that Lucius B. Truesdell (1873–1974) of DeLand took the classic late portraits of HPL when RHB felt that his own attempt was unsatisfactory.

[41]   [CAS to RHB] [TNS]

[Postmarked Auburn, Cal.,
8 July 1934]

Dear Ar-Éch-Bei: Take your time with the pictures—glad to hear that you like them, and that several of them appeal to you for purchase.

Not much news. Wright finally took Xeethra.

Yrs, Klarkash-Ton

[42]   [CAS to RHB] [TLS]

[Postmarked Auburn, Cal.,
1 August 1934]

Dear Ar-Éch-Bei: Thanks for the P. O. order. The instalment plan on the pictures will be perfectly o.k. Will answer your letter before long and give further genealogical data relative to the Old Ones. Official portrait of Cthulhu is a deuced fine thing. Am much impressed by Miss Moore's drawing of Shambleau,[1] which is really rather neat. It *could* have a more poisonous and serpentine abandonment, perhaps. Nevertheless it is good. Yrs for the unsealing of Solomon's djinn bottles. (Excuse semi-inadvertent pun—I was going to say araq anyhow).

CAS

Notes

1. C. L. Moore, "Shambleau" (*WT,* November 1933), illustrated by James M. Wilcox Wilcox. Presumably Moore's drawing circulated privately.

[43]   [CAS to RHB] [TLS]

Auburn, Calif.
Sept. 10th, 1934.

Dear Ar-Éch-Bei:

I fear you have thought me damnably remiss in regard to the letter which I promised you so long ago. But the truth is that my energy has been below par this summer, and the demands upon it have been increased sevenfold. I wrote practically no letters during August, and am now just beginning to resume the neglected epistolary threads.

In a day or two, I shall return by express the muchly appreciated excerpts of The Metal Monster and The Blind Spot,[1] and shall enclose with them a few mss. and autograph items for your collection. I thought the M.M. a tremendous thing, but did not care half so much for the Hall–Flint opus. For one thing, there was too little differentiation of the people beyond The Blind Spot from humanity. However, as tales go, it is far from negligible. The mystery was admirably worked up in the first part[.]

As my card informed you, your offering for the drawings was quite comme il faut. I shall, needless to say, be very glad indeed to receive photos of the items retained. I was interested to note that you had decided on two—the Witch's Tower and Lemurian Landscape—which were particularly admired some years ago by F. B. Long, Jr. Malanoth, concerning whom you inquire, is a master wizard from the world Pnidleethon, which revolves about Yamil Zacra, central sun of evil, and its dark companion, Yuzh.[2]

Your portraits of Cthulhu and Chaugnar certainly grow upon me with a baleful and archean potency! Great stuff, and I hope that you'll do others, since it would seem that the bas-relief is particularly adapted to your talents. Thanks for the photo of C. L. Moore's remarkable drawing of Shambleau. I have been so doubtful of my ability toward bettering this from any angle, that I have not yet tried the pencil sketch that you suggested. Perhaps I'll have it to send in my next. C. L. Moore certainly must be a genius—I liked her Dust of Gods[3] almost better than any of the tales so far published. My one objection is the omnipresent ray-gun, whose use seemed particularly unnecessary in this tale, since the dust could better have been ignited by some secret device installed aeons ago to protect it from desecration. Thanks too for giving me her address—I'd like to write her, but hesitate to do so at present because of my accumulated Ossa and Pelion[4] of correspondence, to which I can hardly do justice.

I'll now try to answer your questions, some of which have necessitated research into archives even darker and more obscure than those of the learned Pnom. Chushax, or Zishaik, of whose lineage I can learn only the most meager and dubious details, was the wife of Tsathoggua. Their offspring, Zvilpogghua, was more male than anything else. The immediate parent of Cthulhu and his race (child of Nug) was Ptmâk. The parent of Yhoundeh or Y'houndeh was the androgyne animal Archetype Zyhumé, which still abides in that cavern of the Archetypes which was visited by the ill-starred Ralibar Vooz on his compulsive itinerations through the Hyperborean underworld. Zyhume is a sort of nebulous and more or less spheroid elk. As to the marriage of Y'houndeh and the flute-player Nyarlathotep, I am inclined to suspect that something of the sort is hinted or adumbrated by Pnom. I quote the reference: "Houndeh in the 3rd cycle of her divinity was covered by that spawn which pipes perennially the dire music of chaos and corruption." If this doesn't refer to the Azathothian fluteplayer, I'll undertake to drink a straight gallon of the next *segur*-whisky that is imported from Mars.

As to the people of your Annals, I think that Yaksh is too bleak and boreal for them. I am inclined to believe that they must have lived on Antanôk, the lost, disrupted planet of which the asteroids are the remnants. This would account for their likeness to humanity, since, in earlier times, there seems to have been a little intercourse between Earth and Antanôk. In fact, there are certain forgotten authorities who claim that mankind as we now know it is descended from Antanôkan colonists. Ulthar, as you have surmised, is indeed conterminous with both Averoigne and Poictesme,[5] the latter lying somewhat to the northeast and the former mainly to the southwest. As to Yondo, I have told that that country is situated many hundred leagues to the south of Dunsany's lands of Wonder. Thus, you will readily perceive, it lies beyond all chartable regions of Earth without quite belonging to any alien planet.

My poetry column only ran for a year or two in the Auburn Journal,[6] and most of the items were reprinted in Sandalwood. I'll dig up some old clippings for you presently. The drama, The Fugitives, concerning which you inquire, was never written aside from a tentative beginning. I did write several songs for it, all of which were included in Sandalwood.

Re the ownership of my sold paintings. I don't know just how many Bender[7] has or did have, and imagine he has given them all to Mills College, a "high-toned" girls' seminary which he seems to favour. I doubt, though if the number is more than 6 or seven. Bio de Casseres and the Russian Jew, Sapanoff,[8] might loan their pictures for photographing, and I'll try to find the present address of the DeCasseres so that you can write them about the matter. They have moved from their old address, 19 E. 31st St., N.Y. Wandrei has three or four paintings, and doubtless a few pencil sketches. Sterling didn't care greatly for my pictorial work but I once gave him an illustration in coloured inks which I made for A Wine Of Wizardry. The picture took its text from the lines: "Silent ghouls whose king hath digged a somber carcanet [/] And necklaces with fevered opals wet." [*sic*][9] I have no idea what has happened to it.

I'd like to see the H.E. when you finish binding it. Ye gods of Pegana, Mhu Thulan, Ulthar and Pnidleethon![10] What an idea! And I certainly look forward to the completion of The Shunned House.

Yrs for the finding of the Black Seal,
Klarkash-Ton

[P.S.] A., however, is directly connected with P. by a long strait winding strip known as L'allée des ans perdus—alley of lost years.

Notes

1. By Austin Hall and Homer Eon Flint.

2. From CAS's "The Infernal Star."

3. "Dust of the Gods" (*WT*, August 1934).

4. Two mountains in Greece, which, according to myth, the Titans piled one upon the other in an attempt to reach the top of Mt. Olympus.

5. The fictional province that forms the setting of the fantasies of James Branch Cabell.

6. CAS's column ran for 100 issues of the *Auburn Journal* between 5 April 1923 and 7 January 1926. It contained his poems (59), epigrams and pensées (341), and translations of selected poems from Charles Baudelaire's *Les Fleurs du mal* (22). His column appeared in part as payment to the printer for *S*.

7. Albert M. Bender (1866–1941), an insurance broker by profession, one of the leading patrons of the arts in San Francisco in the 1920s and 1930s, was a trustee of Mills College in Oakland and a friend and benefactor of CAS and GS. He donated his papers, including some CAS mss., to Mills College.

8. Christopher Sapanoff, a carpet-dealer.

9. GS's celebrated weird poem, first published in *Cosmopolitan* (September 1907) and reprinted in *A Wine of Wizardry and Other Poems* (1909). CAS quotes from ll. 86–88. For *wet* read *set*.

10. Pegāna is an invention of Lord Dunsany, Ulthar of HPL, and Mhu Thulan and Pnidleethon of CAS.

[44]　[CAS to RHB] [TLS]

Averoigne—at the hour of the Sabbat.
[c. 12 September 1934]

Dear Ar-Éch-Bei:

The pictures arrived safely, and I must thank you for the muchly prized transcript of Fungi From Yuggoth.[1] I had written you at De Land a day or two before the arrival of the package, and trust that my letter has been forwarded. In it, I supplied some additional data concerning the lineage and family complications of the Old Ones.

No news here. Wright has ordered drawings for Xeethra and The Dark Eidolon, and I must stir my lazy bones to execute the former within the present week. Have sorted out a bunch of old mss. to send you before long. Hope that Yoh-Vombis has plenty of storage-room!

My lawyer, Miss Weber, succeeded in extracting another fifty from Gernsback—also, a promise to pay the balance of his arrears in trade acceptances at 75 pazoors per *mensis*. Miss Weber must be good!

Later on, I'll loan you another and larger batch of drawings. From your preferences among the lot I sent you, I believe you would like equally well many that I held back.

Here's hoping that you find the plant euphrasy, which was fabled to sharpen and strengthen the eyesight.[2]

Keep the enclosures.

Yrs for the utterance of the ineffable Name,
Klarkash-Ton

[Envelope postmarked 12 September 1934.]

Notes

1. Roy A. Squires sold a TMS of *Fungi from Yuggoth* in the early 1970s. He described the item thus: "12 leaves of typewritten carbon copy; the first 33 sonnets. . . . This copy was sent by Lovecraft to Clark Ashton Smith and contains 11 corrections pen-

ciled in in Smith's hand, including 2 complete lines omitted by the typist. The errors were indicated to Smith by letter, but whether Lovecraft was the typist is unknown" (*Beyond the Bibliographies,* Cat. No. 7, n.d., p. 4). RHB was the typist, and it was he who sent the copy to CAS. A TMS of the poem at JHL contains more than a dozen transcriptional errors, as well as two dropped lines (restored in RHB's hand). When RHB typed it, HPL was still withholding the final two sonnets. In the event he might add more, he wanted them to be last, no matter what. Later—at RHB's suggestion—HPL inserted "Recapture," written earlier and separately, as the antepenultimate sonnet, settling on a sequence of thirty-six sonnets.

2. Euphrasia, also known as eyebright, was used as herbal treatment for eyestrain.

[45]   [CAS to RHB] [ANS]

[Postmarked Auburn, Cal.,
2 April 1935]

Dear Ar-Éch-Bei: If you knew the conditions I have had to contend with, you'd forgive my century-long silence! I'll write as soon as possible and explain. Have done a little work in spite of the devil and high water. Two more of the Zothique series—The Black Abbot of Puthuum and Necromancy in Naat—have sold to WT, along with other yarns. Yrs for the opening of Solomon's bottles, Klarkash-Ton.

[46]   [RHB to CAS] [ANS][1]

June 15, '35
[not postmarked; enclosed in letter by HPL
to CAS postmarked Daytona Beach, Fla.,
16 June 1935]

Dear Klarkash-Ton—

    As you see, I'm again playing host to Randolph Carter,[2] who has recently developed a curious mania for making me work—hence this card (which he supplied.) I merely add a line of greeting, since my intentions are to write you fully—after the first of the month. Anyway, you'll know that I'm still in the running—This being an exceptionally hot day (though I cannot convince my salamander of a visitor) I just drank a bottle of my father's beer, and upon concluding, shall make onslaught on a watermelon.—Write you soon. ¶ By the yellow serpent,
        Ar-Ech-Bei

Notes

1. *Front:* Silver Lakes bordered with cypress and palm, air ever fragrant with flowers and balm, "Come to Florida."

2. HPL was once again visiting RHB in Cassia, this time from 9 June to 18 August. RHB had designed stationery for HPL that he used during his 1935 trip to Florida. In a letter HPL wrote to AWD the same day as his letter to CAS, he labeled the stationery as being that of "Randolph W. Carter." (Note that HPL has nowhere else identified Carter's middle initial or name, including other letters on the same stationery.)

[47]   [CAS to RHB] [TLS]

Hour when the black stars rise
upon Lost Carcosa.[1]
[c. mid- to late June 1935]

Dear Ar-Éch-Bei:

It is good to know that Randolph Carter is again sojourning with you, and I hope that the visit will be a prolonged one.

I should have written you long ago: but perhaps you would forgive me, if you really know the conditions with which I have had to contend. For months my parents were both sick in bed, and I had the duties of a whole corps to fulfill: nurse, cook, housekeeper, errand-boy, and general factotum. Things aren't quite so complicated now; but I am having to fight a most damnable state of staleness and nerve-fatigue, and I fear am putting to poor use my partial and scanty leisure.

There isn't much news. I have started a new Averoigne story, Mother of Toads, which, I fear, will be too naughty for the chaste pages of W.T. There is a slight chance that I might unload it on a new magazine, Spicy Mystery, for which Price has been writing. This mag wants a combination of the lewd and the ghastly. The yarns in it are pretty bad; but, after all, the genre is classic (vide Balzac's The Succubus[2]) and should have possibilities.

I'll welcome your promised letter, and will try to be a more prompt and regular correspondent in future.

I hope you'll like the little carving which I am sending for you together with one for Ech-Pi-El.[3] I am firmly convinced that the ochreish material was once the flesh of a dinosaur! From the outline of the creature, which can still be seen in a railroad cut several miles above Auburn, I'd say that it belongs to the herbivorous type, with a long snaky neck. It is all pretty badly decomposed and mineralized. The stuff is certainly an appropriate medium in which to represent the gods, monsters, wizards and other entities and personages of Hyperborea!

Yours for the Black Kalends,
Klarkash-Ton

Notes

1. A reference to Ambrose Bierce's story "An Inhabitant of Carcosa." Carcosa was also subsequently cited in several stories in Robert W. Chambers's *The King in Yellow*.
2. "Le Succube," a story in *Contes drolatiques* (1832–37).

3. CAS began rock carving c. April 1935, and by summer 1949 had carved about 200 items. AWD had asked CAS in 1959 to write a chapbook about his carvings, to be entitled *Cthulhu and Others in Stone*, but the book was never completed. Carving was by far CAS's primary creative work for the rest of his life. For further information, see Dennis Rickard, *The Fantastic Art of Clark Ashton Smith* (Baltimore: Mirage Press, 1973).

[48]   [RHB to CAS] [ANS][1]

[Postmarked Daytona Beach, Fla.,
29 August 1935]
Aug 28

Dear CAS:

I'm at the termination of a visit to Daytona Beach. You'd enjoy the grotesques frequenting this resort! When I get back, in a few days, I'll actually write, to your boundless amazement.

RHB

[P.S.] Saw HP last in St Aug, starting homeward.

Notes

1. *Front:* Arch and Boardwalk, Daytona Beach, Florida.

[49]   [RHB to CAS] [TLS]

[Postmarked De Land, Fla.,
28 September 1935]

Dear Klarkash-Ton;

May I express my sincerest sympathy for your sorrow?[1] If there is anything that I may do—and I trust that you will not think this is a mere amenity—please call freely upon me. Perhaps I can assist you in preparing typescripts or some similar drudgery at this unfortunate time.

I am sending you various objects, ranging from a photo of my statuette called *Groonta,* to copies of my two publications (one, as you see, taken over from Cook.) Two drawings which were somehow not returned last summer (for which I apologize) & a woodblock I did last year complete this motley assortment. All of them, naturally, are for your retention.

THE GOBLIN TOWER[2] is my cradle-book; done under rather primitive conditions this summer. My future work will surpass it, and I mean to produce a few fine books in small editions, which will be hand-bound in morocco. Naturally, such work will be slow, but it will be Art for Art's Sake with a vengeance. I may not turn out more than a book a year, and only a few copies then, but it will mean the circulation and preservation of worthy material in handsome format. As always, I am driving at something! You have not had a book since Sandalwood, though HP mentioned recently a manuscript book to be called Incantations.[3] May I print it? I must again assure you that the G-T is only a bit of incunabulam [*sic*] compared to current and future results. I would like to issue a large book of your poems—hundreds of pages, if you are willing to abide with my slow work—in quarto or folio size, with press work in judicious decoration and colours. No Hubbardism,[4] but consciously beautiful printing. This could cover all your unpublished poems, as well as collecting from obscure sources, such as the United Amateur.[5] The Baudela[i]rian translations might be in a separate production, or perhaps included. At any rate, this is broaching the subject, and I trust that you will find it agreeable.

While I was in Washington I studied bookbinding, my Opus 1 being your own Star-Treader in green morocco, with esoteric inlay & tooling. I am setting up equipment for hand binding, and will be able to make each copy of your possible volume an individual act of creation. This painstaking type of work naturally does not admit of the large edition E & C had, but I could do between thirty-five and seventy-five copies, and taking it leisurely, not degrade the standard of craftsmanship. Let me know what you think, please.

Thank you for the little dinosaur carving. It occupies a niche among the books of Yoh-Vombis.

I like the two poems The Phoenix and . . . . "When I lay dead &c" (I forget the title)[6] very much indeed. I meant to transcribe them, but HPL somehow got away before I managed to do it. Perhaps I shall print them, instead!

There is not much news, so I shall mail this outrageously-delayed letter at long last. I hope to see *Mother of Toads* in Ms. or print.

With renewed sympathy,

Ever yours,
Ar-Ech-Bei

[P.S.] May I use those clever epigrams you sent me once in my amateur paper?[7] Here is what they would look like. I would appreciate it if you didn't mind.

[P.P.S.] FBL does not yet know of his new book, which was concocted by Abdul & myself as a surprise. So for a couple of weeks, please keep it *sub rosa!* ¶ Being a typographical sow's ear, I bound it in odds & ends, and no silk purse. You will understand it's [*sic*] appearance from the lack of suitable materials all around.

Notes

1. CAS's mother, Fannie (Gaylord) Smith, died on 9 September 1935, at the age of 85.
2. *The Goblin Tower* was a small collection of poetry by Frank Belknap Long selected by HPL and RHB. HPL helped set the type when he visited RHB in the summer of 1935.
3. CAS had intended, since the publication of *S*, that his next collection would be entitled *Incantations*. HPL's letters in *O Fortunate Floridian* discuss RHB's plans to publish

the book, though like many other of his projects, it came to naught.

4. Elbert Hubbard (1856–1915) was an American writer and printer who gained celebrity with the founding of the Roycroft Press, a press specializing in self-consciously "arty" books influenced by William Morris's Kelmscott Press.

5. CAS published seven poems in the *United Amateur* during his short membership of the amateur press association.

6. "In Thessaly."

7. "Epigrams of Alastor" (ms., JHL). RHB published some of the epigrams in *Dragon-Fly* No. 1. *Dragon-Fly* No. 2 contained more epigrams by CAS, under "Pertinence and Impertinence," but RHB's source for these is not known.

[50]   [CAS to RHB] [ANS][1]

[Postmarked Auburn, Cal.,
3 October 1935]

Dear Ar-Éch-Bei: Was glad to get your letter and anticipate the package. Will write before long. Also send your assignment of mss. Your project to print up *Incantations* is great—more anon.

Sure—use the epigrams if *you* like them. Yrs for the transit of Cimmeria, Klarkash-Ton

Notes

1. *Front:* Bear River, Auburn-Grass-Valley Highway, Cal.

[51]   [CAS to RHB] [TLS]

[c. November 1935]

Dear Ar-Éch-Bei: I had meant to write, aeons ago, and thank you for your expression of condolence and offer of assistance in preparing typescripts; also to answer your letter at proper length. I hope you will not think me ungrateful because of the delay, which has been due to nervous demoralization plus a piling up of unfinished (and, alack, unattempted!) tasks.

I appreciated greatly, as a card may have hinted, the gift of The Goblin Tower and The Shunned House.[1] They certainly form a promising beginning for the Dragon-Fly Press and bindery! I liked the first issue of your magazine greatly, too, and hope that you will continue the venture. It would certainly raise the standard of amateur publications. Edkin[s]'s article[2] would have done honor to any of the professional reviews, to mention nothing else.

I hope you received the consignment of mss, etc, which I expressed to you some time ago. Lately, I have been going over the possible material for Incantations, which you have so generously offered to print. A *large* volume seems to me no less impossible than inadvisable, since I have turned out no great body of verse since the publication of Sandalwood; and much of what I have done is in the form of trifling madrigals written for the semi-utilitarian purpose of pleasing the lady or ladies to whom they were addressed. At a rough guess, I'd say the venture will hardly run to more than 60 or 70 compactly printed pages. Very few of my Baudelaire translations are in shape for issue; but perhaps half a dozen items would be worthy of inclusion. I have also racked up some metrical experiments in French, which I was so rash as to attempt several years ago, and may possibly add one or two of these by way of variety. I enclose a specimen, with literal English translation appended. Before long, I'll mail or express you a first selection of items for the volume, to which a few others, held back for revision, might be added later. I admire and applaud your program of Art for Art's sake, and I certainly don't want you to spend time and money on anything unworthy of the labo[u]r.

Your binding of The Star-Treader certainly sounds like a de luxe production! I have, by the way, an S.T. bound by hand in *olive*-green morocco by a Canadian admirer;[3] a fine piece of work.

Éch-Pi-El will relay to you a carving which seems to depict one of the prehuman serpent-eating people of Hyperborea. This carving was found in a much-shattered condition amid the jungle-matted columns of lost Commoriom; and the ingenuity of the finder was taxed in piecing it together . . . Incidentally, Commoriom seems to be a fruitful field for archaeologic labour: I have retrieved therefrom various graven entities, including what is undoubtedly a representation, in some sort of prehistoric bone or ivory, of the woman-breasted cat-goddess, Phauz, whom the Hyperboreans worshipped aeons before Bast was set up in Khem. Also, I have found a strange cameo with edges oddly worn and rounded, bearing the head of that Black Dog who warded the eastern gate of Commoriom against intruders neither brute nor human. . . . Also, there is a bust of the Inquisitor Morghi,[4] who so rashly followed Eibon through the ultra-terrene panel giving on a singular landscape in Saturn; moreover, the head of a dinornis, some cameos depicting obviously unnamable entities, and the head of a creature which is part bird, part insect and part reptile. So much for Commoriom: my researches in Mu and Poseidonis (with the aid of a future-scientific diving-bell) I leave for a later bulletin. Some curious edola have been retrieved; and, emboldened by such success, I may yet venture amid the dreadful purlieus of abysmally sunken R'lyeh!

Yours, by the black pentagram with **two** angles in ascendance,
Klarkash-Ton.

P.S. I append translation of the French poem Revasserie hereunder.

Day-Dream

Here, in the olden wood,
The world is a mirage
More wan and dim
Than the pool wherein is mirrored
In the profound of another sphere
The strange nenuphar.

Scarcely I remember,
I forget my pain:
From this verdant twilight,
I see depart, alike futile
Beneath their varying masks,
Both love and death.

Athwart the foliage,
The sunlit lake
Drowses my dazzled eye
Like a crystal from which passes
The flame of an ecstasy
To the swooning mage.

The incredible oblivion
Plucks at me, ineffable,
From the depth of its lurking-place.
I lose myself, I brush
The thing that takes flight
Too vast of the spirit.

I know not if the oak
Suspires with my breath
Or if I draw air therein;
Sometimes I am the poppy,
And sometimes the mace-reed
Whose down is scattered on the clear stream.

For me, all thought
Is leafed and woodlike,
And mingles itself with the elders:
It flows with the sap,
It ripens the berry,
And spreads out with the branches.

This is very rough and hasty, but renders the thought and imagery.

[P.P.S.] Groonta is good stuff. Thanks for photo.

Notes

1. RHB bound only a few presentation copies of HPL's *The Shunned House*. See CAS to RHB 10n3.
2. E. A. Edkins, "Fragment of a Letter to a Young Poet," *Dragon-Fly* No. 1 (15 October 1935): 11–26. Edkins was an old-time amateur journalist with whom HPL had recently come into contact, and subsequently RHB.
3. John Allan; see CAS to RHB 65n1.
4. A character in "The Door to Saturn."

[52]   [CAS to RHB] [TLS]

> Hour of the Opening of the Sub-
> marine portals, in R'lyeh
> [c. January 1936]

Dear Ar-Éch-Bei:

Many thanks for The Cats of Ulthar.[1] You have done a good job for a good story.

The typescript of Incantations goes forward to you by express. It includes 65 titles: 49 more or less lyric poems, 18 of which are grouped under the subtitle of The Jasmine Girdle; 3 renderings from Paul Verlaine, 9 from Baudelaire; and 4 of my prose pastels at the end.[2] Many pieces have appeared in magazines, and I have made a note of this on the mss. for your private information. I have submitted two other pieces, Ennui and The Sick Muse, to Wright; but if he accepts them, they will no doubt appear in W.T. before the completion of your job on the book.

I hesitated a long time over the inclusions, and spent many hours revising some of them; hence, partly, the delay in sending you the collection. These verses, I feel, are only shards and wraiths of the poems I had once planned to write under the title of Incantations. As to my Baudelaires, most of these were done only in rough, literal prose; and they still need a world of polishing.

I hope that you received, and liked, my little carving of the Hyperborean Snake-Eater. For some time, I have had it in mind to circulate a few of my smaller heads and figurines, as a sort of private loan exhibit, and am wondering if you would care to see them. I don't believe the expressage will amount to much on a small wooden box holding ten or a dozen of these miniature eidola. They would be well worth your while, since they resemble nothing that has been done in sculpture since the foundering of Poseidonis.

> Yrs for the descent into Annwyn,[3]
> Klarkash-Ton

Notes

1. RHB published *The Cats of Ulthar* as his Christmas card for 1935, in an edition of 42 copies.
2. No TMS of *Incantations* is known to exist, although there is an unlabeled table of contents for it, with emendations by RHB, among CAS's papers. CAS had long planned a book entitled *Incantations*. The contents for it and *The Jasmine Girdle*, ultimately published as sections of *SP*, undoubtedly changed over time (see Appendix). See DW's and CAS's letters of 1938 regarding the scuttling of the book.
3. In Welsh mythology, the Otherworld, believed to be located either on an island or underneath the earth.

[53]   [CAS to RHB] [TLS]

Feb. 5th, 1936.

Dear Ar-Éch-Bei:

I was glad to get your recent letter, and to learn that Incantations has arrived safely. Thanks for the pazoors—they were no less welcome because I had almost forgotten that you owed them to me!

It seems to me that the 65 items, which I have carefully arranged as to sequence, should be enough for the volume. After all, I do not intend it to be my final opus in poetry. Perhaps certain omitted items are debatable: for instance, I am leaving out Rêvasserie (Day-Dream) mainly because I think that three poems in French should be fully enough for the present collection. Anything of merit that is left out could go into some future volume, just as certain items omitted from Ebony and Crystal were later included in Sandalwood. Nightfall, which you inquire about, strikes me as being very similar, but inferior, to certain pieces in Ebony and Crystal. It was, in fact, written about the same time as these; and I have never been able to make up my mind that it was worthy of preservation.

Wright has accepted Ennui and The Sick Muse for W.T. but will no doubt print them long before Incantations is ready for distribution. By the way, when the job nears completion, I think it wouldn't be a bad idea to print a small circular to help in selling the book. I could distribute a lot of these for you, to addresses of people who have ordered Ebony and Crystal and The Double Shadow.

Ech-Pi-El's aid in proof-reading should be invaluable—he would be much better at it than I am.

I am pleased to hear that you approved The Hyperborean Snake-Eater. The loan exhibit of carvings will be a little delayed in reaching you, since I am going to start it via New York to get a line on present chances of public exhibition for similar work. I believe you will like these sculptures. Some people seem to prefer them to my paintings and drawings. Later I shall make you a gift of something better than the Serpent-Devourer.

Fungi from Yuggoth[1] and the new Dragon-Fly are certainly something to look forward to. I commend and admire your printing ventures most emphatically.

I'm on the watch for a Sandalwood; but people who own the book seem decidedly unwilling to part with it. Maybe I can scare one up sooner or later. Will do my best.

I'd like to see those snakeskin bindings. The H.E. ms. must be absolutely unique.

Re unpublished stories: I find that I have only about a dozen out of the hundred odd items written since 1929. With the sole exception of the Vathek ending, they are too mediocre to bother about. Several are punk science fiction pieces, and some of the others half-hearted attempts at conventional quasi-realistic fiction[.] Some of the pseudo-science could no doubt be sold by re-writing. One of two novelettes, The Metamorphosis of the World, is based on a far from bad idea, that of the atomic transformation of our planet by people from Venus, into a replica of Venus with all of the latter's atmospheric, geologic and climatic conditions: this in order that it might become inhabitable for the overcrowded Venerians. The other novelette, The Red World of Polaris, unfortunately turns on the notion of brains transferred into metal bodies: a notion original enough with me, since I thought of it thirty years ago! but rendered banal and threadbare by recent repetition in science fiction stories. I'll send you the carbons of these two yarns if you wish to see them; but I don't recommend them.

Perhaps the enclosure will help to "extra-illustrate" your private copy of Incantations. The pencil drawing of the chimera-crowned gentleman was done as an illustration for the nightmare poem, In Slumber. The Maiden Blemmye forms the subject of one of my statuettes, differing considerably, however, in form, expression and color from this drawing. The Sciapod (described in Flaubert's Temptation of St. Anthony) I intend to work up as a figurine sooner or later.

I have made some new carvings, and have sold a few locally, though at prices far from gaudy. Perhaps the best recent one is The Harpy, a vicious female monster with a horny carapace in lieu of wings. The iron oxide in the material makes her look as if her breasts, claws, and the rock on which she crouches, were all ruddled with blood. The piece took on a fine agate-like polish.

I could go on indefinitely with these sculptures but dire necessity is going to drive me back to fiction-writing pretty pronto. Pity me—for I am torn back and forth, hither and yon, by four impulses—those of poetry, prose, painting and carving. Perhaps you can understand my predicament!

Your, by the ever burning tail of the Baboon Omoultakos,

Klarkash-Ton.

Notes

1. RHB began printing HPL's *Fungi from Yuggoth* in mid-1936 but did not complete it.

[54]   [CAS to RHB] [ALS]

[1 June 1936]

Dear Ar-Éch-Bei:

Your welcome letter received. No need of apologies for my delay! I'll answer at length, as soon as a few of my own complications are untangled. Thanks for the new Dragon-Fly, on which you are to be congratulated—I don't see how you did it under the circumstances.

By all means use that little sketch of mine for *Fungi from Yuggoth*.[1] I am pleased and honored to see it in such conjunction. Surprisingly, it seems to have the atmosphere of some of those lonely and eerie and nostalgic sonnets.

A few drawings enclosed. *The Dj[h]ibbi* (*vide Door to Saturn*) was a sketch for a carving, but the carving turned out rather different, showing a more complacent and superior type of apterous avian stylite.

Yrs for the hidden footpath to the Kingdom of Voor,[2]

Klarkash-Ton

Notes

1. The sketch appears in RHB's proofs for the title page (JHL); reproduced in Kenneth W. Faig, Jr., "The Book That Nearly Was," *Xenophile* No. 11 (March 1975): 118–23.

2. A reference to the "Voorish domes" in Arthur Machen's "The White People."

[55]   [RHB to CAS] [TMS (carbon)]

[Envelope postmarked De Land, Fla., 5 July 1936]

R. E. H.
Died June 11, 1936

Conan, the warrior king, lies stricken dead
    Beneath a sky of cryptic stars; the lute
    That was his laughter stilled, and mute[1]
Upon the chilling earth his youthful head.
There sounds for him no more the clamorous fray,
    But dirges now, where once the trumpet loud:
    About him press old memories for shroud,
And ended is the conflict of the day.

Death spilled the blood of him who loved the fight
    As men love mistresses, and fought it well—
    His fair young flesh is marble where he fell
With broken sword than vanquished all but Night.
    And as of mythic kings our words must speak
    Of Conan now, who roves where dreamers seek.

Notes

1. HPL suggested RHB insert the word "sadly" before "mute" (l. 3) to fill out the short line. It appears thus in *WT*.

[56]   [CAS to RHB] [TLS]

Auburn, Calif.
Nov. 23rd, 1936.

Dear Ar-Éch-Bei:

        It would seem that I have been owing you (and nearly every-one else) a letter ever since the fall of Uzuldaroum.[1] To detail the obstacles and impediments, the harassments and bedevilments that have occasioned and prolonged this epistolatory lapse, would require the minor part of a new kalpa; and I shan[']t exhaust my paper or your patience with the execrable catalogue. Suffice it to say that the lapse has been involuntary.

        I hope that I at least thanked you by card of the last Dragon-Fly. I am damnably sorry to learn, both from your letter of last June and Ech-Pi-El's more recent letters, the troubles and difficulties that you have been having. Such matters are beyond our control, and it would seem that misfortunes have a way of "ganging up" on the victim: at least, that has been my own ex-perience. I have had enough grief, the past two years, to founder a dread-nought and am beginning to wonder if sea-bottom has yet been reached!

        Don't worry about Incantations. There's no hurry about presenting it to a world that hasn't yet exhausted the edition of Ebony and Crystal printed nearly 14 years ago, and which has left me about 600 copies of The Double Shadow parked under my bed along with the empty wine-jugs et cetera. In the meanwhile, here's a new poem which you can add to the mss. Wright is using it in W.T. and will no doubt print it before long.[2] Which reminds me, before I pass to other matters, that I greatly liked your sonnet-tribute to R.E.H. in the pages of our old standby.

        In answer to certain queries in your June letter: The projected play, The Fugitives, ran only to 2½ pages of blank verse and several songs that I planned to intercalate in the dialogue. I had these pages laid aside somewhere to send you but seem to have mislaid them again (or *did* I send them?) The plot was a simple and quite romantic one: it began with the mutual dawning of love in an Atlantean boy and girl, soon to be separated. Later, they were to meet again: the boy a wandering poet of recognized genius, the girl a king's concubine. Their old love reawakens, they flee from the Atlantean court and capital, to perish in the wilderness after several days and nights of mad happi-ness. On this framework, much lyric beauty and romantic imagery could have been strung. But somehow, the impetus failed and I never went on with it. I doubt very much if I shall ever write a play.[3] Possibly I shall yet do some imaginative romances of book length; but the dialogue form doesn't appeal to me greatly for personal use.

Éch-Pi-El said that you planned a mimeographed magazine and had expressed a desire to use my ending to 3rd Episode of Vathek in it. By all means go ahead, if you can utilize the thing.[4]

I am glad that the poems of Incantations pleased you so well. Probably any future verse that I write will mark more of a return to, or development of, my older and less lyrically emotional style. I feel in myself an urge and ability to fare even further afield in the cosmic dreamlands than I have yet gone. Also, I believe I could do better paintings of these regions. At present, my new art of sculpture engrosses me immensely. I believe it will be quite possible to make a little money by casting some of my milder grotesques in a hard and durable plaster. The replicas could be sold at fifty cents upward if placed in novelty stores. My originals, if they had been dug up in Guatemala or Cambodia, would be fetching handsome prices from art-collectors! Also, if exhibited in some European capital, they might cause a revolution among the modernists! At present, the only prospect of art-exhibition is at the Crocker Gallery in Sacramento. The director,[5] a personal friend, says that he can give me a showing some time after the first of the year.

I have started to make moulds for five carvings, and if I get some good replicas, will be glad to send you a specimen when I hear from you again and verify your address.

Yrs, by the pipings of Nyarlathotep,

Klarkash-ton

[P.S.] You might like to see the enclosed article by a San Francisco admirer,[6] which appeared a couple of years ago in some Carmel magazine. I was quite touched at reading what G.S. had said about me not long before his end. You can forward the article to Éch-Pi-El, with instructions to return it to me at his leisure.

Notes

1. A city in Hyperborea.
2. "The Song of the Necromancer" (*WT*, February 1937). See CAS to RHB 62.
3. But see *The Dead Will Cuckold You: A Drama in Six Acts* (in verse; 1951).
4. I.e., *Leaves*. RHB did use the story eventually.
5. Harry Noyes Pratt (1879–1944), poet, editor of the *Overland Monthly*, and director of the Crocker Art Gallery.
6. Probably David Warren Ryder, "The Price of Poetry," *Controversy* (December 1934); rpt. by the Futile Press (June 1937) and laid in CAS's *Nero and Other Poems*.

[57]   [RHB to CAS] [ANS; printed Christmas card]

[Postmarked Kansas City, Mo.,
19 December 1936]

[Christmas greetings / and / best wishes / for the New Year
R. H. Barlow]

[58]   [RHB to CAS] [ALS]

[WILLIAM SLOAN HOUSE, Y.M.C.A, New York City]

April 4, 1937

Dear C A S,

I am sending you a book from Howard's library—as you know, he asked me to be his literary executor, & I spent a rather sad week in Providence going over his things & getting his MS together for the book we hope to publish. Someone has probably told you of Derleth's plans.

When I get home I shall write a letter covering all the matter I have been so impolitely silent on. Meanwhile, I am confronted with a tiresome 'bus trip.

Later, Mrs. Gamwell will write you about other books of Howard's. He left you the choice of a good many, after specific bequests.

Yours ever,
Bob

[59]   [CAS to RHB] [TLS]

Auburn, Calif.
April 8th, 1937.

Dear Bob:

I have just received your note from New York, and am hastening to write a line in acknowledgement—also, to make a suggestion which may be hopelessly impractical.

My friends the Sullys and I had debated the idea that permanent preservation of 66 College St. (library and study) would make a fine and fitting memorial to HPL (this before news of his provisions for dividing effects had reached us). It would no doubt necessitate the raising of a memorial fund among admirers; Mrs Gamwell to be the custodian. We are wondering if there are still any possibilities in the plan. I, personally, would be more than happy to waive my claim to any portion of HPL's library if it could be engineered. You, of course will be in a position to judge its practicality far better than I can.

August and Donald have both written me about the projected volume, and I am glad that matters are progressing so well. But I simply can't accustom or in any way harden myself to the idea that HPL is gone.

You will find my poor elegiac ode waiting for you in Kansas City. It will appear in WT.[1]

Please write at length, as soon as you have the time.
Yours always,
Clark Ashton

P.S. I have just read *The Night Ocean*,[2] and wish to congratulate you on an amazing piece of atmospheric writing. More of this anon—the tale calls for re-reading.

Notes

1. "To Howard Phillips Lovecraft." CAS directed that payment for the poem be sent to Mrs. Gamwell.
2. HPL revised the story somewhat.

[60]   [CAS to RHB] [TLS]

Auburn-in-Malebolge,
May 16th, 1937.

Dear Bob:

No doubt you will be astounded to receive so prompt an answer from me. Once in an epoch, I really get the impulse to write a letter; and this time you're the victim.

I received the book on Beddoes which you sent me from HPL's library. Strangely enough, HPL himself sent me a copy of that same book two or three years ago![1] I believe he bought several of them. Do you want the copy that you mailed me—I hardly need duplicates?! The book has certain merits as a critical and psychologic study; though I hardly feel that the author is temperamentally fitted to do full justice to Beddoes, who was a genuinely great and rare poet. As for my receiving other items from HPL's library, I certainly hope that Mrs. Gamwell will take her time. Though I should be glad to have whatever was left to my choice, there is no urgency whatever. I do little reading—and have less room for storage. My bookshelves are jammed full, with sculptures roosting all over the ledges and on the piled volumes at the top!

The typing of HPL's mss. must certainly keep you busy. I have started to type excerpts from his letters to me for August and Donald, and have found it very slow work.[2] A volume of representative letters certainly should establish him as one of the world's great correspondents. There must be a whole library of material buried in his correspondence. The letters to me in one year (1933) must aggregate forty or fifty thousand words if not more.

As to the Sterling letters, I got them together for safe-keeping rather than anything else. They are now in a strong and supposedly fire-proof iron box. I hadn't thought of printing them, and have no money for such a venture anyway. On the whole, they are more personal than literary, and are in no sense comparable to Lovecraft's letters for general value and interest. One of them contains a far from fortunate criticism of Lovecraft's Dagon, which I lent to

G.S. in manuscript. G.S. thought the tale derivative,* and considered that it lacked sufficient "climax." It was, he complained, "all over in 30 seconds, like a rabbit's amour." He made the melodramatic suggestion that the monolith should fall forward and crush the worshipping monster![3] When I passed this suggestion on to HPL, the latter protested very gently and justly that it would hardly be in keeping with the atmospheric development he had intended.[4]

What hurts me more than anything else about HPL's death, is the feeling that he might have lived for many more years with proper recognition, financial recompense, and the nourishing food that his condition must have made doubly imperative. Truly, as you suggest, America has killed her finest artists. And when she hasn't killed them, she has driven them into exile, as in the cases of Hearn and Bierce.[5] Personally I am goddamned sick of the killing process (I seem to die hard) and have fully and absolutely made up my mind to quit the hell-bedunged and heaven-bespitted country when my present responsibilities are over. I haven't any definite plans, but will probably gravitate toward the orient. Anyway, I shall remove myself from Auburn, California and the U.S.A, even if I have to stow away on a tramp steamer.

As you surmised, I am not deeply enamored of the Republican system. On the other hand, I have no faith in *any* political or economic isms, schisms, and panaceas. Theoretically, almost any kind of a system might serve well enough, if human beings were not the stupidest and greediest and most cruel of the fauna on this particular planet. No matter what system you have— capitalism, Fascism, Bolshevism—the greed and power-lust of men will produce the same widespread injustice, the same evils and abuses: or, will merely force them to take slightly different forms. The Marxian motto: From each according to his capacity; to each according to his need, is no doubt a beautiful sentiment; but it is about as impractical, and as likely to be practiced, as the Golden Rule of Jesus Christ. From this, you can see that I am not a likely convert to Communism. I doubt if Communism could be established in this country without prolonged internecine warfare that would make the Spanish embroilment[6] look like a Rotarian barbecue in comparison. The immediate result of revolutionary tactics will be to precipitate a dictatorship of the type now prevalent in Germany and Italy. I don't like to think of what will follow. Whatever ensues will hardly be to the advantage of artists and intellectuals: they'll be damned lucky if they even have pulp magazines to write for. In my opinion, the whole fabric of western civilization is nearly due for a grand debacle; and the spreading class-struggle will hasten rather than avert it. After that—well, it is a familiar platitude that the sun rises in the East.

As to conditions in Russia, I'll admit that I know little about them and do not see how it is possible to know much without visiting the country and circu-

---

*an exhibition of the common fallacy that all weird writing derives from Poe, Bierce, etc. G. wasn't much on nuances.

lating freely among its people. Writers on the subject, whether for or against, are equally open to a strong suspicion of propagandism. Some of the strongest Communists, like Emma Goldman, seem to have soured on the idea after a sojourn in Russia.[7] Though I have no religious beliefs myself, I must confess to a profound distaste for the anti-religious bigotry that forms an avowed feature of the Soviet program. In the name of Iblis, Satan, Thasaidon and Ialdabaoth, why can't they leave religion alone? In trying to suppress it, I believe they have made a similar error to the one made by the late tsar in suppressing vodka. No wonder the mujiks lent themselves to revolt!

One other observation: communism, as practiced in the insect world, is a poor recommendation for its possible effect on humanity. Nothing sickens me more than to watch the mechanistic activities of ants, who have certainly achieved the ultimate in regimentation and operation. I guess I must be an anarchist myself; and I am sure I would be strictly non-assimilable in any sort of co-operative society, and would speedily end up in a concentration camp.

Don't think, from all this, that I am unsympathetic toward the revolutionary spirit, which is the natural reaction of youth when it awakens to the vision of social injustice. My own nature is that of the rebel: if it weren't, I would hardly write, paint and sculp[t] in the manners I have chosen. But, in the political sphere, history has convinced me that revolutions are futile: nothing is changed, except the codes and the masters.

Re certain other matters in your letter. Mrs Gamwell sent me The Californian with your Night Ocean, which HPL had put aside in an envelope addressed to me. I liked your story very much, and also enjoyed the one by Edkins.[8]

I look forward to Leaves, which has a fine program. Offhand, I can't think of any good literate material to suggest. Weiss might have something. He has written some good tales, such as The Smell in Strange Tales and The Dancer in the Crystal in W.T.[9] My stories, Red World of Polaris and Metamorphosis of the World were passably written, but suffer from triteness of plot: this because I wrote them at a time when I had not read enough science fiction to avoid the more obvious plot-ideas. Mother of Toads is a sort of carnal and erotic nightmare and I can't decide on its merits. Spicy Mystery Stories rejected it after holding the ms. for nearly two months. I have now shipped it to Esquire, which, judging from the two issues I have read, will sometimes print stuff that would hardly make the grade with an honest pulp. Wandrei's tales, and one by Arthur Davison Ficke, are the only good ones that I have found in aforesaid issues.[10] The magazine seems aimed at a rather naive class of readers who like to feel that they are wicked and sophisticated. I believe that a yarn like Mother of Toads would arouse considerable Sound and Fury if printed in that quaint periodical (Sound and Fury is the name of the letter department, as you may know. It's a good name—one of the best things about Esquire—particularly when one recalls the Shakespearian passage from which it is taken. However, I must correct myself here—they no doubt took it from Hemingway.)[11]

I have sold one yarn to W.T. recently (The Death of Ilalotha) and have others under way. Ilalotha is quite good, I believe, especially in style and atmosphere. It is unusually poisonous and exotic. Writing is hard for me, since circumstances here are dolorous and terrible. Improvement in my father's condition is more than unlikely, and I am more isolated than ever. Also, I seem to have what psychologists call a "disgust mechanism" to contend with: a disgust at the ineffable stupidity of editors and readers. I think that some of my best recent work is in sculpture: and I find myself confronted with another blank wall of stupidity. Oh well and oh hell: some one will make a "discovery" when I am safely dead or incarcerated in the bughouse or living with a yellow gal in Cambodia.

Yours for the bombing of Philistia and Boe[o]tia with Chinese stinkpots
Clark Ashton

P.S. On glancing over this letter, I note a few asperities of tone, and, in places, a lack of Arnoldian "sweetness and light."[12] In extenuation, I must plead that I have been pretty much at the boiling point lately.

I believe the late R. E. Howard and I would have had a grand time together lambasting civilization; that is, if I have not been misinformed as to his views. Barbarism, barbaric art, barbaric peoples, appeal more and more to me. I could never live in any modern city, and am more of an "outsider" than HPL. His "outsideness" was principally in regard to time-period; mine is one of space, too.

Notes

1. By Royall H. Snow. See HPL to CAS, 11 January 1934 (*Dawnward Spire* 512).

2. CAS eventually abandoned the typing of extracts from HPL's letters and turned over his entire cache of letters to AWD and DW for transcription.

3. Cf. GS to CAS, 13 February 1923: "I've a suggestion to make—a valuable one, I think. The tale is disappointing at its climax, because there's not enough detail, enough suspense, enough action. It's all over in ten seconds, like a rabbit's amour. My advice is that he have the monster uprear, approach the monolith with horrible sounds of worship, and prostrate itself. Then have the mire quake and Dagon fall upon the monster, slaying it, just as other heads of its kind rise from the slime." *The Shadow of the Unattained* 227.

4. See HPL to Edwin Baird: "A friend of mine—Clark Ashton Smith, the California poet of horror, madness and morbid beauty—shewed this yarn to George Sterling, who declared he liked it very much, though suggesting (absurdly enough, as I view it!) that I have the monolith topple over and kill the 'thing' . . . a piece of advice which makes me feel that poets should stick to their sonneteering" (*WT,* October 1923; rpt. HPL, *Letters to Woodburn Harris and Others* [New York: Hippocampus Press, 2022], 41). Publication of the letter was no small embarrassment to HPL.

5. Lafcadio Hearn (1850–1904) moved to Japan as a newspaper correspondent in

1890 and never returned to the US. Bierce (1842–1914?), after retiring from journalism in 1909, headed to Mexico in late 1913 and was never heard from again; he probably died in the course of the Mexican Civil War.

6. I.e., the Spanish Civil War (1936–39).

7. The Russian-born anarchist and atheist Emma Goldman (1869–1940) came to the US in 1885. Although she became a US citizen, she was deported to Russia in late 1919. Initially she spoke favorably of the Russian revolution, but her views later changed, and she left Russia in 1921.

8. E. A. Edkins, "The Affair of the Centaurs," *Californian* 4, No. 3 (Winter 1936): 15–26.

9. Francis Flagg, "The Smell" (*Strange Tales*, January 1932); "The Dancer in the Crystal" (*WT*, December 1929). *Leaves* No. 2 contains Weiss's poem, "Flower of War" (106).

10. DW, "The Eye and the Finger" and "The Painted Mirror"; Arthur Davison Ficke, "Mrs. Morton Buys a Fish" (June 1937).

11. Actually, the title of William Faulkner's novel, *The Sound and the Fury* (1929); from *Macbeth* 5.5.27.

12. The phrase was popularized by British critic Matthew Arnold (1822–1888) to refer to the infusion of beauty and intelligence in verse; but many commentators interpreted it as a synonym for bland conventionality.

[61]   [RHB to CAS] [ALS]

4 July 1937

Dear Clark Ashton—

Your little book has arrived, to my surprise and pleasure . . . thanks very much indeed for it. The printer (who is he?) had produced a neat, tasteful tome, on a nice paper; & I hope to see further productions issue from his anything but futile press.[1] The selection of poems is very pleasing—all (except THE WINDS, which eludes me) being familiar,[2] & several of them favorites of mine. He should go on, & make a little book of the Hashish-Eater. It occurs to me that he might be interested in illustration for forthcoming volumes—I wonder if he'd be interested in any of my junk? I've taken up the graphic arts—notably lithography (of which I'll shortly forward a specimen) & would be more than glad to cooperate if he happened to be interested. Perhaps you could give me his address.

Most of my time, outside of school work, has gone into cutting the stencils for LEAVES, which I hope to have complete & ready for running off by the time I go south (c. July 20) so that my "publisher" can whack away at the job during my absence. This venture, while it entails a lot of sweat on my part, gives me peculiar satisfaction; & in spite of the probable financial holocaust I believe it will continue to appear as an annual or semi-annual, depending on cash & time at my disposal. Your Vathek conclusion, together with Beckford's fragment, is already completed, & yesterday I looked over the copies. Certainly if I keep it up you must be a star contributor, & with my usual forehandedness, I am speculating on material for #2 (MSS, probably.)

Of course, there is your *Overland* story which will probably be reprinted,[3] but what I'd really like is some new production, done at leisure & with an eye to articles subtlely [*sic*] done. What are the prospects for this? You'll probably want some kind of guarantee that said #2 will materialise, but I thought this not too premature a time for making the suggestion.

Leaves is designed to give writers an opportunity—though regrettably non-remunerative—for serious exploration of the fields of exotic writing. It will not be 100% weird & fantastic, since I mean to use other material . . . . library catalogues, essays, & comprising about 1/10th of the complete product, but then additional items will be subordinated even more than they were in RECLUSE, & ought to please rather than disturb. There is not a great deal of material of high enough standard for such a magazine, & the Editor will probably have to drum up trade. If you could find a chance, during the next six months, to play around with a very "arty" opus, designed solely for imaginative effect, & as subtle & atmospheric as possible . . . . eschewing the pitfalls of pulp standard (surprise ending, horrible monsters, &c) LEAVES would be, Sir, your eternal & rejoicing debtor! Speaking of your stories . . . . what became of MOHAUN LAUS [*sic*]? I do not remember seeing it printed.

Nothing exciting here—just the customary wrestling with AWD & the masses of MS., which are about in order now. Do you have a copy of HPL's GREEN MEADOW (1920), NYARLATHOTEP (1920) & *Alchemist* (1908)? I cannot locate copies of these.

Incidentally, where do you mean to insert the new poems since INCANTATIONS was arranged? I shall tackle that as soon as I get back from vacation, & may try to present it to a waiting (too long waiting) world while 1937 yet graces the calendar.

Enough—enough. My real thanks for NERO—& best wishes for its sale. Do you ever send review copies to N.Y. papers? I'll bet the Times would give it a notice, in spite of its slender (physical) dimensions.

Yours ever & ever,
Bob

104 3rd Ave Leavenworth, Ks

Notes

1. *Nero and Other Poems,* printed by Claire Beck for the Futile Press. "The Winds" was indeed in *ST*. The Press also published HPL's *Notes and Commonplace Book,* edited by RHB, and printed GS's *After Sunset* for John Howell, also edited by RHB. RHB had hoped the press could complete his edition of HPL's *Fungi from Yuggoth.*

2. All the poems in *Nero* were reprinted from *ST*.

3. "The Abominations of Yondo" did not appear in *Leaves,* and CAS had nothing in the second number.

[62]   [CAS to RHB] [ALS]

Auburn, Calif.
July 12th, 1937.

Dear Bob:

I was on the point of writing when your last letter came. Glad to hear that the booklet impressed you so favourably. (Mr.) Claire P. Beck, aged nineteen, is the printer; address, Box 27, Lakeport, Cal. It was his own idea to reprint a selection from The Star-Treader. I, however, made the selection of titles and revised several of the poems, particularly Song of a Comet, which now contains some brand-new lines and passages. Beck is one of the higher-grade science fiction enthusiasts, and prints a magazine, Science Fiction Critic, which "pans" the popular magazine junk with proper severity. He is very partial to pure fantasy—and, incidentally, has been an enthusiastic customer for several of my carvings. So far, I don't believe he has used any illustrations; but you might get in touch with him. He is desirous of bringing out a book of R. E. Howard's stories, and also a selection of mine. Later on, a reprint of The Hashish Eater[1] might be a good idea, especially since I have made a number of alterations in the poem, designed, for the most part, to vary the cadence of the verse.

This brings me to the bound mss. of The H.E., which came some time ago with your painting and copies of my grotesques. The viper-skin makes a beautiful back-strip; but you should really have a few contrasting reptile-skins (Gila monster preferably!) to cover the rest of the binding. If you don't mind my keeping the ms. till fall, I may be able to return it with one or two pictorial embellishments. Incidentally, I can add some more [to it].

Thanks for the painting, which seems very expressive. The photos and copies of my grotesques were certainly a surprise—I had totally forgotten several of them! You seem to have done a very good job—at first glance I took some of the pictures for the originals!

I look forward to Leaves, and hope that the sale will at least partially reimburse you for the outlay. I'll try to write something of a purely artistic type for No. 2, but can't positively promise that anything of magnitude will materialize. Shapes of Adamant,[2] which still sticks at about 1000 words, might fill the gap if I can complete it. There is small chance that any professional magazine would care for an opus of such mystical and fantastic nature, involving four avatars in a future continent. . . . The Letter from Mohaun Los, concerning which you inquire, was published in Wonder Stories several years ago under the title Flight into Super-Time—a title for which Gernsback was no doubt to blame.

Regarding Incantations: there are a couple of changes that you might make in the ms. Please change the title of Alienation to *The Outer Land*. The first title seems rather inadequate and inexpressive. Also, in A Fable, the two lines next to the last should read: "And raise from ream-deep ice the boreal cities pale / With towers that man has neither built nor overthrown." As to the placement of new poems: I can't at the moment find my list of titles, but think that Farewell to Eros might come at the very end of the verse-items. Song of the Necromancer wouldn't be bad as an opening, to set the tone of the whole collection. The poem to HPL should be placed toward the last— perhaps after *Revenant*. Did I send you a new Baudelaire—La Beatrice? I can't quite remember. This would do well for the parting squirt of Baudelairian vitriol in Incantations. I enclose a sonnet, Outlanders, which you can place after The Envoys. This, I think, is the last item I'll try to add to the volume; it should be quite enough for you to wrestle with now. By the way, speaking of lithographs, I wonder if you could make anything out of my pencil drawing for In Slumber? I always thought this drawing one of my best.

Not much news at this end either. My writing goes on like the progress of a broken-backed snail. The Garden of Adompha, in which some unusual grafting occurs, is partly written. I make an occasional sculpture, and am inclined to think that my growing collection of such opuses is one reason for the falling-off in visitors. "Hideosities" . . . "chamber of horrors." . . . "nightmares" . . . . such are the key-notes of local art-criticism. Evidently the stuff has a kick. If I were in Paris, I might give the surrealists some competition . . . To date I have made about $40.00 from the sale of carvings.

I hadn't thought of sending any copies of Nero to reviewers, but may gamble one on the N.Y. Times. Thanks for the suggestion. Derleth is giving the booklet some reviews (one in Voices) and probably Stanton Coblentz will mention it in Wings,[3] since a copy was sent to him by a mutual friend. I have mailed one to Alexander Woollcott,[4] at the instigation of a girl-friend. Beck, in his last letter, said that he had already sold about 50 copies, which is certainly a good beginning. At that rate, he won't lose anything on the venture. He has an ad. in W.T.

Your arguments for bolshevism are about the best that can be put up, I imagine; and I must admit that you put them well. Perhaps communism will eventually become universal—perhaps not: I don't feel able to predict. I could never embrace it, since, as far as humanity is concerned, I see little good in anything but development of the exceptional individual, and am unable to think in terms of mass-values and numbers. My feeling is, that communism could not really favour the genius, the "sport," the exception: it would stamp him out as a traitor to the party, since he would inevitably react against it. The present system is bad and cruel enough, but at least one has a fighting-chance, with liberty in speech and press. Such liberty is plainly non-existent under any form of dictatorship, proletariat or otherwise. Any system of government that can't stand honest criticism and opposition is strictly n.g. in my opinion. To hell with it. You may argue that censorship and the other rigors are only temporary, and necessary for the establishment of the new regime; but I'm damned if I can subscribe to any regime that would find them necessary. Russia has been trying it out for nearly a generation, and from the recent whole-sale murder of generals and other officials, it doesn't seem that there can really be much "belt-loosening." Russia might well blow up, if she becomes internally divided, and is assailed by Japan on one hand and Germany on the other.

On the other hand, as I admitted before, Communism *may* be the future of the race. The effect on human development will remain to be seen; but my own feeling is, that it will favour the mediocre, the uniform, the materialistic, at the expense of anything rare and exceptional and spiritual. If this is true, it might be better if civilization collapsed in a general Armageddon, leaving the remnants of the race to start again from scratch in complete barbarism. This, from present indications, becomes more and more the most probable of all the possible eventuations. Maugre what I have said above, I confess that I am almost disinterested in regard to the whole business; and, being a sort of spectator from Mars or Yuggoth, I really have little desire to convert you to monarchism. What is to be will be; and no man, unless he were Attila, will weigh much in the sweep of cosmic forces and temporal tides.

Yrs for the epiphany of Satan,
Clark Ashton.

P.S. I enclose a little squib on Communism by Ben De C. Of course, it would surprise the "workers" to find themselves labelled "parasites";[5] nevertheless, Ben covers the biological aspects with his usual neatness.

Notes

1. None of these three projects was ever realized.
2. "Shapes of Adamant" does not appear to have been completed (see *SS* 131–32).
3. AWD, "The Poets Sing Frontiers," *Voices* No. 91 (Autumn 1937): 44–46; [Stanton Coblentz], [review of *Nero*], *Wings* 3, No. 6 (Summer 1938): 27–28.
4. Alexander Woollcott (1887–1943), American critic, commentator for the *New Yorker*, and a member of the Algonquin Round Table. He did not review *Nero*.
5. Possibly *The Individual Against Moloch* (1936).

[63]   [CAS to RHB] [ALS]

Auburn, Calif.
Sept. 9th, 1937.

Dear Bob:

I was glad to get your letter, enclosing Mrs. Barbauld's fragment (which I had never seen before); also, the much appreciated copies of Leaves. I'd have written sooner; but August was a particularly crowded month, since, in addition to homework and writing, I took on the care of the Sullys' extensive flower-garden while they were away. I did the watering mostly at night, and acquired the general habits of a hoot-owl; incidentally avoiding much of the deadly ultra-violet radiation.

That suggestion about The Last Sabbat is a good one, and I may attempt the subject some time. HPL, however, should have written the story himself. I can't hope to compete with him when it comes to New England setting and atmosphere; though perhaps the actual orgies of the Sabbat would be a little more in my line. As to Sir Bertrand, I must admit that there would be some possibilities in an amplification of the fragment, whose present banal ending seems no more than the deceptive curtain of horrors to come. If you don't mind a delay (possibly of months) I will undertake to extend the piece. The opening is the best piece of Gothic writing that I have seen, and is worthy of the praise given it in the monograph on Supernatural Horror.[1]

Leaves certainly contains a distinguished line-up, and I was especially glad to see the opus on Cats and Dogs and the reprint of Merritt's best story, The People of the Pit. HPL's article is delighting the Sullys who, like myself, are fervent ailurophiles. Dead Houses forms a good foil for the fantastics. If it should get the magazine barred from the mails, Leaves will become a precious collectors' item overnight. However, barred or unbarred, it is going to be valuable. . . . . Regarding E. A. Edkins'[s] comments on weird fiction: it seems to me that he doesn't quite get the point in the use of fantastic names; such nomenclature being necessary (if one is to use names at all) when introducing unknown gods and places and people outside of terrene geography or historic time.[2] However, I will readily grant that the nomenclature should be subtilized, with an eye (or ear) to find onomatopoetic values and phonetic or verbal associations. But to cavil at said nomenclature in itself is too much like denying the runner his starting-place. Too many people approach the weird and fantastic—if they approach it at all—with a grudging attitude. However, what can one expect? The modern mind takes the local illusions of Maya with such deadly seriousness; and the writer or artist who prefers to invent his own illusions is, I suspect, regarded as being slightly immoral or, at least, reprehensible.

The Garden of Adompha, a tale which I am inclined to like, was finished and promptly sold to W.T. Wright spoke of a possible cover-design by Finlay to go with the story.[3] He also took Mother of Toads, from which I had excised the more overt erotic details as being unsuitable for the chaste perusal of the PTA.[4] The tale remains a passable weird, with a sufficiently horrific ending, in which the hero is smothered to death by an army of diabolic toads after which he had refused the second dose of aphrodisiac offered him by the witch, La Mère des Crapauds. Wright has also taken a slightly abridged and pruned version of The Maze of the Enchanter which I had previously submitted to Esquire under the restored original tile, The Maze of Maal Dweb (I think it should be admitted that some of my nomenclature achieves certain nuances or suggestive and atmospheric associative value.) The Esquire editor thought it "reminiscent of both Burroughs and Cabell;" a criticism that amazed and disgusted me. I was not aware that Burroughs had any copyright on jungle hunters, or that Cabell had acquired a monopoly of irony. *******!!******** I fear that Mr. Gingrich[5] is a better judge of garbage than of literature.**********!!

The H.E. ms. will go back to you before long with some additions, including the fragment of The Fugitives: a play which I am never likely to continue, having long forfeited the romanticism that is prerequisite for such work.

I am enclosing a copy of La Béatrice, which can go anywhere among the Baudelaires in Incantations. Re edition of this book: I'd suggest a small one, as originally planned. Claire P. Beck (from whom you should have heard ere this) had sold only 75 of Nero at last report. Sandalwood, of which I printed 250, was the only volume of mine that completely sold out in any reasonable or semi-reasonable length of time; and I doubt if Incantations (though probably a better book) will rival its popularity. The fewer you print, the more the collectors of 1987 will pay for a copy of the volume . . . . and the fewer you'l[l] have to store in the attic or basement. I still have about 600 of The Double Shadow parked under my bed with the empty wine-jugs.

The sonnets you quote in your letter seem slightly prosy and didactic; not enough poetic yeast in them. Otherwise, I find it hard to lay my finger on any specific fault. Technically, some of the lines seem too slow in their movement; a phrase such as "by *ceaseless feet worn deep*"⁶ being an example. The two spondees and the three long ees make it a bit heavy. However, this wouldn't matter greatly by itself. If I were you, I'd try other forms than the sonnet, and would proceed from the basis that imagery is more valuable than philosophic ideas. As Ambrose Bierce once said, the thought in any poem never really amounts to much.⁷ The fallacy that it does amount to something seems to be widespread at the present time: "life," "reality," "psychology" and such like fetiches having taken the place of the moral didacticism of earlier days in America.

I'll look through the Sterling letters some day and see if there is anything suitable for your use. The iron box containing them is at present buried under magazines and old mss.

I wrote three poems in August (counting a burlesque item in vers libre) and will send copies presently. One of them, The Prophet Speaks, was accepted by Wright. It described the doom and destruction of an unnamed seaport city. The best one, Desert Dweller, I am submitting to the "quality" magazines, beginning with Yale Review, which took one of my poems in the rather remote past.⁸

Glad you liked Ilalotha, a story in which I seem to have slipped something over on the PTA. The issue containing it, I hear, was removed from the stands in Philadelphia because of the Brundage cover.⁹ Query: why does Brundage try to make all her women look like wet-nurses? It's a funny, not to say tiresome, complex.

I was amused by your account of the nudist camp. If I were you, I'd do most of my nuding at night or in shady places: ultra-violet is no good for a white man. I believe that I am finishing the summer in far better shape than usual because of my avoidance of *U.V.*

Too bad about Robert S. Carr.[10] At present indications, it seems not impossible that we'll all have to take our turn at dodging Fascistic bombs and bullets: that is to say, if Japan and her European allies start a world-war. It will be hard for the U.S. to keep clear. . . . Incidentally, the word "civilization" would make a jackal vomit in view of the general situation.

Since it is now time for the evening chores, I shall bring this rather lengthy screed to a conclusion.

Yrs, in the name of AntiChrist and under the sign of the Beast 666,
Clark Ashton

P.S. I hope you got the Whitehead mss. and will use them in Leaves.[11]

I hope the suggestion for an illustrated edition of the H.E. will materialize. Beck seemed favorably disposed toward it.

Notes

1. See HPL's "Supernatural Horror in Literature" on "Sir Bertrand" by Mrs. Anna Letitia Barbauld (1743–1825), "in which the strings of genuine terror were truly touched with no clumsy hand" (35). "Sir Bertrand" is a section of an essay, "On the Pleasure Derived from Objects of Terror," in *Miscellaneous Pieces in Prose* (London: J. Johnson, 1773) by John and Letitia Aikin (later Mrs. Barbauld).

2. E. A. Edkins, quoted in RHB, "Obiter Scriptum; or, Succotash without Seasoning": "So many writers of weird fiction lean so heavily on grotesque nomenclature that I really think a study might be profitably made of the whole terminology, with a view to divesting it, as far as possible, from its grosser grotesqueries. Surely none but infantile minds are thrown into a state of receptive coma or condition of shivering ecstasy by such faintly comic vocables as Zuggoth [*sic*], to mention the first one that comes to my mind. . . . It would therefore seem that weird names and titles should be chosen with the utmost artfulness and with a fine discrimination, different from known terms, but not *too* different" (63).

3. Virgil Finlay did indeed do a cover based on CAS's story.

4. CAS alludes to the furor caused by an Indiana branch of the Parent Teacher Association upon publication of C. M. Eddy's "The Loved Dead" (revised by HPL) in *WT* (May–June–July 1924). HPL had referred to the incident in a letter to CAS c. 8 February 1931, and even ten years later Farnsworth Wright was still reluctant to publish certain stories for fear of reprisal. "The Death of Ilalotha" contains some scenes suggestive of necrophilia.

5. Arnold Gingrich (1903–1976) was co-founder and editor of *Esquire*.

6. Cf. "Cycle from a Dead Year" (1936) I.3: "Now on this ledge by tortured feet worn deep" (*Eyes of the God* 363).

7. Cf. Ambrose Bierce, "Thought and Feeling" (1903): "I had supposed that [the poet Robert Loveman's] aim was to produce an emotion, a feeling. That is all that a poet— as a poet—can do. He may be philosopher as well as poet—may have a thought, as profound a thought as you please, but if he do not express it so as to produce an emotion in an emotional mind he has not spoken as a poet speaks. It is the philoso-

pher's trade to make us think, the poet's to make us feel" (*Collected Works of Ambrose Bierce* 10.274).

8. *Yale Review* published only "The Nereid," in July 1913. The burlesque is unidentified.

9. Margaret Brundage did a cover for Seabury Quinn's story "Satan's Palimpsest" (*WT,* September 1937).

10. Robert S[pencer] Carr (1909–1994) published his first novel, *The Rampant Age* (1928), at 17. A convert to communism, he lived in the Soviet Union from 1932 to 1937, working for an agency to promote tourism to the nation. When he returned to the US in late 1937, he worked briefly for various film companies, including the Walt Disney Co.

11. *Leaves* No. 2 contains only Whitehead's "The Tree-Man" (120–32), reprinted from *WT.*

[64]   [RHB to CAS] [TNS]

[Postmarked Leavenworth, Kan.,
18 October 1937]

Dear Clark Ashton, I've just pulled in from the East and am in a hustle getting back to school and getting a cussed typing job off to the *Californian.*[1] I will write more elaborately, but having discovered your request for another Leaves, I wanted to assure you it will be forthcoming with my compliments. Only thing, they cost *24¢* mailed separately, *6¢* ea/ in bales of 20. Do you mind if I wait until I'm ready to send yours in a batch? Hope you will do a continuation of Sir B— am gleefully anticipating it.

Bob

[P.S.] Wish Beck would write if the HE idea attracts him—I shall be doing intro. work again in a week or so.

Notes

1. Probably HPL's "Mrs. Miniter—Estimates and Recollections," a lengthy piece published in the Spring 1938 issue.

[65]   [CAS to RHB] [ALS]

Auburn, Calif.
Dec. 5th, 1937.

Dear Bob:

When you are ready to mail out a bunch of *Leaves,* please send a copy to John Allan,[1] 46 Stanley Ave., Hamilton, Canada, and one to A. Scott (Allan's nephew) at the same address. I insist on paying for these, and enclose 70¢.

When I am able to write at length, I shall tell you more about these men, with whom I have recently gotten in touch. At present I shall say only that J. Allan is, in my estimation, one of the greatest weird and imaginative artists of the Occident. He has also made numerous translations from Baudelaire and has written some fine original poetry.

My father has been seriously ill (heart trouble and general weakness) ever since Armistice Day. I am keeping him alive with wine and liquor, since his stomach tolerates little else. The prescription of the doctor (a teetotaler!) nearly finished him.[2] You can imagine the stress of the situation, since I am day and night nurse as well as the rest of the household staff.

I'll express the H.E. mss. volume to you at first opportunity, along with some new illustrations and scripts. You might like to use the fragment of *The Fugitives* in the next Leaves.

Yrs, in the name of Umr-at-Tawil, the Prolonged of Life,[3]
Clark.

[P.S.] Oh, yes, here's a little blurb that Ben De Casseres wrote about me. Claire Beck has printed 70 copies of it—25 for Ben, 25 for me, and the rest for himself to distribute.[4]

Notes

1. John Allan (1875–1958), Canadian painter and poet.
2. CAS's father Timeus Smith (b. 1855) died 26 December 1937.
3. From "Through the Gates of the Silver Key."
4. Benjamin De Casseres, *Clark Ashton Smith, Emperor of Shadows* (Lakeport, CA: Futile Press, 1937); rpt. as the introduction to *SP*.

[66]   [RHB to CAS] [ALS]

Dear CAS—

I have been wondering how things are going for you, but did not want to compel you to write in the midst of your anxiety. Now, however, I fear I must intrude. Beck is preparing to do the HE, & tells me to go ahead with the lithos from your drawings, & of course I must get the loan of the originals before doing so. I have written Loveman & asked to see his—which request I hope he'll accommodate—but I believe that you have a few of the series yet in your possession. If such is the case, might I borrow them? We want to do you honour on the project—which may be my swan-song as a graphic artist, since my eyes are giving out on me, & the doctors say I must stop all literary & artistic activities. [What a bum farmer I'll make! In about a month, if the HE job is completed, mother & I mean to pull out of KC. There is a chance we may land on the west coast.]

I hope that things are better for you, & that you can unearth the drawings without undue inconvenience.

Ever yours,
Bob

4338 Locust St
    K C Mo
Feb. 14 '38

[67]   [RHB to CAS] [ALS]

Dear Clark,

I would have written weeks ago, but I was trying to get a line out of Love-man. This having now arrived proves to be something of a damper—I quote—

> "Dear Barlow, I've been sick for many months & much of my corre-spondence has suffered, hence my non-reply to your letter. Those draw-ings by Clark are packed away with my other effects in storage, so much so, I could not grapple the task of discovering them unless I withdraw all my wares from the place I am keeping them. It would be impossible to promise them to you for examination in anything approaching the remote future—"

He asks to be remembered to you & thereon signs off. ¶ This news seems a little discouraging—I am sending the letter to Beck & meanwhile speculate on what alternative course we have. It would be devilish unfortunate to be compelled to postpone the venture, & yet those drawings seem to me rather essential. Did you keep any preliminary sketches, or could you at this late date improvise draughts of them supposedly indicative of their nature to provide a basis for litho development? I never expected that we'd be held up in the N Y sector of the battlefield, & am momentarily stumped. Meanwhile, I have been tinkering with the material you sent & hope to have some results to show with my next, along with returned originals. Thanks immeasurably for the ad-ditional MSS—I was especially pleased with the Nora May French piece,[1] since the poem evokes my particular delight. The fragment of *The Fugitives* is tantalising—one can only wish that more had been told of the trans-Magapanic region! Next time I have an attack of mimeographic editorship I hope that the segments may be incorporated into the job.

I am drifting, rather, & cursing my optician & my optics; but at the same time toying with the notion of experimenting with the cinema. Cameras suit-ed to the amateur are becoming less expensive & more readily handled as time goes on, & it is an old interest of mine. Maybe I can get away with it and use it as an outlet for bottled-up creative impulses. Years ago Howard & I discussed a movie version of The Outsider—it would be enormous fun to try, though buying film will would keep me pretty damn poor, I judge.

This isn't a letter at all, really, just a dispatch from the scene of combat. When you feel like writing, I shall eagerly receive any comments or suggestions on the Hashish E–Beck–SL situation; & meanwhile subscribe myself

In all sincerity,
Yours,
Bob

March 28, 1938

Have you ever crossed the border into Mexico? If Standard Oil hasn't booked some local Franco before I get the chance, I shall certainly mosey around Popocatepetl & Ixticahuatl [*sic?*] & the other jaw-breakers ere long![2]

Notes

1. The Nora May French item is unidentified, but may have been the ms. of CAS's poem "To Nora May French." GS and several friends saw to the posthumous publication of her *Poems* (San Francisco: Strange Co., 1910). French (1881–1907) was a young poet and part of GS's circle of writers. She committed suicide in his house in Carmel, CA.
2. Popocatépetl and Iztaccihuatl are two of the tallest volcanoes in Mexico. Cf. RHB's essay "Parícutin" (*Eyes of the God* 517–23) regarding another Mexican volcano.

[68]   [CAS to RHB] [TLS]

Auburn, Calif.
May 10th, 1938.

Dear Bob:

I know I should have written you months and months ago. But the death of my father (Dec. 26th) after a long term of single-handed nursing left me pretty much exhausted; and I have been slow to recuperate. Letters have piled up in the manner of Ossa on Pelion; and I fear that many of them never *will* be answered.

I am sorry that the H.E. volume has temporarily fallen through. Perhaps, with recovered energy, and time, I may eventually be able to make some fresh illustrations for the poem. I did not keep any sketches of those presented to Loveman; and have only the vaguest memory of most of them.

Beck seems eager to go on and print something else in the meanwhile; and I am suggesting a selection from Sandalwood, the least circulated of my volumes.[1] Beck's idea (I believe he has written you) is to use reproductions of half a dozen of my paintings or drawings in the volume, irrespective of whether or not they illustrate any of the pieces. I wonder how this appeals to you, and whether you could make lithos from pictures of mine that you have on hand or wish me to loan you others. I don't believe I have ever done any pictures based on the lyrics in this volume, which are largely amatory; so the designs used would probably afford contrast rather than complement. . . . Incidentally, the originals that I sent you with the returned H.E. ms. volume are to be retained. I'd gladly go ahead and do some special illustrations *now:* but from sad experience I am convinced that my drawings are nothing if not inspirational and I must wait upon the mood, which has not visited me in years. Some of my WT illustrations were a horrible example of what happens when I try to work in cold blood and without definite impetus.

I hope that your optical trouble has been mitigated. Eyestrain is certainly hell: I suffer from more or less of it, though my sight is fairly good. I hope too that your proposed experiments with the cinema will materialize. The Outsider should be tremendous if properly filmed.

Some of my carvings are on exhibition at Gumps, in San Francisco; and one piece, at least, has been sold. But I have done little work of any sort recently. Poverty, and the pressure of debts, are conspiring to drive me into literary hackwork. I have just bought and perused a brand new "science fiction" magazine, Marvel Science Stories, which fathoms new depths in the mental muck of Moronia.[2] However, I believe it pays on acceptance. . . . This magazine, by the way, exhibits a covert trend toward "spiciness" in one or two of its yarns; brassières and step-ins (ripped from the heroine by some salacious monster) divide the interest with space-ships and ray-guns. The next thing will be a magazine specializing in futuristic or ultra-planetary eroticism, entitled Spicy Marvel Stories or Snappy Wonder Stories. We will see such titles as Rape in Utopia and The Whorehouse on the Moon. Henry Kuttner, who wrote an opus called Hollywood on the Moon,[3] should oblige with the latter subject!

Yrs for the Red Apocalypse,
Clark

Notes

1. The planned booklet was not published.
2. *Marvel Science Stories* (August 1938–April 1941; revived November 1950–May 1952) was a pulp magazine initially published by Postal Publications (later Western Publishing [1939–41] and Stadium Publishing [1950–52]). No editor was credited for the initial series (1938–41); the later series was edited by Robert O. Erisman.
3. Henry Kuttner (1915–1958), "Hollywood on the Moon" (*Thrilling Wonder Stories,* April 1938).

[69]   [CAS to RHB] [ALS]

Auburn, Calif.
July 5th, 1938.

Dear Bob:

Finally, though with some doubt as to their suitability for your purpose, I am mailing you a few of my smaller landscape paintings and drawings. Perhaps you have enough anyway, for the illustrating (or should one say illuminating?) of Sandalwood. I should have mailed these weeks ago; but, as usual, have suffered from the infernal dilatoriness consequent on several and sundry kinds of exhaustion. The crayon drawings are the most recent, having been done since I began my sculptures; and I am sending them along because they may interest you rather than with any idea to reproduction. I am also including, in a separate envelope, some of the photographs of aquarelles and drawings by John Allan which he has sent to me in folios of typed verse of his own composition. The verse does not quite show the technical mastery and imaginative genius of the pictures, though it is highly interesting, romantic and with many fine lines and phrases. I believe you will agree with me that the Italian monograph in appreciation of Allan's work[1] (typed translation enclosed with the pictures) is thoroughly deserved and even somewhat moderately phrased. I copy hereunder the sonnet in which Allan describes L'Évocation de Scorphael, which seems to be his supreme pictorial masterpiece:

> The Spirit's profanation who would know:—
> Behold, eclipsed are heaven's last rays, that light
> Its sculptured fane, and in Cimmerian night
> It shall lie desolate, a Mystery of Woe;
> Archdemons of abandonment shall haunt
> Its holiest shrine; nor death nor dread shall daunt
> Their blood-wrought ritual, evoking so
> A strange creation, shaped in Heaven's despite.
>
> Convened by Death, who knows no exorcism,
> Shall come the adepts of Abaddon and Baal,—
> Ecstaticii whose trance unlocks the Abysm;
> Then pale, resplendent, from the accursed travail,
> Shall crawl Hate's sublimate, Hell's fairest microcosm,—
> The scorpion-seraph, demoness Scorphael!

Allan and his nephew, A. Scott (also an artist) were very appreciative of Leaves, and I believe you have heard from J.A. before now. I must remember to pay you for those numbers, and shall put aside for that purpose the next paper dollar that falls, flutters, or otherwise comes within reach of my Satampran digits.

I have recently enjoyed a visit from Claire P. Beck, who stopped here overnight on his way to Reno. His brother, as you doubtless know, will continue the printing press in Lakeport. The copy of HPL's notebook, which reached me the other day, seems a worthy job and rather attractively bound.[2] As to Sandalwood, it seems to me that we should by all means retain the original title. Add the poem entitled Sandalwood, and the fragment of The Fugitives if you like. As to The Jasmine Girdle, or other material from Incantations, it seems to me that there is no hurry whatever. Perhaps, with indefinite delay, I could do some special illustrations for these later and uncollected poems. Horace (or was it Virgil?) said that poetry should be kept for at least 9 years before publication. Personally, I feel like naming an astronomical figure for the period for which most modern verse should be retained in cold storage.

Thanks for the photo of the beautiful Khmer head. This sort of thing makes most modern Occidental sculpture look like the Indian on a 5¢ piece.

I have done a little work (science fiction) but continue to loaf abominably. Thanks for the suggestion about historical fiction. This might offer possibilities but would require research. Egypt has been overworked; but there seem to be many fields of ancient history and archaeology that have been little touched in fiction.

I am glad your eye-trouble has been somewhat mitigated. John Allan, by the way, seems to have quite ruined his eyes by drawing and painting late at night and tells me he has had to give up art work. This is a tragedy. His best pictures, in my opinion deserve a place beside the highest imaginative art of any land or time. Pictures such as L'Évocation de Scorphael and The Sorceress seem to render (as the art of no other artist quite does) the very essence of black magic and Satanry.

I am hoping to strengthen my own eyes (the left is the weakest) by persistent exercise and massage of the surrounding muscles; this being part of a general plan of physical improvement. I don't expect to become a Sandow or a John L. Sullivan;[3] but I believe that I can correct a few defects and ward off the encroachments of middle age. I spring from a tough and long-lived stock, and therefore should have some material to work on. My height is close to 5 feet eleven; weight at present somewhere around 140 lbs; chest measurement 37 inches; waist 30. I am neither phtysical [*sic*][4] nor obese by tendency, but should like to gain about 10 lbs of permanent muscle together with renewed nervous vitality and driving-power. The last five years have been hard on me, both emotionally and physically; and much of the time I have consumed habitually an amount of alcohol (some of it of rather poor quality) which most authorities on the subject would consider dangerous. Recently, for a while, I have abstained entirely; but find now that the continuance of a moderate amount of table wine is desirable.

Charles D. Hornig, of Fantasy Fan renown, expects to stop in Auburn this month on his way East from a vacation in Hollywood. I certainly look forward to seeing him. E.H. Price and his mother may run up during the summer, and perhaps bring with them a girl friend of mine whom I have corresponded with regularly, but have not seen, for more than twenty years.

As ever,

Clark

P.S. Take your time about returning the pictures. No hurry whatever.

Notes

1. Vittorio Pica, "Il pittore dell'occultismo: John Allan," *Emporium* 21 (February 1905): 142–53.
2. *The Notes and Commonplace Book.*
3. Eugen Sandow (1867–1925), British proponent of health and fitness; John L. Sullivan (1858–1918), American boxer.
4. I.e., phthisical, or consumptive.

[70]   [RHB to CAS] [ALS]

Dear Clark,

This isn't going to be very elegant, either in point of composition or calligraphy, since it is being produced on what is known as a "bed of pain" & with a ruined pencil at that, whose snoggled lead may give way any moment.

What I have done is the usual thing in this country where meals are an adventure & water a downright hazard—come down with typhoid. In the process I have lost weight beyond all bounds—they only give me pink gelatin to eat, & I feel like a Portuguese Man-o-War as far as my innards are concerned. However, I shall be out shortly, & am promptly fleeing the country—coming up to your state. This autumn I am going to work with the Beck or Becks—depending on who's home—& hope we can wear out a few presses & mimeographs. First I shall finish up Leaves #2—for which I want a contribution of yours.[1] What can you send me? Please be thinking something up—I ought to be at work in the middle of September. Then we have a number of books which Claire & I discussed plans for. All in all it should be a busy & useful winter. My mother joins me later, & we shall be in Calif indefinitely. Of course I shall make an effort to see you when I have got on my feet. You won't be far away, I should judge.

Did you get the pictures & letter sent from K C as I left? How do you like the portfolio proposition?

Lead has busted as I feared. Write me please, % Becks.

Ever,
Bob

Mexico, Sept 2 '38

Notes

1. *Leaves* No. 2 contained nothing by CAS.

[71]   [postcard by RHB to CAS, nonextant][1]

[c. early December 1938]

Notes

1. See CAS to DW 142 (10 December 1938): "Barlow wrote me a card some days ago, saying that they were now ready to begin work on the book. This card I consigned to the stove."

[72]   [ALS, on RHB microfilm][1]

[c. mid-December 1938]

R. H. Barlow:

Please do not write me or try to communicate with me in any way. I do not wish to see you or hear from you after your conduct in regard to the estate of a late beloved friend. Clark Ashton Smith.

Notes

1. RHB has written "Please return" on the item, indicating he had lent it to someone to read. In *On Lovecraft and Life* 21. RHB retained this card and the first letter from CAS (the rest of his correspondence from CAS being deposited at JHL). It was microfilmed after his death.

Donald Wandrei
(Photo courtesy Dwayne Olson)

Letters: R. H. Barlow and Donald Wandrei

[1] [RHB to DW] [TLS, MHS]

[17 December 1932]

Dear Mr. Wandrei:—

Recently I heard from H. P. Lovecraft that you had had two books of poetry published—DARK ODYSSEY and a previous volume.

Could you tell me how to obtain copies of first editions of each?

Your work I consider of the highest merit—both prose and poetry.

Hoping for an answer at your convenience

I am

Yours sincerely
R. H. Barlow
7019 Ga. Ave., N.W.
Washington, D.C.

[2] [DW to RHB] [TLS]

84 Horatio St.,
New York, N.Y.
Dec. 22, 1932

Dear Mr. Barlow:

My first book ECSTACY [sic] has long been out of print, but I believe there were five or six copies among my books in St. Paul. So far as I know, the second book (DARK ODYSSEY) is not in stock in any bookstore since it was a small, semi-privately printed and limited edition.[1]

I have written home asking for copies of books to be forwarded. They should arrive early next week.

They are priced at 2.00 each, but you may have them both for 3.50 if you want them.

Thank you for your kind words about my work—personally I would make many changes if I could do it over again,[2] but I think this feeling is a natural result of progressive development or at least, I like to flatter myself that it is!

There was a third volume (BROKEN MIRRORS) gotten out by some friends and me, but only eighty copies or so were printed and they are now impossible to obtain. I have one copy but I have tried in vain to secure others, and, of course, I would not part with my personal copy.

Yours ever truly,
Donald Wandrei

Notes

1. DW was 19 when W. Paul Cook's Recluse Press published *Ecstasy and Other Poems* in 1928. The book was illustrated by his brother HW, then 18. It is not known if DW subsidized the publication, but given that he paid in part for publication of CAS's *Sandalwood* in 1925, it is likely that he did. *Dark Odyssey* was printed by Webb Publishing Co. of St. Paul in 1931, publisher of agricultural magazines. Presumably, DW also financed its publication.

2. DW's personal copy of *Ecstasy and Other Poems* was described thus by a dealer: "The book is heavily rewritten throughout [. . .] with hundreds of words in his hand. Some of the poems are totally re-written in red pencil" (Pepper and Stern, 1988, p. [30]).

[3]   [RHB to DW] [TLS, MHS]

[30 December 1932]

Dear Mr. Wandrei:

I enclose three dollars fifty cents for the books ECSTASY and DARK ODYSSEY.

I would appreciate it if you would sign them to me, (on the fly-leaf) but of course that is optional. . . .

Sorry to hear I can't get BROKEN MIRRORS—if you ever find any extra copies, I would like a chance at one.

Do you ever write any Ms. out in long-hand?

Please send them to me at:

De Land, Volusia County,

Florida,

—for I am going to move there in a few days.

Yours sincerely,

R. H. Barlow
(7019 Ga. Ave NW
Wash. D.C.)

[4]   [RHB to DW] [TLS, MHS]

March 28[, 1933]

Dear Mr. Wandrei:

I am gathering material for a LETTERS of the late Henry S. Whitehead, which I propose to issue mainly for his friends on a small hand-press. I do not know whether you knew him or not, but if so, would you have any for inclusion? All contributors will be presented with a copy of the final product.

Yours sincerely,

R. H. Barlow
Box 88
DeLand
Florida

[5]   [DW to CAS] [TLS]

84 Horatio St.,
New York, N.Y.
April 6, 1933

Dear Mr. Barlow:

No, I was never in contact with Whitehead, and have no letters of his. But I wish you all success with your project. I do know that the following people were in communication with him; H. P. Lovecraft, 10 Barnes St., Providence, R.I.; Farnsworth Wright, 840 N. Michigan Ave., Chicago, Ill.: August W. Derleth, Sauk City, Wis.; and A. A. Proctor, editor of ADVEN-TURE. The last name is only a surmise, but Whitehead's stories appeared in the magazine.

Sorry I can't help you further, but doubtless you could obtain still other names by writing to these persons.

Yours sincerely,
Donald Wandrei

[6]   [RHB to DW] [TLS, MHS]

January 10 1934
P. O. Box 88,
DeLand, Fla.

Dear Mr. Wandrei:

You may recall early last year I purchased your two books ECSTASY and DARK ODYSSEY. Were you able to locate a copy of BROKEN MIR-RORS? If you by any chance have one, I'm interested in obtaining it. Could you tell me a few details about this volume? The other contributors, publish-er, date, et cetera?

HPL mentioned, when I asked if he knew of any that might be so kind as to further my bibliomania, that you were a possible victim. So that is, frankly, my main purpose in writing, though several other matters also prompt this letter! Would you be so infinitely kind as to donate to me for my fantastic tale collection . . in which CAS, and others of the WT group are included . . some of your first drafts of weird & fantastic stories? I'd really appreciate it im-mensely, and did I not have admiration for your work, I should not ask you; so you can perceive I have no ulterior motive! I trust this is not too presumptuous!

Regarding your tales in Ast. The hermaphroditic race you portray is high-ly practical and perhaps even probable.[1] In a recent scientific article I read,

(I forget where), someone predicted not only that evolutionary change but the gradual optical merging into a Cyclopean orb! Such changes might well be advantageous! . . . "and yet by no sunset and no moonrise shall make thee man to ease a woman's sighs, or make thee woman for a man's delight.?. ."[2] The increasing preponderance of aberrations tending to the pseudohermaphroditic may well have significance. It is interesting for speculation, at any rate!

Trusting my request is not overly annoying, I am

Sincerely,

R. H. Barlow

Notes

1. In "Farewell to Earth."
2. Algernon Charles Swinburne, "Hermaphroditus," ll. 35–37.

[7]   [DW to RHB] [TLS]

84 Horatio St.,
New York, N.Y.
Feb. 3, 1934

Dear Mr. Barlow:

If I can find a draft of one of my weird tales, I'll send it on. The majority of them are in my St. Paul home, and all my stuff there is packed away at the present time. Sooner or later I'll get at it and see what there is.

I doubt whether a copy of BROKEN MIRRORS will ever turn up. My own copy is in St. Paul, hence I can't even tell you who the contributors were and what was in it, though I believe there was little or nothing of a fantastic nature. Only 84 copies were printed,[1] each of the five contributors and the artist receiving 13 apiece, the others going for copyright and 4 joint presentation copies. The volume sold at $5 but there weren't nearly enough to fill the demand. However, even if a copy should turn up, I don't think it would be worth adding to your library at that price, unless one of the contributors should achieve fame, which doesn't look likely. But I'll notify you in case I do hear of a copy obtainable.

Sincerely yours,
Donald Wandrei

Notes

1. The book's colophon states that 82 copies were published. See DW to RHB 15.

[8]   [RHB to DW] [TNS, MHS]

[Postmarked De Land, Fla.,
19 February 1934]

Dear Mr. Wandrei,

I shall be more than grateful if you will give me one of your manuscripts, and it will be very much appreciated.

So Broken Mirrors was extremely limited? Even if it is costly I want one some day (take your bow!) because you contributed.

I presume Recluse was first time you appeared in cold type?[1]

H. P. L. tells me you are very busy, so I shall not bother you further, except to again express my thanks for the prospective ms.

Yours sincerely,

R. H. Barlow—Bx 88 De Land—Fla

Notes

1. It was not. DW had had his poems and prose poems published in the *Minnesota Quarterly* as early as 1926, admittedly a college publication. His essay "The Emperor of Dreams" appeared in the *Overland Monthly* for December 1926. His poem in the *Recluse* also appeared in *Midwest Student* (May 1927).

[9]   [DW to RHB] [TLS]

84 Horatio St.,
New York, N.Y.
April 4, 1934

Dear Mr. Barlow:

Inclosed is the draught of ATOM-SMASHER[1] which appeared in last month's ASTOUNDING STORY. [*sic*] The sheets are a hopeless mess, as you can see by the typewritten line, the many pencilled changes, and the additional revisions made during the typing and which appear in the published story. However, this is the best I can do, since my mss. are generally far worse than this. At any rate, you can add it to your collection.

You can, in return, do a considerable favor for me, if you will. For years, Lovecraft, Cook, and others have been promising me a set of the unbound sheets of The Shunned House, which I want to bind specially for myself. Lovecraft now tells me that the sheets have been shipped to you, and that I am welcome to a set if you care to send it on. I would greatly appreciate your doing so, since I want to have them leather-bound and tooled,[2] whereas the volume will probably be cloth-bound as issued, and it would be more trouble and less satisfactory to have the covers ripped off and the contents re-bound.

If you do have the sheets, and care to do the favor, I will be greatly appreciative.

Cordially yours,
Donald Wandrei.

Notes

1. The draft of "The Atom-Smasher" apparently does not survive. In *Selections from the Archive of Donald Wandrei,* a story titled "Schonheim" was offered for sale (as by DW and Roy Davis Calverton), "Accompanied by two later versions, the first entitled 'The Decomposer' . . . and the second, 'Atom Smasher . . .'" (p. 15). JHL has two manuscripts that may have been given to RHB: "The Sleeper" (3 pp.) and "A Queen in Other Skies" (3 pp.), a poem.
2. Unbound sheets of *The Shunned House* were found among DW's effects.

[10]   [RHB to DW] [TLS, MHS]
[R. H. Barlow
Bibliomaniac]

Apr 8 34

Dear Mr. Wandrei;
            I am really most indebted for the manuscript, which was a very clever tale, also, in the printed version. Might I ask if the manuscripts of THE RED BRAIN, ECSTASY, and DEAD TITANS WAKE still exist? You will note HPL told me of your novel which I most sincerely hope will appear in book form in the none-too-distant future.
        Whenever the SHUNNED HOUSE arrives I shall of course send you the sheets of a copy. I had considered a specially-bound edition of about 25 copies along with the trade-edition, but you shall have a copy in sheets if you wish it. I can't tell when it will get here, though, for Cook is not wholly prompt!
        May I again render thanks for the donation?
                Most sincerely yours,
                R H Barlow
88
DeLand
Florida

[11]   [HPL and RHB to DW]   [ANS/TNS][1]
[Postmarked De Land, Fla.,
7? May 1934]
Hail, Melmoth! Grandpa is in the tropics at last, & having a great time. Feel 50 years younger than usual . . . . almost as spry as you boys! My host is a gifted artist, fantaisiste, & bibliophile, & has a marvellous collection in the crypt which he calls the Vaults of Yoh-Vombis. Delightful region here—& such an array of felidae . . . . & opossums! A blue lakelet (which we call the Moon Pool)

stretches behind the house, & on its glassy surface we row each evening. You'd have liked this place in your misanthropic 1927 period—it's out of sight of any other human habitation. Hope all prospers in the arctic! Regards to Sonny & the gang.

      Yr obt Grandsire—Melmoth III.

Might I add great appreciation for the manuscript you sent, which enters into Yoh-Vombis with due interment.[2] I'm behaving as should anyone who had not seen a strictly human being for fourteen months!

                      R. H. Barlow 𝕭

[By HPL:] Explored Savannah 8½ hrs. on trip south. Great place!

Notes

1. *Front:* A beautiful Southern Sunset Scene. N.B.: RHB's part of the card is typed.
2. Unknown, but probably the ms. entitled "Poems from *Broken Mirrors*" (TMS, JHL; deposited there by RHB). RHB had been unsuccessful in obtaining a copy of *Broken Mirrors*, which contained DW's work. There is also a TMS at JHL (also deposited by RHB) entitled "Poems from *Weird Tales*."

[12]   [RHB to DW] [TLS]

                    [R. H. Barlow
                    Bibliomaniac]

                                May 19 1934

Dear Mr. Wandrei,

    Recently Farnsworth Wright told me he was sending out a group of the original WT drawings to the authors whose stories they illustrate. Apparently this is the result of several years' saving-up, so that you will receive a considerable batch at once. Would it be too great a nuisance or impertinence to enquire whether there are any of these which could be spared to an ardent collector of such things . . . . myself, for instance? If any can be spared, would you be so kind as to quote a price on them?

    Another matter about which I am emboldened to pester you is that of your own manuscripts—especially rough draughts of stories or poems. Original MSS. of material as meritorious as yours has a permanent value to me, so that I hate to think of its being discarded or destroyed. Might I ask that you save any scripts which you would otherwise throw away, and send them to me at my expense?

    I presume Mr. Lovecraft has written you of my tentative plan for the photographic publication of your gifted brother's marvellous weird drawings.

Please remember me to him, and use your good offices to incline him to the venture if you can conscientiously do so.

   With expressions of the most profound esteem, I remain
                Yours most sincerely,
                           R H Barlow

[13]   [DW to RHB] [TLS]

                                    84 Horatio St., N. Y. C.
                                    May 22, 1934

Dear Mr. Barlow:

   Just after writing to Mr. Lovecraft yesterday, my brother dropped in (grammar poor but you get the sense) and told me of the joint letter he had received. Today came your double letter to me.

   Much as my brother and I appreciated your offer about the drawings, I am afraid I'll have to be a wet blanket. For some years, I have been planning to issue a book of Howard's drawings. I am deeply interested in photography, and as soon as I acquire an enlarging camera or a studio camera, I shall issue a photographic volume of all his good work. I feel that such a volume would not be helped by previous distribution of individual reproductions; and also; reproduction may themselves be re-photographed, so that if sent around, anyone who wanted to could make another negative and issue as many copies as he pleased. Until the drawings and reproductions are protected by copyright, and until I have issued the volume I planned, I can not honestly endorse the scheme you suggest. It is entirely up to Howard, of course, whether he wishes to accept or not. I hope you won't feel offended, and I think you will understand the very personal feeling I have toward Howard's work, and my desire to make the volume representative of his striking talent, and of such more limited ability as I may be able to bring to it.

   Right now, I am in the midst of great rushing around, packing, seeing friends, taking care of innumerable details, etc., in preparation for my summer wanderings. Hence, I must shorten this. But I hope to see you this fall when you come North. In the meantime, best wishes. I appreciate the sincere interest you have in Howard's work and trust you will comprehend my motives in upholding my own plans.

                           Sincerely yours,
                           Donald Wandrei

[14]   [RHB to DW] [TLS, MHS]

[R. H. Barlow
Bibliomaniac]

May 26 1934

Dear Mr. Wandrei,

I am of course sorry that you do not favour the proposition I made, but I can see your side of the matter. The adequate reproduction of the pictures is the essential point, so I suppose it doesn't matter extremely much that I have to give up the idea, although I naturally somewhat regret it. However, let me thank you for your kind letter. I've not yet heard from your brother but shall probably shortly.

May I ask, though, while I write, if you have the original Rankin heading for SONNETS OF THE MIDNIGHT HOURS? I ask, naturally, with ulterior motive. Wright says a bunch of these original drawings are going out to the authors soon.

With best wishes, and regrets, I am
Yours most faithfully and sincerely,
R H Barlow

[15]   [DW to RHB] [TLS]

1152 Portland Ave.,
St. Paul, Minn.
June 16, 1934

Dear Mr. Barlow:

Well, the miracle has happened. A copy of the excessively rare BROKEN MIRRORS, of which only eighty-two were printed, can be bought for $5.00. I don't have the volume, except for my personal copy, but if you want it I'll send you the name of the seller. Or you can order it through me. This might be a better idea, since I can check up on the book at first hand and be sure it's a perfect copy. There were five loose woodcut illustrations which are sometimes missing from the very infrequent copies that turn up. Frankly, though, I don't see why you want the volume, since it has nothing weird or scientific in it. My contributions consist of a very short suicide sketch, a satiric short story, and a dozen or so sonnets and lyrics.[1] About the only reason for buying it is the remote possibility that one of the five co-authors might some day achieve fame, in which case I suppose the thing might command a premium as a collector's item. At present, the price that Johnson quotes is exactly what the original price was.

Remember me to HPL if he is still on the scene.

Yours very truly,
Donald Wandrei

Notes

1. See Bibliography. The book did not contain "a dozen or so sonnets" by DW. He may have been thinking of "Dead Fruit of the Fugitive Years: Ten Sonnets" published in the *Minnesota Quarterly*.

[16] [RHB to DW] [TLS, MHS]

> [R. H. Barlow
> Bibliomaniac]

> > June 29 1934
> > Box 88 DeLand
> > Fla.

Dear Mr. Wandrei;

I am very contrite at my delay in replying to your letter. It was kind of you to remember my desire for BROKEN MIRRORS, and, (after frantically raising the money!) I should like to ask you to inspect the copy, and, if it is a perfect copy, to inscribe and send it to me. This way, if it[']s not right, the trouble of transferring & re-transferring the money will be avoided. This will complete my set of Vandreiana, will it not?

Lovecraft was here for six weeks, and I enjoyed his visit. I hope to get to NY this winter—I may call on him—or even you may be inflicted with my presence!

I take the liberty to send your contributions to RECLUSE, which I'd be grateful to you for signing. I simply dismembered my copy & shall later reassemble it, when I have it bound. In the meantime I am trying to make up a dummy copy of the second abortive issue. You were, I understand, to have two things: a tale THE FACE [*sic*] AT THE WINDOW[1] and an article on M. G. Lewis.[2] Are these still in existence? If you would be so kind as to loan the ms. to me I would be very much indebted, and should provide you with extra copies when I made mine. I want to fill in the missing gaps of my issue No. 2, and while Cook has helped to some extent, he has little left of the unfortunate episode. It would be a vast favour, I assure you, and one for which I would be grateful.

And (while I'm on the subject!) do you-all have any mo' manuscripts for you-all's collector? I would like to place a few judicious hints for first draughts ..... I suppose all the manuscripts of ECSTASY and the other volumes have perished?

Trusting that the book will prove satisfactory, and that this letter is not too much of a bother, I am, with best wishes,

> > Sincerely yours,
> > R H Barlow

[P.S.] May I ask just how many Klarkashtonic drawings you have?

Notes

1. Actually "The Woman at the Window," a prose poem.
2. Titled "The Monk, The Monk, and the Monk." Apparently nonextant.

[17]   [RHB to DW] [TLS, MHS]
                    [R. H. Barlow
                    Bibliomaniac]

                                          Box 88 DeLand
                                          Fla
                                          July 19, 1934

Dear Mr. Wandrei;
    I have not heard from you regarding the book, so, just in case you did not receive my letter, I repeat that I will take it at $5.00, and will appreciate it if you will inscribe it and send it C. O. D. or any manner you choose.
    W. Paul Cook says that proofs were furnished you of your Lewis article and copy of proofs of the tale THE FACE AT THE WINDOW. I desire very much to obtain these two things for my dummy second RECLUSE, as I have all but five of the items necessary to complete it. Would you be willing to let me have these two things in return for a *typed copy and carbon* of each item? I would appreciate hearing on the subject, for it is of particular interest to me.
                        Yours most sincerely,
                        R H Barlow

[P.S.]—And I brazenly repeat that any manuscripts you care to donate will be indeed welcome!

[18]   [DW to RHB] [TLS]

                                          1152 Portland Ave.,
                                          St. Paul, Minn.
                                          July 21, 1934

Dear Mr. Barlow:
    Excuse the delay in answering your letter. As usual, I have been swamped with work, and let mail and correspondence accumulate.
    I have the BROKEN MIRROR for you, but haven't had time to get to the post office and mail it to you. However, I expect to finish my current work in a day or two, hence the book ought to reach you shortly after this note.
    If you don't already have it, get on the trail of LAST AND FIRST MEN, by Olaf Stapledon. It's the best cosmic novel yet written.

Sincerely yours,
Donald Wandrei

[19]   [RHB to DW] [TLS, MHS]

Box 88 DeLand Fla
August 10[, 1934]

Dear Mr. Wandrei,

I hate to plague you again, but I am leaving on the first of September for Washington, D. C[.], and consequently, I'd like to have BROKEN MIRRORS before that date. So may I apologetically ask you to . . . duly autographed . . . send it this month? I am not quite certain whether or not you have it, else I'd send the money now. Ship it either C. O. D. or anyway [*sic*] you wish.

W. Paul Cook has been helping me in compiling a dummy copy of the abortive second RECLUSE, and I lack, (among four or five other things), your two contributions: THE FACE AT THE WINDOW and your article on M. G. Lewis. He thinks you have a copy of one, proof of another. If this proof has no particular sentimental value . . (it would to me) would you exchange your copies of the two things for a typed copy and a carbon copy of each? *This is very important to me, for I wish very much to complete my copy.* Any help you could offer would be highly appreciated.

Trusting this letter is not too presumptuous,

I am
Most faithfully yours,
R H Barlow

[20]   [DW to RHB] [TLS]

1152 Portland Ave.,
St. Paul, Minn.
Aug. 14, 1934

Dear Mr. Barlow:

You should have received BROKEN MIRRORS by now. It was sent by insured parcel post. The illustrations (5) are inserted loose, one at the final page of each section.

Cook sent me the Recluse items, but I don't know where they are now. They may be among stuff I stored in N.Y.C., or somewhere around here. I leave this week for Rainy Lake, and doubt whether I'll have a minute to do any searching before the trip.

If the book is not in your hands by the time this letter reaches you, notify me at this address and I'll take the matter up with the post-office when I return from the trip.

Sincerely,
Donald Wandrei.

[21]   [RHB to DW] [TLS, MHS]

August 30[, 1934]

Dear Mr. Wandrei;

The volume arrived at last, and I am well pleased with it. You will find enclosed the money. Thanks for your trouble and humoring of my whims! . . . . This, now, gives me all your work original in books, does it not? The anthology reprints were from WT, I believe. I intend to get them in time . . CREEPS BY NIGHT has THE RED BRAIN, I think, and the Selwyn & Blount volumes have things, too, if I am not mistaken.[1]

I would be most sincerely appreciative if you would find the two RECLUSE items, and would be doubly your debtor if you would allow me to provide you a typed copy & carbon of each in exchange for the original galley & copy. I wish very much to complete my dummy RECLUSE, and your two items are vitally essential. Cook has helped as much as he can; now I must impose on the kindness of others for assistance.

In the mangled *Fantasy* article[2] a series of poems is mentioned, (similar, I suppose, to SONNETS OF THE MIDNIGHT HOUR in length and style?) which remain unpublished. My printing activities are curtailed at present because of my damn eyes, but I hope to get them cured up in Washington this winter, and resume my abortive publishing. If the series is not of Homeric length, I might well consider issuing them for a small circulation, in something like broadside form (But, of course, on good paper and with as good printing as I could muster.) Would you be interested? Of course, this can all be discussed later, but I simply make the suggestion. I hope to be able to get to NY this winter, after the D.C. sojourn, and see you in person while there.

If you are willing to let me have the RECLUSE items, (and I should be indeed grateful were it so) my address will be from Sept 1. *7019 Ga. Ave. N. W. Washington, D. C.*

Thanks again for the book!

Faithfully yours,

R H Barlow

Notes

1. DW had no stories reprinted in the anthologies edited by Christine Campbell Thompson for Selwyn & Blount.

2. The "article," an interview of DW (see Appendix), has numerous typographical errors, but is not "mangled." RHB may be referring to the fact that DW considered himself to be badly misquoted in the rendering of his anecdote about HPL correcting his pronunciation of *Cthulhu*.

[22]   [DW to RHB] [TLS, JHL]

88 Horatio St.,
New York, N.Y.
Jan. 7, 1936

Dear Mr. Barlow:

Because of my recent absence for a month on a trip home for the holidays, the copies of "The Goblin Tower" and "The Dragon-Fly" did not come to my attention in time for me to acknowledge their receipt before now.

I am delighted to have both. HPL, who came to New York for a short visit at the same time that I returned, and I were discussing your work a few nights ago, and reached the conclusion that you will probably found one of America's celebrated private presses if your publications continue to develope [*sic*] along the lines that they have already shown.[1] In one respect, however, I take issue with HPL. I understand that he grouped and arranged the poems of "The Goblin Tower" according to mood. Whatever esthetic unity a volume of separate lyrics may achieve by such grouping is, I feel, completely offset by the typographical distortions that it necessarily entails. For instance, there would be a marked improvement from the standpoint of typography if "Advice", now on page 5, had been placed at the bottom of page 4. Then "Stallions of the Moon" could have been printed entire on page 5. Type and the handling of type-forms are virtually an art in themselves, but neither the material to be printed nor the format to be employed is mutually exclusive. Each must take into consideration, and effect an appropriate compromise with, the other. Considering the obvious care and infinite patience that you have devoted to the volume, I hesitate even to offer this criticism, but I think the point worth mentioning and bearing in mind because it will crop up again every time you publish a volume of poetry. The best method, I suppose, would be to arrange the poems by mood in setting up the type, and then to make such readjustments as are advisable for pagination and typographic harmony.

Are there any remaining copies of the volume available, and if so, at what price?

Your own "A Dream" is the best item in "The Dragon-Fly". You have a very fine sense of style that I hope you will continue in other writings.

Sincerely
Donald Wandrei

Notes

1. RHB abandoned his plans for his own private press, but not entirely. He bought a printing press for printing the journal he published in later years, *Tlalocan: A Journal of Source Materials on the Native Cultures of Mexico.*

[23]   [RHB to DW] [ALS, MHS]

[January 17, 1936]

Dear Wandrei:

Thanks for the kind words regarding my efforts! I agree with your criticism regarding arrangement, but HP is invincible and unconvincible! It would take a braver one than I to defy his plans! But I *shall* remedy certain of the G. T. defects in my next. *Yuggoth* offers no problems, because it will be all sonnets: *Incantations,* as Opus III, will have its problems partly solved by previous work. My press won't be very prolific, but I mean to make it good. There will be a special, fine-paper-and-binding edition (very small—20 or 30) of each product, and a larger edition in wrappers on plainer stock to cover both audiences. I am interested only in making a fine book, but the great public, I fear, must be served!

Would that I might have been in N.Y. during the Yule festivities! This year I hope that I can make it. Bearing the triumphs of my "rural pen" and press, of course, as credentials!

I can supply the G. T. At 1$\underline{^{00}}$ bound. Poor Belknap hasn't even received the *review copies,* yet! I have been very much under the weather since August, hence my numerous failings.

Again, thanks for your honest letter—and criticize any of publications which needs improvement! I'm glad to hear opinions.

Ever yours,

Bob Barlow

[24]   [DW to RHB] [TLS, JHL]

88 Horatio St.,
New York, N.Y.
Jan. 22, 1936

Dear Barlow:

Inclosed is a money-order for $2.25 for two copies of THE GOBLIN TOWER. The extra quarter will be enough, I hope, to cover the mailing costs. Let me know when you issue other publications, especially the Lovecraft and Smith items, as I shall undoubtedly want two or three copies of each.

Much as I admire Lovecraft, and I consider myself a staunch and loyal friend of his, I feel in all sincerity that you should completely disregard anything and everything he may say with regard to typography and book-making. He has repeatedly and consistently said that he cares nothing about the appearance of a book, that he has no interest in fine press-work, that he simply wants the written material whether it be printed on wrapping-paper or tissue. Since that is the case, he will always disregard the requirements of type, format, paper, binding, etc., and advocate arrangement of poems solely by mood or continuity. But fine press-work and typography are an art that must effect a compromise between the material and the printing. You know this yourself, but I mention it again to drive home the fact that you ought to go upon your own judgment and ignore HPL entirely on all questions of fine printing and binding. It is a typographic sin to begin a long poem like the "Ballad of Saint Anthony" in the middle of a page, at the end of a preceding poem. It is another typographic sin to print from the middle of one page to the middle of another a lyric like the "Ballad of Mary Magdalene" which could be printed entire on one page. As long as HPL remains oblivious to fine printing, so long will you need to remain oblivious to HPL with regard to topographic matters.

I hate to seem like a carping critic, but I feel that HPL gave you some extremely bad advice about "THE GOBLIN TOWER", and I like so well the direction in which you are going on your own initiative, and the improvements would have been so simple and easy to make, that I consider the issue worth fighting for. I said before, and I say again, that I criticize because I thoroughly approve of your undertakings, approve so thoroughly that I want them to get better until they reach perfection.

Most sincerely,
Donald Wandrei

[25]   [RHB to DW] [TLS, MHS]

Jan. 30, 1936

Dear Wandrei;

Many thanks for the order: I am sending two copies of the GT by Parcel Post. I hasten to add that they are all different, being bound in every texture and hue of material known to man!

Everything you say is well founded, I realize. Those specific defects are corrected in the Fungi (which is in press) and a few touches of improvement added. I think that you will approve of Opus II! HP did rather influence the GT, I am afraid—he sort of yelled me down. But recently I've asserted my independence (through the U.S. Mails) in such a positive way that I begin to fear I've mortally offended him![1] His reply has not arrived, but I can imagine what it will be like. I think that he is actually *greived* [*sic*] by a handsome book. I can see a little of his point, to the effect that a *gew-gawed* book overshadows the text—but who wants a gew-gawed book? The finest printing that I have seen was simple—It's getting it correct, perfect, reasoned, that makes a fine book. By the way, do you have that fine Cheshire House Georgics?[2] It is a grand book, perhaps a bit large for convenience, but a monument of restrained dignity. I got mine at remainder.

Koenig[3] has just been through this region, but missed me. I'm sorry that he couldn't stop by, for I like him. Price speaks of a possible Florida jaunt, later.

Did you know that Edna St. Vincent Millay has a Baudelaire translation coming out this spring? I'm using nine more of CAS' in his book INCAN-

TATIONS. Wonder whether hers will be the definitive.[4] Because she is a great poet doesn't mean that she is a good translator.

Ever yours,

R H B

[P.S.] The picture *Ah, Wilderness* is not as spirited as the play.[5]

Notes

1. HPL had been traveling and thus could not reply to any letters from RHB. It is not certain how RHB "asserted [his] independence," but he had recently (and secretly) printed *The Cats of Ulthar*, and so did the work without guidance from HPL.

2. *The Georgics of Virgil*, tr. John Dryden (New York: Cheshire House, 1931).

3. H[erman] C[harles] Koenig (1893–1959) of New York was a collector of weird and occult books who graciously lent them to HPL and others. He spearheaded the rediscovery of the work of William Hope Hodgson.

4. RHB refers to *Flowers of Evil* (1936).

5. *Ah, Wilderness!* (MGM, 1935), directed by Clarence Brown; starring Wallace Beery, Lionel Barrymore, and Mickey Rooney. Based on the play by Eugene O'Neill, which premiered on 2 October 1933.

[26]   [DW to RHB] [TLS]

1152 Portland Ave.,
St. Paul, Minn.
Oct. 26, 1936

Dear Mr. Barlow:

In going over my library just now, I discovered to my great dismay that the sheets of "The Shunned House" which I obtained from you a year ago are lacking the signature comprising pp. 48–56 [*sic*].[1] I am at a loss to account for it, since the sheets were kept in the package that they arrived in.

Can you send me the missing signature? Or if not that, a complete set?

I will send you promptly by return mail the price of the postage and mailing charges.

Yours very sincerely,
Donald Wandrei

P.S.—Have you published the Smith poems yet, or work by other members of the gang?

D. W

Notes

1. DW means the eight-page signature containing pp. 49–56.

[27]   [RHB to DW] [TLS, MHS]

Election Eve.
[2 November 1936]¹

Dear Wandrei;

The Shunned House sheets are in a DeLand bank; it will probably be several months before I can get at them. When I do, I shall, of course, be entirely willing to send you a complete set. I am sorry those you have are not all there.

A prolonged and complete family bust-up has interfered with my printing—the half-done Fungi is also in storage, and I have the manuscripts of others, including CAS' Incantations, with me here. They'll just have to keep a little longer.

This summer I visited Howard for a month, moved on to New York, spent a most pleasant evening in alcoholic pursuits with your brother and Belknap; and wound up in my native region of Leavenworth–K.C. Technically, I am now one of Mr. T. Benton's² students at the Art Institute here, but I have yet to set the Thames on fire.

When do you mean to return to New York? Or have you emigrated for keeps? Sometimes I wish I'd stayed there, but Sodom is a dismal place to spend the winter. It's so much nicer to live off my relatives, even if they are Republicans!

The Last Puritan, if you haven't read it, is worth tackling, and in a less serious class, the remarkable melodrama Gone With the Wind.³ Mitchell could make a pile of dirty dishes seem interesting. I'm apathetically winding up the last two spasms of Remembrance of Things Past,⁴ which I have neglected too long. Speaking of Marcel, I discovered, in Ellis' RO[U]SSEAU TO PROUST, that the same man served as model for des Entees [*sic*] (I hope I got that right!) and C[h]arlus.⁵ He must have been a fabulous character.

Sorry I can't help just now about the sheets, but I won't forget you.

Ever yours,
R H Barlow

810 West 57th Terrace, K.C. Mo.

Notes

1. Someone has written the date November 4 on the manuscript.
2. Thomas Hart Benton (1889–1975), the noted American muralist and painter. He taught at the Kansas City Art Institute from 1935 to 1941. His most famous student was Jackson Pollock.
3. By George Santayana and Margaret Mitchell, respectively.
4. In English, these would have been *The Sweet Cheat Gone* (1930) and *Time Regained* (1931).
5. RHB refers to Duc Jean Floressas des Esseintes in J.-K. Huysman's *À Rebours* and Baron de Charlus in Marcel Proust's *Remembrance of Things Past*. Marie Joseph Robert Anatole, Comte de Montesquiou-Fézensac (1855–1921), French aesthete, Symbolist poet, art collector, and dandy, was the basis for both characters.

[28]   [DW to RHB] [TLS]

1152 Portland Ave.,
St. Paul, Minn.
Dec. 24, 1936

Dear Mr. Barlow:

Thanks immensely for the missing signature of Lovecraft's THE SHUNNED HOUSE. I hope that you weren't put to much bother. The season's greetings, and the best of luck when you resume your ventures in publication.

Sincerely,
Donald Wandrei

[29]   [RHB to DW] [TLS, MHS]

[19 April 1937]

Dear Wandrei,

Derleth tells me that you are headed back for St. Paul, so I judge this will catch you there. I hope you saw the raft of stuff I sent—now, I am assembling a larger shipment. But that wasn't the point of this letter. You said, once, that you would show me your excavated Cosmic series, and the two things you were to have in RECLUSE. I would appreciate it if you would lend them to me for a brief while, before you go to New York and haven't them available. Everybody seems to be lending manuscripts to everybody else, so I trust you won't raise violent objections to this request! Needless to say, I shan't make confetti out of the Ms, and will endeavour to return them A-1, as soon as I've seen them.

Your brother was doing the HP jacket when Belknap and I called on him[1]—of which I have supplied certain photographs. Hope it comes along nicely. Give him my best when you see him; and Belknap too.

Yours ever,
Barlow

810 W 57 Ter K C Mo

[P.S.] Isn't this swell ink!

Notes

1. HW was to design the dust jacket for Arkham House's edition of HPL's *The Outsider and Others,* but the work ultimately was done by Virgil Finlay.

[30]   [DW to RHB] [TLS]

1152 Portland Ave.,
St. Paul, Minn.
April 22, 1937

Dear Mr. Barlow:

I'll be glad to lend you the mss. if you can be a little more specific. Of the so-called Cosmic Series, one part was represented by the full-length horror novel, "Dead Titans[,] Waken!" I have no copy of this, my New York agents having requested it and received it last fall. They're sending it around to publishers, though it's of such limited appeal that I see no chances for its appearance.[1] The other part of the Cosmic Series consisted of three linked abstractions, of which "The Red Brain" formed the only one that could be called a story. The other two are very short. I have them, if they are the ones you mean.[2]

As for The Recluse, my memory completely fails me. Was it prose or poetry? I have gone through my files, and located the proof-sheets of an article on "Monk" Lewis, the Gothic novelist of late 18th and early 19th centuries. This evidently had been set up for a second copy of The Recluse. I also located a fantasy, more or less a prose-poem, called "The Woman At The Window", which has a line in Cook's handwriting. I have several copies of this latter. You can keep it if it's what you're after. The Lewis article exists only in the one set of proof-sheets which I'd like back for my own file.

Drop me a line if these are the things you want to see, and I'll send them on.

Do you happen to possess extra copies of, or know of anyone who wants to sell, the following issues of Weird Tales? I've been checking all my files, and discover to my dismay that losses through loans have depleted my once complete set by no less than SIX issues—du lieber himmel!

WEIRD TALES—May, 1923 (Vol. 1, no. 3)
June, 1923 (Vol. 1, no. 4)
Sept., 1923 (Vol. 2, no. 2)
Jan., 1924 (Vol. 3, no. 1)
Sept. 1932 (Vol. 20, no. 3)

The sixth is a recent number that I am ordering through Wright. I will gladly pay a premium for the earlier issues, some of which I understand have become collectors' items.

Derleth and I are up to our necks in the HPL material, and will be for a long time to come. What a task we have set for ourselves!

I'm told you've taken to art—good luck with the brush and the pigments!

Sincerely,
Donald Wandrei

Notes

1. Indeed, it was not published until 1948 (as *The Web of Easter Island*), and then by Arkham House. Copies were still available from the publisher in the 1970s.
2. DW refers to "The Twilight of Time" (i.e., "The Red Brain"), "On the Threshold of Eternity," and "A Legend of Yesterday." RHB published them in *Leaves*.

[31]   [RHB to DW] [TLS, MHS]

[24 April 1937]

Dear Wandrei,

Thanks for your prompt reply. The stories I wanted to see are those related to the RED BRAIN. Howard spoke highly of these connected stories— giving the impression that there were several of them—and particularly of one about the dust of worlds stretching through eternity. I did not know that DEAD TITANS, AWAKE! [*sic*] was part of this Cosmic Series; although from what I have been told of that, it must be pretty swell; since it's not available, my bothersome request won't extend that far! You said once that the Red Brain was cut in publication, but that you had a set of unbutchered proofs. I would like to see this also, if you don't mind.

Your Recluse contributions were the Lewis article and the Woman at the Window, Cook tells me. I would indeed be grateful for a donation of one of the extra copies of the latter—thanks a lot. I have most of the stuff that was to go into the second Recluse, and am anxious to see the remainder represented by your stuff. Munn had a feature article[,] A STRANGE ADVENTURE, which seems to have vanished from human ken. It has always struck me as unfortunate that the venture fell through—a high-grade literary magazine leaning toward the esoteric is something really needed . . . a sentiment you probably share. Considerable talent has wandered into the less imaginative fields, simply because there existed no reliable outlet for serious work in the genre. But to get back to my sheep, if you will be good enough to lend me the complete Red Brain and allied stories, and the two Recluse items, I shall certainly appreciate it, and return the batch before an undue time elapses.

Sorry, I do not know of any WT for sale . . . it is a damn shame that your file got riddled that way. I have had trouble in completing my own set, and can only offer my sympathy! I don't know what you'll have to pay for those early issues, but they tell me 1923–24 issues come unreasonably high. If I hear of any I'll let you know.

What have you been writing recently? Any poetry? You ought to produce another volume with your brother as illustrator. Incidentally, I think that should any customer arise, I'd hock my BROKEN MIRRORS and eat it. Do you know of any applicants? That Providence trip depleted my slim exchequer.[1]

You and AWD are certainly faced with an Augean task—but that isn't exactly the word I meant!—going over the vast accumulations of HPL letters. Are you transcribing *everything*? Or just choice specimens? An old lady poet recently gave me the ten-year series he wrote her,[2] and I shall forward them to Sauk City. They contain some interesting analyses of verse technique. As for my own activities in that line, I have been copying the collection of poems . . . 34 pp . . called THE ANCIENT TRACK, which he compiled and gave to me last spring . . . And a fragment of a draught of Innsmouth, both of which I shall send along in a day or two. I have been expecting comment from AWD on the first samples, but none coming, will do up a larger installment.

Yes, I'm studying here under Thomas Benton; a swell painter and a swell guy. The KC Art. Inst., I am firmly convinced, is one of the topnotchers. It certainly beats hell out of the Corcoran, where I spent a year learning nothing. If I don't pick up something, it'll be native stupidity, and not the fault of the school. But I think I am learning something, as a current student exhibit seems to bear out, since I have four pieces out of about 15.

(This would never be condoned by Mrs. Post, but who cares?)[3]

Belknap was pretty low when I saw him, although we managed to inhale several buckets of beer and wander about the town a bit, calling on your brother as I think I mentioned. He (Belknap) has a peck of troubles, particularly new trouble with his operation, which has broken open and compels him to wear a truss. Poor guy! And Howard's death got him down terribly, as it did all of us. That is something that will strike closer when we can accept it as a reality . . . our present grief is reluctant to face the actual loss as a permanent thing. Howard was sort of like Gibralter [*sic*] or Karl Marx, an accepted fact that nothing would change.

But enough of your good time has been wasted. I'll surely refund whatever the postman soaks you in lending the Ms, and remain something of a debtor.

Yours ever,
Barlow

810 W 57 Ter KC Mo

[P.S.] When do you hit Providence?

Notes

1. RHB had gone to Providence immediately following HPL's death to secure his papers and such volumes of his library as he desired (per HPL's instructions).
2. HPL corresponded with Elizabeth Toldridge (1861–1940) beginning in 1928. Although many HPL letters were sent to Sauk City for transcription after his death, Toldridge's letters from HPL—though well-represented in *Selected Letters*—are not

among the Arkham House transcripts save for a single letter identified only as "to a poet." The letters are now held by JHL.

3. RHB had typed on both sides of the sheet, a supposed breach of etiquette.

[32]   [DW to RHB] [TLS]

1152 Portland Ave.,
St. Paul, Minn.
April 26, 1936 [*sic*]

Dear Mr. Barlow:

Herewith are THE TWILIGHT OF TIME (THE RED BRAIN), ON THE THRESHHOLD [*sic*] OF ETERNITY, A LEGEND OF YESTER-DAY, (which three comprised the entire cosmic group), THE WOMAN AT THE WINDOW, and THE MONK. Half the set of proofs of THE RED BRAIN has vanished with other irreplaceable items from my library. The only complete copy is the one enclosed, with all changes, from which the full story was typed and sent to Wright some ten years ago. The galleys of THE MONK are also unique. You can keep THE WOMAN, of which I have other copies, but I want the other four items back for my personal file. I'd like them returned as soon as possible because I leave for the east early in May, and expect to arrive at Providence between the middle and the end of May. Typing of the HPL material, and furious work in trying to complete and straighten out my entire library, ms. files, and correspondence are all that hold me back. I've lost so damned much of my collection through loans that I'm rapidly getting to the point of simply refusing to make any more. First editions of Crawford's WANDERING GHOSTS, Blackwood's THE LISTENER, Shiel's THE PALE APE, Fort's BOOK OF THE DAMNED, and my entire set of the weird-horror numbers of the old BLACK CAT magazine are only a sample of losses.

I occasionally receive phone-calls about BROKEN MIRRORS, though none since last fall. I'll let you know when the next inquiry or purchaser comes along. The usual price is around $5.00. . . . No, I don't have SIR BERTRAND, but I never made any attempt to get other than the few outstanding Gothic novels. . . . Sam Loveman, 104 Fifth Ave., N.Y., might be interested in THE VAMPIRE, which I presume is the Polidori tale. It normally sells around $2.50, hence it would seem that a dealer would pay less for it, and the extra costs of shipping would hardly make it worth your while.

What was Belknap's operation? Your reference was news to me.

Good luck on the painting. Benton is one of America's best.

Sincerely yours,
Donald Wandrei.

[33]   [RHB to DW] [TLS, MHS]

May Day 1937

Dear Wandrei,

I was very pleased to discover your envelope of stories in the postman's loot; and have just finished with them in order to shoot them back pronto. Thanks tremendously for the loan, and particularly, for the gift of THE WOMAN AT THE WINDOW; a provocative piece. Your essay on Monk Lewis was good, and useful in pointing out that the MONK is the only thing of his worth tackling. I had not realized his really overwhelming plag[i]arisms, although I was familiar with certain admissions along that line. Too damn bad the thing didn't see print. As a matter of fact, I continue to bewail the sinking of THE RECLUSE, which might have become a fairly solid institution. Last summer Howard and I discussed at length the possibilities of a venture to supplement and continue its general lines; which would include specific items designed for the fiasco, and add other things of merit; to be published as an annual in a small edition.[1] This has taken my wayward fancy, and has got to the stage where I am tentatively selecting items, from Catherine Moore and HP and Edith Miniter's unpublished things.[2] Such a magazine would probably survive only a brief while, maybe an issue or two, but it would undeniably be a good thing, since it could thumb its nose at commercial requirements, and circulate about 60,000 words of A-1 material at a throw. Would you be willing for me to include the Cosmic Episodes in this contemplated venture? I think it will not flicker out, for various reasons; and you will not be disgraced by the company, since I'm only after top-notch exotic material. It will be fun to produce one issue, at least, of what a good weird-fantastic magazine could be. In the rather sanguine hope that you will let me use them, I have taken the liberty of transcribing the enclosed episodes, although very naturally I can be squelched!

The TWILIGHT OF TIME begins on page 50—which leads me to conclude that while these are the *cosmic* portions, there must have been terrestrial antecedents . . . an assumption which links up with dim recollections of HP speaking about a "Last Man" story[3] beginning the series. Am I right? And if so, may I suggest the same fate for any such earlier portions? As I have said, there's yards and yards of room in this magnum opus, so that the whole work could be contained in its proper order, and as originally written. I'd like to know your reaction.

Belknap is suffering with further trouble from the appendix-removal of some while back; the muscles have not healed where they were cut, and it seems to be a considerable, though not particularly painful, nuisance—very naturally depressing to him.

Your misfortunes with your library are certainly annoying. I can see why you consider nailing up an OUT FOR LUNCH sign when borrowers arrive: but, damn it, when one has something difficult to obtain, and others want to read it, it's hard to be cold-blooded and turn them down. I had my GOLEM[4] read to death in circulation, and lending hasn't helped some of my Blake colour-plate tomes. Ars longa, libra breva est![5]

Thanks for the suggestion about my Vampyre. I don't esteem the work very highly. Have you ever seen his other weird story, and the book of pomes dated 1816?[6]

Yours ever,
Barlow

Notes

1. HPL had remarked to RHB "if you ever started a southern counterpart of the Recluse Press there's a lot of stuff I'd be glad to have printed . . . . besides a lot by others that I could recommend" (*OFF* 63). *Eyes of the God* (p. 586) lists some twenty "still-born projects" that RHB had planned but never completed.
2. Edith Miniter (1867–1934) was an amateur colleague of HPL. The first issue of *Leaves* included her marginally weird story "Dead Houses."
3. RHB's "'Till A' the Seas'" was itself a "last man" story.
4. By Gustav Meyrink.
5. "Art is long, a book is short" (i.e., the lifetime of a book is short). A parody of the Latin tag *Ars longa, vita brevis* ("Art is long, life is short"). For *libra* RHB should have written *liber.*
6. Polidori did not write any other "weird story." He did write a short novel, *Ernestus Berchtold; or, The Modern Oedipus* (1819). His poetry volume is *Xinemenes, the Wreath, and Other Poems* (1819).

[34]   [RHB to DW] [TLS, MHS]

[c. 21 July 1937]

Dear Wandrei,

I had an idea that you were in the east by this time, or would have written you before. Being on the verge of a southern trip myself I must make this short and snappy.

If you received the stories back o.k. . . . and I hope that you did . . . you may or may not have investigated the envelope and discovered a letter from me, requesting your permission to use the three connected tales in a successor to the RECLUSE which I am just completing. I would be very grateful indeed for such permission (!), and it would give you a chance to circulate the unabridged text, instead of the Wright-mangled version. Can you be wheedled into this? The opus, entitled LEAVES, has contributions by HPL CAS AWD FBL REH Merritt Edkins Kat Moore and the whole shebang, and to this galaxy I am more than anxious to affix your own name.

Perhaps Wright would have the final say insofar as copyright goes . . . as a tentative move, awaiting your own permission, (which I hope will be granted) I am also writing him.

The anthology or annual magazine or whateveritis, consists of 100 copies, and is expected to be a financial failure. I have taken the liberty of making transcriptions of the items mentioned.

Your[s] ever,
Barlow

104 3 Ave Leavenworth Ks

[35]   [DW to RHB] [TLS]

1152 Portland Ave.,
St. Paul, Minn.
July 22, 1937

Dear Mr. Barlow:

Yes, you have my permission to use the three connected tales concerning the Red Brain. It will be a pleasure to see the key story printed in its original form. Your venture sounds ambitious, and though it may be a financial failure, it will certainly be a prodigal one.

Best wishes, and let me know when LEAVES is issued.

Derleth has probably kept you informed on progress of the HPL volumes. I postponed my eastern trip until fall, and am immersed with a play which I hope will eventually supply funds to complete the project in full detail.

Sincerely,
Donald Wandrei

[36]   [RHB to DW] [ALS, MHS]

Aug. 16, 1937

Dear Wandrei,

I am having two copies of *Leaves* mailed to you from Leavenworth. It was gratifying to be able to include the early versions of your three tales, & I hope that you will find them accurate. A discovery concerning postage rates forced me to omit Kat Moore's Werewoman, whose pages—already completed—are set aside to begin Issue II, in January. Perhaps you will contribute to this also? I aim at putting out a good many issues (which is possible solely through this unambitious format, the work being done by myself) of a Reclusish Repository, wherein all sorts of writings from ms. & rare printed sources can be assembled. Although I do not admire the typographic effect much,[1] the text is, after all, the vital thing, & if Leaves wins any support (I doubt that it will!) printing may be possible later. *Story* began in just such a way, & the only thing to do is to give it a trial. I can offer this—a magazine which is almost snobbishly indifferent to popular demand—& *Leaves* may foster some worth-while material before it expires. I hope to use the original Moon-Pool & perhaps The Metal Emperor in time.

If you are not wholly disgusted by this timid initial number, I would like to use The Woman at the Window & any or all short prose decorations you have in your files. I assume that you must have done several in this vein, & recall at least two others which I hope are eligible—"The Messengers" & "The Pursuers". How about it? Wouldn't it be agreeable to you to make a clean sweep of all your short experiments in prose poetry? I have a strange penchant for *assembling things,* so I must be an editor at heart!—Wasn't there a series of poems called *Post-Historian Legends,* too?

Clark Ashton promises an art-for-art's[-]sake tale to be used in #2— probably called *Shapes of Adamant,* & I have an Orton poem (intended for the second Recluse) as well as the rare & provocative Sir Bertrand, which I shall reprint. There will be Whitehead material also. Anything you can send, or any serious fantasy-writer whose work you know of, & could recommend, would be avidly welcomed.[2]

Have been spending the past couple of weeks in a nudist camp, but it is monotonous, & I shall pull on to Miami, staying there until the Art Inst. reopens.

How goes the play? Is it of the battle of the sexes or the class-conscious variety? One wonders that so few effective weird plays have ever been turned out—you ought to go in for that.

I've got a hell of a lot of deciphering & typing to do on HPL ms, as well as on the letters to me, but the resultant books will place him high, I think. His letters rival Walpole & Sevigne & Chesterfield[3] & the whole shootin'-match.

Thanks again for the stories, & let me know your reactions to Leaves I.

Ever yours,

Barlow

[P.S.] I actually had a letter from Belknap before I pulled out on my travels!

Address
104 3 Ave,
Leavenworth Ks

Notes

1. The two issues of *Leaves* were typed on a typewriter and mimeographed.

2. DW's "The Woman at the Window" and Vrest Orton's poem "Winter Night" did appear in *Leaves* No. 2, but there was nothing by CAS. Whitehead's "The Tree-Man" and RHB's "A Checklist of the Published Weird Stories of Henry S. Whitehead" also appeared in the issue.

3. Horatio Walpole, 4th Earl of Orford (1717–1797); Marie de Rabutin-Chantal, Marquise de Sévigné (1626–1696); and Philip Dormer Stanhope, 4th Earl of Chesterfield (1694–1773), all noted letter writers.

[37]   [DW to RHB] [TLS]

303 West 4th St.,
New York, N.Y.
June 23, 1938

Dear Barlow:

Your letter arrived just one day too late. I was in St. Paul for most of May and part of June, and started back to New York on June 18, with a stop-over at Sauk City where your letter was waiting for me. If it had been sent direct to me in St. Paul it would have caught me in time. Well, there's no use wasting time on regrets. My CAS material is in storage in St. Paul, and can't be got at until my next visit home, which probably won't be until next spring.

Some of the water colors and colored drawings would probably photograph fairly well, but one of his best pieces I'm afraid couldn't be used in any way. It's a strange and morbidly haunting painting, in metallic inks, on black silk. The metals have begun to oxidize, and I doubt whether the fabric could survive packing and shipping. In fact, I was never able to hang the painting at all, because the metal flakes simply scaled off. There would be no trouble with the other items, however, since they are on handmade or sturdy papers and could be easily flat-backed. I suppose Beck's project[1] will be done long before next Spring but perhaps I'll have the pieces photographed anyway. Who, by the way, is Beck and where? He's a new one to me.

As for the WEIRD TALES, I am still lacking that issue and want it. Do you care to sell it? or have you some other exchange or swap in mind?

By the way, for future reference, I make a visit to St. Paul every year in early May and stay until the middle of June. The bulk of my books, files, and weird material is there. In case anything else comes up, my St. Paul address is always the best one.

Yours sincerely,
Donald Wandrei

[P.S.] What happened to the printing projects you started in Florida? Weren't you doing Lovecraft's FUNGI? Was it ever finished?[2]

Notes

1. RHB shunted CAS's *Incantations* to Beck's Futile Press when he found he could not print it himself.
2. RHB, who was unable to complete printing of his edition of *Fungi from Yuggoth,* had asked the Futile Press to finish the work, but the book remained unfinished.

[38]   [RHB to DW] [ALS, MHS]

June 25, '38

Dear Wandrei—

It is too damn bad I missed you by such a narrow margin, since (despite the slow functioning of amateur presses) Beck will certainly have the book ready before spring. However, there may be some later collection in which your drawings could be reproduced . . . . in which event I observe your migratory time-table. Perhaps the metallic painting could be photographed then in St. Paul if shipping seemed dangerous. Can you give me an idea of the number of formal & finished pieces you have?

Beck is a young California fellow who has printed a revised small selection from *The Star-Treader*, a critical booklet, &c & whose plans are extensive.[1] He has good taste & industry, & may produce some nice little books of a fanciful trend.

I'll send you the WT (Jan. '24) anyway, if you tell me where you want it. St. Paul or NYC? No, there isn't any other swap I can think of, unless you happen to have got DEAD TITANS WAKE back from the rounds, & would let me read it. HP spoke pretty well of this, citing the last half in particular.

My publishing ventures went smash because the household collapsed—all presses & type being inaccessible now. But the omnipresent Beck will finish the partly-done *Fungi* sheets when Wright has used all he intends to in WT.[2]

Sorry I failed to make contact, but let me know where to ship the W.T.

Ever yours,

R H Barlow

(~~4344~~ 4334! Locust KC Mo)

[P.S.] Is your brother in NY? What happened to the jacket for the HP collection? FB intimated he'd given it up—I hope not.

Notes

1. The CAS book was *Nero and Other Poems* (1937) and Beck's book was *Hammer and Tongs* (1937). Beck later published RHB's edition of HPL's commonplace book.
2. Wright took seven sonnets from *Fungi from Yuggoth* (years before he took ten).

[39]   [RHB to DW] [TLS, MHS]

Dear Wandrei,

You asked me a year ago to notify you if duplicate copies of the early Weird Tales came my direction. Well, that is what I am doing . . . having recently acquired an extra of JANUARY 1924, Vol. Three, No. 1, in good shape.

I'll present you with this, in exchange for the favour I'm about to ask. Beck, in California, is getting out a C.A.S. book, mostly Sandalwood reprints, and wants it illustrated with the poet's own graphic work. At first I was supposed to make lithographs from CAS originals, but soon discovered that the spirit of the original went by the board as soon as any tinkering was done. So now it will be photographs, I judge, and you have a good collection of his paintings. Would you lend me these if I put up a substantial enough bond, so that I could have them photographed and printed by a friend here? The book ought to represent a variety of his product, not only what is at hand in his and my possession.

Let me know, will you? I am not sending the WT because I'm doubtful of your address. Derleth said he was seeing you recently, hence this goes in his care.

Ever yours,

R H B

Barlow.

4338 Locust KC Mo
June ? 38[1] [*sic*]

Notes

1. Someone has written the date "[July 16, 1938]" on the ms., but that is incorrect.

[40]   [DW to RHB] [TLS]

303 West 4th St.,

New York, N.Y.

June 27, 1938

Dear Barlow:

Thanks greatly for the WT in advance—that Jan., 1924 issue will fill in a long-present gap in my file of the magazine. I'd rather have it sent here, where I expect to accumulate several items for taking home with me next year. I'll be glad to lend you DEAD TITANS WAKEN when I can get at it—it also is under lock and key in St. Paul. It is too damned bad your letter couldn't have reached me out there. I was home for about six weeks, and thoroughly went through my files and library, packing away such items as might fall prey to moths and mice and the ravages of semi-annual house-cleaning.

My Smith material is not nearly as extensive as the collection of Loveman, which you saw when you were in New York. The painting on black silk was a fine piece, though by nature perishable. I have also the original sculpture DAGON, which I consider his best sculpture up [to] the time I bought it a couple of years ago. Then there are four painted plaster casts of other sculptures, and three brilliantly colored tinted drawings about eight by ten in size and approximately two dozen of the grotesque heads in pencil and watercolor.

Tough luck about the press. I hope you can re-establish it in time. There seems to have been a hoodoo attending every venture to publish anything by Lovecraft in book form during his lifetime.

My brother is now at 319 West 14th St., here.

Nothing more can be done about a jacket for THE OUTSIDER until the typescript is completed, which will be done this summer, and the book accepted for publication, which time is still in the lap of the gods.

Do you know of the work of Vernon Hill? He made a dozen and a half or two dozen full page illustrations for two quartos, BALLADS WEIRD AND WONDERFUL, and THE NEW INFERNO, published in England in 1910 and 1913 or 1914.[1] Very fine work somewhat in the Blake tradition. Also, an artist named Don Cordry did a half-dozen full pages in color and a good many head and tail-pieces for the West High Senior Annual of Minneapolis for 1924, perfectly amazing decadently weird work for a high-school kid. Entered in a national competition, the annual was at once tossed out on the ground that a professional artist had been hired, because no high school student could possibly have done such brilliant and imaginative work.[2] It's in the vein of Alastair, Kay Nielsen, ad Harry Clarke. The volume will probably prove hard to get, but shouldn't cost more than $.50 or a $1.00 if it is available. If interested you might write to the Century Book Store, Hennepin near 8th, or Oudal's Book Store, Marquette near 2nd., Minneapolis.

As Ever,
Donald Wandrei

Notes

1. Vernon Hill (1887–1972), British book illustrator and sculptor. Of the two books cited, the first is by Richard Pearse Chope, the other by Stephen Phillips.
2. Donald Cordry (1907–1978), artist and ethnographer. His collection of Mexican masks is in the Nettie Lee Benson Latin American Collection at the University of Texas.

[41]   [RHB to DW] [ALS, MHS]

[5 July 1938]

Dear Wandrei,

Your WT is in the mail, & I hope it will arrive in good shape. I'll take a rain check on DEAD TITANS, though God knows where I'll be next spring! Right now I am preparing to leave for the City of Mexico, where I hope to spend some months.

No, I don't know Vernon Hills' [*sic*] work, but next time I have a chance at the Congressional Library, or the similar edifice in your town, shall try to find samples. This will be sometime in the future, but I shall certainly put my word in sooner at one of the bookstores you mention, for that High School Annual. What became of the boy afterward? His eviction from the contest reminds me of the amateur poet (in the U.A.P.A?) whose verse entry for a laureateship was judged best, but who wasn't given the prize because of his less poetic cognomen of Tubbs! A policy as outrageous as those of Neville Chamberlain!!!

Hope the WT proves satisfactory—& in case we lose touch, I'll keep your date of westerly travel in mind for next spring.

Ever yours,

Barlow

[42] [DW to RHB] [ALS]

303 West 4th St.,

New York, N.Y.

July 8, 1938

Dear Barlow:

This is just a short note to thank you again with the greatest pleasure for the WT, which came today together with your note. I will repay you in the future—I don't know exactly how or when, but perhaps I can perform some service when I have access to my files in St. Paul next spring.

Don Cordry was the artist who illustrated the high school annual. He then became interested in grotesque wood carvings of the African primitive kind, and for some years went in for puppet & marionette shows. I've heard that he married & settled here, but I haven't seen him for eight or ten years, and don't know of anything more that he did in the same weirdly fantastic vein as his illustrations in the annual.

City of Mexico? You might run into some of my friends—Glen and Francis Mitchell, of the Minneapolis Art School, who are there with an art group. I believe they've settled in Taxco; south of but not far from Mexico City for the summer.

Let me know what your new, permanent address is—and best wishes for a colorful, adventurous trip.

As ever,

Donald

[43] [James F. Morton, E. Hoffmann Price, and RHB to DW] [ANS, MHS][1]

[Postmarked San Francisco, Cal.,

3 July 1939]

Stopping a couple of days with Price, and enjoying every minute. Yudotta come out here and see some of the big sights.

James F. Morton.

Maintaining an ancient tradition—the compound postal card—In the old manner, but unhappily an old signature is lacking. E H P

R H Barlow

Notes

1. PA8:—Home of Former President Hoover, Stanford Campus, Palo Alto, California.

BROKEN MIRRORS

AVON PRESS
1938

Howard Wandrei (Photo courtesy Dwayne Olson)

Letters: R. H. Barlow and Howard Wandrei

[1]   [HW to RHB] [TLS]

320 West 11th Street, NYC, May 23, 1934

Dear Mr. Barlow

I don't know when I have been so overwhelmed by any letter as by yours. There must be something about the climate in DeLand, all the benefits of which seem to have descended on you and Mr. Lovecraft. I can return HPL's enthusiasm, as he is undoubtedly the master of his craft in America. However, I am sure I can tell you nothing about that which you do not already know since you have the man himself in your house. As for surpassing Beardsley, I cannot help feeling that good people have done me a great kindness, without any false modesty. You and Lovecraft together are enough to turn any man's head, but I can't forget certain significant markings in my own work which I do not detect in an equal degree in the great [*sic*] you mention. Some things of mine I feel might stand with the best, but hardly all of them; I am interested to see that you have chosen what the interested few have called my best drawings.

You have a rather formidable plan; I feel that a boon has been conferred on me by the interest of someone of your apparent energy. The plan has everything in its favor, and is practically the one method outside of outright recognition for an artist to become known. I am not questioning your sincerity in the slightest and for my part am not so much interested in immediate profit as in having the members of an intelligent, understanding group find copies of these drawings available, no matter how small the group may be.

As I have explained to HP in the letter which this accompanies, I am ready to send down such drawings as you may desire when I am able to do so. I have nothing here now but a few juvenilia that would not do anyone a particle of good. A current exhibit has taken the best of the collection, some of the framed pieces have been loaned in the process of my moving from my old address. At the moment I can lay my hands on only one of the drawings you requested, and feel that I had better wait, don't you think?—until I am in a better position to co-operate with you. Your 11 × 14 size would be quite ample. I feel, though, that even at the price of two dollars each not many people would feel able to afford a full folio of reproductions. It is true, too, that I was compelled to leave my best drawings at home in St. Paul when I moved to New York. I refer specifically to THE WHISPERING KNOLL, which has been exhibited a score of times, and NIGHT, DEATH, AND THE DEVIL, which has been exhibited just once, and which I have never ceased to regret letting out of my hands. There are also several extremely large drawings which I would hardly dare ship because of their size alone. NIGHT, DEATH, AND THE DEVIL is my finest drawing, and you have suggested a good excuse for my attempting to get it back into my hands, if only temporarily. If you are interested in photographing this drawing, which none of you have ever seen and can only take my word on, please let me know, and I shall try to get in touch with the purchaser at once. I may not succeed, since the buyer, a Minnesota schoolteacher, has ignored my attempts at communicating with her before.

My felicitations to you. An appreciation like yours makes the day yet a little longer.

Most cordially yours,
H E Wandrei

P.S. Apologies for delay. Your letters underwent a long forwarding.

[2]   [RHB to HW] [TLS]

[R. H. Barlow
Bibliomaniac]

#88 DeLand Fla
May 26 1934

My dear Mr. Wandrei;

It pleases me exceedingly that you will permit your excellent drawings to be reproduced for the benefit of the weird group. After all, I think professional photography will be more adequate than any amateur work, no matter how enthusiastic & ambitious. The size I decided would be best, after some consideration. The important thing—aside from permitting circulation of the pictures—is to have them securely done up in pantographic gelatin, so that no matter what might happen to the originals, good copies will exist. I shall of course have them copyrighted in your name. So I urge you, by all means, to send for NIGHT, DEATH AND THE DEVIL for immediate use when you can get hold of it, and any others you can obtain. As for the admirable WHISPERING KNOLL, did you not think (inasmuch as a fairly distinct reproduction is in *Dark Odyssey*) it would [be]better to use some of the unissued work first? And then, when your finest hal[f]-dozen are done, others (accessible elsewhere) can be included in the series.

When do you suppose you'll be able to lay hands on some for reproduction? I couldn't overstate my admiration for your excellent work . . . it makes me envious of your ability to use eyesight to that extent. I'm virtually purblind, and comically, have artistic ambitions forbidden by the doctor! Heigh-ho!

I'll surrender this letter to HPL for a time, and then resume. (didn't take advantage of his generosity, but am sticking to an epistle of my own!—HP)

I see I got fooled! but—

I'll resume with an enquiry. If I send my DARK ODYSSEY to you would you object animatedly to signing it for me? I would really appreciate this.

I must cease so that this letter can be mailed. I am late now, I fear.

I trust I shall hear from you more on this subject of mutual interest, and meantime remain

Most sincerely and faithfully yours
R H Barlow

[3]   [HW to RHB] [TLS]

320 West 11th Street, NYC, June 15, 1934

My dear Mr. Barlow:

I am apologizing on all hands for the break in my correspondence, so to you. There is little to say of importance, however, even after all this time. The Macy show is still on, and I have not heard from Minnesota. I am sending another short note today. The first note was not returned, so I assume it was received. The woman is a procrastinator, or worse, of the worst kind.

My father, to whom I commented on your scheme, concurs with you, or shall I say with us. There can be no harm done, perhaps some good. A copyright, his comment, is advisable, as you say.

Will be glad to sign DARK ODYSSEY for you; send it up whenever you find it convenient. I expect to be at this address for some time. As to an old point, which I neglected to address last time, the artist you asked about, the one I spoke of to HPL, is John Austen as he is represented in his illustrations for Shakespear's Hamlet. Only therein. Finest wo[r]k of its kind I have ever seen.[1]

I honestly do not know when I will have my hands on any of the pictures again, but hope to soon now. I have uncovered one here, an illustration called FOOL! FOOL!, which you may have seen. It is a figure, with cape, suspended in air, background an elaborate circle, the torso of a distorted shape in lower right foreground. I am afraid the drawings cannot be described very well. The others you asked about are on display.

Best regards,

Howard Wandrei

Notes

1. British artist John Archibald Austen (1886–1948) illustrated many more volumes than just Shakespeare's *Hamlet, Prince of Denmark* (New York: E. P. Dutton, 1922).

[4]   [RHB to HW] [TLS]

[R. H. Barlow
Bibliomaniac]

June 29, 1934
Box 88 DeLand
Fla.

Dear Mr. Wandrei:

I repent me, as Twain said, in sackcloth and ashes. I am a very bad correspondent, though I like to *receive* mail!

I have sent the DARK ODYSSEY, and will be truly grateful if you will sign it for me. Right now I'm horribly broke, trying to get Brother Donald's BROKEN MIRRORS! If you will trust my kleptomania, and send FOOL! FOOL! I shall do my damn[e]dest to have it photographed. I shall put the case entirely frankly.

The original glass plate will cost one dollar fifty cents. It will be 8 × 10. From it each enlargement to 9 × 12 will cost another 1.50. If they are sold at two dollars each the extra fifty cents will cover the costs of mailing (they should be practically sent in a crate, to prevent damaging!) and eventually cover the cost of the original plate & copyright copies. You see this way is by no means profit-making, but it will get the drawings preserved so that nothing can happen to them even if the originals are injured later. I'm a frightful fanatic on that preparedness theme!

How beautifully you can draw! I'm profoundly jealous—or, rather, envious of your eyesight. You see, I have always had artistic ambitions, but I may never be able to do anything because of sight. It's a hell of a life! You can perhaps imagine how irksome it would be if you were deprived of use of your eyes! But no. That is not a fair comparison—you have talent, and I have not. Once in a while—like yesterday—I toy with the nearest materials, to see if I still know which end to hold a pen or pencil, if I ever had the opportunity. The result of my recent disobedience I enclose. It is not a drawing in any finished sense, but for some obscure reason I'm prompted to enclose it. Is it too much to ask for your frank, brutal (it must be brutal!) opinion? You must remember I am terribly out of practice, and never was much.

I am interested only in the fanciful—as far as creative line goes, though I admire other types of art to a great degree. And in this line you are incomparable. You will get some here, and it won't take long.

FOOL! FOOL! is not the one with the spider-thing and the elaborate circles? From your brief description I think not, I trust you will send this in time, or anything you prefer.

I shall use the Chinese water-torture on that woman if she doesn't send your drawing. If you get absolutely no results, would you let me have her address?

After suitable photographing (when I recuperate financially) I should like ineffably to possess one of your weird drawings. Can you give me an idea of what you get? I'm afraid I'm too po' to pay anything like what they deserve in merit! But I mus[t]n't scare you off.

Well, I have effused enough. Pour a bottle on [*sic*] ink on the picture of mine, paper the cracks with my letter, and send a reproving postcard—that's the only way to get rid of my parasitic attention. . . . .

Most sincerely and cordially yours,

[his sign] R H Barlow

[P.S.] HPL is NY bound. Left St Aug today, lord knows where he'll stop long enough to catch between there and NYC!

[P.P.S.] Here is your drawing you asked me to return for him. Lucky I didn't steal it!

[5]   [RHB to HW] [TLS]

[R. H. Barlow
Bibliomaniac]

Last day of June [1934]

Dear Mr. W:

As postscript, I thank you for the signing of D.O[.], and send as donation the Official Portrait of Lovecraft's Cthulhu—a mud-pie I made during his visit.[1]

[RHB's stylized signature]

And in mad hurry hasten to correct a gross error I made in my letter. The enlargement of your drawings will be eleven by fourteen inches, *not* 9 × 12.!

Notes

1. RHB's "mud-pie" appears to be a clay bas-relief (see RHB to CAS 32). Cf. HPL's celebrated drawing of Cthulhu, dated 11 May 1934, is inscribed "To R. H. Barlow, Eſq., whoſe Sculpture hath given Immortality to this trivial Deſign of his oblig'd obdt Servt. H. P. Lovecraft." Presumably the statuette given HW was a copy of one made for HPL.

[6]   [HW to RHB] [TLS]

320 West 11th Street, NYC, July 3, 1934

Dear Mr. Barlow,

Many thanks for Cthulhu. It goes in collection. By this you see I am in receipt of both your notes, for which thanks. The much-attenuated exhibit, containing the picture you have asked for is at this date unhung, reversing English; I may go uptown any time I please now and collect. As I remember it, that picture is entitled simply BEETLE. When I have them here I shall proceed to unframe them and send you one or two down, which is the way I believe you wanted it done. Perhaps you are a little sanguine even in the expectation of making expenses, but time will bear that out in one way or another. Pictures should be copyrighted, and I should like a copy of each as it is taken. This may prove to be more expensive than you think. . . .

No word from the Minnesota woman. I shall write her again today. If there is no reply this time, I shall be pleased to let you have what I think is her address. If it is not, someone holds mail which is not his, or hers.

Don't waste time envying eyesight. What's left of mine isn't much good for drawing. I have done very little but an occasional illustration such as the one you have just returned. No longer write in longhand, even first drafts of manuscripts.

Yes I expected to see HPL on his way through NY; sorry he is taking another way around, but I suppose he will be in NY again before very long, so long as he has the free foot. I wrote to him at your address, but I suppose he will not receive the letter till he is back in his own bailiwick.

You spoke of wanting one of my drawings. A number of them are not for sale; my attitude is one of thorough selfishness, hailing from my own certain knowledge that I will never do this work with such gusto again. All the drawings, save for an illustration or two in DO, were done in a space of a year and a half or two years, '28, '29, and a month or two in '30. I must say they were done for my own amusement when I had time on my hands. There being no commercial outlet, most of my time is spent in other channels; opportunities for playing with pen and ink are very few. The group of fantastic drawings, of which you have seen a few, remain a unity with the exception of a half dozen which have gone to friends and an importunate buyer or two, other floating specimens having been recollected. I don't think I care to break the group further, though I am quite willing to make drawings on commission. The buyer then selects practically what price he chooses. My drawings have been showed to a few experts; I gave one of them to S. Chatwood Burton[1] for estimating the work as a whole, including the batiks. Prices apparently range between ten or twelve dollars to top, whatever that is. A real estate broker in the Twin Cities offered twelve hundred for a large color drawing on a full sheet, but of course these things do not interest you. I received only twenty-five dollars from the schoolteacher.

I am in your debt for rearousing my interest in what is probably my best talent. In the next few days I plan to get off a decoration or two to send out, and that's something after all this time.

Cordially,   H E Wandrei

P.S. Re pencil sketch,—don't you feel that animals in broadsides are never satisfactory, even as pure decoration? It is impossible to say much, of course, of a drawing in first stages. Foliage becomes birds, and a shadow turns out to be a threatening face, if that is the drawing's mood.

Notes

1. Samuel Chatwood Burton (1881–1955), American artist and etcher.

[7]   [RHB to HW] [TLS]

[R. H. Barlow
Bibliomaniac]

July 8[, 1934]

Dear Mr. Wandrei;

A hasty note. If, in sending the drawings, you have no vast preference, please send the two of crowded figures; (one with things emerging from floor before vast window and other outdoors with things pouring and limping and riding strange mounts from forest as I recall it.) I esteem these two above all I've seen.

Faithfully,

RHB

They are great-great-great!

[8]   [HW to RHB] [ALS]

7/19/34
Dear R H B—
They are already suffering minor damage, as you see.
Hope these are the ones you want.
Sorry for delay

Wandrei

[9]   [RHB to HW] [TNS][1]

[Postmarked De Land, Fla.,
27 July 1934]

Drawings arrived in good condition, will write fully in a few days.

Faithfully

RB [stylized]

Notes

1. *Front:* 207 Moonlight on a Southern River.

[10]   [HW to RHB] [TLS]

320 West 11th Street, N.Y. 8/20/34

Dear Barlow,

I have your card and note. Glad that things are progressing.

You may be interested in knowing that all the drawings I have done in NY were sent home, to my home in St. Paul, some time ago, and that no word has been received of them. They seem to have been lost in the mail. This is months of work destroyed, and is very disturbing news, to say the least. I can't say that I have noticed any peculiar safety or efficiency in the mailing of government mail.

You spoke of returning the drawings you have within a week. They have not as yet arrived, and if you have not yet sent them off, I wish you would exercise as much care as possible in wrapping them. It would be better to mail them flat, cardboard, and insure. Unluckily, the work I sent home was not insured, so is a total loss. I am expecting to see prints of the three drawings, which with cardboard should make a package stiff enough to defy the vandalism of the most asinine postman.

I hope to hear from you soon, and see the first results of the project. Yours with best regards,

H E Wandrei

[11]   [RHB to HW] [TNS][1]

8/24/34 Daytona Beach, Fla.

Dear H.E.—

My orgy here is prolonged till Sunday, when I'll return home, settle the drawing matter (and return them wrapped in chain-mail for protection!) and other things, for Sept 2 finds me in Washington, my favorite city, for ocular reasons. Later I hope to get up to N.Y. / Have you any customers for the photo's? [*sic*] 11 × 14 seems to win disfavor, so I shall have to put out 8 × 10 prints too. I think, former 2.00 later 1.25. // Am profoundly sorry the NY drawings were lost on St. Paul route . . . it is sickening.[2] Hope they turn up & will offer prayers to Tulu and Tsathoggua for their safety. How many were there? Include any of your really best ones? Was O'MECCA illus. among them?[3] Mainly weird, I suppose? My sincerest sympathy.

¶ E'ch-Pi-El mentions advertising border used by Dutton's some year[s] ago. Where was it reproduced?

Laconically, inquisitively, and truly yrs,

ar-éch-bei [and sign]

Notes

1. *Front*: No picture.
2. RHB wrote to HPL about the matter. An envelope addressed to him (postmarked Providence 30 August 1934), forwarded by Annie Gamwell to Nantucket, where HPL was at the time, bears a note on the outside in HPL's hand: "Wandrei difficulties" along with other notes. HPL's letter to RHB of 1 September addresses the matter: "Sorry H. E. is such a sharp business-man about his pictures—I hardly expected he'd turn out to be that type! When I write him I'll see if I can indicate the need for a little leniency on his part."
3. Perhaps an unpublished drawing by HW. Jack Binder had illustrated the appearance of HW's story "The Hand of the O'Mecca" in *WT* (April 1935).

[12]   [HW to RHB] [TLS]

320 West 11th Street, N.Y. Sept. 6, 1934

Dear Mr. Barlow:

I have been more or less expecting the return of the three drawings sent you, particularly since the above is not to be my address very much longer. I am going west. Busy with clearing up business here, I have not been able to write or answer your card.

I find your letter of a month ago saying drawings would be on way here within a week. I suppose all photographing has been done by now and copyrights taken. Received the first. I wish you would take care of sending the drawings at once, as I do not propose to entrust the post office department with forwarding from this address no matter how well a parcel may be secured or insured. I have lost too many items of mail in moving.

Best regards. I hope you settle with my brother on the Broken Mirrors, and that you will send along copies of the photographs. I want very much to see what the work is like.

Yours sincerely,
H E Wandrei

[13] [RHB to HW] [TLS]

[R. H. Barlow
Bibliomaniac]

7019 Ga. Ave, N.W.
Washington, D. C.
[c. September 1934]

Dear Mr. Wandrei:

How I loathe letter-writing! And, correspondingly, how I like receiving them! This time, however, I think I have a legitimate excuse, for I have been in the process of transferring my abode to Washington, and I am exceedingly glad to get back. My purpose is to have my rotten eyes treated, and to vainly hope to get them in shape to permit attending an art school. (By the way, where did *you* go?) I suppose it will never happen though, unless they show a decided & unfor[e]seen improvement.

I left SIDI's No. 29 and THE WOMAN AT THE WINDOW with my mother, accompanied by explicit directions for wrapping, insuring, etc. Please let me know if they arrive o. k. The WITCHE'S [*sic*] SABBATH, on the dim hope I might be able to find some sort of colour photography that wasn't too high in cost, I took the liberty of bringing along. I'll scout around, and if I have any luck, will announce the fact, and in any event realize I must reluctantly relinquish this magnificent drawing to the rightful owner in the near future. Since I cannot yeild [*sic*] to kleptomania, and keep it, I want particularly to have a colour reproduction. Black and white does it so little justice. Some time I'd like you to make two or three little drawings on order for me, if as you say, estimates to value are $10 and up. In my state the lowest would be about my highest! To continue with the topic of your drawing, w[hat] about NIGHT, DEATH AND THE DEVIL? Is the owner going to loan it? Who else, aside from yourself, has important specimens of your work? I think you said you gave one to S. Chatwood Burnam [*sic*], and one or two were sold in the past.

I shall send, with the original of WITCHE'S SABBATH, a life-size print of The Woman At the Window. It printed a little dark, but I am told next trial will be better. Making such tremendous photo's is, I imagine, a job. Which brings me to another topic. I really hate to have to mention the subject, but I am financially incapable of supplying you with life-size prints of all hypothetical future photo's. You see, until a few sales are made, I have the expense of having the negatives made, the copyright fee, and various incidentals, which makes it so confoundedly expensive I don't know how I am going to keep it up. And at the same time I admire them so highly, I wish very much to get reproductions afloat. Would it be too much to ask that you wait until sales justify the price of prints for you? I don't see how I can keep it up, and I don't see how I could do otherwise!

There is an exhibit at the Congressional that you'd like very much . . . MASTERPIECES OF ORIENTAL BOOKMAKING. One of them—a case of illuminated pages from the Koran—consists of apparently coloured paper with immensely involved pen-work and ornamentation. The astonishing thing is, they are not ink, but unbelievably delicate paper cuttings, made by some unknown and highly skilled craftsman, and *pasted* on. Such a tremendous task would be right up your alley!

I understand you are going to visit HPL. I'm sure you will hav[e] a very pleasant time there. I enjoyed his visit to me. But I'm sorry you are leaving NY, for I hoped to get up there this winter, and frankly, among the greatest attractions was your talented self! Will you go back, or return to St. Paul?

I got the BROKEN MIRRORS and was well pleased with it. I suppose he rece[ived th]e money which I sent some time ago.

Did you [ev]er locate the missing package of drawings? It would be a frightful sha[me] if they were lost . . . You didn't tell me if the O'Mecca drawing was among them. Could you enumerate them?

Apologising for this delay, and assuring you that I will reluctantly return your splendid drawing, which is carefully kept, I am

Most admiringly yours,

[RHB's stylized signature]

[P.S.] If you want me to, I'll send it to St. Paul . . ?

[14] [HW to RHB] [TLS]

320 West 11th Street, N.Y. Sept. 13, 1934

Dear Mr. Barlow:

Letter writing is a necessary labor, and we wouldn't get far with[out?] some slight indulgence in it. I have no feeling about it one way or another, but have gotten into the habit of answering any letters that appear on my desk.

Yes, I received the two drawings, and in good shape, though it was raining that day and they were very damp. As to the WITCHES' SABBATH, please do not yield to the kleptomania, or my brother would be down to cut your ears off or some other pleasant thing. But I hope you succeed in the color photography, if only to please yourself. I would be glad to make a small drawing for you, which you speak of, but I think you realize it would have to be around ten dollars. It is hard to measure one's eyesight in dollars and cents, and I have levied heavily on mine in the drawing I have just completed, ALL THE SILENCES. I hope you come out well with your own treatment.

I have received no further word on NDATD, I am sorry. I do not seem to be able to hurry that woman.[1] The only other important work I am missing is a fine wash and line drawing held by one of the Faricy clan in St. Paul. This is called CLARENCE AND THE TWO, my sole Shakespearian illustration. It is a good one, which you will see eventually. Burton (not Burnam. This man is an internationally known etcher and teacher, represented in many of the first galleries, and collected) has only a small plate, though it is good enough.

As to supplying me with prints, we'll let that go until you are in better financial position. I will be pleased to see the print you mention, however. HPL wrote me of the difficulties you are in, and I fully understand, having often been short myself. As to marketing the prints, I can not give you any buyers, I am afraid. I have so much other work which takes up my time, and the extraneous correspondence would be a little too much for me. I do believe, however, that August Derleth, in Wisconsin, might be interested in making up a folio of reproductions, as he has shown a marked interest in my work. You might inquire of him if you know him. His address is Sauk City, Wisconsin.

Yes, Don remarked he had heard from you—and gotten your check. Glad you are pleased with the book, which is rather a queer one.

The package of drawings came back safely, after taking a jaunt down some blind alley in the mails, apparently. The O'MECCA drawing was the least among them. I have three others now that are equal or superior to anything I have done in the past. One is a falling figure, an illustration, one EPILUDE, one ATS, which I mention above. You will eventually see these also.

I will be here until October first. Send the TWS to St. Paul if you do not finish it before then, and allowing for the time it will take to send it here.

Best regards. I look forward to seeing HPL again.

Cordially,

H E. Wandrei

Notes

1. HW ultimately did hear from the teacher. See HW to HPL, 23 July 1934 (*Letters with Donald and Howard Wandrei and to Emil Petaja* [New York: Hippocampus Press, 2019], p. 374): "there is a piece of news that pleases me a great deal, and which arrived this morning. I received a fat letter from the Minnesota school teacher. My letters caught up with her in Onamia, Minnesota, which is in the northern section. She advises me that the drawing in question hangs in a bedroom of hers in Milaca, wherever that is, and that when she can get over there or get in touch with someone who can do it for her, she will have the picture packed and sent on forthwith." It is unknown, however, if HW ultimately received the painting.

[15]   [HW to RHB] [TLS]

1152 Portland Avenue, St. Paul, Minnesota. November thirtieth 1934

Dear Mr. Barlow:

Rather expecting to hear from you. How is your project going? I have been working very hard at writing, have little time for anything else. Did not get up to see Lovecraft, and in many respects the trip here was an unlucky one. I hope you are well and that you are having success. This is to remind you that I never did get the large print you mentioned; I wish you would send it on here with THE WITCHES' SABBATH, unless things are unfortunate enough that the print might be too expensive. I hope that is not so.

I expect to be returning to the east in early next year.

Sincerely

Howard Wandrei

[16]   [HW to RHB] [TLS]

155 West 10th Street, NYC, January 12, 1935

Dear Barlow:

It was my understanding that you would have the Witches' Sabbath drawing delivered to this address by this morning at the latest. The idea, of course, was that the picture was to be taken uptown this morning to be framed so that it could be showed [*sic*] at a celebration my brother and I planned for tomorrow. We had attached some importance to having the picture here, as I did not bring any of my drawings along.

The celebration and exhibition has been called off, postponed until you can get the drawing up here. Please send it along at once.

Yours sincerely
Howard Wandrei

[17]   [RHB to HW] [TLS]

7218 16th St NW
Washington D C
[c. mid-January 1935]

Dear Mr. Wandrei;

I was rather startled at your letter, as the drawing was mailed to you late Thursday. You must surely have received it by now; I had the address 115 W 10, and to make assurance doubly sure, I added *"Julius', Greenwich Village"*.[1] Please let me know right away if it has not come and I'll have it traced. I'm very much surprized it hadn't come by the time you wrote, since it was sent first class, special delivery.

I regret that I was unable to try yet another method of reproduction on it . . . I wanted to keep on trying until something satisfactorily representing the original could be obtained. There is nothing I want quite so much as a colour photograph of the W- S-; I did everything within my power to get it. Let's hope your brother manages something of the kind ultimately.

I am afraid I annoyed you a great deal in NY with my incessant quizzing, but you will realize the spirit of sincere interest that prompted it.

. . . Please let me hear about the delivery of the picture.

Yours most sincerely and faithfully,
R H Barlow

Notes

1. The Wandreis had an apartment above Julius's, now recognized as the oldest continuously operating gay bar in New York City.

[18]   [HW to RHB] [TLS]

155 West 10th Street, NYC, 1/15/1935

Dear Barlow:

The picture had not arrived this morning, but at about noon the mailman came up with it. Your addressing was correct, but since you put Julius' on the address, the saloon-keeper kept it and was holding it for my call. I couldn't call for the drawing, of course, not knowing where it was.

Yes, it's too bad that you haven't had much success with the reproductions, and I suppose I shall have to content myself with the small snapshots I have of the pictures. Some day when I have the money I will have Limborg of St. Paul make up a group for me. In the past his work has been highly professional; he has taken large shots of my big batiks, for example, and gotten everything into them but the color. The color is only one step further, but these things can wait until my exchequer is in a more blooming state. I'm still busy with the pulp writing, and won't be doing any drawing for some little while.

Best regards, and all success in whatever you're doing. Send up samples of what you have in the line of reproductions if it is within your means. You must realize that I have not yet seen a single one of the photographs.

Yours sincerely,

H W

[19]　[HW to RHB] [ANS][1]

21 Bethune Street, New York City, March 24, 1937

Dear Barlow:

Am in touch with August Derleth, who has commendable plan of getting a reputable publisher (likely Scribner's) to publish omnibus edition of H.P.L's tales. Don't know whether you are communicating with Derleth or not, but hope you share my highest conviction that all of us should get together on this thing and do our utmost to establish H. P. in his deserved place in literature. I trust you will agree with me in that here is an excellent opportunity to do justice in memory of H. P., a scholar, a brilliant intellect, and master of prose. For it is plain that Derleth has publishing contacts possessed by none of the rest of us, and will exhaust his exchequer if necessary to finance this noble gesture.

Will you please write me and let me know how things are going up there—and how you feel about Augie's preparing Howard's tales for publication? I would appreciate an early reply.

Yours cordially,

[Howard] Wandrei

Notes

1. *Front:* Blank.

[20]　[HW to RHB] [ALS]

21 Bethune Street, New York City, April 15, 1937

Dear Barlow—

Many thanks for the negatives and prints, especially the latter. You may have the group back any time you say, but I should like a little while to run off copies—I am very busy now, too. I should like a larger, clearer print of ms. 66 if possible, but I can make this one do.

No I have no pictures of Howard at all. If you have a portrait and perhaps a couple of full-length snaps, I could certainly use them. You are doing well. Come again.

In appreciation,
[Howard] Wandrei

[21] [HW to RHB] [ALS]

21 Bethune Street, New York, N.Y. April 27, 1937

Dear Barlow:

My sincere thanks for the photographs, especially the smaller one, which relieves me of the burden of relying on memory alone. You need not worry about the safety of the pictures: I believe they are in good hands. If you are not coming back this way (I am about to pay my annual visit to Minnesota), you must let me know at this address whether you can be reached in the next three months at the one I have for you.

I think the jacket will be a good one. The best I can do in tribute to the outsider, at any rate.

Best regards,

As ever,
[Howard] Wandrei

P.S. The negatives are really excellent.

Appendix

Benjamin De Casseres

And a Little Book Shall Lead Them

Selected Poems. By George Sterling. Henry Holt & Company.
Ebony and Crystal. By Clark Ashton Smith. Printed by the Auburn Journal, Auburn, Cal.

I bunch these two books together because they came together and because George Sterling wrote the preface to the Ashton Smith poems.

It is hard for me to review books of poetry. In the first place, I am a poet myself; in the second place, I have so saturated my life since boyhood with the great poets and the great prose writers, that I have gone stale on poetry. In a word, I am simply tired of it—at least to-day. I prefer to take my poetry, now, in prose or music or the curves of women's bodies. The poets writing to-day in America are mere echoes. After Whitman and Poe, Swinburne and Francis Thompson, Verlaine, Hugo, and D'Annunzio, what is there to be said? Nothing. And there is no new way of saying the old things.

I have always been an admirer of George Sterling since that day he burst upon us in the old *Cosmopolitan* yahooed by Ambrose Bierce. But his was never great poetry. No rebellion, no real terror, too much rhyming, too much perfection, too much artistry—no real personality. No one would, necessarily, want to know Sterling after reading his poetry. No one would be curious about him. And the test of all great art is personality. But I know no better poetry of its kind being written in present-day America than Sterling writes.

The poetry of Ashton Smith is out of an unearthly imagination. It is morphinated, hallucinated poetry. It is gemmed and jeweled stuff. Some of it is as ethereal as Poe's. It is a book I am always picking up and finding in it gorgeous adventures.

But, gentlemen, poetry is dead the world around.

Donald Wandrei

The Emperor of Dreams

In 1912 there came from the press of A. M. Robertson, in San Francisco, a slender book of poems. Had that volume come from a well-known writer, it would have ranked him with the immortals. Had it come from a rising author, it would have spread his fame far and wide. It came from neither. It was little advertised, for it had no financial backing and the author had neither influential friends nor acquaintances among those who determine what the public may read. No attempt was made to popularize it. The book shortly passed from sight, almost unknown save to a few fortunate people who possessed copies. The book was, "The Star-Treader and Other Poems;" its author, Clark Ashton Smith, a young poet, not yet twenty, who had already dreamed and dared to dream as few men have in a lifetime. That book of poems is one of the great contributions to American literature. It contains some of our finest pure poetry, some of our best imaginative lyrics. A few of them would now be famous, had they been written by a Keats or Shelley, and a cause of laurels. The critics have ignored the volume. The literary pontiffs have passed it over. Today, not many persons know it, even by title. Yet the same critics decry the anaemic state of American letters, its lack of enduring works. A genius—in the true, not abused, sense—appears, his eyes on the other side of eternity, his poems of eternity, his work the kind that endures. He is unnoticed. He is given no encouragement. American poetry is still anaemic.

A thousand years hence, when the people of that distant time survey the accumulated mass of all literature, they will place high up on the role of honor the name, Clark Ashton Smith; and looking backward, they will ask why the world of that age long ago did not appreciate him when it had him. Perhaps this is as it ought to be. The man of letters should be the possession of those who do appreciate him. It is not given to ordinary man to walk with the gods; nor, when it is so given, does he usually avail himself of the opportunity unless he is one of that group which is the justification of himself, the cornerstone of the arts, and the prophet of immortality.

A poet can not live on visions, on dreams, on a prospect of future fame. He must live on something more material. And one can not write when it is necessary to earn a sustenance. Perhaps this was the reason that ten years elapsed before another book appeared under the poet's name. Or perhaps it was the neglect, popular, which is of little importance, and critical, which may be of the greatest importance, given his first book. Or perhaps the dreamer lived in his own realm, indifferent to ephemeral external life, writing seldom and then mainly for his own pleasure. Or perhaps . . . One trembles at the thought. "Ebony and Crystal" was published by the author in 1922. Its fate is akin to that of "The Star-Treader." Not many persons know it. Those who do regard it as worshippers a sanctum sanctorum, as connoisseurs a rare tapestry, as jewellers a priceless pearl.*

There is no place in contemporary prose and poetry for genius.

---

*I have since been informed that the silence was due to the destruction of imperfect poems, and to ill-health. It is hard to believe this statement in a day when the least is treasured by those whose best is mediocre. But it explains the uniform excellence of his work, the lack of a single weak poem.

Was "Ebony and Crystal" worth the labor of ten years? It is a larger volume than the first and contains twice as many poems, one hundred and fourteen against fifty-five. Did eleven poems a year, and those not of unusual length, with one exception, justify the author a place among the front-rank poets? If fame is the criterion, no. If excellence, yes. "Ebony and Crystal" is the finest volume of pure poetry that has appeared in America since the opening of the twentieth century, perhaps the finest since the time of Edgar Allan Poe. Not until its publication did any of our poets approach him in imaginative power. "Ebony and Crystal" belongs on that shelf with Poe, Coleridge, Blake, Shelley, Baudelaire. In that group where each is coequally supreme, he may justly take his place.

Imagination is his god, beauty his ideal; his poems are an offering to both. He is the poet of the infinite, the envoy of eternity, the amanuensis of beauty. For even as beauty was deity to Keats and Shelley, so it is to him, and in its praise has he written. But he has not celebrated it as an abstract term or an aesthetic quality, but as a more tangible substance. He has constructed entire worlds of his own and filled them with creations of his own fancy. And his beauty has thus crossed the boundary between that which is mortal and that which is immortal, and has become the beauty of strange stars and distant lands, of jewels and cypresses and moons, of flaming suns and comets, of marble palaces, of fabled realms and wonders, of gods, and daemons, and sorcery. Time and Space have been his servants, the universe his domain; with the stars his steeds and the heavens his tramping ground, he has wandered in realms afar; and he has found there a wondrous beauty and a strange fear, the goal of his early dreams and the enchanted road to greater, all manner of things illusory and fantastical.

Some of his poems are like shadowed gold; some are like flame-encircled ebony; some are crystal-clear and pure; others are as unearthly starshine. One is coldly wrought in marble; another is curiously carved in jade; there are a few glittering diamonds; and there are many rubies and emeralds aflame, glowing with a secret fire. Here and there may be found a poppy-flower, an orchid from the hot-bed of Hell, the whisper of an eldritch wind, a breath from the burning sands of regions infernal. The wizard calls, and at his imperious summons come genie, witch, and daemon to open the portal to the haunted realms of faery; and their wonder is transmuted so that those who can open the door may listen to the murmuring waters of Acheron, or watch the passing of a phantom throng; and the fen-fires gleam; and the slow mists arise; and heavy perfumes, and poisons, and dank odors fill the air. A marble palace rises in the dusk, a treasure-house of gold, and ebony, and ivory; soft lutes play within; fair women, passionless and passionate, wander in the corridors; silks and tapestries adorn the walls, and fuming censers burn a rare incense. And fabulous demogorgon and hippogriff guard the golden gateway to the hoarded wealth. The sky is black. But now and again white comets blaze, or suns of green, of crimson, of purple, flame across the firmament with silver moons. The sky is burning. Stars hurtle to destruction or waste away. All mysteries are uncurtained. One may watch a landscape of the moon, the seas of Saturn, the sunken fanes of old Atlantis, wars and wonders on some distant star.

There is no place in the poetry of Clark Ashton Smith for the conventional, the trite, the outworn. It is useless to search his work for offerings to popular desire. Some authors pander to the public taste; their books may have a huge sale, but die with the author. Some writers have skill and ability but desire wealth or immediate fame; their work has not so great a popularity but endures longer. A very few have what is called "genius." They write primarily for themselves, or with a certain small group of people who know literature in mind. They are artists, word artists; and they fashion their prose or poetry with care and labor. They are seldom appreciated in their lifetime, and never have widespread popularity, but the highest minds of every age enjoy their work. These are ones who speak to us across the ages, who will speak across the ages to come. It is to this class that Clark Ashton Smith belongs. One will examine his poems in vain for the commonplaces that have so largely crept into our literature; and by so much as he has avoided ephemeral and written of immortal things, by so much the longer will his work endure.

II

"The Star-Treader" was his earliest volume, and it shows the effects of imagination in its first exuberance. Stars and suns and comets parade in all their majesty; Chaos, Infinity, and "the eldritch dark" are ever present; and the wonder, the inexplicable mystery of the Universe form the background of the book. It was then that the young poet wrote "The Song of a Comet;" it was then that he fashioned "The Song of the Stars;" and from his pen came "The Wind and the Moon." Of the fixed forms, the sonnet was his favorite, and nearly a third of the poems have its form. In most of them he strove to obtain single, dominant effects, to limn one unforgettable scene, as in "The Last Night," "The Medusa of the Skies," and "Averted Malefice." Occasionally, he was content with a single quatrain, or a pair, as "The Maze of Sleep" and "The Morning Pool." But he had a greater chance to display his power in the longer, more sustained poems, such as "Saturn," "The Star-Treader," and "The Masque of Forsaken Gods." They would have been accomplishments for a man of maturity, for one who had long written poetry, as the work of a youth they are remarkable achievements. The entire book has this note of maturity; it was a world-weary youth wise beyond his years who wrote these poems beautiful, fantastic, sometimes bitter and more than once inexpressibly terrible in their suggestion.

"The Star-Treader" was published in 1912. Not for ten years did another book come from the poet.* What had he been doing those ten long years? Had the neglect of his first book compelled him to turn his mind into other channels? It is hard to say, but "Ebony and Crystal" is not a large volume for the work of ten years.

There is a great difference between the two, in imagery, in tone and subject, and in metrical skill. The first was, to some extent, experimental; the second, a fulfillment of the promise in the foreshadowing work. The craftsmanship of these later poems is well-nigh flawless; the volume is rich in perfectly planned, perfectly fashioned jewels. It is jewel-cutting that he was engaged in those ten years. Here may be found "such stuff as dreams are made of," and the dreams themselves; here the utterance of god and witch, the harmony of the spheres, the strains of immortal music, the unveiling of an imagery unparalleled. The beauty of these poems is intoxicating, for the poet who wrote them was haunted and intoxicated by loveliness immaculate and incarnate, by all beauty. And the poems are couched, not in ordinary language, but in an English filled with curious and archaic forms, rare or obsolete words, unusual diction; and they have been given flowing rhythms and unforgettable melodies; and they move in measured intonation, and in cadence, and in musical sweep that are seldom found in poetry. They are whispers of the unearthly, rather than mortal work. They are enduring forms of unenduring dreams and ideals and desires. They are the unattainable, set in deathless words of gold. They are time-outlasting marble; they are lotus and poppy; they are fadeless amaranth and asphodel, pure, perfect shadows of the pure and perfect, eternal, aeonian. They are star-dust and starshine, caught by a dreamer of the ages, fashioned in ebony and crystal. They are nectar and ambrosia, nepenthe, Lethean draughts to drown the world in forgetfulness and oblivion. They are the waters of paradise.

The poems are laden with a pagan, exotic beauty and imagery. Sometimes this takes the form of light and shadow, as in "Arabesque." Sometimes it deals with the lands of romance, as in "Beyond the Great Wall:"

> Beyond the far Cathayan wall,
> A thousand leagues athwart the sky,
> The scarlet stars and mornings die,
> The gilded moons and sunsets fall.
>
> Across the sulfur-colored sands
> With bales of silk and camels fare,
> Harnessed with vermil and with vair,
> Into the blue and burning lands.

---

*"Odes and Sonnets" was privately issued by the Book Club of California in 1918. The odes are from "The Star-Treader"; the sonnets were included in "Ebony and Crystal."

And, ah, the song the drivers sing,
To while the desert leagues away—
A song they sang in old Cathay,
Ere youth had left the eldest king.

Ere love and beauty both grew old,
And wonder and romance were flown,
On fiery wings to worlds unknown,
To stars of undiscovered gold.

And I their alien words would know,
And follow past the lonely Wall,
Where gilded moons and sunsets fall,
As in a song of long ago.

Occasionally it reverts upon itself as in "The Melancholy Pool" and "Solution:"

The ghostly fire that walks the fen,
Tonight thine only light shall be;
On lethal ways thy soul shall pass.
And prove the stealthy, coiled morass,
With mocking mists for company.

On roads thou goest not again.
To shores where thou hast never gone,—
Fare onward, though the shuddering queach
And serpent-rippled waters reach
Like seepage-pools of Acheron,

Beside thee; and the twisten reeds,
Close-raddled as a witch's net,
Enwind thy knees, and cling and clutch
Like wreathing adders; though the touch
Of the blind air be dank and wet,

As from a wounded Thing that bleeds
In cloud and darkness overhead—
Fare onward, where thy dreams of yore
In splendour drape the fetid shore
And pestilential waters dead.

And though the toads' irrision rise,
As grinding of Satanic racks,

And spectral willows, gaunt and grey,
Gibber along thy shrouded way,
Where vipers lie with livid backs,

And watch thee with their sulphurous eyes,—
Fare onward, till thy feet shall slip
Deep in the sudden pool ordained,
And all the noisome draught be drained,
That turns to Lethe on the lip.

But usually it takes the form of a rich imagery, oriental in its profusion and splendour, unlimited in its concept and scope, imperishable by reason of its supreme, its unearthly, its alien perfection. "In Saturn"—

Upon the seas of Saturn I have sailed
To isles of high, primeval amarant,
Where the flame-tongued sonorous flow'rs enchant
The hanging surf to silence: All engrailed

With ruby-colored pearls, the golden shore
Allured me; but as one whom spells restrain,
For blind horizons of the sombre main,
And harbors never known, my singing prore

I set forthrightly: Formed of fire and brass,
Immenser skies divided, deep on deep
Before me,—till, above the darkling foam,

With dome on cloudless adamantine dome,
Black peaks no peering seraph deems to pass,
Rose up from realms ineffable as Sleep!

"The Kingdom of Shadows," "The Land of Evil Stars," "A Precept," "Chant of Autumn," Requiescat in Pace,"—but it is useless to try to select fine poems from a volume which has room for none other.

There is one long poem, however, that deserves special attention. It is "The Hashish-Eater," containing many hundred lines of blank verse. But it is far different from what is usually called blank verse, from what one knows as ordinary iambic pentameter. This has always been a stately metre, capable of impressive effects; and in his hands, with the aid of his boundless imagination and descriptive powers, besides his technical skill, it has become the implement of a poem-colossus, gigantic in theme and treatment, told in a heavy, sonorous English that sweeps onward in measured roll with an ever-swelling rhythm from the Imperial summons of the opening lines:

Bow down: I am the emperor of dreams;
I crown me with the million-colored sun
Of secret worlds incredible, and take
Their trailing skies for vestment, when I soar,
Throned on the mounting zenith, and illume
The spaceward-flown horizons infinite.

And at the very end of a volume which will one day be a prized literary heritage is the sombre and morbidly magnificent prose-poem, "The Shadows," a poem told with such care that no word is lost or wasted, and so well that it lingers in the memory as a sable fantasy enshrined, a rare perfume, darkly odorous and darkly poisonous, clinging to a bit of strangely shapen ebony.

III

In October, 1925, came the third of his published books, "Sandalwood," a volume which, though slender, contains more poems than his first. After "Ebony and Crystal," not much could be added to his laurels, but had that volume not existed, "Sandalwood" might have taken its place to a large extent. It is different from "Ebony and Crystal" in that the poems are less ambitious with regard to the depicting of strange, vast splendour, but more songlike, lyrical, and spontaneous, though the mastery of technique and the metrical skill displayed admit of neither spontaneity nor its attendant roughnesses. The poems may be divided into several classes, including nineteen translations from Baudelaire, and four songs from the uncompleted romantic drama, "The Fugitives." And there is a poem of six stanzas, "We Shall Meet," told in an original or very rare but very beautiful verse form. But to one who has read the early work of Clark Ashton Smith, his later poems remain beyond praise. One may go into ecstasies at a vision of glory; but the greater glory surpasses description. And he who has sate on the ramparts of Heaven and Hell is mute before magnificence and pageantry that shame the speech.

No critic and no criticism can do justice to the work of this poet. There are some things which are beyond the reach of both, and in this rare group belongs the work of Clark Ashton Smith. For there are books so distinctive, so excellent, that they cannot be compared with others of their class, by reason of their perfection. For them, there is no standard of judgment, and one can only admire what one is helpless to censure or to sanctify. To use homely language in estimating such work is to do it an injustice; and yet, superlatives are equally useless, for they have been so carelessly employed that nowadays they deprecate the work they are meant to extol.

Earlier in this essay, certain other poets of the romantic-imaginative group were mentioned. But Clark Ashton Smith cannot be associated with any particular one. Each within that class was original, and by virtue of a similar originality, this modern poet deserves his rank. The great poets neither follow nor imitate; they create. And he has created, on a cosmic scale. The greatest indictment of contemporary verse is its lack of form, its deliberate exclusion of the most vital quality of a work of art, a quality which every book that aspires to greatness must have, above all else, if it is to endure. Substance–form; form–substance; of the two, form is by far the most important. And this element—including, as it does, diction, style, presentation, euphony, craftsmanship—is present in the poems of Clark Ashton Smith to such an extraordinary degree that, had there been no substance, had he produced only rainbows and iridescent bubbles, he would still have deserved lasting attention. Indeed, the sole flaw in his poems is occasionally form in too great a degree. His gifts are so much beyond those of average poets, and his vocabulary is of such enormous content that the desired word is often an uncommon one. Yet even this lends a curious charm, a singularly effective atmosphere to the poem, at worst, it may only be considered what would be a god-send to the lamentably word-base verse of the Philistines. It is an example of his innate power of concentration, his ability to say best and to say beautifully the things that deserve to be clothed in costly raiment.

Just where the place of this emperor of dreams will ultimately be fixed in poetry cannot, of course, be foretold, save that it should be very high. Nor can one prophesy the day he shall receive the recognition he has earned. It took the world forty years to appreciate Thomas Lovell Beddoes; it took longer for it to appreciate William Blake; Arthur O'Shaughnessy is still almost unknown; and few even of those occasional persons who have read "The Book of Jade" could tell the name of its author, Park Barnitz. And now, Clark Ashton Smith—

Announcement

Commencing in 1975, the Autobiography of Donald Wandrei will be published in three volumes of approximately 350 pages each, illustrated, covering the periods 1908 to March 17, 1942; March, 1942 to July 4, 1971; and July 1971 to date.

This work, with a general title still to be chosen, will be a permanent factual record and completely documented chronicle of the author's interlocking relationships and his participation in important segments of American literary and art trends of the twentieth century, of special interest in the realm of imaginative writing, both supernatural cosmicism and science-fiction.

Circumstances of birth produced the brothers Donald Wandrei and Howard Wandrei. Happenstance, coincidence, chance and a rare overlapping of lifetimes resulted in long correspondence and friendships with both H. P. Lovecraft (from 1926 to 1937 in Providence and New York) and Clark Ashton Smith (from 1926 to 1961 in Auburn, California).

The Autobiography gives full details never before disclosed of the author's visits with Lovecraft; direct accounts of Lovecraft's aunts, Mrs. F. C. Clark and Mrs. A. E. Phillips Gamwell; first hand observations on W. Paul Cook, Bernard Dwyer, C. M. Eddy, James F. Morton, Samuel Loveman, Frank B. Long, George Kirk, Rheinhart Kleiner, Alfred Galpin, Arthur B. Leeds, H. C. Koenig, Seabury Quinn, and many others of the Lovecraft group .

The author presents an equally vivid record of Clark Ashton Smith and his parents, friends and environment in the hilltop ranch house, now destroyed, where Smith lived in Auburn, California.

The origins of the author's own development are here for the first time revealed, with hitherto unknown published work identified; his encounters with Farnsworth Wright, editor [*sic*] of *Weird Tales;* F. Orlin Tremaine and Desmond Hall of *Astounding Stories;* Fanny Ellsworth of *Black Mask;* Mort Weisinger of National Comics Publications; Harry Bates, John W. Campbell and more. There are accounts of Dr. Hereward Carrington, T. Everette [*sic*] Harre; experiences as advertising manager for E. P. Dutton & Co. in 1928–9 at the height of the post-war boom in New York of the Prohibition Era, and of living in New York 1932–8 during the Great Depression.

The author's military service from March, 1942, through November, 1945, in the U. S. and in France, Germany and Austria is covered, including two brief chance encounters with General Patton, highly to the General's credit.

Recorded in the Autobiography are the specific origins of stories from real life experiences; an explanation of basic differences in the cosmicism of Lovecraft, of Smith, and of the author; and a partial influence by the author on Lovecraft's own creativity.

Full details are provided of the author's repeated efforts to achieve wider magazine and book publication for Lovecraft's tales from 1927; of his correspondence and relationship with August Derleth; of his part in obtaining an editorial job for Derleth in Minneapolis in 1929; of the collecting and publishing of Lovecraft's tales and the founding of Arkham House by August Derleth and Donald Wandrei in 1939 when no established publisher could be found for Lovecraft's work.

The Autobiography is solidly substantiated by the author's own complete files of all correspondence and memorabilia from H. P. Lovecraft, Clark Ashton Smith, Mrs. Gamwell, Frank B. Long, W. Paul Cook, Samuel Loveman, Bernard Dwyer, August Derleth and many more, as well as drawings, sculptures, watercolors and metallic painting on silk by Clark Ashton Smith; the lifetime correspondence of Howard Wandrei as well as the total lifetime art of Howard Wandrei—batiks, oil paintings, charcoal sketches, sculptures in wood, plaster casts, jewelry and the incredible pen-and-ink nightmares in multiple colors which Lovecraft himself described, after seeing them in New York in 1935 at the Wandrei apartment, as "the greatest fantastic art ever produced."

The illustrations for the 3 volumes of the Autobiography will be selected from the author's own files of letters, memorabilia, art works, and photographs taken by himself at his studio in New York of Lovecraft, Hall, Long, and others, as well as photographs made in St. Paul and at Clark Ashton Smith's ranch house in Auburn. An unusual illustration is the set of palm prints of August Derleth made at the author's residence in St. Paul on June 7, 1971, just four weeks before Derleth's death.

The Autobiography will NOT be published by Arkham House, from which the author severed all connections in May, 1973; nor will any further work by the author, or of his ownership, editorship or control, be published by Arkham House under its present management.

Donald Wandrei
March, 1974

Julius Schwartz and Mortimer Weisinger

Donald Wandrei Interviewed

When the editors of *Weird Tales* published Donald Wandrei's masterful story, "The Red Brain," back in their October, 1927 issue, they were not surprised at the sudden influx of letters from readers all over the country proclaiming the story to be one of the most outstanding weird tales of all time. As a matter of fact, they expected it. Nor were they surprised to learn that Dashiell Hammett had deemed the story so good that it merited reprinting in his anthology of weird tales, *Creeps by Night*. And it seemed only natural for the story to appear in a collection of weird stories published in England.

Followers of fantastic literature were not surprised at all these manifestations of literary approval, we say, because they knew the story was destined to be a classic when they first read it. But, we venture to guess, not a single person of all the thousands who read the tale would have imagined the author to be a lanky lad of sixteen!

This story, extremely mature in expression, and which the author himself considers one of the best of his published output, was originally titled by him "The Twilight of Time." It was Farnsworth Wright, the editor, who gave the story its final caption, and Wandrei was satisfied with it.

Donald Wandrei was born April 20, 1908. He received his B. A. at the University of Minnesota. He put in two years of work towards his Ph.D. degree, but finally decided against it. Later, he taught English at this university for a period of two years. He is not married and emphatically asserts that he "never will be."

At the youthful age of twenty, Wandrei was advertising manager of the Dutton Publishing Company, where he held this position for two years. Now he is a public relations man, and believes there is a great future in the field. His work employs so much of his time that he has little time left for writing.

His mind is seething with an abundance of unusual plots which have not yet found an outlet, due to the aforesaid reason.

Wandrei has flocks of friends who are continually regaling him with plots, usually based on their dreams. Wandrei has [so] many of his own that their suggestions are politely, but firmly, rejected.

Recently Wandrei completed a stupendous, super-science novel, titled "Dead Titans, Waken!" which attempts to explain the pyramids of Egypt, the statues of Easter Island and similar phenomena. Publishers have been fascinated by the idea behind this book, which Wandrei himself says "will drive readers crazy." Essentially, the theme is similar to "Colossus." Wandrei has optimistic hopes concerning this novel.

Unlike other authors, Wandrei does not dash off his stuff. He writes the story out in longhand, putting in about 1000 words a night. Each night he revises the work he wrote the night before. At times he becomes so enthused with a story that he writes it at white heat, and usually at one sitting. This happened with his "A Race Through Time" and "The Tree Men of M'Bwa." This latter story was suddenly inspired, and Wandrei thought it so good that he decided to write it up immediately. He finished the ms. in five hours, and sent the story to *Weird Tales* the next day.

Many of Wandrei's personal experiences furnish fodder for his stories. For example, he wandered one day into a friend's curio shop. There he saw a sealed bottle. He started thinking how long the bottle had been sealed, why it was sealed and what was in it. His answer to these questions appear in "Spawn of the Sea."

On still another occasion, which takes us back to 1925, Wandrei tells of the time when he resided in Minneapolis, where during the winter he was astounded to see a red snowfall. This phenomenon perplexed him to such an extent that he offered his own explanation in "Something from Above."

Wandrei has met many author-celebrities. He knows Seabury Quinn, H. P. Lovecraft, F. B. Long, Jr., Farnsworth Wright, Desmond Hall, and Hugh Rankin. Of Lovecraft he tells us the following anecdote:

"When I met Lovecraft I chanced to comment on his excellent story, 'Call of Cthulhu,' and I pronounced the word as it was spelt. Lovecraft enlightened me on its correct pronunciation, which sounds like a series of witches' whistles. I asked Lovecraft how he could possibly pronounce the name different from my version of it, which was correct phonetically. He then said to me, 'Look here, I ought to know how to say it, don't you think?'"

At one time Wandrei possessed almost a complete file of the rare *Black Cat Magazines,* which published copious amounts of fantastic literature. This magazine might still be existing, were it not for the fact that they once published a story, of such a gruesome nature that the circulation dropped to almost nothing! This story was called "The Pain Thermometer," and told about a scientist who perfected a thermometer which was able to record various degrees of pain. He vivisected dogs and cats and performed various operations on them in an effort to get the thermometer to rise. But his efforts succeeded in raising it only a few degrees. The scientist then decided to try it on a human being. He captured a man, strapped him to the operating table, and proceeded to flay him alive. After a very graphic description of the torture, the author goes on, to show the thermometer bursting from the excessive amount of pain it registered. The story ends with the lifeless mass of the flayed man slowly making its way towards the scientist.

Wandrei would like to do serious writing. He writes fantasy because he is interested in it, and modestly refers to his published work as "a pile of junk." However, our readers will dispute that. His greatest thrill in the writing occurred when he completed the framework for his *Dead Titans, Waken!* His greatest disappointment was the rejection of his series of short fantastic poems, "Post-Historian Legends," which he himself thought really good. His best stories are "The Red Brain," "The Tree Men of M'Bwa," and "The Lives of Alfred Kramer."

His brother, Howard Wandrei, is the author of "Over Time's Threshold" and "In the Triangle," which have appeared in *Weird Tales.* He is also an artist and is the illustrator of Wandrei's book of verse, *Dark Odyssey.* He has also written another book of verse, *Ecstasy.*

One of Wandrei's best stories, "The Fragment of a Dream," appeared in *The Recluse,* a now defunct periodical which also featured material by Lovecraft, C. A. Smith, and H. Warner Munn. He corresponds regularly with Smith, and thinks his stories much above the average weird tale.

He thinks W. Olaf Stapledon's *Last and First Men* is a masterpiece of science fiction. He enjoyed "The Invisible Man" so much that he saw it twice. He sees a great future in scientifilms. He thinks Hugh Rankin's stuff is much above the average pulp magazine artists, and he calls him "my favorite illustrator." His favorite authors are Arthur Machen, C. A. Smith, Lovecraft, and the early H. G. Wells. He does not read his stories over after they are published, and does not save acceptance slips.

Ms. Enclosures Smith Sent to Donald Wandrei

Abandoned Plum-
  Orchard
After Armageddon
Amithaine
Amor Aeternalis
Au bord du Léthé
Avowal
Borderland
But Grant, O Venus
Calenture
Canticle
Cats in Winter Sunlight
Concupiscence
Un Couchant
Cumuli
Dans l'universe lointain
December
Declining Moon
Didus Ineptus
Dominion
Éloignement
Enchanted Mirrors
Enigma
Ennui [My days are as a
  garden, where the dust]
L'Ensorcellement
The Envoys
Essence
L'Espoir du néant
A Fable
Feast of St. Anthony
Fence and Wall
Foggy Night
La Fontaine de Sang
The Funeral Urn
Geese in the Spring Night
The Ghost of Theseus
Growth of Lichen
Haiku
Harvest Evening
The Hill of Dionysus
The Hill-Top

Humors of Love
A Hunter Meets the
  Martichoras
Illusion
Improbable Dream
In a Distant Universe
Incognita
The Incubus of Time
Interim
Late Pear-Pruner
Lichens
The Limniad
Loss
Love and Death
Love in Dreams
Luna Aeternalis
Madrigal
Un Madrigal
Madrigal of Memory
Maya
Mithridates
The Monacle
Morning on an Eastern
  Sea
Mors
Necromancy
Nevermore
Night of Miletus
Nightmare of the Lilli-
  putian
Nocturnal Pines
"Not Altogether Sleep"
October
Odysseus in Eternity
The Old Water-Wheel
On a Chinese Vase
One Evening
Ougabalys
The Pagan
Paphnutius
Passing of an Elder God
Phallus Impudica

Philtre
Poet in Hades
Quintrains
Revenant
Satiety [A weary Juan,
  smothered in boudoirs,]
The Saturnienne
The Sciapod
Seeker
Shadows
Sinbad, It Was Not
  Well to Brag
Some Blind Eidolon
Someone
Song at Evenfall
Song of the Necromancer
Sonnet [Empress with
  eyes more sad and au-
  reate]
Sonnet for the Psycho-
  analysts
Sonnet lunaire [French]
Souvenance
The Sparrow's Nest
Spectral Life
Surréalist Sonnet
Swine and Azaleas [i.e.,
  The Thralls of Circe
  Climb Parnassus]
To Howard Phillips
  Lovecraft
To One Absent
Trope
Unicorn
Untold Arabian Fable
Venus
Une Vie spectrale
Warning
The Whisper of the
  Worm
Willow-Cutting in Au-
  tumn

Epigrams
The Devil's Note-Book
  (10-page typescript)
Epigrams of Alastor (9-
page typescript

Translations of Baudelaire
XXI. Le Masque
XXVI
Sed Non Satiata (2)
XXXIII
L. Le poison
L'aube spirituelle
Evening Harmony
Spiritual Dawn
The Wine of Lovers
The Irreparable
Chant d'automne

Les hiboux
XCII. A une Malabaraise
CVIII. Paysage
CIX. Le soileil
A une mendiante rousse
The Love of Falsehood
Rêve Parisien
CXXXI. Le vin du soli-
  taire
Epigraph pour un livre
  condamné
CXXXV. Une martyre
La Béatrice
CXLVI. La mort des
  amants
CXLVIII. La mort des
  artistes

Les bijoux*
Lethe (verse)*
Le Lethe (prose)
Femmes damnes*
Les metamorphosis du
  vampire*

*From *Les Épaves* (Jetsam)

Prose Poems
Chinoiserie
The Lotus and the
  Moon
The Mirror in the Hall
  of Ebony
The Muse of Hyperborea
Preference

Ms. Enclosures Smith Sent to R. H. Barlow

The Abominations of Yondo
The City of the Singing Flame
The Colossus of Ylourgne*
The Devotee of Evil
The Disinterment of Venus*
The Double Shadow
The Dweller in the Gulf*
The End of the Story
The Epiphany of Death*
Epigrams of Alastor
The Flower-Women*
The Hashish-Eater
The Holiness of Azédarac
In the Book of Vergama*
The Last Incantation
The Monster of the Prophecy
A Night in Malneant*
The Ninth Skeleton
One Evening

The Passing of Aphrodite
Pertinence and Impertinence (epi-
  grams)
A Rendezvous in Averoigne
The Seed from the Sepulcher*
The Seven Geases (page 1 only,
  signed by CAS)
The Tale of Satampra Zeiros
The Testament of Atthamaus*
The Third Episode of Vathek
To Nora May French
The Uncharted Isle
The Vaults of Yoh-Vombis
The Weaver in the Vault
The Willow Landscape
Xeethra*

*From "Typed copies of CAS stories
~~in my files~~" among RHB's papers.

R. H. Barlow

The Time Machine

(A Bibliographical Note)

The first publication of the tale that later became Wells' most famous short novel, was in a paper issued at his school. The magazine, The Science Schools Quarterly, serialized a story of the same underlying plot, dealing with a Welesh [*sic*] professor. This was, broadly speaking, the debut of the story. It was later re-written, and some decade afterwards, after being published in both the National Observor and The New Review, appeared in a modest little volume published by Wm. Heinomann. [*sic*] Preceding it were two text-books and Conversations With An Uncle came out the dan [*sic*] immediately before.

The book in its first English edition, was a modest duodecimo volume measuring approximately $7 \times 5 \times 1$ ins. It was bound in a coarse linen-like grey cloth, and bore in purple lettering as well as the title a peculiar device of a rather emaciated sphinx. It contained pages 152 and XVI. The text, besides the title page was virtually the same as that recently issued in Short Stories of H. G. Wells, but differed in several respects from that Amazing Stories used in their May, 1927 issue.

It appeared simultaneously both in the bound edition and wrappers, the former at the price of 3s, and the latter at 2s 6d.

About H. G. Wells

By Daniel McPhail

A short while ago, H. G. Wells had a dream of the future which inspired the writing of his new semi-fantasy book, "The Shape of Things to Come." It is an outline of the next century and a half, forecasting a World State eventually after destructive wars. Published by Macmillan.

Wells writes in an almost invisible small hand.

A slightly demented person has been suing him for a decade, charging that he stole his "Outline of History" from an unpublished manuscript of his. Wells has had all the bills to pay, to say nothing of the annoyance.

Wells and Arthur Machen were both asked to contribute to an abortive magazine published in the '90s, and in one of the few issues appeared Wells' "The Cone"—Machen's didn't get in because the magazine expired. Wells' "The Time Machine" and Machen's effective horror story, "The Three Impostors" were both quite in the limelight at the time. The short lived magazine was somewhat of a forerunnrr [*sic*] of the modern weird magazines. Machen was the subject of many amusing attacks, more fully reported in his autobiographical "Far Off Things" and "Things Near and Far," even being accused of being deliberately unpleasant by some prudish ladies' magazine for his "Great God Pan."

The three H. G. Wells stories featured in Weird Tales during 1925 and 1926 were reprints, though not mentioned as such when published. They were written about a quarter of a century before.

David E. Schultz

Smith's Unpublished Poetry Collections

Readers of Clark Ashton Smith's *Selected Poems* must have wondered a bit at the method by which the book was compiled. Those familiar with Smith's poetry know well that *The Star-Treader*, *Ebony and Crystal*, and *Sandalwood* were his earliest books, and that *The Hill of Dionysus* was his last, though written more than a decade before it saw partial publication. Thus, those titles constitute the opening and closing sections of *Selected Poems*. Other sections obviously were not published books, but merely gatherings of like poems: "Translations and Paraphrases," "Experiments in Haiku" (all previously unpublished) and the like. But what of the sections titled "Incantations" and "The Jasmine Girdle"? Their titles are not explanatory as to content but seem to be named groupings of poems, on the order of his published books.

The two items were in fact planned as books two decades before. In July 1925, Smith informed Donald Wandrei "I am planning a new book which will contain nothing but pure poetry—no sentimentalities, no philosophical aridities—nothing but the strange, the magical, and the gorgeous! 'Incantations' might be a good title for this book ... which, in all likelihood, I will have to print at my own expense." At the time, he had little more than an idea and a title. Smith mentioned "Incantations" to correspondents for the next decade but did not have any concrete contents. In early 1929, he informed Wandrei that he had "put my new volume of verse, which I have entitled 'The Jasmine Girdle and Other Poems,' in the hands of a N.Y. literary agent," with hope that an eastern publisher might publish the book. In this case, he had prepared a typescript, though whatever became of it is not known, although when he was preparing the typescript of *Selected Poems*, he mentioned to Wandrei that a collection called "The Jasmine Girdle" was incorporated into the typescript. Needless to say, no eastern publisher deigned to publish the book.

The editors have seen two lists prepared by Smith with titles for "The Jasmine Girdle." The first given below seems to coincide with the manuscript he had his agent circulate among eastern publishers. Note that the list contains some poems that did appear in the "Jasmine Girdle" section of *Selected Poems*. Also, "The Jasmine Girdle" in *Selected Poems* contains thirteen poems (two in French) not on Smith's list. The seven poems listed under the "Incantations" subheading and the four under "Mandragoras" are all in the "Incantations" section of *Selected Poems*. Of the nine translations of Baudelaire on Smith's list, only seven were published in *Selected Poems*.

The Jasmine Girdle

1. The Chatelaine of Dream [The Nevermore-to-Be?]
2. Fantaisie d'antan
3. Un Madrigal
4. One Evening
5. Song at Evenfall
6. Trope
7. Canticle
8. Answer
9. Madrigal of Evanescence
10. Tristan to Iseult
11. Souvenance
12. Venus
13. To Antares
14. Immortelle
15. Amor Autumnalis
16. Temporality
17. Offering [a prose poem]
18. Song
19. Credo
20. The Autumn Lake
21. November
22. Chanson de Novembre
23. Sonnet lunaire
24. Exorcism

Nine Poems from Charles P. Baudelaire
1. L'Irremediable
2. Les Hiboux
3. Sed non satiata
4. Spleen (LXXX)
5. Le Revenant
6. Brumes et pluies
7. Epigraphe pour un livre condamné
8. Chant d'automne
9. Le Balcon

Incantations
1. The Nightmare Tarn
2. Warning
3. Necromancy
4. The Saturnienne
5. Sonnet

6. A Fable
7. After Armageddon

Mandragoria
1. October
2. December
3. Au bord du Léthé
4. L'Espoir du néant

The Jasmine Girdle and Other Poems

Euphrasees
1. On a Chinese Vase
2. Jungle Twilight
3. Nyctalops
4. The Envoys
5. Le Refuge

Four Poems from P. Verlaine
1. Clair de lune
2. En Sourdine
3. Le Faune
4. IX Ariettes Oubliées

Madrigals and Memories
1. Septembral
2. Ode
3. Poplars
4. Un Couchant
5. L'Ensorcellement

Interregnum
1. Ennui
2. Bâillement
3. A Mi-Chemin

Likewise, "Incantations" was not published, although for a brief time, it seemed that it might be. The intrepid boy publisher R. H. Barlow, whose legacy is littered with many uncompleted projects, offered to publish the book (just as he offered to publish Lovecraft's *Fungi from Yuggoth* and a collection of Wandrei's poems). Barlow was quick to put aside—somewhat inexplicably—the Lovecraft book, which he had typeset and even printed in part, in order to take up the Smith book. Barlow's only book printing and binding experience until that time was the somewhat amateurish *The Goblin Tower* of Frank

Belknap Long, but as he gained more experience, he sought to take on more ambitious projects. Barlow obviously persuaded Smith to let him have a try at *Incantations,* and so in a letter to Barlow of January 1936, Smith writes "The typescript of Incantations goes forward to you by express. It includes 65 titles: 49 more or less lyric poems, 18 of which are grouped under the subtitle of The Jasmine Girdle; 3 renderings from Paul Verlaine, 9 from Baudelaire; and 4 of my prose pastels at the end." Curiously, *Incantations* includes a subsection titled "The Jasmine Girdle." The typescript of *Incantations* that Smith mentions seems no longer to exist. When Wandrei persuaded Smith to cut ties with Barlow, who had in the meantime decided that the Beck brothers of The Futile Press, who had published Smith's *Nero and Other Poems,* were perhaps better suited to the project, Smith requested the typescript back from the Becks under a thin pretext, and so it was not to be found among Barlow's other manuscripts received from Smith.

However, among Smith's own papers, there is a typescript labeled "Contents." No book title is specified, but it is evident that it was intended for *Incantations* for several reasons. First, it lists, as Smith stated, 49 lyric poems (18 of which were under "The Jasmine Girdle"), 16 translations, and 4 prose pastels. In subsequent letters to Barlow, Smith suggested some changes and additions, and these can be seen in Barlow's hand on the typescript, where two poems are added to the main section, another is added (mistakenly) under "The Jasmine Girdle," and one poem is given a new title. Furthermore, the table of contents contains all the titles, though scattered somewhat differently, in *Selected Poems.* For example, there are five poems by Verlaine rather than merely three, there are twenty-four poems under "The Jasmine Girdle" (and so there were *three* proposed lists of poems for "The Jasmine Girdle"), the prose pastels are omitted, and there are considerably more Baudelaire items and also lyrics under "Incantations." The following table compares the items intended for the original Dragon-Fly Press/Futile Press edition of *Incantations* with the corresponding parts of *Selected Poems,* assembled roughly ten years after scrubbing *Incantations.*

Contents [for *Incantations*]

Incantations [Dragon-Fly Press]	*Incantations* [in *Selected Poems*]
	Ennui
	Apostrophe
	Sonnet
	The Saturnienne
	Revenant
	Un Vie Spectrale [Fr.]
	Song of the Necromancer
	In Thessaly
	Lines on a Picture
	Hellenic Sequel
	Refuge
	Only to One Returned
	But Grant, O Venus
	Town Lights
	Strange Girl
	Some Blind Eidolon
	If Winter Remain
	Pour Chercher du Nouveau
	Anteros

The Jasmine Girdle [Dragon-Fly Press]	*The Jasmine Girdle* [in *Selected Poems*]
The Chatelaine of Dreams [= The Nevermore-to-Be]	The Nevermore-To-Be
Fantaisie d'Antan	Fantaisie d'Antan
One Evening	One Evening
Canticle	Trope
Song at Evenfall	Canticle
Trope	Venus
November	November
Le Miroir des Blanches Fleurs [Fr.]	Le Miroir des Blanches Fleurs [Fr.]
The Autumn Lake	Le Marees [Fr.]
Madrigal of Evanescence	The Autumn Lake
Moon-Sight	Winter Moonlight
Calendar	To Antares
September	Connaissance
Indian Summer	Exorcism
The Dragon-Fly	Calendar
Sufficiency	Madrigal of Evanescence
Mystery	September
Dominion	Indian Summer
	The Dragon-Fly
Farewell to Eros*	Touch
	Sufficiency
	Ineffability

| | Mystery |
| | Dominion |

Three Poems from Paul Verlaine

En Sourdine	En Sourdine
Le Faune	The Faun
IX (Ariette Oubliees)	IX (Ariette Oubliees)

Nine Poems from Charles Pierre Baudelaire

The Balcony	—
Sed non Satiata	Sed non Satiata
The Phantom	The Phantom
Spleen (LXXX)	Spleen (LXXX)
Song of Autumn	Song of Autumn
Mists and Rains	Mists and Rains
The Sick Muse	The Sick Muse
The Owls	The Owls
Epigraph for a Condemned Book	—

Prose Pastels

Chinoiserie	—
The Lotus and the Moon	—
The Mirror in the Hall of Ebony	—
The Passing of Aphrodite	—

Notes:
I = "Incantations"; JG = "The Jasmine Girdle";
1 = as planned in 1935   2 = as published in *SP.*
1. Items marked * (I1) are added in RHB's hand, per CAS's instructions in his letters, although RHB erroneously placed "Farewell to Eros" under "The Jasmine Girdle."
2. I2 contained 28 poems not initially planned for I1 (62 total). JG2 contained 8 poems not planned for JG1.
3. "Ode" (I1) remained uncollected; "Ougabalys" (I1) is an earlier version of "Tolometh" (I2). "Song at Evenfall" (JG1) and the translations "The Balcony" and "Epigraph for a Condemned Book" were not collected; "Moon-Sight" (JG1) remained unpublished. Otherwise, all poems intended for I1 are in *SP,* and all the uncollected poems may be found in *The Complete Poetry and Translations.*

Poems & Translations
By Clark Ashton Smith

These poems and translations
are, for the vast majority, uncollected.
Some will appear in a volume to be called
INCANTATIONS, whose date of publication is (1937) as yet undetermined.

[Written by RHB on the typescript of "One Evening," JHL.]

Glossary of Frequently Mentioned Names

Ackerman, Forrest J (1916–2008), American agent, author, editor. Ackerman had been a science fiction fan since the late '20s; he corresponded sporadically with HPL from around 1931 onward. He was the instigator of the feud chronicled in "The Boiling Point."

Barker, Eric W[ilson] (1905–1973), American poet born in England, awarded the Shelley Memorial Award of the Poetry Society of America in 1963. His wife was the dancer Madelynne F. Greene. CAS dedicated *Selected Poems* to them.

Barnitz, [David] Park (1878–1901), American poet, best known for his collection of decadent and nihilistic verse, *The Book of Jade* (1901), published anonymously.

Bates, Hiram Gilmore (Harry) III (1900–1981), editor of *Strange Tales* for the Clayton chain of pulp magazines.

Beck, Claire P. (1919–1999), of Lakeport, CA, published the science fiction fanzine *The Science Fiction Critic.* His brother **Groo Beck** (1914–1978; "Groo" was mother's surname) edited some of the later issues of the magazine and printed *After Sunset* (1939), a posthumous collection of the poetry of George Sterling, edited by RHB. **Clyde F. Beck** (1912–1986), fan and critic who wrote the first work of criticism devoted to American science fiction: *Hammer and Tongs* (1937), assembled from four essays and reviews contributed to *The Science Fiction Critic.* With Roy A. Squires, he published CAS's *The Hill of Dionysus: A Selection* (1962). The brothers constituted The Futile Press, which published CAS's *Nero and Other Poems* (1937) and H. P. Lovecraft's *Notes and Commonplace Book* (1938, edited by RHB). RHB lived with the Becks briefly before attending college.

Cook, W. Paul (1880–1948) of Athol, MA, publisher of the *Monadnock Monthly,* the *Vagrant,* the *Recluse,* and other amateur journals and proprietor of the Recluse Press. He published poetry books by Donald Wandrei, Frank Belknap Long, and Samuel Loveman and printed (but did not publish) H. P. Lovecraft's "The Shunned House." Clark Ashton Smith approached him about publishing *Sandalwood* but he was unable to do so.

Crawford, William L[evy] (1911–1984), editor of *Marvel Tales* and *Unusual Stories* and publisher of the Visionary Publishing Company, which issued HPL's *The Shadow Over Innsmouth* (1936).

De Casseres, Benjamin (1873–1945), poet, critic, long-time associate of CAS, and author of the preface to Smith's *SP.* **Bio** (Adele Mary Jones, née Terrill) **De Casseres** (1875?–1963) and Benjamin met in 1902. Bio divorced her husband Harry O. Jones in 1919 and married Benjamin that year. De Casseres published a collection of the letters written during their courtship, *The Love Letters of a Living Poet* (1931).

Derleth, August W[illiam] (1909–1971), author of weird tales and also a long series of regional and historical works set in his native Wisconsin. After HPL's death, he and Donald Wandrei founded the publishing firm of Arkham House to preserve HPL's work in book form. For the joint correspondence of HPL and Derleth, see *Essential Solitude.*

Dwyer, Bernard Austin (1897–1943), weird fiction enthusiast and would-be writer and artist, living in West Shokan, NY.

Eldridge, Paul (1888–1982), American poet, novelist, short story writer and teacher. Best known for collaborating with George Sylvester Viereck on a trilogy of exotic fantasy novels from 1928 to 1932.

French, Nora May (1881–1907), California poet and member of the bohemian literary circles of the Carmel Arts and Crafts Club. She died by suicide, and her friends published her *Poems* in 1910.

Galpin, Alfred (1901–1983), amateur journalist and correspondent of HPL. He studied music in Paris and was also a scholar in French literature.

Gamwell, Annie E[meline] P[hillips] (1866–1941), HPL's younger aunt, living with him at 66 College Street (1933–37).

Gernsback, Hugo (1884–1967), editor of *Amazing Stories, Wonder Stories,* and other pioneering science fiction pulps.

Greene, Madelynne F. (1907–1970), dancer, artist, and wife of Eric Barker. In 1962, she founded the Mendocino Folklore Camp. CAS dedicated *Selected Poems* to her and Eric Barker. According to Greene, CAS "dedicated *The Hill of Dionysus* to me." CAS referred to her in his poems as "Bacchante."

Hall, Desmond (1909–1992), assistant editor of *Astounding Stories of Super-Science* under Harry Bates, and also under F. Orlin Tremaine when Street and Smith revived the magazine as *Astounding Stories.*

Hamilton, Edmond (1904–1977), popular and prolific author of "weird-scientific" stories for *Weird Tales.*

Hearn, Patrick Lafcadio (1850–1904), international writer born in Greece. Known in the U.S. for his writings about the city of New Orleans based on his ten-year stay in that city. Best known for his books about Japan, especially collections of Japanese legends and ghost stories, such as *Kwaidan: Stories and Studies of Strange Things.*

Hornig, Charles D[erwin] (1916–1999), editor of the *Fantasy Fan* (1933–35) and associate editor of *Wonder Stories.*

Howard, Robert E[rvin] (1906–1936), prolific Texas author of weird and adventure tales for *Weird Tales* and other pulp magazines; creator of the adventure hero Conan the Cimmerian. He and HPL corresponded voluminously from 1930 to 1936. He committed suicide when he heard of his mother's impending death.

Jacobi, Carl (1908–1997), of Minneapolis, prolific author of weird, weird menace, and science fiction stories for the pulp magazines. Undergraduate classmate of Donald Wandrei at University of Minnesota from 1927 to 1930. His early writings appeared in the *Minnesota Quarterly.*

Kirk, George W[illard] (1898–1962) corresponded with CAS in 1920–22. He was a close friend of HPL and presented HPL with a copy of *OS.*

Kleiner, Rheinhart (1882–1949), amateur poet and longtime friend of HPL. He visited HPL in Providence in 1918, 1919, and 1920, and met him frequently during the heyday of the Kalem Club (1924–26).

Kline, Otis Adelbert (1891–1946), prolific writer for *Weird Tales* and other pulp magazines; also a literary agent for Robert E. Howard and others.

Leeds, Arthur (1882–1952?), an associate of H. P. Lovecraft in New York and member of the Kalem Club. He was the author (with J. Berg Esenwein) of *Writing the Photoplay* (1913).

Long, Frank Belknap (1901–1994), fiction writer and poet; close friend and correspondent of H. P. Lovecraft and member of the Kalem Club. RHB published his book, *The Goblin Tower.*

Lovecraft, H[oward] P[hillips] (1890–1937), pioneering writer of weird fiction who came into correspondence with CAS in 1922. They never met. Lovecraft also corresponded with DW, HW, and RHB.

Loveman, Samuel (1887–1976), poet, writer, and bookdealer, and member of the Kalem Club. He corresponded with Ambrose Bierce, George Sterling, CAS, H. P. Lovecraft, and several other well-known writers, including Hart Crane. Loveman introduced HPL to the work of CAS, and it was through Loveman that HPL began corresponding with him. CAS dedicated *Ebony and Crystal* to him.

Markham, Edwin (1852–1940), American poet and associate of George Sterling and Ambrose Bierce. From 1923 to 1931 he was Poet Laureate of Oregon. His most famous poem was "The Man with the Hoe" (1898).

Merritt, A[braham] (1884–1943), writer of fantasy and horror tales for the pulps.

Monroe, Harriet (1860–1936), poet and editor, founded *Poetry: A Magazine of Verse* in 1912. Although she published some poems by CAS and George Sterling, she preferred the Modernist poets (Eliot, Pound, and the like).

Moore, C[atherine] L[ucille] (1911–1987), prolific American science fiction and fantasy writer. Married to Henry Kuttner, with whom she collaborated on many stories published pseudonymously.

Morton, James Ferdinand (1870–1941), amateur journalist, author of many tracts on race prejudice, free thought, and taxation, longtime friend of H. P. Lovecraft, and member of the Kalem Club.

Munn, H[arold] Warner (1903–1981), prolific contributor to the pulp magazines, living near W. Paul Cook in Athol, MA.

Nicolson, J[ohn] U[rban] (1885–1944), American poet and writer, author of *King of the Black Isles: Poems* (1924), an edition of the *Canterbury Tales* in modern English (1934), and the supernatural novel *Fingers of Fear* (1937).

Price, E[dgar] Hoffmann (1898–1988), prolific pulp writer of weird and adventure tales.

Saltus, Francis (1848–1889), American poet, musician, linguist, and scholar. Leader of a group of bohemians in New York that included his brother Edgar (1855–1921) and James Huneker.

Seymour, George Steele (1878–1945), American poet and head of a literary circle, the Bookfellows. He edited 12 volumes of *A Bookfellow Anthology* (1925–36).

Sterling, George (1869–1926), American poet, was the founder of the Carmel, CA, artists' colony, protégé of Ambrose Bierce, and CAS's mentor. He was an early champion of CAS's poetry and assisted CAS in proofreading *ST* (1912). CAS dedicated *Sandalwood* to him.

Sully, Genevieve K[noll] (1880–1970), close friend of CAS in Auburn. **Helen V. Sully Trimble** (1904–1997) and **Marion Sully Schenk** (1911–1994) were her daughters.

Swanson, Carl W. (1902–1974), a bookdealer from Washburn, ND, who wrote to several authors of weird and science fiction asking for contributions to a magazine he planned to publish, to be called the *Galaxy*. It was never realized.

Talman, Wilfred Blanch (1904–1986), correspondent of HPL and late member of the Kalem Club. HPL assisted Talman on his story "Two Black Bottles" (1926) and wrote "Some Dutch Footprints in New England" for Talman to publish in *De Halve Maen*, the journal of the Holland Society of New York. Late in life he wrote the memoir *The Normal Lovecraft* (1973).

Wandrei, Albert Christian (1872–1942), DW's father. Chief editor of West Publishing Company, America's leading publisher of law books.

Wandrei, David G. (1906–1959), DW's older brother. The only member of DW's family not interred at the Acacia Park Cemetery, Mendota Heights, MN.

Wandrei, Jeannette Adelaide Guernsey (1878–1972), DW's mother.

Wandrei, Jeannette Alberta (1913–1972), DW's sister.

Whitehead, Henry S[t. Clair] (1882–1932), author of weird and adventure tales, many of them set in the Virgin Islands. HPL corresponded with him and visited him in Florida in 1931. HPL wrote a brief eulogy of Whitehead for *Weird Tales*.

Wright, Farnsworth (1888–1940), editor of *Weird Tales* (1924–40). He rejected some of HPL's best work of the 1930s, only to publish it after HPL's death upon submittal by August Derleth. Referred to as Satrap Pharnabozus, Pharnabeezer, etc., by Smith and Lovecraft. Satrap signifies a petty or secondary ruler.

Chronology

Sender	Recipient	Number*	Date
Smith	D. Wandrei	CAS 1	11 December 1924
Smith	D. Wandrei	CAS 2	30 January 1925
Smith	D. Wandrei	CAS 3	25 June 1925
Smith	D. Wandrei	CAS 4	10 July 1925
Smith	D. Wandrei	CAS 5	4 August 1925
Smith	D. Wandrei	CAS 6	7 August 1925
Smith	D. Wandrei	CAS 7	25 August 1925
Smith	D. Wandrei	CAS 8	12 September 1925
Smith	D. Wandrei	CAS 9	27 September 1925
Smith	D. Wandrei	CAS 10	26 October 1925
Smith	D. Wandrei	CAS 11	15 November 1925
Smith	D. Wandrei	CAS 12	4 December 1925
Smith	D. Wandrei	CAS 13	1 January 1926
Smith	D. Wandrei	CAS 14	12 February 1926
Smith	D. Wandrei	CAS 15	18 April 1926
Smith	D. Wandrei	CAS 16	9 May 1926
Smith	D. Wandrei	CAS 17	4 July 1926
Smith	D. Wandrei	CAS 18	3 August 1926
Smith	D. Wandrei	CAS 19	23 August 1926
Smith	D. Wandrei	CAS 20	3 September 1926
D. Wandrei	Smith	CAS 21	18 September 1926
Smith	D. Wandrei	CAS 22	27 September 1926
Smith	D. Wandrei	CAS 23	26 October 1926
Smith	D. Wandrei	CAS 24	11 November 1926
Smith	D. Wandrei	CAS 25	13 November 1926
D. Wandrei	Smith	CAS 26	27 November 1926
Smith	D. Wandrei	CAS 27	6 December 1926
Smith	D. Wandrei	CAS 28	26 December 1926
D. Wandrei	Smith	CAS 29	28 December 1926
Smith	D. Wandrei	CAS 30	13 January 1927
D. Wandrei	Smith	CAS 31	20 January 1927
Smith	D. Wandrei	CAS 32	9 February 1927
Smith	D. Wandrei	CAS 33	13 March 1927
D. Wandrei	Smith	CAS 34	25 March 1927
Smith	D. Wandrei	CAS 35	5 April 1927

CAS = Smith/D. Wandrei series; RHB = Smith/Barlow; DW = D. Wandrei/Barlow; HW = H. Wandrei/Barlow

Sender	Recipient	Number	Date
D. Wandrei	Smith	CAS 36	14 April 1927
Smith	D. Wandrei	CAS 37	7 May 1927
D. Wandrei	Smith	CAS 38	26 May 1927
Smith	D. Wandrei	CAS 39	8 June 1927
D. Wandrei	Smith	CAS 40	7 July 1927
Smith	D. Wandrei	CAS 41	9 July 1927
D. Wandrei	Smith	CAS 42	15 July 1927
Smith	D. Wandrei	CAS 43	27 July 1927
D. Wandrei	Smith	CAS 44	11 August 1927
Smith	D. Wandrei	CAS 45	19 August 1927
D. Wandrei	Smith	CAS 46	24 August 1927
D. Wandrei	Smith	CAS 47	1 September 1927
D. Wandrei	Smith	CAS 48	5 September 1927
Smith	D. Wandrei	CAS 49	18 September 1927
D. Wandrei	Smith	CAS 50	22 September 1927
Smith	D. Wandrei	CAS 51	26 September 1927
D. Wandrei	Smith	CAS 52	2 October 1927
Smith	D. Wandrei	CAS 53	8 October 1927
D. Wandrei	Smith	CAS 54	16 October 1927
Smith	D. Wandrei	CAS 55	9 November 1927
Smith	D. Wandrei	CAS 56	10 December 1927
Smith	D. Wandrei	CAS 57	17 January 1928
Smith	D. Wandrei	CAS 58	9 February 1928
Smith	D. Wandrei	CAS 59	8 March 1928
Smith	D. Wandrei	CAS 60	13 April 1928
Smith	D. Wandrei	CAS 61	20 April 1928
Smith	D. Wandrei	CAS 62	26 August 1928
Smith	D. Wandrei	CAS 63	21 October 1928
Smith	D. Wandrei	CAS 64	26 November 1928
Smith	D. Wandrei	CAS 65	20 March 1929
D. Wandrei	Smith	CAS 66	11 May 1929
Smith	D. Wandrei	CAS 67	7 June 1929
Smith	D. Wandrei	CAS 68	17 September 1929
D. Wandrei	Smith	CAS 69	17 January 1930
Smith	D. Wandrei	CAS 70	24 January 1930
D. Wandrei	Smith	CAS 71	28 March 1930
Smith	D. Wandrei	CAS 72	4 June 1930
Smith	D. Wandrei	CAS 73	9 October 1930
Smith	D. Wandrei	CAS 74	18 November 1930
Smith	D. Wandrei	CAS 75	18 January 1931
Smith	D. Wandrei	CAS 76	24 March 1931
Smith	D. Wandrei	CAS 77	14 April 1931

Sender	Recipient	Number	Date
Smith	Barlow	RHB 1	8 June 1931
Smith	D. Wandrei	CAS 78	7 August 1931
D. Wandrei	Smith	CAS 79	18 August 1931
Smith	D. Wandrei	CAS 80	29 August 1931
Smith	D. Wandrei	CAS 81	14 September 1931
D. Wandrei	Smith	CAS 82	18 September 1931
Smith	D. Wandrei	CAS 83	7 October 1931
D. Wandrei	Smith	CAS 84	18 November 1931
Smith	D. Wandrei	CAS 85	21 November 1931
Smith	D. Wandrei	CAS 86	22 November 1931
D. Wandrei	Smith	CAS 87	22 December 1931
Smith	D. Wandrei	CAS 88	31 January 1932
Smith	D. Wandrei	CAS 89	17 February 1932
Smith	D. Wandrei	CAS 90	1 March 1932
Smith	D. Wandrei	CAS 91	2 April 1932
Smith	D. Wandrei	CAS 92	6 April 1932
Smith	D. Wandrei	CAS 93	14 April 1932
Smith	D. Wandrei	CAS 94	4 May 1932
Smith	D. Wandrei	CAS 95	1 September 1932
Smith	Barlow	RHB 2	1 September 1932
Barlow	Smith	RHB 3	14 September 1932
Smith	Barlow	RHB 4	30 September 1932
D. Wandrei	Smith	CAS 96	31 October 1932
Smith	D. Wandrei	CAS 97	10 November 1932
Smith	Barlow	RHB 5	17 November 1932
Barlow	Smith	RHB 6	30 November 1932
Smith	Barlow	RHB 7	13 December 1932
Barlow	D. Wandrei	DW 1	17 December 1932
D. Wandrei	Barlow	DW 2	22 December 1932
Smith	D. Wandrei	CAS 98	c. 24 December 1932
Barlow	D. Wandrei	DW 3	30 December 1932
Smith	Barlow	RHB 8	8 February 1933
Smith	Barlow	RHB 9	19 February 1933
Smith	Barlow	RHB 10	15 March 1933
Smith	Barlow	RHB 11	20 March 1933
Barlow	D. Wandrei	DW 4	28 March 1933
D. Wandrei	Barlow	DW 5	6 April 1933
Barlow	Smith	RHB 12	10 April 1933
D. Wandrei	Smith	CAS 99	24 May 1933
Smith	Barlow	RHB 13	31 May 1933
Smith	D. Wandrei	CAS 100	7 June 1933
Smith	D. Wandrei	CAS 101	15 June 1933

Sender	Recipient	Number	Date
Smith	D. Wandrei	CAS 102	28 June 1933
Smith	D. Wandrei	CAS 103	6 August 1933
Smith	Barlow	RHB 14	6 August 1933
D. Wandrei	Smith	CAS 104	20 August 1933
Smith	D. Wandrei	CAS 105	28 August 1933
Smith	D. Wandrei	CAS 106	c. September 1933
Smith	Barlow	RHB 15	19 September 1933
Smith	Barlow	RHB 16	4 October 1933
Smith	Barlow	RHB 17	25 October 1933
D. Wandrei	Smith	CAS 107	c. 20 December 1933
Barlow	Smith	RHB 18	1 November 1933
Smith	Barlow	RHB 19	16 November 1933
Smith	Barlow	RHB 20	17 November 1933
Barlow	Smith	RHB 21	19 November 1933
Smith	Barlow	RHB 22	5 December 1933
Barlow	Smith	RHB 23	13 December 1933
Barlow	Smith	RHB 24	13 December 1933
Smith	Barlow	RHB 25	30 December 1933
D. Wandrei	Smith	CAS 108	9 January 1934
Barlow	D. Wandrei	DW 6	10 January 1934
D. Wandrei	Smith	CAS 109	12 January 1934
Smith	D. Wandrei	CAS 110	23 January 1934
D. Wandrei	Barlow	DW 7	3 February 1934
Smith	Barlow	RHB 26	11 February 1934
Barlow	D. Wandrei	DW 8	19 February 1934
D. Wandrei	Smith	CAS 111	20 February 1934
Barlow	Smith	RHB 27	21 February 1934
Smith	Barlow	RHB 28	23 March 1934
Smith	D. Wandrei	CAS 112	24 March 1934
Barlow	Smith	RHB 29	29 March 1934
D. Wandrei	Barlow	DW 9	4 April 1934
Barlow	D. Wandrei	DW 10	8 April 1934
Smith	Barlow	RHB 30	30 April 1934
Smith	Barlow	RHB 31	1 May 1934
Barlow	D. Wandrei	DW 11	7 May 1924
Barlow	Smith	RHB 32	10 May 1934
Smith	Barlow	RHB 33	18 May 1934
Barlow	D. Wandrei	DW 12	19 May 1934
Smith	Barlow	RHB 34	19 May 1934
Smith	Barlow	RHB 35	21 May 1934
D. Wandrei	Barlow	DW 13	22 May 1934
H. Wandrei	Barlow	HW 1	23 May 1934

Sender	Recipient	Number	Date
Barlow	D. Wandrei	DW 14	26 May 1934
Barlow	H. Wandrei	HW 2	26 May 1934
Barlow	Smith	RHB 36	2 June 1934
Smith	Barlow	RHB 37	15 June 1934
Smith	Barlow	RHB 38	15 June 1934
H. Wandrei	Barlow	HW 3	15 June 1934
D. Wandrei	Barlow	DW 15	16 June 1934
Smith	Barlow	RHB 39	16 June 1934
Smith	Barlow	RHB 40	c. late June 1934
Barlow	D. Wandrei	DW 16	29 June 1934
Barlow	H. Wandrei	HW 4	29 June 1934
Barlow	H. Wandrei	HW 5	30 June 1934
H. Wandrei	Barlow	HW 6	3 July 1934
Smith	Barlow	RHB 39	8 July 1934
Barlow	H. Wandrei	HW 7	8 July 1934
Barlow	D. Wandrei	DW 17	19 July 1934
H. Wandrei	Barlow	HW 8	19 July 1934
D. Wandrei	Barlow	DW 18	21 July 1934
Barlow	H. Wandrei	HW 9	27 July 1934
Smith	Barlow	RHB 42	1 August 1934
Barlow	D. Wandrei	DW 19	10 August 1934
D. Wandrei	Barlow	DW 20	14 August 1934
H. Wandrei	Barlow	HW 10	20 August 1934
Barlow	H. Wandrei	HW 11	24 August 1934
Barlow	D. Wandrei	DW 21	30 August 1934
H. Wandrei	Barlow	HW 12	6 September 1934
Smith	Barlow	RHB 43	10 September 1934
Barlow	H. Wandrei	HW 13	c. September 1934
Smith	Barlow	RHB 44	12 September 1934
H. Wandrei	Barlow	HW 14	13 September 1934
D. Wandrei	Smith	CAS 113	3 October 1934
Smith	D. Wandrei	CAS 114	16 October 1934
D. Wandrei	Smith	CAS 115	20 October 1934
Smith	D. Wandrei	CAS 116	27 October 1934
H. Wandrei	Barlow	HW 15	30 November 1934
Smith	D. Wandrei	CAS 117	c. 20 December 1934
D. Wandrei	Smith	CAS 118	11 January 1935
Smith	D. Wandrei	CAS 119	11 January 1935
H. Wandrei	Barlow	HW 16	12 January 1935
Barlow	H. Wandrei	HW 17	mid-January 1935
H. Wandrei	Barlow	HW 18	15 January 1935
Smith	D. Wandrei	CAS 120	28 February 1935

Sender	Recipient	Number	Date
Smith	Barlow	RHB 45	2 April 1935
Barlow	Smith	RHB 46	15 June 1935
Smith	Barlow	RHB 47	mid- to late June 1935
Smith	D. Wandrei	CAS 121	24 June 1935
Barlow	Smith	RHB 48	28 August 1935
D. Wandrei	Smith	CAS 122	7 September 1935
D. Wandrei	Smith	CAS 123	21 September 1935
Barlow	Smith	RHB 49	28 September 1935
Smith	Barlow	RHB 50	3 October 1935
Smith	Barlow	RHB 51	c. November 1935
Smith	D. Wandrei	CAS 124	c. 15 December 1935
Smith	Barlow	RHB 52	c. January 1936
D. Wandrei	Smith	CAS 125	7 January 1936
D. Wandrei	Barlow	DW 22	7 January 1936
Barlow	D. Wandrei	DW 23	17 January 1936
D. Wandrei	Barlow	DW 24	22 January 1936
Barlow	D. Wandrei	DW 25	30 January 1936
Smith	Barlow	RHB 53	5 February 1936
Smith	D. Wandrei	CAS 126	6 March 1936
Smith	Barlow	RHB 54	1 June 1936
D. Wandrei	Smith	CAS 127	29 June 1936
Smith	D. Wandrei	CAS 128	23 [May] June 1936
Barlow	Smith	RHB 55	5 July 1936
D. Wandrei	Smith	CAS 129	15 July 1936
Smith	D. Wandrei	CAS 130	16 August 1936
Smith	D. Wandrei	CAS 131	7 September 1936
D. Wandrei	Barlow	DW 26	26 October 1936
Barlow	D. Wandrei	DW 27	2 November 1936
Smith	D. Wandrei	CAS 132	17 November 1936
Smith	Barlow	CAS 56	23 November 1936
D. Wandrei	Smith	CAS 133	8 December 1936
Barlow	Smith	RHB 57	19 December 1936
Smith	D. Wandrei	CAS 134	c. 20 December 1936
D. Wandrei	Barlow	DW 28	24 December 1936
Smith	D. Wandrei	CAS 135	23 March 1937
H. Wandrei	Barlow	HW 19	24 March 1937
Smith	D. Wandrei	CAS 136	3 April 1937
Barlow	Smith	RHB 58	4 April 1937
Smith	Barlow	RHB 59	8 April 1937
H. Wandrei	Barlow	HW 20	15 April 1937
D. Wandrei	Smith	CAS 137	19 April 1937
Barlow	D. Wandrei	DW 29	19 April 1937

Sender	Recipient	Number	Date
D. Wandrei	Barlow	DW 30	22 April 1937
Barlow	D. Wandrei	DW 31	24 April 1937
D. Wandrei	Barlow	DW 32	26 April 1937
H. Wandrei	Barlow	HW 21	27 April 1937
Barlow	D. Wandrei	DW 33	1 May 1937
Smith	Barlow	RHB 60	16 May 1937
Smith	D. Wandrei	CAS 138	17 May 1937
Barlow	Smith	RHB 61	4 July 1937
Smith	Barlow	RHB 62	12 July 1937
Barlow	D. Wandrei	DW 34	c. 21 July 1937
D. Wandrei	Barlow	DW 35	22 July 1937
Barlow	D. Wandrei	DW 36	16 August 1937
Smith	Barlow	RHB 63	9 September 1937
Barlow	Smith	RHB 64	18 October 1937
Smith	Barlow	RHB 65	5 December 1937
Barlow	Smith	RHB 66	14 February 1938
Barlow	Smith	RHB 67	28 March 1938
Smith	Barlow	RHB 68	10 May 1938
D. Wandrei	Barlow	DW 37	23 June 1938
Barlow	D. Wandrei	DW 38	25 June 1938
Barlow	D. Wandrei	DW 39	late June 1938
D. Wandrei	Barlow	DW 40	27 June 1938
Smith	Barlow	RHB 69	5 July 1938
D. Wandrei	Barlow	DW 41	5 July 1938
Barlow	D. Wandrei	DW 42	8 July 1938
Barlow	Smith	RHB 70	2 September 1938
D. Wandrei	Smith	CAS 139	26 September 1938
Smith	D. Wandrei	CAS 140	30 September 1938
D. Wandrei	Smith	CAS 141	2 October 1938
Barlow	Smith	CAS 71	c. early December 1938
Smith	D. Wandrei	CAS 142	10 December 1938
Smith	Barlow	RHB 72	c. mid-December 1938
Barlow etc.	D. Wandrei	DW 43	3 July 1939
Smith	D. Wandrei	CAS 143	25 July 1941
Smith	D. Wandrei	CAS 144	29 October 1941
D. Wandrei	Smith	CAS 145	18 January 1942
D. Wandrei	Smith	CAS 146	14 April 1942
D. Wandrei	Smith	CAS 147	24 February 1943
D. Wandrei	Smith	CAS 148	27 February 1943
D. Wandrei	Smith	CAS 149	18 July 1943
Smith	D. Wandrei	CAS 150	13 August 1944
Smith	D. Wandrei	CAS 151	9 September 1944

Sender	Recipient	Number	Date
D. Wandrei	Smith	CAS 152	14 March 1946
D. Wandrei	Smith	CAS 153	2 October 1946
Smith	D. Wandrei	CAS 154	8 October 1946
D. Wandrei	Smith	CAS 155	27 June 1948
Smith	D. Wandrei	CAS 156	17 October 1948
Smith	D. Wandrei	CAS 157	20 October 1949
D. Wandrei	Smith	CAS 158	17 November 1949
Smith	D. Wandrei	CAS 159	22 November 1949
D. Wandrei	Smith	CAS 160	1 December 1949
Smith	D. Wandrei	CAS 161	10 December 1949
D. Wandrei	Smith	CAS 162	10 August 1950
D. Wandrei	Smith	CAS 163	1 November 1950
D. Wandrei	Smith	CAS 164	8 November 1950
D. Wandrei	Smith	CAS 165	12 November 1950
D. Wandrei	Smith	CAS 166	26 November 1950
D. Wandrei	Smith	CAS 167	13 December 1950
D. Wandrei	Smith	CAS 168	14 May 1951
D. Wandrei	Smith	CAS 169	9 November 1955
D. Wandrei	Smith	CAS 170	17 October 1957

Bibliography

A. Works by Clark Ashton Smith

Books

The Abominations of Yondo. Sauk City, WI: Arkham House, 1960. *Contents:* The Nameless Offspring; The Witchcraft of Ulua; The Devotee of Evil; The Epiphany of Death; A Vintage from Atlantis; The Abominations of Yondo; The White Sybil; The Ice-Demon; The Voyage of King Euvoran; The Master of the Crabs; The Enchantress of Sylaire; The Dweller in the Gulf; The Dark Age; The Third Episode of Vathek (with William Beckford); Chinoiserie; The Mirror in the Hall of Ebony; The Passing of Aphrodite.

The Averoigne Chronicles: The Complete Averoigne Stories of Clark Ashton Smith. Edited by Ronald S. Hilger. New York: Hippocampus Press, 2021.

The Black Book of Clark Ashton Smith. Edited by D. Sidney-Fryer and Rah Hoffman. Sauk City, WI: Arkham House, 1979.

Born under Saturn: The Letters of Clark Ashton Smith and Samuel Loveman. Edited by S. T. Joshi and David E. Schultz. New York: Hippocampus Press, 2020.

The Collected Fantasies. Edited by Scott Connors and Ron Hilger, San Francisco: Night Shade Books.

> *Volume 1: The End of the Story* (2006). *Contents:* Introduction by Ramsey Campbell; A Note on the Texts [by Connors and Hilger]; To the Daemon; The Abominations of Yondo; Sadastor; The Ninth Skeleton; The Last Incantation; The End of the Story; The Phantoms of the Fire; A Night in Malnéant; The Resurrection of the Rattlesnake; Thirteen Phantasms; The Venus of Azombeii; The Tale of Satampra Zeiros; The Monster of the Prophecy; The Metamorphosis of the World; The Epiphany of Death; A Murder in the Fourth Dimension; The Devotee of Evil; The Satyr; The Planet of the Dead; The Uncharted Isle; Marooned in Andromeda; The Root of Ampoi; The Necromantic Tale; The Immeasurable Horror; A Voyage to Sfanomoë; *Appendixes:* Story Notes [by Connors and Hilger]; The Satyr: Alternate Conclusion; From the Crypts of Memory; Bibliography; About the Editors.

> *Volume 2: The Door to Saturn* (2007). *Contents:* Introduction by Tim Powers; A Notes on the Texts [by Connors and Hilger]; The Door to Saturn; The Red World of Polaris; Told in the Desert; The Willow Landscape; A Rendezvous in Averoigne; The Gorgon; An Offering to the Moon; The Kiss of Zoraida; The Face by the River; The Ghoul; The Kingdom of the Worm; An Adventure in Futurity; The Justice of the Elephant; The Return of the Sorcerer; The City of the Singing Flame; A

Good Embalmer; The Testament of Athammaus; A Captivity in Serpens; The Letter from Mohaun Los; The Hunters from Beyond; *Appendixes:* Story Notes [by Connors and Hilger]; Alternate Ending to 'The Return of the Sorcerer'; Bibliography; About the Editors,

Volume 3: A Vinage from Atlantis (2007). *Contents:* Introduction by Michael Dirda; A Note on the Texts [by Connors and Hilger]; The Holiness of Azédarac; The Maker of Gargoyles; Beyond the Singing Flame; Seedling of Mars; The Vaults of Yoh-Vombis; The Eternal World; The Demon of the Flower; The Nameless Offspring; A Vintage from Atlantis; The Weird of Avoosl Wuthoqquan; The Invisible City; The Immortals of Mercury; The Empire of the Necromancers; The Seed from the Sepulcher; The Second Interment; Ubbo-Sathla; The Double Shadow; The Plutonian Drug; The Supernumerary Corpse; The Colossus of Ylourgne; The God of the Asteroid; *Appendixes:* Story Notes [by Connors and Hilger]; The Flower-Devil; Bibliography.

Volume 4: The Maze of the Enchanter (2009). *Contents:* Introduction by Gahan Wilson; A Note on the Texts [by Connors and Hilger]; The Mandrakes; The Beast of Averoigne; A Star-Change; The Disinterment of Venus; The White Sybil; The Ice-Demon; The Isle of the Torturers; The Dimension of Chance; The Dweller in the Gulf; The Maze of the Enchanter; The Third Episode of Vathek; Genius Loci; The Secret of the Cairn; The Charnel God; The Dark Eidolon; The Voyage of King Euvoran; Vulthoom; The Weaver in the Vault; The Flower-Women; *Appendixes:* Story Notes [by Connors and Hilger]; Alternate Ending to 'The White Sybil'; The Muse of Hyperborea; The Dweller in the Gulf: Added Material; Bibliography.

Volume 5: The Last Hieroglyph (2010). *Contents:* Introduction by Richard A. Lupoff; A Note on the Texts [by Connors and Hilger]; The Dark Age; The Death of Malygris; The Tomb-Spawn; The Witchcraft of Ulua; The Coming of the White Worm; The Seven Geases; The Chain of Aforgomon; The Primal City; Xeethra; The Last Hieroglyph; Necromancy in Naat; The Treader of the Dust; The Black Abbot of Puthuum; The Death of Ilalotha; Mother of Toads; The Garden of Adompha; The Great God Awto; Strange Shadows; The Enchantress of Sylaire; Double Cosmos; Nemesis of the Unfinished; The Master of the Crabs; Morthylla; Schizoid Creator; Monsters in the Night; Phoenix; The Theft of the Thirty-nine Girdles; Symposium of the Gorgon; The Dart of Rasasfa; *Appendixes:* Story Notes [by Connors and Hilger]; Variant Temptation Scenes from 'The Witchcraft of Ulua'; The Traveller; Material Removed from 'The Black Abbot of Puthuum'; Alternate Ending to 'I Am Your Shadow'; Alternate Ending to 'Nemesis of the Unfinished'; Bibliography.

The Complete Poetry and Translations. Edited by S. T. Joshi and David E. Schultz. New York: Hippocampus Press.

    1. *The Abyss Triumphant,* 2008.
    2. *The Wine of Summer,* 2008.
    3. *The Flowers of Evil and Others,* 2007.
The Dark Chateau. Sauk City, WI: Arkham House, 1951.
Dawnward Spire, Lonely Hill: The Letters of H. P. Lovecraft and Clark Ashton Smith. Edited by David E. Schultz and S. T. Joshi. New York: Hippocampus Press, 2017.
The Devil's Notebook: Collected Epigrams and Pensées of Clark Ashton Smith. Compiled by D. Sidney-Fryer. Edited by Don Herron. Mercer Island, WA: Starmont House, 1990.
The Double Shadow and Other Fantatasies. Auburn, CA: [Auburn Journal Print,] 1933. *Contents:* The Voyage of King Euvoran; The Maze of the Enchanter; The Double Shadow; A Night in Malnéant; The Devotee of Evil; The Willow Landscape.
Ebony and Crystal: Poems in Verse and Prose. Auburn, CA: Auburn Journal, 1922.
Eccentric, Impractical Devils: The Letters of Clark Ashton Smith and August Derleth. Ed. David E. Schultz and S. T. Joshi. New York: Hippocampus Press, 2020.
Genius Loci and Other Tales. Sauk City, WI: Arkham House, 1948. *Contents:* Genius Loci; The Willow Landscape; The Ninth Skeleton; The Phantoms of the Fire; The Eternal World; Vulthoom; A Star-Change; The Primal City; The Disinterment of Venus; The Colossus of Ylourgne; The Satyr; The Garden of Adompha; The Charnel God; The Black Abbot of Puthuum; The Weaver in the Vault.
Grotesques and Fantastiques. Saddle River, NJ: Gerry de La Ree. 1973.
The Hill of Dionysus: A Selection. Pacific Grove, CA: [Roy A. Squires,] 1962.
In the Realms of Mystery and Wonder: Collected Prose Poems and Artwork of Clark Ashton Smith. Ed. Scott Connors. Lakewood, CO: Centipede Press, 2017.
The Last Oblivion: Best Fantastic Poems of Clark Ashton Smith. Edited by S. T. Joshi and David E. Schultz. New York: Hippocampus Press, 2003.
Lost Worlds. Sauk City, WI: Arkham House, 1944. *Contents:* The Tale of Satampra Zeiros; The Door to Saturn; The Seven Geases; The Coming of the White Worm; The Last Incantation; A Voyage to Sfanomoë; The Death of Malygris; The Holiness of Azédarac; The Beast of Averoigne; The Empire of the Necromancers; The Isle of the Torturers; Necromancy in Naat; Xeethra; The Maze of Maâl Dweb; The Flower-Women; The Demon of the Flower; The Plutonian Drug; The Planet of the Dead; The Gorgon; The Letter from Mohaun Los; The Light from Beyond; The Hunters from Beyond; The Treader of the Dust.
The Miscellaneous Writings of Clark Ashton Smith. Edited by Scott Connors and Ron Hilger. San Francisco: Night Shade Books, 2011. *Contents:* Foreword, by Connors and Hilger; Introduction: The Sorcerer Departs, by D. Sidney-Fryer; The Animated Sword; The Red Turban; Prince Alcouz and

the Magician; The Malay Krise; The Ghost of Mohammed Din; The Mahout; The Rajah and the Tiger; Something New; The Flirt; The Perfect Woman; A Platonic Entanglement; The Expert Lover; The Parrot; A Copy of Burns; Checkmate; The Infernal Star; Dawn of Discord; House of the Monoceros; *The Dead Will Cuckold You; The Hashish-Eater; or, The Apocalypse of Evil;* Bibliography; O Amor atque Realitas! Clark Ashton Smith's First Adult Fiction, by D. Sidney-Fryer.

Nero and Other Poems. Lakeport, CA: The Futile Press, May 1937.

Odes and Sonnets. San Francisco: Book Club of California, 1918.

Out of Space and Time. Sauk City, WI: Arkham House, 1942. *Contents:* Clark Ashton Smith: Master of Fantasy, by August Derleth and D. Wandrei; The End of the Story; A Rendezvous in Averoigne; A Night in Malnéant; The City of the Singing Flame; The Uncharted Isle; The Second Interment; The Double Shadow; The Chain of Aforgomon; The Dark Eidolon; The Last Hieroglyph; Sadastor; The Death of Ilalotha; The Return of the Sorcerer; The Testament of Athammaus; The Weird of Avoosl Wuthoqquan; Ubbo-Sathla; The Monster of the Prophecy; The Vaults of Yoh-Vombis; From the Crypts of Memory; The Shadows.

Other Dimensions. Sauk City, WI: Arkham House, 1970. Futurity; The Immeasurable Horror; The Invisible City; The Dimension of Chance; The Metamorphosis of Earth; Phoenix; The Necromantic Tale; The Venus of Azombeii; The Resurrection of the Rattlesnake; The Supernumerary Corpse; The Mandrakes; Thirteen Phantasms; An Offering to the Moon; Monsters in the Night; The Malay Krise; The Ghost of Mohammed Din; The Mahout; The Raja and the Tiger; Something New; The Justice of the Elephant; The Kiss of Zoraida; A Tale of Sir John Maundeville; The Ghoul; Told in the Desert.

The Red World of Polaris: The Adventures of Captain Volmar. Edited by Ronald S. Hilger and Scott Connors. San Francisco: Night Shade Books, 2003. *Contents:* The Magellan of the Constellations (introduction), by Hilger and Connors; Marooned in Andromeda; A Captivity in Serpens; The Red World of Polaris; The Ocean-World of Alioth; Captain Volmar and Crew: An Afterword, by D. Sidney-Fryer.

Sandalwood. Auburn, CA: Auburn Journal, 1925.

The Shadow of the Unattained: The Letters of George Sterling and Clark Ashton Smith. Edited by David E. Schultz and S. T. Joshi. New York: Hippocampus Press, 2005.

Selected Poems. Sauk City, WI: Arkham House, 1971. Prepared in the late 1940s.

Spells and Philtres. Sauk City, WI: Arkham House, 1958.

The Star-Treader and Other Poems. San Francisco: A. M. Robertson, 1912.

Strange Shadows: The Uncollected Fiction and Essays of Clark Ashton Smith. Ed. Steve Behrends with D. Sidney-Fryer and Rah Hoffman. Westport, CT: Greenwood Press, 1989.

Tales of Science and Sorcery. Sauk City, WI: Arkham House, 1964. *Contents:* Clark Ashton Smith: A Memoir by E. Hoffmann Price; Master of the Asteroid; The Seed from the Sepulcher; The Root of Ampoi; The Immortals of Mercury; Murder in the Fourth Dimension; Seedling of Mars; The Maker of Gargoyles; The Great God Awto; Mother of Toads; The Tomb-Spawn; Schizoid Creator; Symposium of the Gorgon; The Theft of the Thirty-Nine Girdles; Morthylla.

The Unexpurgated Clark Ashton Smith. Series editor, Steve Behrends. West Warwick, RI: Necronomicon Press. Comprises: *The Dweller in the Gulf* (1987); *The Monster of the Prophecy* (1988); *Mother of Toads* (1987); *The Vaults of Yoh-Vombis* (1988); *The Witchcraft of Ulua* (1988); *Xeethra* (1988).

Zothique: The Final Cycle, ed. Ron Hilger. New York: Hippocampus Press, 2022.

Stories

"The Abominations of Yondo." *Overland Monthly* 84, No. 4 (April 1926): 100–101, 114, 126. In *AY, CF* 1.

"An Adventure in Futurity." *Wonder Stories* 2, No. 11 (April 1931): 1230–51, 1328. In *OD, CF* 2.

"Alkahest" (syn.). In *BB.*

"The Amazing Planet." See "A Captivity in Serpens."

"The Beast of Averoigne." *WT* 21, No. 5 (May 1933): 628–35. In *LW, CF* 4.

"Beyond the Singing Flame." *Wonder Stories* 3, No. 6 (November 1931): 752–61. *Tales of Wonder* No. 10 (Spring 1940): 6–31 (combined with "The City of the Singing Flame"). In *OST. Startling Stories* 11, No. 1 (Summer 1944): 90–99. In *CF* 3.

"The Black Abbot of Puthuum." *WT* 27, No. 3 (March 1936): 308–22. In *GL, CF* 5.

"The Cairn." See "The Secret of the Cairn."

"A Captivity in Serpens." *Wonder Stories Quarterly* 2, No. 4 (Summer 1931): 534–51, 569 (as "The Amazing Planet"). In *RW, CF* 2.

"The Chain of Aforgomon." *WT* 26, No. 6 (December 1935): 695–706. In *OST, CF* 5.

"The City of the Singing Flame." *Wonder Stories* 3, No. 2 (July 1931): 202–13. *Tales of Wonder* No. 10 (Spring 1940): 6–31 (combined with "Beyond the Singing Flame"). *Startling Stories* 5, No. 1 (January 1941): 98–106. In *OST* (combined with "Beyond the Singing Flame"), *CF* 2.

"The Colossus of Ylourgne." *WT* 23, No. 6 (June 1934): 696–720. In *GL, CF* 3.

"The Coming of the White Worm." *Stirring Science Stories* 1, No. 2 (April 1931): 105–14. In *LW, CF* 5.

"The Death of Ilalotha." *WT* 30, No. 3 (September 1937): 323–30. In *OST, CF* 5.

"The Death of Malygris." *WT* 30, No. 3 (April 1934): 488–96. In *LW, CF* 5.

"The Demon of the Flower." *Astounding Stories* 12, No. 4 (December 1933): 131–38. In *LW, CF* 3.

"The Devotee of Evil." In *DS. Stirring Fantasy Fiction* (February 1941): 109–17. In *AY*, *CF* 1.

"The Disinterment of Venus." *WT* 24, No. 1 (July 1934): 112–17. In *GL*, *CF* 4.

"The Door to Saturn." *Strange Tales of Mystery and Terror* 1, No. 3 (January 1932): 390–403. In *LW*, *CF* 2.

"The Double Shadow." In *DS. WT* (Feb. 1939). In *OST*, *CF* 3.

"The Dweller in the Gulf." *Wonder Stories* 4, No. 10 (March 1933): 768–75 (as "The Dweller in Martian Depths"). In *CF* 4.

"The Eidolon of the Blind." See "The Dweller in the Gulf."

"The Empire of the Necromancers." *WT* 20, No. 3 (September 1932): 338–44. In *LW*, *CF* 3.

"The End of the Story." *WT* 15, No. 5 (May 1930): 637–48. In *OST*, *CF* 1.

"The Epiphany of Death." *FF* 1, No. 11 (July 1934): 165–68. In *AY*, *CF* 1.

"The Eternal World." *Wonder Stories* 3, No. 10 (March 1932): 1130–37. In *GL*, *CF* 3.

"The Flower-Women." *WT* 25, No. 5 (May 1935): 624–32. In *LW*, *CF* 4.

"The Garden of Adompha," *WT* 31, No. 6 (June 1938): 393–400. In *GL*, *CF*.

"Genius Loci." *WT* 21, No. 6 (June 1933): 747–58. In *GL*, *CF* 4.

"The Ghoul." *FF* 1, No. 5 (January 1934): 69–72. In *OD*, *CF* 2.

"The Ghost of Mohammed Din." *Overland Monthly* 51, No. 5 (November 1910): 519–22. In *OD*, *MW*.

"The Gorgon." *WT* 19, No. 4 (April 1932): 551–58. In *LW*, *CF* 2. Original title: "Medusa" or "Medusa's Head."

"Helman Carnby." See "The Return of the Sorcerer."

"The Holiness of Azédarac," *WT* 22, No. 5 (November 1933): 594–607. In *LW*, *CF*.

"The House of Haon-Dor." *Crypt of Cthulhu* No. 27 (Hallowmas 1984 [special issue: *Untold Tales*]): 12–14. In *SS*.

"The Hunters from Beyond." *Strange Tales of Mystery and Terror* 2, No. 3 (October 1932): 292–303. In *LW*, *CF* 2.

"In a Hashish-Dream" (frag.). *Crypt of Cthulhu* No. 27 (Hallowmas 1984 [special issue: *Untold Tales*]): 15–16. In *SS*.

"The Ice-Demon." *WT* 21, No. 4 (April 1933): 484–94. In *AY*, *CF* 4.

"The Immeasurable Horror." *WT* 18, No. 2 (September 1931): 233–42. In *OD*, *CF* 1.

"The Immortals of Mercury." *The Immortals of Mercury*. New York: Stellar Publishing Corp., 1932. In *TSS*, *CF* 3.

"The Infernal Star." In *SS*, *MW*.

"The Invisible City." *Wonder Stories* 4, No. 1 (June 1932): 6–13. In *OD*, *CF* 3.

"The Isle of the Torturers." *WT* 21, No. 3 (March 1933): 362–72. In Christine Campbell Thomson, ed. *Keep On the Light!* London: Selwyn & Blount, 1933. 237–54; *LW*, *CF* 4.

"The Kingdom of the Worm." *FF* 1, No. 2 (October 1933): 17–22. In *OD* (as "A Tale of Sir John Maundeville"), *CF* 2.

"The Last Hieroglyph," *WT* 25, No. 4 (April 1935): 466–77. In *OST, CF.*

"The Last Incantation." *WT* 15, No. 6 (June 1930): 783–86. In *LW, CF* 1.

"The Letter from Mohaun Los." *Wonder Stories* 4, No. 3 (August 1932): 218–29 (as "Flight into Super-Time"). In *LW, CF* 2.

"The Light from Beyond." See "The Secret of the Cairn."

"The Mahout." *Black Cat* 16, No. 11, (August 1911): 25–30. In *OD, MW.*

"The Maker of Gargoyles." *WT* 20, No. 2 (August 1932): 198–207. In *TSS, CF* 3.

"The Malay Krise." *Overland Monthly* 51, No. 4 (October 1910): 354–55. In *OD, MW.*

"Marooned in Andromeda." *Wonder Stories* 2, No. 5 (October 1930): 390–401, 465. In *OD, RW, CF* 1.

"The Martian." See "The Seedling of Mars."

"The Master of Destruction." *Crypt of Cthulhu* No. 27 (Hallowmas 1984 [special issue: *Untold Tales*]): 28–31. In *SS.*

"The Maze of Maal Dweb" *DS* (as "The Maze of the Enchanter"); rpt. *WT* 32, No. 4 (October 1938): 475–83. In *LW, CF* 4 (as "The Maze of the Enchanger").

"Medusa." See "The Gorgon."

"The Metamorphosis of the World." *WT* 43, No. 6 (September 1951): 62–79 (as "The Metamorphosis of Earth"). In *OD* (as "The Metamorphosis of Earth"), *CF* 1.

"The Monster of the Prophecy." *WT* 19, No. 1 (January 1932): 8–31. In *OST, CF* 1.

"Morthylla." *WT* 45, No. 2 (May 1953): 41–46. In *TSS, CF* 5.

"Mother of Toads," *WT* 32, No. 1 (July 1938): 86–90; In *TSS, CF* 5.

"Murder in the Fourth Dimension." *Amazing Detective Tales* 1, No. 10 (October 1930): 908–37. In *TSS, CF* 1.

"The Nameless Offspring." *Strange Tales of Mystery and Terror* 2, No. 2 (June 1932): 264–76. In *AY, CF* 3.

"Necromancy in Naat." *WT* 28, No. 1 (July 1936): 2–15. In *LW, CF* 5.

"A Night in Malnéant." In *DS. WT* 34, No. 3 (September 1939): 102–5. In *OST, CF* 1.

"The IX Chapter of Eibon." See "The Coming of the White Worm."

"The Ninth Skeleton." *WT* 12, No. 3 (September 1928): 363–66. In *GL, CF* 1.

"The Planet Entity." See "The Seedling of Mars."

"The Plutonian Drug." *Amazing Stories* 9, No. 5 (September 1934): 41–48. In *LW, CF* 3.

"The Raja and the Tiger." *Black Cat* 17, No. 5 (February 1912): 12–18. In *OD, MW.*

"The Red World of Polaris." In *RW, CF* 2.

"A Rendezvous in Averoigne." *WT* 17, No. 3 (April–May 1931): 364–74. *WT* 33, No. 1 (January 1939): 112–22. In *OST, CF* 2.

"The Return of the Sorcerer." *Strange Tales of Mystery and Terror* 1, No. 1 (September 1931): 99–109. In *OST, CF* 2. Original title: "The Return of Helman Carnby."

"Sadastor." *WT* 16, No. 1 (July 1930): 133–35. In *OST, CF* 1.

"The Satyr." *La Paree Stories* 2, No. 5 (July 1931): 9–11, 48. In *GL, CF* 1.

"The Second Interment." *Strange Tales of Mystery and Terror* 3, No. 1 (January 1933): 8–16. In *OST, CF* 3.

"The Secret of the Cairn." *Wonder Stories* 4, No. 11 (April 1933): 823–29 (as "The Light from Beyond"). In *LW* (as "The Light from Beyond"), *CF* 4.

"The Seed from the Sepulcher." *WT* 22, No. 4 (October 1933): 497–505. In *TSS, CF* 3.

"Seedling of Mars." *Wonder Stories Quarterly* 3, No. 1 (Fall 1931): 110–25, 136 (as "The Planet Entity"). In *TSS, CF* 3. Originally titled "The Martian."

"The Seven Geases." *WT* 24, No. 4 (October 1934): 422–35. In *LW, CF* 5.

"Shapes of Adamant." In *SS*.

A Star-Change." *Wonder Stories* 4, No. 12 (May 1933): 962–69 (as "The Visitors from Mlok"). *Tales of Wonder and Super-Science* No. 15 (Autumn 1941): 57–67 (as "Escape to Mlok"). In *GL, CF*.

"The Supernumerary Corpse." *WT* 20, No. 5 (November 1932): 693–98. In *OD, CF* 3.

"The Tale of Satampra Zeiros." *WT* 18, No. 4 (November 1931): 491–99. In *LW, CF* 1.

"A Tale of Sir John Maundeville." See "The Kingdom of the Worm."

"The Testament of Athammaus." *WT* 20, No. 4 (October 1932): 509–21. In *OST, CF* 2.

"The Third Episode of Vathek" (with William Beckford). *Leaves* No. 1 (Summer 1937): 1–24. In *AY, CF* 4.

"The Tomb-Spawn." *WT* 23, No. 5 (May 1934): 634–40. In *TSS, CF* 5.

"The Treader in the Dust." *WT* 26, No. 2 (August 1935): 241–46. In *LW, CF* 5.

"Ubbo-Sathla." *WT* 22, No. 1 (July 1933): 112–16. In *OST, CF* 3.

"The Uncharted Isle." *WT* 16, No. 5 (November 1930): 605–8, 710–14. In *OST, CF*.

"The Vaults of Yoh-Vombis." *WT* 19, No. 5 (May 1932): 599–610. In *GL, CF* 3.

"A Vintage from Atlantis." *WT* 22, No. 3 (September 1933): 394–99. In *AY, CF* 3.

"The Voyage of King Euvoran." In *DS*. *WT* 39, No. 12 (September 1947): 4–13 (as "Quest of the Gazolba"; abridged). In *AY, CF* 4.

"A Voyage to Sfanomoë." *WT* 18, No. 1 (August 1931): 111–15. In *LW, CF* 1.

"The Weaver in the Vault." *WT* 23, No. 1 (January 1934): 85–93. In *GL, CF* 4.

"The Weird of Avoosl Wuthoqquan." *WT* 19, No. 6 (June 1932): 835–40. In *OST, CF* 3.

"The Willow Landscape," *Philippine Magazine* (May 1931). In *DS. WT* 34, No. 1 (June–July 1939): 87–90. In *GL* 21–25; *CF* 2.

"The Witchcraft of Ulua." *WT* 23, No. 2 (February 1934): 253–59. In *AY, CF* 5.

"Xeethra." *WT* 24, No. 6 (December 1934): 726–38. In *LW, CF* 5.

Prose Poems. All titles are in *In the Realms of Mystery and Wonder.*

"Chinoiserie." *Philippine Magazine* 27, No. 12 (November 1931): 728, 752, 756. *FF* 1, No. 8 (April 1934): 116 (as "Prose Pastels 1"). *Acolyte* 1, No. 4 (Summer 1943): 3. In *AY, PP.*

"From the Crypts of Memory." *Bohemia* 2, No. 3 (April 1917): 27. In *EC, OST. Fantasy Sampler* No. 4 (June 1956): 12–13. In *PP.*

"The Lotus and the Moon." *FF* 2, No. 1 (September 1934): 7 (as "Prose Pastels IV"). *Acolyte* 1, No. 4 (Summer 1943): 3. In *PP.*

"The Mirror in the Hall of Ebony." *FF* 1, No. 9 (May 1934): 140, 144 (as "Prose Pastels 2"). *Acolyte* 1, No. 4 (Summer 1943): 3–4. In *AY, PP*

"Offering." In *SS.*

"The Passing of Aphrodite." *FF* 2, No. 4 (December 1934): 59–60 (as "Prose Pastels: 5"). *Acolyte* 1, No. 4 (Summer 1943): 4–5. In *AY, PP.*

"The Shadows." In *EC, OST, PP.*

Plays

The Dead Will Cuckold You. In *In Memoriam: Clark Ashton Smith* (Baltimore: Mirage Press, 1963), *SS, CP* 2.

The Fugitives. In *CP* 1. Verse drama begun 17 September 1922 but never completed. CAS published four "songs" separately, as follows:

"The Song of Aviol." *AJ* 23, No. 25 (5 April 1923): 6. *Lyric West* 3, No. 11 (March 1924): 28. In *S, SP, SS* (as "Song").

"Song." *AJ* 23, No. 33 (31 May 1923): 6. *Wanderer* 2, No. 1 (January 1924): 1 (as "The Fugitive"). In *S, SP.*

"The Love-Potion." *AJ* 23, No. 29 (3 May 1923): 6. In *S. Step Ladder* 13, No. 5 (May 1927): 135. In *SP.*

"The Song of Cartha." *AJ* 23, No. 29 (3 May 1923): 6. *Wanderer* 2, No. 8 (August 1924): 103. In *S, SP.*

Poetry

"Alexandrines." In *OS, EC, SP, CP* 1.

"After Armageddon." *Recluse* No. 1 (1927): 15. In *CP* 1.

"Alienation." See "The Outer Land."

"Alternative." *Raven* 2, No. 2 (Summer 1944): 13. In *SP, S&P, CP* 2.

"Amor Autumnalis." In Derleth, *Dark of the Moon* (q.v.), *SP, CP* 1.

"Answer." In *CP* 2.

"Anteros." In *SP, S&P, CP* 2

"Apostrophe." In *SP, CP* 1.

"Au Bord tu Léthé." In *SP, CP* 2.

"The Autumn Lake." In *SP, CP* 2

"Bond." In *SP, HD, CP* 2.

"But Grant, O Venus." In *SP, CP* 2.

"Calendar." *Troubadour* 2, No. 6 (February 1930): 11. In *SP, CP* 2.

"Calenture." *Arkham Sampler* 2, No. 4 (Autumn 1949): 17–18. In *SP, DC, CP* 2.

"Cambion." In *SP, DC, CP* 2

"Canticle." *Troubadour* 3, No. 8 (July 1931): 26. In *SP, CP* 2.

"Chance." *Auburn Journal* 23, No. 35 (14 June 1923): 6. *Bloodstone* 1, No. 2 (November 1937): [4]. In *SP, CP* 1.

"Chanson de Novembre." In *CP* 2.

"Connaissance." In *SP, CP* 2.

"Concupiscence." In *SP, CP* 1.

"Credo." In *CP* 2.

"Cumuli." *Interludes* 8, No. 1 (Spring 1931): 11. In *SP, CP* 2.

"Dans l'universe lointain." In *CP* 2.

"The Dark Chateau." In *DC, CP* 2.

"Day-Dream." An English translation of "Rêvasserie." In *CP* 2.

"December." *Auburn Journal* 24, No. 8 (6 December 1923): 6. *Poetry* 33, No. 3 (December 1928): 123. In *SP, CP* 1.

"Desert Dweller," *WT* 36, No. 12 (July 1943): 71. In *SP, CP* 2.

"Dialogue." *WT* 36, No. 11 (May 1943): 67 (as by "Timeus Gaylord"). In *SP, S&P, CP* 2.

"Dissonance." *Thrill Book* 2, No. 6 (15 September 1919): 149. In *EC, SP, CP* 2.

"Dominion." *WT* 36, No. 11 (May 1943): 67 (as by "Timeus Gaylord"). In *SP, S&P, CP* 2.

"Dominium in Excelsis." In *DC, BB, CP* 2.

"Don Quixote on Market Street." In *DC, BB. WT* 45, No. 1 (March 1953): 11. In *CP* 2.

"The Dragon-Fly." In *SP, CP* 2.

"A Dream of the Abyss." *FF* 1, No. 3 (November 1933): 41. In *SP, CP* 2.

"Ennui." *WT* 27, No. 5 (May 1936): 547. In *SP, CP* 2.

"The Envoys." *AJ* 26, No. 13 (7 January 1926): 4. *Overland Monthly* 84, No. 5 (June 1926): frontispiece. *Overland Monthly* 84, No. 7 (July 1926): 230 (corrected version). In Derleth, *Dark of the Moon* (q.v.), *SP, CP* 1.

"L'Espoir du Néant." In *SP, CP* 2.

"Exorcism." *Troubadour* 3, No. 5 and 6 (February–March 1931): 6. In *SP, CP* 2.

"A Fable." *WT* 10, No. 1 (July 1927): 76. In *SP, CP* 2.

"Fantaisie d'Antan." *WT* 14, No. 6 (December 1929): 724. In *SP, CP* 2.

"Farewell to Eros." *WT* 31, No. 6 (June 1938): 759. In *SP, S&P, CP* 2.

"La Forteresse." In *CP* 2.

The Hashish Eater; or, The Apocalypse of Evil. In *EC; DM* 321–38; In *SP.*

"Hellenic Sequel." *Arkham Sampler* 1, No. 2 (Spring 1948): 12. In *DC, SP, CP* 2.

"Hesperian Fall." In *DC, HD, CP* 2.

The Hill-Top." In The Edwin Markham Poetry Society, ed. *The Laureate's Wreath: An Anthology in Honor of Dr. Henry Meade Bland, Poet Laureate of California.* San Jose: The Edwin Markham Poetry Society, 1934. 108. In Rufus Rockwell Wilson, ed. *The Golden Year: A Calendar of the Poets.* New York: Wilson-Erickson, 1936. 15. In Stanton A. Coblentz, ed. *The Music Makers.* New York: Bernard Ackerman, 1945. 225–26. In *SP, CP* 2.

"If Winter Remain." In *SP, CP* 2.

"Immortelle." *Auburn Journal* 25, No. 10 (18 December 1924): 14. In *CP* 1.

"In a Distant Universe." In *CP* 2.

"In Slumber." *WT* 24, No. 2 (August 1934): 253. In *CP* 2.

"In Thessaly." *WT* 26, No. 5 (November 1935): 551. In Derleth, *Dark of the Moon* (q.v.), *SP, CP* 2.

"Indian Summer." In *SP, CP* 2.

"Ineffability." In *SP, CP* 2.

"The Isle of Saturn." In *DC, BB, SZ.*

"Jungle Twilight." *Oriental Stories* 2, No. 3 (Summer 1932): 420 (15 lines only). In *SP, S&P, CP* 2.

"Lamia." *Arkham Sampler* 1, No. 1 (Winter 1948): 20. In *SP, DC, CP* 2.

"Lichens." *Wings* 1, No. 2 (Summer 1933): 7. In *SP, CP* 2.

"Lines on a Picture." *Raven* 2, No. 1 (Spring 1944): 22. In *SP, CP* 2.

"Un Madrigal." In *CP* 1.

"Madrigal of Evanescence." *Kaleidoscope* 2, No. 11 (March 1931): 3. In *SP, CP* 2.

"La Mare." In *SP, CP* 2.

"Le Marées." In *SP, CP* 2.

"The Medusa of Despair." *Town Talk* No. 1113 (20 December 1913): 8. In *OS, EC, SP, CP* 1.

"Le Miroir des Blanches Fleurs." In *CP* 2.

"The Mirrors of Beauty." In *EC, SP, CP* 1.

"Moly." *New Atheneum* (Fall 1950): [25]. In *SP, DC, CP* 2.

"Moon-Sight."

"Mors." In *SP* (as a translation of "Christophe des Laurières"), *CP* 1.

"Mystery." In *SP, CP* 2.

"Necromancy." *FF* 1, No. 12 (August 1934): 188. *WT* 36, No. 10 (March 1943): 105. In *SP, S&P, CP* 2.

"The Nereid." *Yale Review* 2, No. 4 (July 1913): 685–86. In *EC.* In *California Poets: An Anthology of 224 Contemporaries.* New York: Henry Harrison, 1932. 665. In *SP, CP* 1.

"The Nevermore-To-Be." In *SP, CP* 2.

"Night of Miletus." In *SP, CP* 2.

"Nightfall." *Auburn Journal* 24, No. 13 (10 January 1924): 13. In *CP* 1.

"The Nightmare Tarn." *WT* 14, No. 5 (November 1929): 624; in *SP, CP* 2.

"November." In *SP, CP* 2.

"Nyctalops." *WT* 14, No. 4 (October 1929): 516. In The Edwin Markham Poetry Society, ed. *The Laureate's Wreath: An Anthology in Honor of Dr. Henry Meade Bland, Poet Laureate of California.* San Jose: The Edwin Markham Poetry Society, 1934. 109. In Dudley Chadwick Gordon, Vernon Rupert King, and William Whittingham Lyman, ed. *Today's Literature.* New York: American Book Co., 1935. 449. In Derleth, *Dark of the Moon* (q.v.). In *SP, CP* 2.

"October." *Westward* 4, No. 5 (May 1935): 5. In Hans A. Hoffmann, ed. *Poets of the Western Scene.* San Leandro, CA: Greater West Publishing Company, 1937. 89. In *SP, S&P, CP* 1.

"Ode" [O young and dear and tender sorceress!]. *Agenbite of Inwit* 2, No. 4 (September 1945): [6]. *SP, HD, CP* 2.

"Ode on Imagination." In *ST, SP, CP* 1.

"The Old Water Wheel." *Poetry* 61, No. 3 (December 1942): 492. In *SP, DC, CP* 2.

"On a Chinese Vase." *Oriental Stories* 2, No. 2 (Spring 1932): 174. In *SP, CP* 2.

"One Evening." In *SP, CP* 2.

"Only to One Returned." *Arkham Sampler* 1, No. 4 (Autumn 1948): 13. In *SP, CP* 2.

"Ougabalys." *WT* 15, No. 1 (January 1930): 135. Later revised as "Tolometh." Both in *CP* 2.

"The Outer Land." *Supramundane Stories Quarterly* 1, No. 2 (Spring 1937): 3–4 (as "Alienation"). In *SP. Spearhead* 2, No. 2 (Spring 1951): 3–5. In *DC, CP* 2.

"Outlanders." In *Nero* (as one-page broadside). *WT* 31, No. 6 (June 1938): 746. In Derleth, *Dark of the Moon* (q.v.), *SP, CP* 2.

"Paysage Païen." In *SP, CP* 2.

"The Phoenix." *WT* 35, No. 3 (May 1940): 94. In *SP, S&P, CP* 2.

"Pour chercher du nouveau." *Arkham Sampler* 2, No. 4 (Autumn 1949): 28–29. In *SP, DC, CP* 2.

"The Prophet Speaks." *WT* 32, No. 3 (September 1938): 348–49. In *SP, S&P, CP* 2.

"The Pursuer" (Climbing from out what nadir-fountained sea,). In *SP. Portals* (November 1957): 7–9. In *CP* 2.

"Refuge." In *SP, CP* 2.

"Le Refuge." In *CP* 2.

"Resurrection." *WT* 39, No. 11 (July 1947): 85. In *DM* 345–46. In *SP, HD, CP* 2.

"Rêvasserie." In *CP* 2.

"Revenant." *FF* 1, No. 7 (March 1934): 106–7. In *SP, DC, CP* 2.

"The Saturnienne" [Beneath the skies of Saturn, pale and manymooned,]. *WT* 10, No. 6 (December 1927): 728. In *SP, CP* 2.

"Seeker." In *DC, SP* 2.

"September." In *SP, CP* 2.

"Shadows." *WT* 15, No. 2 (February 1930): 154. In *SP, CP* 2.

"Shapes in the Sunset." In *DC, BB, CP* 2.

"Silent Hour." *Wings* 5, No. 2 (Summer 1941): 15. In *SP, HD, CP* 2.

"Soliloquy in an Ebon Tower." In *DC, CP* 2.

"Some Blind Eidolon." *Kaleidograph* 19, No. 2 (June 1947): 2–3. In *SP, DC, CP* 2.

"Song" [Vagrant from the realms of rose,]. *Auburn Journal* 23, No. 33 (31 May 1923): 6. *Wanderer* 2, No. 1 (January 1924): 1 (as "The Fugitive").In *S, SP, CP* 1.

"Song at Evenfall." *Overland Monthly* 88, No. 5 (May 1930): 149. In *CP* 2.

"The Song of a Comet." In *ST, Nero, SP, CP* 1.

"Song of the Necromancer." *WT* 29, No. 2 (February 1937): 220. In *SP, CP* 2.

"Sonnet" [Empress with eyes more sad and aureate]. *WT* 13, No. 4 (April 1929): 542. In *SP, CP* 2.

"Sonnet for the Psychoanalysts." In *SP, DC. WT* 44, No. 2 (January 1952): 73. In *CP* 2.

"Sonnet Lunaire." In *CP* 1.

"Souvenance." In *CP* 2.

"Strange Girl." *Wings* 6, No. 3 (Autumn 1943): 12–13. In Stanton A. Coblentz, ed. *The Music Makers*. New York: Bernard Ackerman, 1945. 224–25. In *SP, CP* 2.

"Sufficiency." In *SP, CP* 2.

"A Sunset" [Far-falling from a wounded heaven,]. English translation of "Un Couchant." In *CP* 1.

"Surréalist Sonnet." In *SP, DC, CP* 2.

"Swine and Azaleas." See "The Thralls of Circe Climb Parnassus."

"Temporality." In *CP* 2.

"The Thralls of Circe Climb Parnassus." In *SP, CP* 2.

"To Antares." In *SP, CP* 2.

"To George Sterling" [Deep are the chasmal years and lustrums long]. In *SP, CP* 1.

"To George Sterling: A Valediction." *Overland Monthly* 85, No. 11 (November 1927): 338. In *SP, CP* 1.

"To Howard Phillips Lovecraft." *WT* 30, No. 1 (July 1937): 48. In Lovecraft, *Marginalia, SP, CP* 2.

"To Omar Khayyam." In *EC. Lyric West* 5, No. 8 (May–June 1926): 216–17. In *SP, CP* 2.

"To the Chimera." *AJ* 24, No. 25 (3 April 1924): 6; *United Amateur* 23, No. 1 (May 1924): 7. In *S. Helios* 1, No. 3 (August–September 1937): 10. *WT* 40, No. 6 (September 1948): 79. In *SP, CP* 1.

"To the Daemon Sublimity." In *SP;* Derleth, *Fire and Sleet and Candlelight* (q.v.); *CP* 1. First title: "To the Spirit Sublimity."

"Tolometh." In *SP, S&P, CP* 2. Final version of "Ougabalys" (q.v.).

"Touch." In *SP, CP* 2.

"Town Lights." *Wings* 5, No. 8 (Winter 1943): 15. In Stanton A. Coblentz, ed. *The Music Makers.* New York: Bernard Ackerman, 1945. 223–24. In *SP, CP* 2.

"Tristan to Iseult." *Westward* 4, No. 4 (April 1935): 7. In *SP* (as a translation from "Christophe des Laurières"). In *CP* 2.

"Trope." In *SP, CP* 2.

"The Unremembered." In *ST* (as "The Unrevealed"), *SP, CP* 1.

"The Unrevealed." See "The Unremembered."

"Vaticinations." In *SP, CP* 2.

"Venus." In *SP, CP* 2.

"Une Vie Spectrale." In *SP, CP* 2.

"Warning." *WT* 12, No. 4 (October 1928): 525. In Derleth, *Dark of the Moon* (q.v.), *SP, CP* 2. In *SP, CP* 2.

"We Shall Meet." *AJ* 23, No. 28 (26 April 1923): 6. *Wanderer* 2, No. 5 (May 1924): 60–61. In *S, SP, CP* 1.

"The Winds." In *ST, SP, CP* 1.

"Winter Moonlight" [After our fond, reiterate farewells]. In *SP, CP* 2.

"Witch-Dance." *WT* 36, No. 1 (September 1941): 104–5. In *The Hill of Dionysus, SP, CP* 2.

"The Witch With Eyes of Amber." *Auburn Journal* 23, No. 32 (24 May 1923): 6. *Agenbite of Inwit* 2, No. 5 (November 1945): [16]. *Epos* 1, No. 4 (Summer 1950): 14. In *SP, DC, CP* 1.

"Wizard's Love." *Alchemist* (1941; i.e., *Deventioneer Alchemist* [not seen]). *Golden Atom* No. 11 (1954–55): 91. In *The Hill of Dionysus, SP, CP* 2.

Translations from Charles Baudelaire. All titles are in *CP* 3.

"The Balcony." *Auburn Journal* 25, No. 50 (24 September 1925): 4 (as "Le Balcon"). *Bacon's Essays* 2, No. 1 (Spring 1929): [1] (as "Le Balcon").

"Beatrice." In *SP*.

"Brumes et pluies." See "Mists and Rains."

"Chant d'automne." See "Song of Autumn."

"Une Charogne." *WT* 12, No. 2 (August 1928): 262–63 (as one of "Three Poems in Prose").

"Epigraph for a Condemned Book." *WT* 11, No. 3 (March 1928): 385 (as "Epigraphe pour un Livre Condamné").

"Femmes damnées."

"La Fontaine de sang." See "The Fountain of Blood."

"The Fountain of Blood." In *S* (as "La Fontaine de Sang"), *SP*.

"Les Hiboux." See "The Owls."

"Horreur Sympathétique." See "Sympathetic Horror."

"Hymne à la beauté." See "Hymn to Beauty."

"Hymn to Beauty." *AJ* 25, No. 48 (10 September 1925): 8 (as "Hymne à la Beauté"). In *S* (as "Hymne à la Beauté"). *WT* 29, No. 6 (June 1937): 719. In *SP*.

"L'Irréparable." *WT* 12, No. 12 (August 1928): 261 (as one of "Three Poems in Prose").

"Mists and Rains." *AJ* 26, No. 6 (19 November 1925): 5 (as "Brumes et Pluies"). *Recluse* No. 1 (1927): 60. In *SP*.

"The Owls." *Auburn Journal* 25, No. 51 (1 October 1925): 4 (as "Les Hiboux"). *Step Ladder* 13, No. 5 (May 1927): 138 (as "Les Hiboux"). *WT* 36, No. 2 (November 1941): 120 (as translated by "Timeus Gaylord"). In Derleth, *Dark of the Moon* (q.v.). In *SP*.

"Parisian Dream." In *S* (as "Rêve Parisien"), *SP* (as "A Parisian Dream").

"The Phantom." *WT* 13, No. 5 (May 1929): 720 (as "Le Revenant"). In *SP*.

"Rêve Parisien." In *S*. In *SP* as "Parisian Dream."

"Le Revenant." See "The Phantom."

"Sed non Satiata." *Arkham Sampler* 2, No. 2 (Spring 1949): 24. In *SP*.

"Les Sept Vieillards." *WT* 12, No. 2 (August 1928): 261–62 (as one of "Three Poems in Prose").

"The Sick Muse." *AJ* 25, No. 37 (25 June 1925): 10 (as "La Muse Malade"). *WT* 27, No. 4 (April 1936): 485. In *SP*.

"Song of Autumn." *WT* 26, No. 4 (October 1935): 506. In *SP, S&P*.

"Spleen." *WT* 7, No. 2 (February 1926): 254. In *SP*.

"Sympathetic Horror." *AJ* 25, No. 46 (27 August 1925): 6 (as "Horreur Sympathique"). In *S* (as "Horreur Sympathétique"). *WT* 7, No. 5 (May 1926): 664 (as "Horreur Sympathétique"). In Baudelaire's *Flowers of Evil*. Ed. James Laver. London: Limited Editions Club/Fanfare Press, 1940. 134 (as "Magnetic Horror"). In *SP*.

Translations from Paul Verlaine. All titles are in *SP* and *CP* 3.

"IX (Ariette Oubliées)."

"Claire de lune." *WT* 36, No. 6 (July 1942): 49 (as "Moonlight"; as translated by "Timeus Gaylord").

"En Sourdine."

"The Faun."

Nonfiction

"A Cosmic Novel: *The Web of Easter Island*." *Arkham Sampler* 1, No. 4 (Autumn 1948): 88–89. In *PD*.

"The Epigrams of Alastor." *Dragon-Fly* No. 1 (15 October 1935): [10]. *International Observer* (January 1937) (same as first appearance, but including one item from "Pertinence and Impertinence" [q.v.]). In *The Devil's Notebook*.

"The Family Tree of the Gods." *Acolyte* 2, No. 3 (Summer 1944): 9–10 [includes a "Genealogical Chart of the Elder Gods"]. Reprinted in T. G. L. Cockcroft, "Addendum: Some Observations on the Carter Glossary" [i.e., Lin Carter, "H. P. Lovecraft: The Gods"], in Lovecraft et al. *The Shuttered Room and Other Pieces.* Sauk City, WI: Arkham House, 1959. 274–76 (without the chart). In *PD.*

"George Sterling: An Appreciation." *Overland Monthly* 85, No. 3 (March 1927): 79–80. In *PD.*

"Pertinence and Impertinence." *Dragon-Fly* No. 2 (15 May 1936): 61.

"The Weird Work of M. R. James." *FF* 1, No. 6 (February 1934): 89–90. In *PD.*

B. Works by Donald Wandrei

Books

Broken Mirrors (with Francis Bosworth, Karl Litzenberg, Gordon Louis Roth, and Harrison Salisbury; illustrated by Leo Henkora). [St. Paul, MN:] Avon Press, 1928. *Contents* [by DW]: The Victor Loses; The Suicide; Fling Wide the Roses; Drink!; The Dead Mistress; My Lady Hath Two Lovely Lips; Aftermath; The Moon-Glen Altar; Credo; The Sleeper.

Colossus: The Collected Science Fiction of Donald Wandrei. Edited by Philip J. Rahman and Dennis E. Weiler. Minneapolis, MN: Fedogan & Bremer, 1989. Contents: Editors' Note; Introduction (Colossus); The Red Brain; The Holiday Act; Something from Above; Raiders of the Universes; A Race Through Time; Farewell to Earth; Colossus; Colossus Eternal; The Atom-Smasher; The Blinding Shadows; Life Current; The Whisperers; Murray's Light; Earth Minus; Finality Unlimited; Infinity Zero; Black Fog; The Crystal Bullet; On the Threshold of Eternity; A Trip to Infinity; Requiem for Mankind; Selected Bibliography, by D. H. Olson.

Dark Odyssey. With five illustrations by Howard Wandrei. St. Paul, MN: Webb Publishing Co., [1931].

A Donald Wandrei Miscellany. Edited by D. H. Olson. St. Paul. MN: Sidecar Preservation Society, 2001.

Don't Dream: The Collected Horror and Fantasy Fiction of Donald Wandrei. Edited by Philip J. Rahman and Dennis E. Weiler. Minneapolis, MN: Fedogan & Bremer, 1997. *Contents:* Editor's Note by Philip J. Rahman and Dennis E. Weiler; Introduction (Don't Dream) by Helen Mary Hughesdon; A Fragment of a Dream; The Shadow of a Nightmare; The Green Flame; The Tree-Men of M'Bwa; When the Fire Creatures Came; The Lives of Alfred Kramer; The Fire Vampires; Spawn of the Sea; The Lady in Gray; The Man Who Never Lived; The Nerveless Man; The Chuckler; A Scientist Divides; The Destroying Horde; The Monster from Nowhere; The Witch-Makers; The Eye and the Finger; The Painted Mirror; Uneasy Lie the Drowned; Giant-Plasm; Don't Dream; It Will Grow On You; Strange Harvest; Nightmare; The Crater; Delirium of the Dead; Prose Poems, Essays, and Marginalia: Introductory Note (uncredited); The

Messengers; The Pursuers; The Woman at the Window; The Purple Land; Dreaming Away My Life; Black Flame; The Shrieking House; The Phantom City; The Kingdom of Dreams; Lotus and the Poppy; Unforgotten Night; Santon Merlin; Cigarette Characterization; The Imaginative Element in Modern Literature; Of Donald Wandrei, August Derleth and H. P. Lovecraft, by D. H. Olson.

Ecstasy and Other Poems. Athol, MA: Recluse Press, 1928.

The Eye and the Finger. Sauk City, WI: Arkham House, 1944. *Contents:* Introduction; The Lady in Gray; The Eye and the Finger; The Painted Mirror; It Will Grow on You; The Tree-Men of M'Bwa; The Lives of Alfred Kramer; The Monster from Nowhere; The Witch-Makers; The Nerveless Man; Black Fog; The Blinding Shadows; A Scientist Divides; Earth Minus; Finality Unlimited; The Crystal Bullet; A Fragment of a Dream; The Woman at the Window; The Messengers; The Pursuers; The Red Brain; On the Threshold of Eternity.

Letters [of H. P. Lovecraft] *with Donald and Howard Wandrei and to Emil Petaja.* Edited by S. T. Joshi and David E. Schultz. New York: Hippocampus Press, 2019.

Poems for Midnight. Sauk City, WI: Arkham House, 1964.

Sanctity and Sin: The Collected Poems and Prose Poems of D. Wandrei. Edited by S. T. Joshi. New York: Hippocampus Press, 2007.

Strange Harvest. Sauk City, WI: Arkham House, 1965.

Dead Titans, Waken!; Invisible Sun, ed. S. T. Joshi. Lakewood, CO: Centipede Press, 2011; rpt. as *Dead Titans, Waken!* Minneapolis, MN: Fedogan & Bremer, 2017.

The Web of Easter Island. Sauk City, WI: Arkham House, 1948.

Fiction

"Black Fog." *Thrilling Wonder Stories* 9, No. 1 (February 1937): 33–41.

"Bone Crusher." *Clues Detective Stories* 35, No. 5 (April 1936): 58–81.

"The Destroying Horde." *WT* 25, No. 6 (June 1935): 711–23. In *DD*.

"The Door to the Room." See "Nightmare."

"Ebony and Silver." In *DWM, Sanctity and Sin.*

"The Eye and the Finger." *Esquire* 6, No. 6 (December 1936): 70, 319–20. In *EF, DD*.

"Farewell to Earth." *Astounding Stories* 12, No. 4 (December 1933): 98–115. In *C.* There is also a lengthy letter by Wandrei in *Astounding* under "Brass Tacks" (140–41) discussing the story.

"The Fire Vampires." *WT* 21, No. 2 (February 1933): 179–89. In *SH, DD*.

"Fragment of a Dream." *Minnesota Quarterly* 4, No. 2 (Winter 1926): 28–34. *Recluse* No. 1 (1927): 18–21. In *EF, DD*.

"Giants in the Valley." *Clues Detective Stories* 35, No. 3 (February 1936): 52–81.

"The Green Flame." *WT* 16, No. 1 (July 1930): 47–48.

"It Will Grow on You." *Esquire* 17, No. 4 (April 1942): 70–73. In *EF, DD.*

"Killer's Bait." *Clues Detective Stories* 36, No. 6 (November 1936): 102+.

"The Lady in Gray." *WT* 22, No. 6 (December 1933): 764–67. In *EF, DD.*

"A Legend of Yesterday." *Leaves* No. 1 (Summer 1937): 79. In *Sanctity and Sin.*

"The Lives of Alfred Kramer." *WT* 20, No. 6 (December 1932): 817–29. In *EF, DD.*

"The Messengers." *Minnesota Quarterly* 4, No. 1 (Fall 1926): 58–59. In *EF, DD.*

"A Midsummer Knight." Nonextant.

"The Monster from Nowhere." *Argosy* 260, No. 2 (23 November 1935): 28–49.

"Nightmare" [formerly "The Door to the Room"]. In *SH, DD.*

"On the Threshold of Eternity." *Leaves* No. 1 (Summer 1937): 76–79 (under "Three Stories"). In *EF, C.*

"The Painted Mirror." *Esquire* 7, No. 5 (May 1937): 50–118. In *EF, DD.*

"Paphos." In *Sanctity and Sin.*

"The Pursuers." *Minnesota Quarterly* 4, No. 1 (Fall 1926): 59. In *EF, DD.*

"Raiders of the Universes." *Astounding Stories* 11, No. 1 (September 1932): 63–77. In *C.*

"The Red Brain" [formerly "In the Billionth Aeon" and "The Twilight of Time"]. *WT* 10, No. 4 (October 1927): 531–37. *WT* 27, No. 5 (May 1936): 626–28, 630–33. *Leaves* No. 1 (Summer 1937): 71–76 (as "The Twilight of Time"; under "Three Stories"). In *EF, C.*

"The Rod and the Staff." *Black Mask* 19, No. 12 (February 1937): 124+.

"A Sea Change." See "Uneasy Lie the Drowned."

"Something from Above." *WT* 16, No. 6 (December 1930): 763–78. In *SH, C.*

"Spawn of the Sea." *WT* 21, No. 5 (May 1933): 567–76. In *SH, DD.*

"The Tree-Men of M'Bwa." *WT* 19, No. 2 (February 1932): 220–27. In *EF, DD.*

"The Twilight of Time." See "The Red Brain."

"Uneasy Lie the Drowned." *WT* 30, No. 6 (December 1937): 740–44. In *SH, DD.* Originally "A Sea Change."

"When the Fire Creatures Came." In *DD* (first appearance).

"The Witch-Makers." *Argosy* 264, No. 1 (2 May 1936): 34–56.

"The Woman at the Window." *Leaves* No. 2 (1938): 98–99. In *EF, DD.*

Poetry. All poems are in *Sanctity and Sin.*

"After Farewell." Nonextant.

"The Challenger." *Minnesota Quarterly* 4, No. 3 (Spring 1927): 36. In *E, PM.*

"The Corpse Speaks." *Midwest Student* (May 1927) (as "In the Grave"). *Recluse* No. 1 (1927): 76 (as "In the Grave"). In *PM.*

"The Cypress-Bog." *WT* 16, No. 5 (November 1930): 714.

"Dark Odyssey." In *Dark Odyssey, PM.*

"Dead Fruit of the Fugitive Years: Ten Sonnets." *Minnesota Quarterly* 7, No. 2 (Winter 1929): 27–31. Contains: The Dream Changes; Surrender; Though All My Days; The Second Beauty; Twice Excellent Perfection; This Larger

Room; The Woman Answers; The Deadly Calm; Corroding Acids; With Cat-like Tread.
"Early Harvest." Nonextant.
"Ecstasy." In *E*.
"In Mandrikor." In *E, PM*. (The version in *E* is found under "Uncollected Poems" in *Sanctity and Sin.*))
"In Memoriam: George Sterling." In *E, PM*.
"Marmora." *WT* 15, No. 5 (May 1930): 636.
"Moon Magic." *Minnesota Quarterly* 7, No. 1 (Fall 1929): 27–30.
"On Some Drawings." In *E, PM*.
"Out of the Grave." See "The Corpse Speaks."
"Paphos."
"A Queen in Other Skies." *WT* 19, No. 1 (January 1932): 109.
"The Roaring of the Sea." Nonextant.
"Sanctity and Sin." In *E*.
"Song of Oblivion." *Minnesota Quarterly* 4, No. 3 (Spring 1927): 33 (as "The Song of Oblivion"). In *E* (as "The Song of Oblivion"), *PM*.
"Summer Roads." Nonextant.
"To a Friendship Broken." Nonextant.
"Valerian." In *E*.
"The Worm-King." *WT* 15, No. 6 (June 1930): 734. In *PM*.

Nonfiction
"Announcement." Flyer circulated by the Minnesota Science Fiction Society c. 1974. Authorship by Wandrei is uncertain.
"Arthur Machen and *The Hill of Dreams*." *Minnesota Quarterly* 3, No. 3 (Spring 1926): 19–24. *Studies in Weird Fiction* No. 15 (Summer 1994): 27–30.
"The Emperor of Dreams." *Overland Monthly* 84, No. 12 (December 1926): 380–81, 407, 409. *Klarkash-Ton* No. 1 (1988): 3–8, 25.
"Lovecraft in Providence." In H. P. Lovecraft et al. *The Shuttered Room and Other Pieces*. Ed. August Derleth. Sauk City, WI: Arkham House, 1959. 124–40.
[Brief untitled autobiography (369–80) in DW's *Don't Dream* under "Of Donald Wandrei, August Derleth, and H. P Lovecraft" by D. H. Olson, pp [367]–91.

C. Works by R. H. Barlow

Annals of the Jinns. West Warwick, RI: Necronomicon Press, 1978.
The Dragon-Fly and Leaves. Edited by S. T. Joshi. Seattle: Sarnath Press, 2020.
The Eyes of the God. Edited by S. T. Joshi, Douglas A. Anderson, and David E. Schultz. New York: Hippocampus Press, 2002, 2022.

On Lovecraft and Life. [Edited by S. T. Joshi.] West Warwick, RI: Necronomicon Press, 1992.

All fiction, nonfiction, and poetry by RHB are contained in *Eyes of the God.*

Fiction

"A Dream." *Dragon-Fly* No. 1 (15 October 1935): 1–6.

"The Experiment." *Unusual Stories* 1, No. 1 (May/June 1935): 35–40.

"The Night Ocean" [with H. P. Lovecraft]. *Californian* 4, No. 3 (Winter 1936): 41–56. The last two paragraphs appeared as "A Fragment." *Californian* 3, No. 3 (Winter 1935): 43.

Annals of the Jinns

1. "The Black Tower." *FF* 1, No. 2 (October 1933): 28.
2. "The Shadow from Above." *FF* 1, No. 3 (November 1933): 19.
5. "The Tomb of the God." *FF* 1, No. 6 (February 1934): 90–91.
6. "The Flower God." *FF* 1, No. 9 (May 1934): 139–40.

Nonfiction

"About H. G. Wells." *FF* 1, No. 9 (May 1934): 143–44 (as by Daniel McPhail).

"Henry S. Whitehead." In Henry S. Whitehead, *Jumbee and Other Uncanny Tales.* Sauk City, WI: Arkham House, 1944. vii–xii.

"Parícutin." *Eyes of the God.*

"The Time Machine: A Bibliographical Note." *FF* 1, No. 7 (March 1934): 109.

Verse

"R. E. H." *WT* 28, No. 3 (October 1936): 353.

Other

The microfilms made by George Smisor of Barlow's papers following his death are held by the John Hay Library, Brown University, Providence, RI. They contain letters to Barlow, Barlow's poetry, fiction, and nonfictions, and were the source for many items contained herein.

Dragon-Fly

No. 1 (15 October 1935). *Contents:* [Errata]; Barlow, "A Dream"; Elizabeth Toldridge, "Expectancy"; J. Vernon Shea, Jr. "On Writing in Bed"; Clark Ashton Smith, "The Epigrams of Alastor"; E. A. Edkins, "Fragment of a Letter to a Young Poet"; August W. Derleth, "First Scylla"; R. H. B., "Obiter Dictum"; Eugene B. Kuntz, "The Sea: Yesterday and Today"; E. A. Edkins, "Bizarres."

No. 2 (15 May 1936): *Contents:* Barlow, "Pursuit of the Moth"; E. Toldridge, "Locusts and Wild Honey"; E. A. Edkins, "What Is Poetry?"; J. Vernon

Shea, Jr., "Four Playwrights"; C. A. S., "Pertinence and Impertinence"; August W. Derleth, "Bluebirds."

Leaves

No. 1 (Summer 1937). *Contents:* "The Story of the Princess Zulkais and the Prince Kalilah: An Unfinished Episode from William Beckford's *Vathek*"; Clark Ashton Smith, "Conclusion to Wm. Beckford's Story of Princess Zulkais and Prince Kalilah"; Robert E. Howard, "With a Set of Rattlesnake Rattles"; Lewis Theobald, Jun. [H. P. Lovecraft], "Cats and Dogs"; Elizabeth Toldridge, "Mist"; Edith Miniter, "Dead Houses"; Clark Ashton Smith, "Sandalwood"; Frank Belknap Long, Jr., "The Beautiful City"; A. Merritt, "The People of the Pit"; R. H. B., "Obiter Scriptum; or Succotash without Seasoning"; Elizabeth Toldridge, "H. P. Lovecraft" and "Ephemera"; August W. Derleth, "The Panelled Room"; Arthur Goodenough, "It Will Be Thus"; Donald Wandrei, "Three Stories" ("The Twilight of Time," "On the Threshold of Eternity," "A Legend of Yesterday"); Arthur H. Goodenough, "Autumnus and October."

No. 2 (1938). *Contents:* C. L. Moore, "Werewoman"; Vrest Teachout Orton, "Winter Night"; D. Wandrei, "The Woman at the Window"; H. P. Lovecraft, "From a Letter"; [H. P. Lovecraft and Barlow], "Collapsing Cosmoses"; Howard Davis Spoerl, "Haunted"; Samuel Loveman, "The Faun"; Henry George Weiss, "Flower of War"; H. P. Lovecraft, "Three Fragments" (I. "Azathoth"; II. "The Descendant"; III. "The Book"); Frank Belknap Long, Jr., "O Is There Aught in Wine and Ships?"; Frank Belknap Long, Jr., "Futility"; Fritz Leiber Jr., "The Demons of the Upper Air"; H. P. Lovecraft, "In Defense of 'Dagon'"; Jonathan Lindley [i.e., R. H. Barlow], "The Unresisting" and "March"; Henry S. Whitehead, "The Tree-Man"; Th. Weelkes, "Thule"; [R. H. Barlow], "A Checklist of the Published Weird Stories of Henry S. Whitehead"; R. H. Barlow, "Origin Undetermined"; [R. H. Barlow], "Colophon or Epitaph."

D. Works by Howard Wandrei

Books

The Eerie Mr. Murphy: The Collected Fantasy Tales of Howard Wandrei. Volume 2. Edited by Dwayne Olson. Minneapolis, MN: Fedogan & Bremer, 2003.

The Last Pin. Ed. D. H. Olson. Minneapolis, MN: Fedogan & Bremer Mystery, 1996.

Time Burial: The Collected Fantasy Tales of Howard Wandrei. Volume 1. Edited by Dwayne Olson. Minneapolis, MN: Fedogan & Bremer, 1995.

E. Works by Others

Andersen, Hans Christian (1805–1875). *Fairy Tales*. Illustrated by Harry Clarke. New York: Brentano's, 1916.

———. *Fairy Tales*. Illustrated by Kay Nielsen. New York: George H. Doran Co., 1924.

Applegate, Bergen Weeks (1865–?). *Paul Verlaine, His Absinthe-Tinted Song: A Monograph on the Poet, with Selections from His Work*. Chicago: R. F. Seymour/The Alderbrink Press, 1916.

Apuleius, Lucius (123?–180? C.E.). *The Golden Asse of Lucius Apuleius*. Tr. William Adlington. Illustrated by Jean de Bosschère. London: Bodley Head, 1923.

Asbjørnsen, Peter Christen (1812–1885), and Jørgen Engebretsen Moe (1813–1882), ed. *East of the Sun and West of the Moon: Old Tales from the North*. Illustrated by Kay Nielsen. London: Hodder & Stoughton, 1914.

Balzac, Honoré de (1799–1850). *Droll Stories*. <1832–37> Tr. George Robert Sims. London: John Camden Hotten, 1874.

Barker, Eric. "Clark Ashton Smith—In Memory of a Great Friendship." In Donald Sidney-Fryer. *Emperor of Dreams: A Clark Ashton Smith Bibliography*. West Kingston, RI: Donald M. Grant, 1978. 29–31.

[Barnitz, David Park] (1878–1901). *The Book of Jade*. New York: Doxey's, [1901]. Rpt. with additional material as *The Book of Jade: A Critical Edition*. Ed. David E. Schultz and Michael J. Abolafia. New York: Hippocampus Press, 2015.

Baudelaire, Charles Pierre (1821–1867). *Baudelaire: His Prose and Poetry*. Ed. T. R. Smith. New York: Boni & Liveright (Modern Library), 1919.

———. *Les Épaves*. Bruxelles: Chez tout les libraries, 1866.

———. *Flowers of Evil*. Tr. George Dillon and Edna St. Vincent Millay. New York: Harper & Brothers, 1936. A selection.

———. *Les Paradis artificiels: Opium et haschisch*. Paris: Poulet-Malassis et de Broise, 1860.

———. *The Poems of Charles Baudelaire*. Selected and Translated from the French, with an Introductory Study, by F. P. Sturm. London: Walter Scott Publishing Co., 1906.

Beckford, William (1759–1844). *The Episodes of Vathek*. <1912> Translated from the Original French by Sir Frank T. Marzials. London: Chapman & Dodd, 1922.

———. *Vathek*. With an Introduction by Ben Ray Redman. Illustrated by Mahlon Blaine. <1786> New York: John Day Co., 1928.

Beddoes, Thomas Lovell (1803–1849). *Death's Jest Book; or, The Fool's Tragedy*. London: William Pickering, 1850.

Bennett, Arnold (1867–1931). *The Old Wives' Tale*. <1908> London: Johnathan Cape, 1934.

Bierce, Ambrose (1842–1914?). *The Collected Works of Ambrose Bierce*. Washington, DC: Neale Publishing Co., 1912. New York: Gordian Press, 1966.

12 vols.

——. *The Devil's Dictionary.* <1906/1911> New York: Albert & Charles Boni, 1925.

Blackwood, Algernon (1869–1951). *The Listener and Other Stories.* London: Eveleigh Nash, 1907.

Blake, William (1757–1827). *Pencil Drawings.* Ed. Geoffrey Keynes. New York: Random House, 1927.

Bland, Henry Meade (1863–1931), ed. *A Day in the Hills: A Poetical Competition of the Edwin Markham Chapter of the English Poetry Society Held at Villa Montalvo, Saratoga, Santa Clara County, California, September 18, 1926, Including a Short Anthology of California Poems Specially Contributed by Their Authors.* San Francisco: Taylor & Taylor, 1926.

Boni, Albert (1892–1981), ed. *The Modern Book of French Verse in English Translations.* New York: Boni & Liveright, 1920.

Browne, Sir Thomas (1605–1682). *Hydriotaphia.* London: Peter Davies, 1927.

Brooke, Rupert (1887–1915). *The Collected Poems of Rupert Brooke.* New York: John Lane, 1920.

Cabell, James Branch (1879–1958). *Figures of Earth.* New York: Robert M. McBride & Co., 1921.

Chambers, Robert W. (1865–1933). *The King in Yellow.* <1895> New York: Harper & Brothers, 1902. [Contains "The Yellow Sign."]

Chope, Richard Pearse (1862–1938). *Ballads Weird and Wonderful.* Illustrated by Vernon Hill. New York: John Lane; London: The Bodley Head, 1912.

Crawford, F. Marion (1854–1909). *Wandering Ghosts.* New York: Macmillan, 1911. London: T. Fisher Unwin, 1911 (as *Uncanny Tales*).

De Casseres, Benjamin (1873–1945). *The Shadow-Eater.* New York: American Library Service, 1923.

De Quincey, Thomas (1785–1859). *Confessions of an English Opium-Eater.* <1821> London: J. M. Dent & Sons, 1925.

Dell, Floyd. "Literature and the Machine Age." *Liberator* 7, No. 9 (September 1924): 29–30. Rpt. in Dell's *Intellectual Vagabondage.* New York: George H. Doran, 1926. 214–19. Also in Barnitz, q.v.

Derleth, August (1909–1971). *Someone in the Dark.* Sauk City, WI: Arkham House, 1941.

Derleth, August, ed. *Dark of the Moon: Poems of Fantasy and the Macabre.* Sauk City, WI: Arkham House, 1947.

——, ed. *Fire and Sleet and Candlelight.* Sauk City, WI: Arkham House, 1961.

Drayton, Michael (1563–1631). *Poly-Olbion; or, A chorographical description of tracts, rivers, mountaines, forests, and other parts of this renowned Isle of Great Britaine, with intermixture of the most remarquable stories, antiquities, wonders, rarityes, pleasures, and commodities of the same: digested in a poem. With a table added, for direction to those occurrences of story and antiquitie, whereunto the course of the volume easily leades not.* London: Printed by H. L. for Mathew Lownes, 1612.

Dunsany, Lord (Edward John Moreton Drax Plunkett, 18th Baron Dunsany, 1878–1957). *The Book of Wonder* <1912> [and *Time and the Gods* <1906>]. New York: Boni & Liveright (Modern Library), [1918].

———. *A Dreamer's Tales and Other Stories.* New York: Boni & Liveright (Modern Library), [1917], [1919], or [1921]. [Contains "Idle Days on the Yann."]

Eldridge, Paul (1888–1982). *Vanitas.* Boston: Stratford Co., 1920.

Ellis, Havelock (1859–1939). *From Rousseau to Proust.* Boston: Houghton Mifflin, 1935.

Flaubert, Gustave (1821–1880). *La Tentation de St. Antoine.* <1874> Tr. by Lafcadio Hearn as *The Temptation of St. Anthony.* New York: Alice Harriman Co., 1910.

Fort, Charles (1874–1932). *The Book of the Damned.* New York: Boni & Liveright, 1919.

French, Nora May (1881–1907). *Poems.* San Francisco: Strange Co., 1910.

Givler, Robert Chenault (1884–1975). *Poems.* n.p., 19——.

Goethe, Johann Wolfgang von (1749–1832). *Faust.* Illustrated by Harry Clarke. New York: Dingwall Rock, 1925.

Greene, Madelynne. "Letter." In Donald Sidney-Fryer. *Emperor of Dreams: A Clark Ashton Smith Bibliography.* West Kingston, RI: Donald M. Grant, 1978. 154.

Grillot de Givry, Émile-Jules (1870–1929). *Witchcraft, Magic and Alchemy.* Tr. J. Courtenay Locke; with 10 plates in colour and 366 illustrations in the text. London: George G. Harrap, 1931.

Grimm, Brothers [Jacob (1785–1863) and Wilhelm (1786–1859)]. *Hansel and Gretel and Other Stories.* Illustrated by Kay Nielsen. London: Hodder & Stoughton; New York: George H. Doran Co., 1925.

Hall, Austin (1885?–1933), and Homer Eon Flint (1892–1924). *The Blind Spot. Argosy* (14 May–18 June 1921). Philadelphia: Prime, 1953.

Hearn, Lafcadio (1850–1904). *Fantastics and Other Fancies.* Ed. Charles Woodward Hutson. Boston: Houghton Mifflin, 1914.

———. *Gleanings in Buddha Fields: Studies of Hand and Soul in the Far East.* Boston: Houghton, Mifflin, 1897.

———. *Life and Letters.* Ed. Elizabeth Bisland. Boston: Houghton Mifflin, 1923. 3 vols.

———. *Stray Leaves from Strange Literature: Stories Reconstructed from the Anvari-Soheïli, Baitál Pachísí, Mahabharata, Pantchatantra, Gulistan, Talmud, Kalewala, etc.* Boston: James R. Osgood, 1884.

Hecht, Ben (1893–1964). *Fantazius Mallare: A Mysterious Oath.* Illustrated by Wallace Smith. Chicago: Covici-McGee, 1922.

Hoffmann, Rah (1920–2013). "Letter." In Donald Sidney-Fryer, *Emperor of Dreams: A Clark Ashton Smith Bibliography.* West Kingston, RI: Donald M. Grant, 1978. 192–95.

Huneker, James Gibbons (1857–1921). *Steeplejack.* New York: Charles Scribners Sons, 1920–21. 2 vols.

James, M. R. (1862–1936). *The Collected Ghost Stories of M. R. James.* London: Edward Arnold, 1931.

———. *Ghost-Stories of an Antiquary.* London: Edward Arnold, 1904.

———. *A Warning to the Curious.* London: Edward Arnold, 1925.

Jerome, Jerome K. (1859–1927). *Three Men in a Boat.* London: Simpkin, Marshall, Hamilton, Kent, 1889.

Leopardi, Giacomo (1798–1837). *Essays, Dialogues and Thoughts (Operette morali and pensieri) of Giacomo Leopardi.* Tr. James Thomson. Ed. Bertram Dobell. London: George Routledge & Sons, 1880.

Lévi, Eliphas (pseud. of Alphonse Louis Constant, 1810–1875). *Histoire de la magie.* <1860> Tr. Arthur Edward Waite (1857–1942) as *The History of Magic, Including a Clear and Precise Exposition of Its Procedure, Its Rites and Its Mysteries.* London: William Rider & Son, 1913.

Lewis, Matthew Gregory (1775–1818). *The Monk.* <1796> London: Brentano's, [1924]. 3 vols. in 1.

Lolme, Jean Louis de (1740–1806). *Heath's French and English Dictionary: Compiled from the Best Authorities In Both Languages.* Boston; New York; Chicago: D. C. Heath & Co., 1903.

Long, Frank Belknap (1901–1994). *The Goblin Tower.* Cassia, FL: Dragon-Fly Press, 1935.

Louÿs, Pierre (1870–1925). *Aphrodite.* <1892> n.p.: Privately printed, 1919.

Lovecraft, H. P. (1890–1937). "The Alchemist." *United Amateur* 16, No. 4 (November 1916): 53–57.

———. *The Annotated Supernatural Horror in Literature.* Ed. S. T. Joshi. New York: Hippocampus Press, rev. ed. 2012.

———. *At the Mountains of Madness. Astounding Stories* 16, No. 6 (February 1936): 8–32; 17, No. 1 (March 1936): 125–55; 17, No. 2 (April 1936): 132–50.

———. "Beyond the Wall of Sleep." *Pine Cones* 1, No. 6 (October 1919): 2–10. *FF,* 2, No. 2 (October 1934): 25–32.

———. "The Call of Cthulhu." *WT* 11, No. 2 (February 1928): 159–78, 287.

———. *The Cats of Ulthar.* Cassia, FL.: Dragon-Fly Press, 1935.

———. *Collected Essays.* Ed. S. T. Joshi. New York, Hippocampus Press, 2004–06. 5 vols.

———. "The Doom That Came to Sarnath." *Scot* No. 44 (June 1920): 90–98. *Marvel Tales of Science and Fantasy* 1, No. 4 (March–April 1935): 157–63.

———. "The Dunwich Horror." *WT* 13, No. 4 (Apr. 1929): 481–508.

———. "From Beyond." *FF* 1, No. 10 (June 1934): 147–51, 160.

———. *Fungi from Yuggoth: An Annotated Edition.* Ed. David E. Schultz. New York: Hippocampus Press, 2017.

———. "The Haunter of the Dark." *WT* 28, No. 5 (Dec. 1936): 538–53.

———. "The Lurking Fear." *Home Brew* 2, No. 6 (January 1923): 4–10; 3, No. 1 (February 1923): 18–23; 3, No. 2 (March 1923): 31–37, 44, 48; 3, No. 3 (April 1923): 35–42. *WT* 11, No. 6 (June 1928): 791–804.

———. *Marginalia.* Ed. August Derleth. Sauk City, WI: Arkham House, 1944.

———. "Mrs. Miniter—Estimates and Recollections." *Californian* 5, No. 4 (Spring 1938): 47–55.

———. *The Notes and Commonplace Book Employed by the Late H. P. Lovecraft Including His Suggestions for Story-Writing, Analyses of the Weird Story, and a List of Certain Basic Underlying Horrors, &c., &c., Designed to Stimulate the Imagination.* [Ed. Barlow.] Lakeport, CA: Futile Press, 1938. West Warwick, RI: Necronomicon Press, 1978.

———. "Nyarlathotep." *United Amateur* 20, No. 2 (November 1920): 19–21. *National Amateur* 43, No. 6 (July 1926): 53–54.

———. *O Fortunate Floridian: H. P. Lovecraft's Letters to R. H. Barlow.* Ed. S. T. Joshi and David E. Schultz. Tampa, FL: University of Tampa Press, 2007.

———. "The Outsider." *WT* 7, No. 4 (April 1926): 449–53. *WT* 17, No. 4 (June–July 1931): 566–71.

———. *The Outsider and Others.* Ed. August Derleth and Donald Wandrei. Sauk City, WI: Arkham House, 1939.

———. "Psychopompos: A Tale in Rhyme." *Vagrant* No. 10 (October 1919): 13–22.

———. "The Rats in the Walls." *WT* 3, No. 3 (March 1924): 25–31. *WT* 15, No. 6 (June 1930): 841–53.

———. *Selected Letters.* Ed. August Derleth, Donald Wandrei, and James Turner. Sauk City, WI: Arkham House, 1965–76. 5 vols.

———. "The Shadow out of Time." *Astounding Stories* 17, No. 4 (June 1936): 110–54.

———. *The Shadow over Innsmouth.* Everett, PA: Visionary Publishing Co., 1936.

———. "The Strange High House in the Mist." *WT* 18, No. 3 (October 1931): 394–400.

———. "Supernatural Horror in Literature." *Recluse* No. 1 (1927): 23–59. Rev. ed. in *FF* (October 1933–February 1935).

———. "To Clark Ashton Smith, Esq., upon His Fantastic Tales, Verses, Pictures, and Sculptures." *WT* 31, No. 4 (April 1938): 392 (as "To Clark Ashton Smith").

———. "The White Ship." *United Amateur* 19, No. 2 (November 1919): 30–33. *WT* 9, No. 3 (March 1927): 386–89.

———. "The Whisperer in Darkness." *WT* 18, No. 1 (Aug. 1931): 32–73.

———, and Winifred V. Jackson. "The Green Meadow." *Vagrant* (Spring 1927): 188–95 (as by "Elizabeth Neville Berkeley and Lewis Theobald, Jr.").

———, and E. Hoffmann Price (1898–1988). "Through the Gates of the Silver Key." *WT* 24, No. 1 (July 1934): 60–85.

Loveman, Samuel (1887–1976). *The Hermaphrodite: A Poem.* With a Preface by Benjamin De Casseres. Athol, MA: W. Paul Cook, 1926.

———. *The Hermaphrodite and Other Poems.* Caldwell, ID: Caxton Printers, 1936.

———. *Out of the Immortal Night: Selected Works of Samuel Loveman.* Ed. S. T. Joshi and David E. Schultz. New York: Hippocampus Press, 2004, 2021.

———. *The Sphinx. Ghost* No. 2 (July 1944): 19–41.

Machen, Arthur (1863–1947). *The Hill of Dreams.* (Blue paper edition.) London: Martin Secker, [1922].

———. *The House of Souls.* <1906> New York: Alfred A. Knopf, 1923. [Contains "The Great God Pan."]

Marguerite of Navarre (1492–1549). *The Heptameron: Tales and Novels of Marguerite, Queen of Navarre.* Tr. Arthur Machen. London: George Routledge, 1911.

Masuccio, Salernitano (1410–1475). *The Novellino of Masuccio.* Tr. W. G. Waters. London: Lawrence & Bullen, 1895. 2 vols.

Merritt, A[braham] (1882–1943). *The Metal Monster. Argosy All-Story Weekly* (7 August–25 September 1920). New York: Hippocampus Press, 2002. Rev. as *The Metal Emperor. Science and Invention* (October 1927–August 1928).

———. "The Moon Pool." *All-Story Weekly* (22 June 1918).

Meyrink, Gustav (1868–1932). *The Golem.* <1915> Tr. Madge Pemberton. London: Gollancz; Boston: Houghton Mifflin, 1928.

Mifflin, Lloyd (1846–1921). *Collected Sonnets of Lloyd Mifflin.* London: Henry Frowde, 1905.

Mitchell, John Ames (1845–1918). *The Last American.* New York: Frederick A. Stokes, 1889.

Mitchell, Margaret (1900–1949). *Gone with the Wind.* New York: Macmillan, 1936.

Moore, Thomas (1779–1852). *Lalla Rookh: An Oriental Romance.* <1817> New York: Thomas Y. Crowell & Co., 1888.

Nicolson, J. U. (1885–1944). *King of the Black Isles.* Chicago: Covici-McGee Co., 1924.

Pepper & Stern Rare Books, et al. *Selections from the Archive of Donald Wandrei: Manuscripts, Letters, Printed Ephemera, and Original Art.* Santa Barbara, CA: Pepper & Stern Rare Books, 1994.

———. *Selections from the Library of Donald Wandrei.* Santa Barbara, CA: Pepper & Stern Rare Books, 1988.

Petronius (T. Petronius Arbiter, fl. 1st c. C.E.). *The Complete Works of Gaius [sic] Petronius.* Tr. Jack Lindsay, with one hundred illustrations by Norman Lindsay. London: Fanfrolico Press, 1927. New York: Rarity Press, 1932.

Phillips, Stephen. *The New Inferno.* Illustrated by Vernon Hill. New York: John Lane, 1910.

Poe, Edgar Allan (1809–1849). *Tales of Mystery and Imagination.* Illustrated by Harry Clarke. <1919> New York: Tudor Publishing Co., 1933.

Polidori, John William (1795–1821). *The Vampyre: A Tale*. London: Sherwood, Neely & Jones, 1819.

Pollard, Percival. *Their Day in Court*. New York: Neale Publishing Co., 1909.

Robertson, William John (1846–1894). *A Century of French Verse: Brief Biographical and Critical Notices of Thirty-Three French Poets of the Nineteenth Century with Experimental Translations from Their Poems*. London: A. D. Innes & Co., 1895.

Rossetti, Dante Gabriel (1828–1882). *The Collected Works of Dante Gabriel Rossetti, Volume II: Translations, Prose—Notices of Fine Art*. Ed. William Michael Rossetti. London: Ellis & Elvey, 1890.

Saltus, Edgar (1855–1921). *The Philosophy of Disenchantment*. Boston: Houghton, Mifflin, 1885.

Saltus, Francis (1848–1889). *The Bayadere and Other Sonnets*. New York: G. P. Putnam's Sons, 1894.

———. *Dreams After Sunset: Poems*. Buffalo, NY: C. W. Moulton, 1892.

———. *Shadows and Ideals*. Buffalo, NY: C. W. Moulton, 1890.

———. *The Witch of En-Dor and Other Poems*. Buffalo, NY: C. W. Moulton, 1891.

Santayana, George (1863–1952). *The Last Puritan: A Memoir in the Form of a Novel*. London: Constable, 1935. New York: Charles Scribner's Sons, 1936.

Schwartz, Julius, and Mort Weisinger. "Donald Wandrei Interviewed." *Fantasy Magazine* 1, No. 3 (May 1934): 10–11, 32.

Shiel, M. P. (1865–1947). *The Pale Ape and Other Pulses*. London: T. Werner Laurie, 1911.

———. *The Purple Cloud*. <1901> Rev. ed. New York: Vanguard Press, 1930.

———. *Shapes in the Fire*. London: John Lane; Boston: Roberts Brothers, 1896. [Contains "Xélucha" and "Vaila" (early version of "The House of Sounds").]

Sidney-Fryer, Donald. *Emperor of Dreams: A Clark Ashton Smith Bibliography*. West Kingston, RI: Donald M. Grant, 1978.

Smith, Thorne (1892–1934). *Topper: A Ribald Adventure*. New York: Robert M. McBride & Co., 1926.

———. *Topper Takes a Trip*. New York: Doubleday, Doran, 1932.

Snow, Royall H. (1898–1976). *Thomas Lovell Beddoes, Eccentric and Poet*. New York: Covici, Friede, 1928.

Spence, Lewis (1874–1955). *The History of Atlantis*. London: Rider, 1926.

Stapledon, Olaf (1886–1950). *Last and First Men*. London: Methuen, 1930.

Stedman, Edmund Clarence (1833–1908). *An American Anthology, 1787–1900: Selections Illustrating the Editor's Critical Review of American Poetry in the Nineteenth Century*. Boston: Houghton, Mifflin, 1900.

Sterling, George (1869–1926). *After Sunset*. [Ed. R. H. Barlow.] San Francisco: John Howell, 1939.

———. *Beyond the Breakers and Other Poems*. San Francisco: A. M. Robertson, 1914.

———. *The House of Orchids and Other Poems.* San Francisco: A. M. Robertson, 1911.

———. *Lilith: A Dramatic Poem.* San Francisco: A. M. Robertson, 1919. San Francisco: Book Club of California, 1920. New York: Macmillan, 1926 (introduction by Theodore Dreiser).

———. *Sails and Mirage and Other Poems.* San Francisco: A. M. Robertson, 1921.

———. *Selected Poems.* New York: Henry Holt, 1923.

———. *The Testimony of the Suns and Other Poems.* San Francisco: W. E. Wood, 1903. San Francisco: A. M. Robertson, 1904, 1907.

———. "A Wine of Wizardry." *Cosmopolitan* 43, No. 5 (September 1907): [551–56].

———. *A Wine of Wizardry and Other Poems.* San Francisco: A. M. Robertson, 1909.

Summers, Montague (1880–1948). *The Geography of Witchcraft.* London: Kegan Paul, Trench, Trübner & Co.; New York: Alfred A. Knopf, 1927

———, ed. *The Supernatural Omnibus.* <1922> London: Victor Gollancz, 1931. Garden City, NY: Doubleday, Doran, 1932.

———. *The Vampire: His Kith and Kin.* London: Kegan Paul, Trench, Trübner & Co., 1928.

———. *The Vampire in Europe.* London: Kegan Paul, 1929.

———, ed. *Victorian Ghost Stories.* London: Fortune Press, 1933.

Symons, Arthur (1865–1945). *Aubrey Beardsley.* London: At the Sign of the Unicorn, 1908.

Thompson, C. J. S. (1862–1943). *The Mysteries and Secrets of Magic.* London: John Lane, 1927. Philadelphia: J. B. Lippincott, 1928.

Tolstoy, Leo (1828–1910). *What Is Art?* Tr. Charles Johnston. Philadelphia: Altemus, 1898.

Walters, L. D'O. (1880–?), ed. *The Year's at the Spring: An Anthology of Recent Poetry.* Illustrated by Harry Clarke. New York: Dodd, Mead, 1920.

Whitehead, Henry S. (1882–1932). *Jumbee and Other Uncanny Tales.* Sauk City, WI: Arkham House, 1944.

Yasuda, Kenneth (1914–2002). *A Pepper-Pod: Classic Japanese Poems Together with Original Haiku.* With a Foreword by John Gould Fletcher. New York: Knopf, 1947. As by Shōson.

Index

www.ingramcontent.com/pod-product-compliance
Lightning Source LLC
Chambersburg PA
CBHW070801030726
47504CB00003B/656